M000200349

ALSO STARRING...

FORTY BIOGRAPHICAL ESSAYS ON THE GREATEST CHARACTER ACTORS OF HOLLYWOOD'S GOLDEN ERA, 1930-1965

BY CYNTHIA AND SARA BRIDESON

Published in the USA by:
BearManor Media
PO Box 1129
Duncan, Oklahoma 73534-1129
www.bearmanormedia.com

ISBN 978-1-59393-296-1

Printed in the United States of America.
Book design by Brian Pearce | Red Jacket Press.

TABLE OF CONTENTS

We dedicate this book to our parents, Amelia and Mark Brideson. Without their support and encouragement, we would have abandoned the idea for this book as insignificant and impossible. Thank you, Mamma and Daddy, for always listening to our monologues about this or that classic actor ever since we were children. Thank you for making us feel that our passions were not interesting only to us, but could be valued by others.

Thank you for your love and patience and for being two people upon whom we could count when there was no one else.

ACKNOWLEDGEMENTS

Thank you to our teachers who taught us the art of research and that nonfiction can be as interesting, if not more so, than fiction. Special acknowledgments go to Ms. Kim Engstrom, who was the first to champion our writing, Professor Edward Cundiff, who taught us the ins and outs of using a library and made us feel as if we really were, in his words, "a boon" to our school, to Dr. Wendy Jorae for making history fun, to Professor Rick Norman for always being able to make us smile, to Professoressa Rosemarie Bertini for showing such compassion to two girls who went through high school as loners, and to Dr. Philip DiMare for making us feel special in a class of hundreds of students. Lastly, thank you to Professor Ruth Buck, who during high school was the main support for our writing and who continues to be a friend and role model today.

We would also like to thank our penpals Austin Carlos, Constance Metzinger, and Michael Ryan, whose friendship and words of encouragement spurred us to expand our blogs about classic film into an entire book of essays. We would also like to acknowledge Charlene Brown Perry, our friend and mentor since junior high, who has stayed a constant support through our roughest patches. Lastly, we would like to extend a thank you to Rabbi Reuven Taff and Taliah Berger for coming into our lives when we needed friends and direction most.

We would additionally like to thank our grandparents, John and Karen Brideson, for teaching us the value of faith and hope and proving that kindness still prevails in the world. Thank you to our grandpa, David Nolan Salter, for passing on the gift of storytelling and a love of classic film. Thank you to our paternal grandmother, Mary Buehler, for passing on to us the love of the written word. We gratefully acknowledge our uncle, James Jervis, for his steadfast presence and our aunt, Sally Jervis, for her generosity, boosting our spirits with her calming influence, and inspiring us with her constant quest for new things to learn.

Finally, thank you to Jerry Murbach for graciously allowing us to use his vast collection of classic Hollywood stills to illustrate this book and to our editor, Ben Ohmart for accepting our book and having faith in its merit!

Cynthia and Sara Brideson
June 2012

INTRODUCTION

"What's her name? I know I've seen her before."
"Hey, it's that man again! He's in everything, isn't he?"

Anyone who has watched enough classic films is sure to have voiced these questions on more than one occasion. It would be a difficult task to know the name of every actor, famous or obscure, who appears on the silver screen. Hollywood's golden era saw countless players appear in hundreds of films, sometimes in only cameos, sometimes in scene-stealing supporting roles. Their names flashed across the screen after the title credits, often lost in a list of a dozen other supporting players. Relatively few audience members would remember that many of these names used to be above the title on theater marquees before changing times and tastes pushed former toasts of Broadway to seek work in moving pictures.

When we think of classic Hollywood, our minds summon the big names: Clark Gable, Jean Harlow, Cary Grant, Marilyn Monroe. However, when reflecting on what we enjoyed most in a given film, it is usually the little scenes and the little actors we remember. The *Collins American Dictionary* defines a character actor as one who "specializes in playing odd or eccentric characters." Indeed, it is character actors' "odd or eccentric" performances that elicit more lively discussion and enthusiasm among film viewers than the performances of leading actors. What would *It's A Wonderful Life* (1946) be without Clarence, the guardian angel, *The Wizard of Oz* (1939) without the Wizard, or *Gone With the Wind* (1939) without Mammy?

From the 1930s through the 1950s, studios produced unequalled numbers of films each year. The studios ran like factories, and thus, many of their products featured leading men and women with characters that could be dull and generic. Yet, whether a film was a grade A production or a low-budget second-billed feature, there was invariably a unique supporting character to save it from being unmemorable. The wise-cracking sidekick, the condescending butler, the cranky maid, and the scatter-brained mother-in-law are only a few familiar types that have enlivened films. Supporting characters such as these provide the backbone to any film, great or otherwise.

Perhaps the reason supporting actors are so endearing to audiences is because viewers do not stand in awe of small players as they do top stars. Rather, viewers see themselves in the relatable situations and realistic idiosyncrasies these actors present on screen. Like the average member of a movie audience, supporting players worked hard, if not harder, than leading stars. They voiced little complaint as to their salaries or the redundancy of their types of roles. Stars like Marilyn Monroe and James Dean, who made relatively few films, are better remembered today than tireless supporting players like Lewis Stone or Harry Davenport, who were ubiquitous in the casts of over a hundred films. There is also a category of supporting players who seemed to remain forever suspended between leading star and character actor: Joan Blondell, Claude Rains, and Shelley Winters, to name a few. They were stars whose names had lucrative drawing power at the box office, but they carried the unique distinction of gaining such fame despite the fact that their roles were almost exclusively secondary ones.

Although it might seem that supporting actors sacrificed quality over quantity, they did so simply to remain employed. Remarkably, their back-to-back assignments did not diminish their abilities to give memorable performances. Rather, the steady stream of jobs gave them the opportunity to hone their own brand of character, and in so doing, gain a loyal audience. *New York Times* journalist Molly Haskell explained: "In the 30's, 40's and even the 50's, each studio's roster of types stood out vividly, icons on the horizon, targets for whom screenwriters could tailor roles and with whom audiences could identify. Hear the name and you could hear the voice, see the face and name the epithet that conjured up that particular presence for all time."[1] The characters the actors created might have limited the actors' scope, but the audiences enjoyed knowing what to expect from each individual. Likewise, the studios relished finding formulas that guaranteed box-office success; thus, they were hesitant to cast supporting players against type.

Once a supporting player reached a certain level of popularity, their weekly salaries could be rather generous. Edward Everett Horton earned up to $7,000 a week. Frank Morgan earned $2,500 a week for his work in *The Wizard of Oz* and Ray Bolger earned $3,000. Billie Burke earned $766 a week for her work as Glinda the Good Witch and Margaret Hamilton earned $1,000 for her work as the Wicked Witch.[2] Hattie McDaniel received $1,000 as well for her work as Mammy in *Gone With the Wind*.[3] During the Depression when these actors were in their heyday, these salaries would seem enormous to the average person. But in comparison to leading stars, they were tiny. In the early 1930s, Constance Bennett commanded the highest salary at $30,000 a week.[4] Character actress Billie Burke once admitted that while she wished for different, bigger, and better roles, "if people will laugh at my work and keep a sound roof over my head, who am I to complain?"[5]

Incidentally, the inspiration for this book can be credited to Billie Burke. When we the authors were seven years old, we pushed aside our Disney cartoons in favor of *The Wizard of Oz*. We were fascinated by Dorothy, but Glinda the Good Witch stood out more than any of the other characters for us. We found that Dorothy was actually Judy Garland and Glinda was actually Billie Burke. We proceeded to hunt down every film we could find in which the actresses had parts. In doing so, we discovered masterpieces featuring Burke like *Dinner at Eight* (1933), *The Man Who Came to Dinner* (1942), and *Topper* (1937) as well as less remembered gems like *The Young in Heart* (1938) and *Merrily We Live* (1938). We discovered the great M-G-M musicals through Judy Garland, including *Meet Me in St. Louis* (1944), *In the Good Old Summertime* (1949), and *The Harvey Girls* (1946). As we discovered Burke's and Garland's films, we also discovered an array of delightful supporting actors. We watched the films so many times that we began to memorize certain names that appeared again and again in the cast credits. Chill Wills was the iceman Garland's sister Tootie befriended in *Meet Me in St. Louis*, but he was also Garland's comical long distance fiancé in *The Harvey Girls*. Spring Byington, Garland's flighty mother in *Presenting Lily Mars* (1943), was also her no-nonsense co-worker in *In the Good Old Summertime*. Roland Young, the actor who portrayed Mr. Topper, was Billie Burke's co-star again in six other films!

As we grew older, we regularly recorded films from the Turner Classic Movie channel and found more supporting players beyond the ones we discovered through Billie Burke and Judy Garland. We began to seek out films with our favorite little actors more so than even the ones with our favorite leading men and women. When we saw Edward Everett Horton, Eric Blore, or Marjorie Main's names (just to mention a few), we experienced the same rush of joy and anticipation one might feel when a favorite aunt or uncle steps through the door on a holiday.

We hope this collection profiling forty outstanding supporting players will bring readers smiles, laughs, and perhaps even tears: feelings akin to poring over a family album with photographs of half-forgotten friends and relatives who, upon remembrance, summon our most sincere fondness and nostalgia.

"WHAT'S THAT, BOSS?"
EDDIE ROCHESTER ANDERSON

EDDIE ROCHESTER ANDERSON IN *CABIN IN THE SKY* **(1943).**

"His charisma was tangible, his pumice-like orations undeniable... he became a Spiro-electronic Messenger of the black city, a rasp unstoppable." [1]

The black messenger of which author R.J. Smith speaks is Eddie Anderson, better known as Eddie Rochester Anderson. He adopted the middle name after he became synonymous with his radio and screen character, Rochester Van Jones, chauffeur to the legendary comedian Jack Benny. He had the distinction of being the first black radio star at a time when white men feigned black dialect on the air waves. Eddie was embraced by the white community for his inimitably delivered comebacks but was also accepted by the black community for his character's lack of subservience to "Mr. Benny." Eddie did not only make radio history, but he also earned a place in film history as a notable character actor. He added his unapologetic humor to screwball comedies like *You Can't Take It with You* (1938) and *Topper Returns* (1941) and to musicals like *Cabin in the Sky* (1943) and *Broadway Rhythm* (1944). Eddie Rochester Anderson broke racial barriers not through activism but through the common experience of laughter.

Eddie Anderson was born in 1905 in Oakland, California. There was little question that he would find his way to show business given that his father, "Big Ed," was a minstrel performer and his mother, Ella Mae, worked as a tightrope walker. Eddie's ancestors had found their way to California after escaping the South through the Underground Railroad. [2] The perseverant spirit of his ancestors was passed on to Eddie, as proven when he, at age twelve, took it upon himself to help keep his family's rent paid after his mother suffered a serious fall. Eddie found work as a newsboy selling papers on street corners in San Francisco. The job did not seem related to performing, but Eddie's experience selling papers was what gave him his most valuable asset in his radio and film work. "We really hawked newspapers when I was a kid in San Francisco," Eddie said. "We thought that the loudest voice sold the papers, which wasn't true of course. Anyway, I ruptured my vocal cords from straining them." [3] The ruptured vocal cords gave him the gravelly rasp that would make him instantly recognizable on radio and on screen.

After two years, Eddie quit selling papers to join his brother, Cornelius, in an all-black vaudeville revue. The brothers received their first significant job at the 1925 World Theater in Omaha, Nebraska. The gig led to jobs up and down the vaudeville circuit until they reached Los Angeles. There, they secured a regular spot singing and dancing at the famed Cotton Club for two years. [4] The regular paychecks Eddie now received gave him the security he needed to start a family. In 1932, he married Mamie Wiggins

Nelson. Though they would remain married for twenty-two years, the only child in the marriage was a son from Mamie's previous marriage, Billy.

When vaudeville's popularity waned in the 1930s, Eddie turned to radio, which was then the favored form of entertainment in America. In 1937, Eddie won a part on Jack Benny's radio program as a Pullman porter. Though the role was small, it garnered much public notice. In Eddie's short segment, Benny asks him when the next train to Albuquerque is due and Eddie laughs as a response, assuming a name as silly as Albuquerque had to be fabricated by Benny. "Eddie was a riot on that show," Benny recalled. "And I was surprised nobody picked him up. We got so much mail. I decided to make him a regular. I made him my butler and chauffeur on the show." [5] At the time, *Amos 'n Andy* was the only popular show centered on blacks, but blacks did not perform on the show and the way in which Amos and Andy were represented was stereotypical and one-dimensional. During the twenty-three-year run of *The Jack Benny Program* (on radio and television), the Rochester Van Jones character deepened and developed into much more than a perfunctory chauffeur. Rochester did possess some attributes typically given to black characters such as loafing, gambling, and drinking, but Eddie made these traits more a part of his character than a criticism of his entire race. The languid nature of Rochester was not far removed from Eddie's actual manner. He was known for his lack of punctuality. After he arrived late several days in a row, Benny began incurring fifty-dollar fines per tardy arrival. Eddie's lateness was most often due to his ardent interest in people and pursuits. He often became so caught up in a conversation or activity that he lost track of time. [6]

Aside from the less desirable stereotypes Rochester embodied, he possessed positive attributes, namely autonomy from his employer and self-respect. Rochester referred to Benny as "Boss" rather than "Sir," which indicated he was not simply a servant but closer to "one man speaking more directly to another." [7] "What's that boss?" became Eddie's most oft-repeated phrase, usually spoken with an incredulous lift to his brows each time Benny invented a new nonsensical scheme such as keeping a baby polar bear for a pet or starting his own laundry service. Much of the humor on the Benny program made Benny the object of ridicule as in this exchange between him and Rochester:

ROCHESTER: *Say Boss, if you win the Academy Award will you give me a raise?*

BENNY: *I certainly will — you'll get a nice, substantial increase.*

ROCHESTER: *Man, I sure wish you was a better actor.* [8]

In another episode, Benny asks Rochester to help him prepare for a boxing match, which ends with Rochester accidentally knocking his boss unconscious. Surprisingly, the Benny program received no protestations concerning the scenario of a black man knocking out a white man. "I like white folks and they like me," Eddie explained. "A colored man's just nacherly gotta laugh. Take me. If I don't laugh I reckon pretty quick I'd die. And other folks ain't no different." [9]

Though Eddie had found his niche in radio, he ventured into films and found success, though it could not compare to that of his radio popularity. His first appearance was as a butler in George Cukor's *What Price, Hollywood?* (1932). His name was not included on the casts of most of his films until the 1936 all-black film based on biblical stories, *The Green Pastures* (1936). Though his roles continued to be small, he began appearing in a higher caliber of film. He showed off his dancing skills while cutting the rug with the Sycamore family's maid in Frank Capra's screwball classic *You Can't Take It with You* (1938) and played Uncle Peter, Aunt Pitty's coachman in *Gone With the Wind* (1939). Many of his early credited roles were as Eddie Anderson; it was not until Jack Benny sold him the copyright to the name "Rochester" for $1 that he began to give his name as Eddie Rochester Anderson. [10] Eddie gradually took on more significant roles, particularly when he began to co-star with Jack Benny in comedies such as *Man About Town* (1939) and *Buck Benny Rides Again* (1940). Eddie soon became a ubiquitous presence in a variety of light fare. His wide-eyed and alternately baffled or sarcastic personality was as funny on screen as on the air waves. One of his most memorable roles was as Eddie, Mr. Topper's chauffeur in *Topper Returns* (1941). The part is a variation on the Rochester character, and the script even included an in-joke referring to Eddie's work with Jack Benny. In one scene, Eddie the Chauffeur is lamenting the strange happenings brought about by a mischievous ghost, played by Joan Blondell:

EDDIE, THE CHAUFFEUR: *Doors opening by themselves. People talkin' to nuthin' and gettin' answers. I'm going back.*

CLARA TOPPER: *Back where?*

EDDIE, THE CHAUFFEUR: *To Mr. Benny. Ain't nuthin' like this ever happened there.* [11]

Eddie received the rare opportunity to step out of the Rochester character when he won the lead role in the all-black musical *Cabin in the Sky* (1943). Directed by Vincent Minnelli, produced by the legendary Arthur Freed, and co-starring Ethel Waters and Lena Horne, it was a top-notch musical. In the film Eddie plays Little Joe, a gambler who, through the help of the Devil, wins a lottery and strays from his faithful wife, Ethel Waters,

EDDIE ROCHESTER ANDERSON WITH ETHEL WATERS ON THE LEFT AND LENA HORNE ON THE RIGHT IN *CABIN IN THE SKY* (1943). COURTESY OF JERRY MURBACH.

and into the arms of temptress Lena Horne. The film boasts now-classic tunes, including "Happiness Is a Thing Called Joe" and "Takin' a Chance on Love." Eddie's delivery of his song, "Life's Full of Consequences," was more comedic than dramatic with his sandpapery voice.

A leading role would not recur in Eddie's career. He played servants and chauffeurs for the remainder of his life, with the exception of his part in *Brewster's Millions* (1945). Eddie plays a war veteran whose white friend from the Army comes to him for advice as to how he should prove himself worthy so he may receive his rightful inheritance. Because Eddie is shown on a somewhat more equal footing with his white friend, the film was banned in many Southern areas. The Memphis Board of Motion Picture

Censors claimed Eddie had "an important role and has too familiar a way about him." [12] Though Eddie was enormously popular with blacks and whites alike, such backlashes occurred more than once. In 1943 when Jack Benny brought Eddie and the rest of his show's crew on tour through Missouri, Eddie was denied a room at the hotel at which Benny reserved rooms. Benny and the rest of the crew refused to stay in the hotel if Eddie was not permitted. [13] The loyalty between Eddie and Benny was a rare and touching one when the era's societal conventions are considered.

Anyone doubting Eddie's worth would find it difficult to argue that he was not an exemplary American citizen. During World War II, he took an active part in politics in hopes of making more opportunities for blacks to defend their country. The black community living in the area surrounding Central Avenue in Los Angles had a long-held tradition of holding a mock election for a black mayor, whom they dubbed "The Mayor of Central Avenue." Eddie ran for the position in 1940, claiming, "If I am elected, I will pave Central Avenue with pancakes and flood it with molasses." [14] However jesting this remark might have seemed, Eddie was serious when discussing his ideas. He called for cleaner streets, more efficient law enforcement, and fair hiring practices in the police force. [15] With the coming of war eminent, Eddie advocated for the training of black aviators. He even took a flying course himself and arranged talks with the Tuskegee Institute. Eddie won the election and, true to his promise, provided pancakes for everyone. During the war, Eddie continued to aid the effort not only by lightening the nation's mood with his comedy but by purchasing the Pacific Parachute Company, a black-owned business that manufactured parachutes for the military. [16]

Eddie's activities outside of acting extended beyond politics to pleasure pursuits — namely horseracing and automobiles. In 1943, Eddie became the first black man to enter a horse in the Kentucky Derby. He declared that his thoroughbred, which he humorously named Burnt Cork, would run the race "even if he doesn't do anything but run around after the others." [17] When the horse eventually won a race, Eddie arrived for work at M-G-M dressed as a Kentucky colonel, insisting he be called "Colonel Rochester." [18] Eddie certainly had the income to live like a colonel; the man who played a chauffeur possessed his own staff as well as a yacht and a sizable mansion. In 1962, *Ebony* cited him as being among the 100 wealthiest blacks in America. [19] Despite his wealth, Eddie enjoyed less genteel pursuits that involved working with his hands. He built his own racing car in 1951 that combined a Cadillac engine with a low-slung body. The vehicle was shown at car shows nationwide. [20]

Eddie's wealth did not make him immune to tragedy in his personal life. His wife of twenty-two years died in 1954, leaving behind his adopted son, Billy. Billy had become a football player for the Chicago Bears, but this high position was lost after he was convicted of assaulting his secretary and for possession of marijuana. [21] Eddie's personal life became more optimistic after he married Evangela Simon in 1956. They had three children. The marriage ended in 1973, but Eddie retained custody of his two minor children.

Eddie's ability to make audiences laugh did not diminish despite his private difficulties. "To the comedian, any area of life is material for comedy," [22] he stated. The 1950s saw Eddie find a new audience on the small screen as he joined Jack Benny on his television program in 1950, again as Rochester Van Jones. Even after the program's end in 1965, Eddie and Jack Benny remained friends. "We always exchange Christmas gifts and he's not as stingy as he pretends to be," [23] Eddie chuckled. Eddie and Benny reunited for a television special in 1968 and both appeared in the film *It's a Mad, Mad, Mad, Mad World* (1963). By that time, Eddie's work in film was over and his screen time on television also slowed. He spent the early seventies behind the camera as the voice of B.J. in the television series *The New Scooby-Doo Movies* (1972-1973).

Show business remained on the periphery of Eddie's life in his senior years as he devoted the bulk of his time to his passion for horses. After the end of *The Jack Benny Program*, he worked as a trainer at the Hollywood Park Racetrack, a position he would hold until his death. It was a job he took as seriously, if not more so, than his performing. When one of his horses, Up and Out, was injured and said to be beyond help, Eddie refused to have the animal shot. Instead, he spent hours at the Paramount Pictures Library studying horses and their anatomy. He sought out a veterinary surgeon and together they saved Up and Out from death. [24]

Eddie still remained a part of show business despite his preoccupation with horseracing. In 1972, he staged a comeback nightclub act in Houston, which led to his being cast in a Broadway revival of the 1920s musical *Good News*. However, Eddie was unable to fill the role due to ailing health. In 1974, his friend and colleague, Jack Benny, preceded Eddie in death. Many were shocked that Eddie was not included in Benny's will, but, despite this omission, Eddie never spoke about his partner with anything but admiration and affection. Two years later, Eddie was admitted to the Motion Picture and Television Hospital for a heart condition. He died three months later of heart failure.

Eddie willed his estate to be used as a home for at-risk substance abusers, but the project was not fully formalized until 1989. Eddie's experience with his adopted son, Billy, was doubtless the inspiration behind this gesture. Eddie's younger son, Eddie Jr., helped establish The Rochester House, which today still strives to give its residents' lives purpose and to help them go on to "their rightful place in society." [25] The foundation was dedicated to Eddie's memory, for he was an example to the at-risk residents of someone who rose above obstacles to find that rightful place in society.

Though he never won any awards, Eddie Rochester Anderson holds a special place in history as the first black entertainer to create a unique character that went beyond the clichéd portrayals of his race. Through "Rochester" and the variations thereof in film, he humanized blacks on the airwaves and on screen. Rochester Van Jones is the antithesis of the submissive servant; he is unafraid to tell his boss his faults and, more often than not, appears more resourceful than his employer. Eddie's success at winning both black and white audiences' favor was a testament to his talent at delivering comedy that was universally appealing. Eddie's portrayal of Rochester endeared him to America to such an extent that he arguably became a more popular a character than Jack Benny. But Benny did not begrudge his friend this honor and even had Amos and Andy comment on it on *The Jack Benny Program*'s first show on CBS:

AMOS: *That Mr. Benny is supposed to be a big comedian…He didn't say nothin' funny.*

ANDY: *Well, it's just like I told ya, he ain't nothin' without Rochester.* [26]

FILMOGRAPHY

1967 *Enter Laughing* .... Subway Rider Who Sits on Box *(uncredited)*
1963 *It's a Mad Mad Mad Mad World*..................... Second Cab Driver
1959 *The Mouse That Jack Built (short)*................................... Rochester
(voice, as Rochester)
1946 *The Show-Off* .... Eddie
1945 *The Sailor Takes a Wife* .... Harry
1945 *I Love a Bandleader* .... Newton H. Newton *(as Rochester)*
1945 *Brewster's Millions* ....Jackson
1944 *Broadway Rhythm* .... Eddie

1943	*Stormy Weather* .... *(scenes deleted)*
1943	*What's Buzzin', Cousin?* .... Rochester
1943	*Calling All Kids (short)* .... Buckwheat *(voice)*
1943	*Cabin in the Sky* ....Joseph 'Little Joe' Jackson
1943	*The Meanest Man in the World* .... Shufro
1942	*Star Spangled Rhythm* ..... Rochester — Sharp as a Tack Number *(as Rochester)*
1942	*Tales of Manhattan* .... Rev. Lazarus
1941	*Birth of the Blues* .... Louey *(as Rochester)*
1941	*Kiss the Boys Goodbye* .... George
1941	*Topper Returns* .... Eddie, Chauffeur
1940	*Love Thy Neighbor* .... Rochester *(as Eddie Anderson)*
1940	*Buck Benny Rides Again* .... Rochester Van Jones
1939	*Gone with the Wind* .... Uncle Peter, Her Coachman *(as Eddie Anderson)*
1939	*Man About Town* .... Rochester *(as Eddie Anderson)*
1939	*You Can't Get Away with Murder* ....Sam *(uncredited)*
1939	*You Can't Cheat an Honest Man* .... Rochester *(as Eddie Anderson)*
1939	*Honolulu* .... Washington, Mason's Hollywood Servant *(as Eddie Anderson)*
1938	*Going Places* ....George — a Groom *(as Eddie Anderson)*
1938	*Kentucky* ....Groom *(as Eddie Anderson)*
1938	*Strange Faces* .... William
1938	*Thanks for the Memory* .... Janitor
1938	*Exposed* .... William
1938	*Five of a Kind* ....Hotel Doorman *(uncredited)*
1938	*You Can't Take It with You* .... Donald *(as Eddie Anderson)*
1938	*Gold Diggers in Paris* ....Doorman *(as Eddie Anderson)*
1938	*Jezebel* ....Gros Bat *(as Eddie Anderson)*
1938	*Reckless Living* ....Dreamboat
1937	*Over the Goal* ....William *(as Eddie Anderson)*
1937	*On Such a Night* ....Henry Clay, Fentridge Handyman *(as Eddie Anderson)*
1937	*Wake Up and Live* .... Elevator Operator *(uncredited)*
1937	*One Mile from Heaven* ....Henry Bangs
1937	*Reported Missing* ....Porter *(uncredited)*
1937	*White Bondage* ....Old Glory *(uncredited)*
1937	*Public Wedding* ....Man Carrying Coat *(uncredited)*
1937	*Melody for Two* .... Exodus Johnson *(as Eddie Anderson)*

1937 *When Love Is Young* .... Taxi Driver *(uncredited)*
1937 *Bill Cracks Down* .... Chauffeur
1937 *Love Is News* .... Man Getting Marriage License *(uncredited)*
1936 *Mysterious Crossing* .... Porter *(uncredited)*
1936 *Rainbow on the River* .... Doctor *(uncredited)*
1936 *Three Men on a Horse* .... Moses, the Elevator Operator
(as Eddie Anderson)
1936 *Two in a Crowd* .... Swipe
1936 *Star for a Night* .... Maid's Boyfriend *(uncredited)*
1936 *The Green Pastures* .... Noah *(as Eddie Anderson)*
1936 *Show Boat* .... Young Black Man *(uncredited)*
1936 *The Music Goes 'Round* .... Lucifer *(uncredited)*
1935 *His Night Out* .... Bellhop *(uncredited)*
1935 *Transient Lady* .... Noxious *(as Eddie Anderson)*
1934 *The Gay Bride* .... Second Bootblack *(uncredited)*
1934 *Behold My Wife* .... Chauffeur *(uncredited)*
1933 *I Love That Man* .... Charlie, Porter *(uncredited)*
1933 *Terror Aboard* .... Seaman *(uncredited)*
1933 *From Hell to Heaven* .... Sam's Pal *(uncredited)*
1933 *Billion Dollar Scandal* .... Railroad Steward *(uncredited)*
1932 *False Faces* .... Chauffeur *(uncredited)*
1932 *Hat Check Girl* .... Walter
1932 *What Price Hollywood?* .... James, Max's Butler *(uncredited)*

MISS VINEGAR
EVE ARDEN

EVE ARDEN, CIRCA 1950. AUTHOR'S COLLECTION

"I've never cared for the characters I generally played in films. I certainly don't think they were me. I really think I'm kinder than that." [1]

One would find it difficult to believe the above words spoken by Eve Arden, so convincing were her portrayals of "the cool, crisp, caustic career-dame who wore brass knuckles on her tongue when she wasn't dipping it in sulfuric acid." [2] The tall, blonde actress, more striking than tradition-ally beautiful in appearance, could potentially have been a leading lady had she not played her type of role so well. As a struggling actress full of quips in *Stage Door* (1937), Joan Crawford's sharp-tongued girlfriend and business partner in *Mildred Pierce* (1945), and the sardonic but loveable schoolteacher on the sitcom for which she is best remembered, *Our Miss Brooks* (1952-1956), she played only slight variations of the same resilient woman. Contrary to her screen image, the real Eve Arden was variously described as "mild" and full of "gentility, warmth, and kindness of spirit." [3] Eve herself declared she had had enough of being "Miss Vinegar year after year" and yearned to portray the soft, domestic woman she was in life. That being said, she also held that to play a role successfully, one has to bring facets of one's own personality to it. [4] It is Eve's genuine warmth of heart behind the sulfur-tongued women she created that makes filmgoers see her barbs as humorous rather than cruel in their unapologetic honesty.

Eve was born Eunice Quedens on April 30, 1908 in Mills Valley, California, but she spent the bulk of her childhood in San Francisco. A child of divorce, she doubtlessly brought aspects of her steel-spined mother to her later film characterizations. Mrs. Quedens did not know the word impossible. She was a successful businesswoman, teacher, and actress. As Eve grew up, her mother brought her to every theater in San Francisco, thus fostering a love of drama in the girl. Eve became so enam-ored of the theater that she transformed the attic of her apartment house into a sort of stage and used neighborhood children as an audience for her one-woman shows. "My plays were drawn from an active imagination, and I played all the parts," [5] Eve explained. After a few years of school in a convent, Eve and Mrs. Quedens settled back in Mills Valley. Eve relished the freedom of the rural environment and more than ever took advantage of chances to showcase her acting abilities. She won a WCTU recitation contest about the horrors of drink, and in school, the leggy teen "appeared in every form of entertainment that offered itself — short plays, song and dance skits." [6]

Eve would receive her first taste of the legitimate theater immediately upon graduation from high school. She became a member of Henry Duffy's stock company in San Francisco and made her debut in a walk-in.

But she climbed the acting ladder with astonishing speed; by her fourth play, she was the lead ingénue. Despite her popularity, Duffy criticized Eve with the observation that she was, "Having too much fun. You'll never be a success in this business. Don't take your work seriously enough." [7] Eve proved Duffy wrong. She moved to Los Angeles and went hungry before finally landing a part in her first film, a backstage musical comedy called *Song of Love* (1929) in which she played a wisecracking show girl. [8]

Next, Eve found work with the Bandbox Repertory Company, a group that gave the actress her first opportunity to ad lib on stage. Broadway mogul Lee Shubert was the most prominent producer to first notice the young actress' scene-stealing, witty improvisations. He promptly cast her in the *Ziegfeld Follies* but advised her to change her name. "Eunice Quedens will never do on the marquee at the Winter Garden," he remarked. Eve created her *nom de plume* using the first name of the heroine in the romance novel she was currently reading and the last name of the maker of the beauty products on her dresser. The newly christened Eve Arden fell in love with her new home in New York from the start. She became friends with co-stars Buddy and Vilma Ebsen and Fanny Brice.

On Eve's opening night in the 1934 *Follies,* she recalled her peculiar lack of fear most novices experience. "I guess something has been left out of me," she remarked. [9] She claimed that the only thing that gave her pause was her singing voice, but she gained confidence when she found the trumpets in the orchestra were "so loud they drowned me out." [10] Drowned out or not, Eve was a sensation and continued to be one in her successive shows. In *Parade,* a musical revue, Eve stated that her number "stopped the show cold." [11] Her skit had her parodying a Vassar graduate attempting to be a salesgirl and a society woman who fancies herself a liberal. She could lampoon every type and class of woman with equal wit and acidity, a talent she would put to good use portraying various characters in her films, from struggling young women to blasé socialites.

Eve's social life became as sensational as her professional one as her star continued to rise. Men of wealth and distinction vied for her affection, namely Lee Shubert and Robert Benchley, member of the Algonquin Round Table. Benchley proposed to Eve, but she was in love with Shubert. Shubert, a married man, offered to make her his mistress. However, she refused to break up his and his wife's union. Though she later professed to seek therapy because of how inferior she felt to her mother's great beauty, men clearly found the 5'7" blonde quite appealing. She never acknowledged her beauty. When told she appeared much thinner than her 129 pounds, she said with self-deprecation, "I have one of those deceptive figures." Upon seeing the eyes of the man who had made the comment begin to wander, she quipped, "Well, not that deceptive!" [12] Eve was a rare specimen in show business; she never "climbed the ladder of success lad by lad" or "knifed a fellow actress." Rather, she was described as "pleasant, easy-going, non-competitive." [13]

EVE ARDEN, IN CENTER ON SOFA WITH KATHARINE HEPBURN AND GINGER ROGERS TO HER LEFT IN A SCENE FROM *STAGE DOOR* **(1938).** COURTESY OF JERRY MURBACH.

Her lack of competitiveness and backstabbing worked in her favor. She was cast in a second edition of the *Follies,* directed by the soon-to-be leading Hollywood director, Vincent Minnelli. With barely time to take a breath after the run of the show, she landed her first significant film role. The film was *Oh, Doctor* (1937) and her laudable performance in it was responsible for her next being cast in the now-classic Edna Ferber-George Kaufman story of acting hopefuls, *Stage Door* (1937). Eve's role was initially a minor one, but it turned into arguably the most memorable role in the film thanks to her ad libs. It was Eve who suggested that her character always have a white cat draped about her neck whom she calls Henry. She renames the kitty Henrietta after "he" has kittens, causing Eve to declare that she has lost all her faith in men (feline ones included).

Director Gregory La Cava was so impressed that he asked Eve for more ideas. By the time the film was ready for release, Eve had a prominent role as the fast-talking, wisecracking friend to Jean, played by leading lady Ginger Rogers. She offers not a few sharp-tongued, but darkly funny bits of dialogue. With irony dripping from her words, she makes a dispiriting reply to Jean on the opening night of their friend's Broadway debut:

JEAN MAITLAND: *Hey, you're not gonna catch the opening tonight, huh?*

EVE: *No, I'm going tomorrow and catch the closing.* [14]

Whenever Eve leaves the screen in *Stage Door*, it is difficult to wait for her next scene and anticipate the next outrageous remark she will make. Apparently audiences and critics felt the same way. Eve became fondly known as "the girl with the cat" [15] after the film. Eve's part in *Stage Door* established her reputation in Hollywood, perhaps too well. For the rest of her career, Eve would play virtually the same part over and over again. One exception was when she was Peerless Pauline, a female acrobat in the Marx Brothers' film *At the Circus* (1939).

Busy as Eve was in the late 1930s, she found time to fall in love and wed. The groom's name was Ned Bergen. "I made picture after picture and had a husband to come home to at night. I seemed to have it all," [16] Eve stated. Among her succession of pictures were *Comrade X* (1940), in which she portrayed Clark Gable's Girl Friday, *Ziegfeld Girl* (1941), in which she was a jaded showgirl, *My Reputation* (1946), a film that had her playing Barbara Stanwyck's commonsensical pal, and *Mildred Pierce* (1945), a film that had her this time as Joan Crawford's friend Ida. The latter role became Eve's shining hour on the screen. As Ida, she played the "brass knuckled career dame" to the hilt. At the same time, she brought sensitivity to her role; many of her barbs only thinly cloaked her longing for a settled home and man to love (not unlike Eve herself). At one moment, she bitterly declares, *Oh, men. I never yet met one of them that didn't have the instincts of a heel. Sometimes I wish I could get along without them.* [17]

At the next moment, she wistfully watches Crawford with her soon-to-be husband and sighs, *When men get around me, they get allergic to wedding rings.* [18]

Eve's multi-dimensional and human performance earned her an Academy Award nomination, but she lost to Anne Revere in *National Velvet* (1945).

Though they had nearly earned her an Oscar, by the late 1940s, Eve had grown tired of her predictable "big hearted dames." She bemoaned that, "I'm always the flip miss who comforts her friend after she had comes in from a rough date...Do I ever get any comforting? Do I ever get a part where I have a rough date?" [19] As little comfort as Eve received on screen, she received less at home. Her husband had joined the Navy, leaving her alone for the majority of the time and making Eve's wish for children impossible to realize. However, she found a solution that gave her "a focus and sense of purpose" [20] for her work when she adopted Liza, a baby girl. The child helped assuage the loneliness Eve faced after she and Ned had "an amicable divorce" [21] in 1947. Her family continued to grow even without Ned. She adopted another little girl, Connie, and a boy, Duncan, before the decade was out.

Though a loving and capable mother, Eve could not overcome the feeling of depression that began to enfold her. She began seeing a psychotherapist with much success. She later reflected on what she learned from their sessions: "There are two types of neurotics, those who take their frustrations out on the world and those who take them out on themselves. I wanted to take them out on me." [22] No longer taking her frustrations out on herself, Eve began to embrace the character she had created in *Stage Door*. Eve played her with her customary excellence, elevating fluffy musicals such as *Tea for Two* (1950), *My Dream Is Yours* (1949), and *Night and Day* (1946) with her intelligent wit.

In 1948, Eve found a new project that would give her the character she had been searching for. She was Miss Connie Brooks, a middle-aged school teacher with Eve's acid wit but also her soft heart, shown through her unrequited crush on fellow teacher Mr. Boynton. [23] *Our Miss Brooks* began as a radio show, but was picked up on television in 1952, where it would enjoy a four-year run. The heart and sincerity she brought to her role even through her wisecracks did not go unnoticed by her fans. She was made an honorary member of the National Education Association and was given an award from the Teacher's College of Connecticut Alumni Association for "humanizing the American teacher." [24]

Flush with success as Miss Brooks, Eve found equal success in her personal life. In 1950, she met fellow actor Brooks West and married him at a farm she had bought for her and her growing family in Massachusetts. They made the farm the home Eve had always hoped for. She filled it with antiques inside while outside she made it a home for unwanted animals. She raised every type of creature from sheep to horses to iguanas. Though animals outnumbered her children, she now had a healthy brood of four kids: Liza, Connie, Duncan, and Douglas. Douglas was her only birth child. She called him the "red head I'd always dreamed of" [25] when he was born to her and Brooks. The family bonded through travel, which Eve called their "third life." They traveled through most of Europe and rented an apartment in Italy for a lengthy period of time. "We wanted to…live as a family sharing new adventures together," [26] Eve explained. She shared her contentment in her new family life in candid interviews, offering her parenting methods to readers. "I try to teach my…children a sense of humor… When they see me laughing at something that I might have been upset about, they laugh, too," she said [27] She went on to philosophize that if everyone took this view of "less grim and more grin," [28] no wars would ever begin.

As much as Eve encouraged a good sense of humor, she found it hard to keep a happy face as her seemingly idyllic family life began to crack. She discovered her husband had a severe drinking problem. She managed to hold the family together by convincing Brooks to enter a detoxification program and plunging into her work. After *Our Miss Brooks* was cancelled, she attempted, but failed, to make a success of *The Eve Arden Show*. Instead, she turned to the stage, where she would land a succession of plum roles perfectly suited for her unique personality. First, she played the optimistic, eccentric Auntie Mame all along the West Coast; next, she launched a one-woman show in Las Vegas. The show gave her an impressive $20,000 a week and earned equally generous reviews. Critics lauded her combination of singing, dancing, telling jokes, reminiscing about her career, and her series of impression of famous figures including Bette Davis and Jackie Kennedy. One reviewer hailed her a "show business phenomenon" who could do just about anything well. [29] Shortly after the success of the show, Eve was cast as a secretary in *Anatomy of a Murder* (1959) with her temporarily sober husband as her co-star. The picture was as warmly met by critics as her one-woman show was.

Eve celebrated her success by traveling. She rubbed elbows with the such British intelligentsia as Rebecca West, appeared at a benefit with luminaries Laurence Olivier and Elizabeth Taylor, and attended numerous Chekhov plays. "If I've learned anything in life, it's to live now, to enjoy nowness," she said, sounding not a little like Auntie Mame herself. Eve continued on an upswing when she returned to the U.S. in 1967 and replaced Carol Channing in the title role of *Hello, Dolly!* She won a Sarah Siddons Award for her achievement. *Hello, Dolly!* paved the way for Eve's return to television. She found a new television series, *The Mothers-in-Law*, in which she played one of several meddlesome and temperamental women who inadvertently complicate their children's lives. Eve loved the "wild, robust humor"[30] of the show and the familiar routine it gave her life. But the show ended after only two seasons. Eve turned her focus away from her work for the majority of the 1970s, instead tending to Brooks, who had again fallen into alcoholism. She helped him rehabilitate by taking up painting with him and attending his AA meetings. She found time to do a bit of theater, most notably with Donald O'Connor in a play entitled *Little Me*. At the close of the decade, Woody Allen approached Eve for a part in a project he was working on but she could not accept it. Brooks suffered a fatal stroke as a complication of his alcoholism. Eve was devastated, but her steel spine was her savoir. She showed her resilience and her immoveable optimism with the words: "I have a childlike faith that what's meant to be will be, as the song puts it, que sera, sera."[31]

It took Eve until she was nearly eighty years old to retire. She penned the story of her life in the cleverly titled 1985 autobiography *The Three Phases of Eve*, recounting her entire career up to her last foray into show business playing the principal in *Grease II* (1982). The seemingly indefatigable Eve succumbed to heart disease five years after the book's publication. Shortly afterward, she was honored with two stars on the Hollywood Walk of Fame, one for radio and one for television. It is a sad oversight that she was not also awarded a star for her contributions to film; indeed, she created a character so distinct that even in her lifetime, many scripts could sum up a role simply by calling it "an Eve Arden part."[32]

Eve once said that for her whole life she felt on the brink of failure. Over the course of her career, she proved herself wrong in every role to which she lent her talent. To every medium, she brought a character whose ripostes could be called catty if they were not spoken with such good humor that audiences could not help but grin. The confidence and independence Eve brought to her roles made her like "one of the boys." She had the distinction of being admired by men not only for her good looks but for her brains and uncompromising persona. Eve was just as strong as the women she portrayed, though she seldom, if ever, admitted it. She maintained a refreshing innocence and humility, even more refreshing when contrasted with the often jaded woman she portrayed in her work: "I am grateful for the many miracles and even, I suppose will be grateful for the pain [in my life]," she said. "At least I will better understand others' pain and be able to contribute something worthwhile to this sad and wonderful world."[33]

FILMOGRAPHY

1982	*Grease 2*	Principal McGee
1982	*Pandemonium*	Warden June
1981	*Under the Rainbow*	The Duchess
1978	*Grease*	Principal McGee
1975	*The Strongest Man in the World*	Harriet Crumply
1965	*Sergeant Dead Head*	Lieutenant Kinsey
1960	*The Dark at the Top of the Stairs*	Lottie Lacey
1959	*Anatomy of a Murder*	Maida Rutledge
1956	*Our Miss Brooks*	Miss Constance 'Connie' Brooks
1953	*The Lady Wants Mink*	Gladys Jones
1952	*We're Not Married!*	Katie Woodruff
1951	*Goodbye, My Fancy*	Miss 'Woody' Woods
1951	*Three Husbands*	Lucille McCabe
1950	*Tea for Two*	Pauline Hastings
1950	*Curtain Call at Cactus Creek*	Lily Martin
1950	*Paid in Full*	Tommy Thompson
1949	*The Lady Takes a Sailor*	Susan Wayne
1949	*My Dream Is Yours*	Vivian Martin
1948	*Whiplash*	Chris Sherwood
1948	*One Touch of Venus*	Molly Stewart
1947	*The Voice of the Turtle*	Olive Lashbrooke
1947	*The Unfaithful*	Paula
1947	*Song of Scheherazade*	Madame de Talavera
1947	*The Arnelo Affair*	Vivian Delwyn
1946	*Night and Day*	Gabrielle
1946	*The Kid from Brooklyn*	Ann Westley
1946	*My Reputation*	Ginna Abbott
1945	*Mildred Pierce*	Ida Corwin
1945	*Patrick the Great*	Jean Mathews
1945	*Earl Carroll Vanities*	'Tex' Donnelly
1945	*Pan-Americana*	Helen 'Hoppy' Hopkins
1944	*The Doughgirls*	Sgt. Natalia Moskoroff
1944	*Cover Girl*	Cornelia 'Stonewall' Jackson
1943	*Let's Face It*	Maggie Watson
1943	*Hit Parade of 1943*	Belinda Wright
1942	*Obliging Young Lady*	'Space' OShea, aka Suwanee Rivers
1941	*Bedtime Story*	Virginia Cole
1941	*Sing for Your Supper*	Barbara Stevens

1941 *Last of the Duanes* .... Kate
1941 *Manpower* .... Dolly
1941 *Whistling in the Dark* .... 'Buzz' Baker
1941 *San Antonio Rose* .... Gabby Trent
1941 *She Knew All the Answers* .... Sally Long
1941 *Ziegfeld Girl* .... Patsy Dixon
1941 *That Uncertain Feeling* .... Sally
1940 *No, No, Nanette* .... Kitty
1940 *Comrade X* .... Jane Wilson
1940 *She Couldn't Say No* .... Alice Hinsdale
1939 *Slightly Honorable* .... Miss Ater
1939 *A Child Is Born* .... Miss Pinty, A Nurse
1939 *At the Circus* .... Peerless Pauline
1939 *Eternally Yours* .... Gloria
1939 *The Forgotten Woman* .... Carrie Ashburn
1939 *Big Town Czar* .... Susan Warren
1939 *Women in the Wind* .... Kit Campbell
1938 *Letter of Introduction* .... Cora Phelps
1938 *Having Wonderful Time* .... Henrietta
1938 *Cocoanut Grove* .... Sophie De Lemma
1937 *Stage Door* .... Eve
1937 *Oh, Doctor* .... Shirley Truman
1933 *Dancing Lady* .... Marcia–the Southern Actress *(uncredited)*
1929 *Song of Love* .... Maisie LeRoy *(as Eunice Quedens)*

LADY FAY
FAY BAINTER

FAY BAINTER, CIRCA 1923, AUTHOR'S COLLECTION

"A very rare personality this! She has no particularly striking beauty, perhaps, and no great single talent, but she has a freshness of feeling and a daintiness of charm that surround her like an atmosphere and win their way by an almost instant magic."[1]

These words, written in 1918 by a *New York Times* dramatic editor, were in regards to a rising young Broadway star by the name of Fay Bainter. Her name may not sound familiar, but when viewing classics of the silver screen, it is hard not to come across her less than a dozen times. The very traits the dramatic editor outlined in 1918 seamlessly translated onto film. Her empathetic eyes, soft face, and motherly build paired with her sophisticated and husky voice are quickly recognizable and difficult to forget in her memorable roles as both maternal figures and independent women. Fay might be remembered simply as a character actress today, but both onstage and onscreen, she was more than a supporting player. At one time she was among Broadway's most acclaimed actresses. In Hollywood, she excelled in her acting to such a degree that in 1939, the Academy of Motion Pictures Arts and Sciences changed its rules so she could receive two nominations in the same category in one year.

Although Fay was famous on Broadway, she began and ended her career in Hollywood. She was born on December 7, 1893, to Charles Bainter and Mary Okell in Los Angeles, California. As is the case in many actresses' histories, it was Fay's mother who pushed her into acting at a very young age. She made her stage debut at the age of six in Oliver Morosco's production *The Jewess*. She remained with Morosco's traveling stock company until 1912. As a child, she received small parts in plays such as *A Little Princess*, *The Prince and the Pauper*, and *Little Lord Fauntleroy*. Fay left Morosco's troupe when she traveled to New York in 1912. She made her Broadway debut in a musical titled *The Rose of Panama* followed by *The Bridal Path* in 1913. With her Mary Pickford-style curls and large, expressive eyes, she made a promising new ingénue even though her first two plays were not hits at the box office.

Fay spent the next five years struggling in traveling stock troupes, a bit discouraged by her lack of success on Broadway. In a 1918 article she wrote for the *New York Times,* she reminisced about her early days as a starving young actress. She explained, "Those were the days when a company would play for one week and be laid off for two without salary before it played another week."[2] Such an uncertain lifestyle was difficult for a young girl, particularly in 1912 during *The Rose of Panama* when she had to celebrate her first Christmas without her family. With her eleven-dollar salary, Fay "like a crazy kid went out and bought books"[3] for everyone in her family. The capricious act left her broke, but the camaraderie between her and her cast mates saved her spending Christmas completely alone. She and a young man named Phil Sheffield had made a habit of dining on oyster stew for dinner so that they could fill up on the crackers that came with it. On that Christmas of 1912, Phil found Fay sobbing in the theater, alone, broke, and hungry. Together, Phil, Fay, and another friend pooled $1.80 and went to a cheap spaghetti cellar for dinner. Fay finished her article, saying, "That [the spaghetti] and the good nature of those two boys was all that saved that Christmas from utter disaster." [4]

The uncertain life as a stock troupe actress eating oyster stew for dinner ended in 1918 when Fay became a member of legendary producer David Belasco's company. Belasco had been responsible for starting the careers of many actresses, most notably Mary Pickford's. It was through her fortuitous association with the producer that Fay was cast in her first hit, *Arms and the Girl*, in 1916. The dramatic editor of *The Toledo Blade* wrote to the *New York Times* editor, concurring with his prophesy that Fay had a promising future: "She is earnest, sincere, unaffected, and ambitious, and beyond doubt your prediction as to her future will be verified." [5] A succession of hits followed, one of which was an Oriental-themed play called *The Willow Tree*. Critics claimed that "she [brought] witchery and a touching tenderness to the role." [6] Fay proved to be equally adept at musical comedies as she was in dramas, and critics lauded her in the spring of 1918 for her role in the Viennese-inspired show *The Kiss Burglar*. Critics claimed she "had no voice to speak of" but that she sang "the purest music," and that she "conveyed [humor] with the subtlest comedy." [7]

Fay became known by all on Broadway after she made her biggest hit yet in *East Is West* in December 1918. Cast in the lead role, she played Ming Toy, an outspoken young lady trying to escape her old-fashioned Oriental upbringing. Despite her overnight success, Fay still suffered from feelings of doubt and homesickness. She later stated that on her opening night at the Astor Theater, "I was terribly worried and nearly dead from rehearsal and almost sorry I was alive at all. I might own up, at this late date that I was not at all optimistic about the play." [8] Fay's anxiety was for naught. She became the darling of Broadway and the acclaimed painter Robert Henri even had her pose for an oil portrait.

Although *East Is West* was the height of her success to date, Fay was not seen frequently on the stage between 1919 and 1925. In 1918, she met a lieutenant commander in the U.S. Navy named Reginald Venable who had become her admirer after he first saw her on stage. The two were engaged for a year before they married in summer 1920 in Riverside,

California. Reginald and Fay were ardent about keeping their marriage out of the press. Fay declared it was in bad taste to make the marriage a public affair. However, the press could hardly stay away when Reginald broke Navy regulations by using the destroyer he was in charge of for his own personal use. He redirected the destroyer so that he could be the first to meet Fay's steamer, which was returning from a trip she had taken to Europe. Navy secretary Daniels was lenient and smilingly said that Reginald was just "a young man courting."[9] Fay and Reginald did not announce their marriage to the press until the following year.

As much as Fay enjoyed being back in her home state and taking on the role of wife, she returned to the stage in 1925 to star in an anti-war drama, *The Enemy*. Her next show was not until 1927, for in 1926, she gave birth to her first and only child, Reginald Jr. Returning in 1927 in Noel Coward's *Fallen Angels*, Fay's career continued to prosper into the early 1930s. She played a variety of roles, including the part Gloria Swanson had done on screen in *The Admirable Crichton* and the part Ginger Rogers would later do on screen in *The Gay Divorcee*. In 1934, Fay did what is now seen as her best stage work when she portrayed the restless wife of Dodsworth in Sinclair Lewis' story of the same name.

This same year marked the end of her Broadway career. M-G-M persuaded her to come to Hollywood to co-star as Lionel Barrymore's wife in *This Side of Heaven* (1934). At first, Fay was not fond of acting for the camera. But, her family resided in California and the movies offered a generous salary. In addition, Depression era audiences flocked to movie theaters more than they did to New York plays. Fay received steady employment in film, her second one being *Quality Street* (1937) with Katharine Hepburn. The film is considered to be in Hepburn's box-office poison era, but Fay was singled out as "the triumph of the production."[10] Her portrayal of Hepburn's flustered and nervous aunt gave life to scenes that otherwise might have seemed stilted. The same year as *Quality Street*, Fay appeared in her most prestigious film to date, *Make Way for Tomorrow* (1937). The Leo McCarey classic tells the story of two displaced seniors during the Depression who must rely on their often selfish children to give them room and board. As Beulah Bondi's daughter-in-law, Fay gives a performance that is both sympathetic and unsympathetic. She perfectly blends the feeling of wishing to help her elderly mother-in-law while at the same time wanting to remain queen of her own household with no criticisms from the older woman.

Though she was not lovable in *Make Way for Tomorrow*, beginning with the role of Priscilla Lane's mother in *Daughters Courageous* (1939),

Fay was most often cast in warm, sympathetic, maternal roles. It was for such a part that she received the 1939 Oscar for Best Supporting Actress for her portrayal of Bette Davis' aunt in *Jezebel* (1938). Davis later claimed, "Her contribution to the film and to my performance was immeasurable. It just wouldn't have been the same picture without her." [11] Although her part was small, she added bits of common sense

FAY BAINTER WITH BETTE DAVIS IN *JEZEBEL* (1938). COURTESY OF JERRY MURBACH.

to offset Bette Davis' sharp tongue. An example of such an exchange is illustrated with this line:

> JULIE: *He had no right to tell me what I could ride and what I couldn't!*

> AUNT BELLE: *The horse showed you what you couldn't! You broke your collarbone and your engagement!* [12]

The same year *Jezebel* was released, the academy changed its rules so that Fay could also be nominated for Best Supporting Actress in *White Banners* (1938) for her performance as a woman trying to help her son's foster family without letting the family know she is the boy's mother.

After winning for *Jezebel,* she had reached a level of prestige that gave her steady employment into the mid-1940s. She played the mother of the number one box office draw of the early 1940s, Mickey Rooney, in *Young Thomas Edison* (1940) and *The Human Comedy* (1940). As adept as Fay was at playing saintly mothers, aunts, or ladies of society, she craved more challenging roles. "I want to be a bad, bad, woman — I'm so tired of being good." Am I doomed to nobleness for the rest of my screen life?" [13] With only a few exceptions, she played variations of the same saintly mother figure or society matron. She was cast against type in *The Shining Hour* (1938), in which she played her first unlikable part as Joan Crawford's spiteful sister-in-law. In *The Heavenly Body* (1944), she further widened her range by playing Hedy Lamarr's phony astrologer. She was a witty career woman, working as a producer's assistant in *Babes on Broadway* (1941). In *Woman of the Year* (1942) as Katharine Hepburn's feminist aunt who ultimately chooses marriage, she blended the independent woman with the domestic one. She was a compassionate and determined social worker in *Journey for Margaret* (1942), and a dress designer in *June Bride* (1948). Among the best of her performances was in the 1946 Rodgers and Hammerstein film, *State Fair.* It is a pleasure to see her in Technicolor and have the opportunity to hear her sing, as she did in her early Broadway career. In each of her films — both the great and the mediocre — her scenes stand out above the rest and turn otherwise formulaic entertainment into touching or humorous scenes that linger in the audiences' memories.

After the success of *State Fair,* Fay left pictures to return to New York for the play *The Next Half Hour.* She was no longer the romantic leading lady, but Fay was accepting of her status as a supporting, older actress. She explained, "There comes a day when the flush of youth disappears from every woman's face. Most women dread it. I did. Like so many things, however, it is worse in anticipation than in actual fact." [14] Fay was satisfied to be a character actress rather the leading lady she had been on Broadway. As was the case in *Quality Street* (1937), Fay often was more memorable than the heroine in her films. In *Presenting Lily Mars* (1943) and *Babes on Broadway* (1941), she managed to steal scenes from such electric personalities as Judy Garland and Mickey Rooney. *New York Times* journalist Molly Haskell aptly described the category into which Fay fell: "There was a character-actress type: not the beauty, but beauty's handmaiden — mothers, servants, sisters, rivals, all revolving around the heroine in a solar system where planets of descending importance were as essential to celestial health and happiness as the sun itself." [15]

When not appearing in film, Fay sometimes received the opportunity to be "the sun" rather than a revolving planet. The majority of Fay's acting in the 1950s was in guest appearances on television or in roles on stage. In 1955 while touring as the lead in the play *Kind Lady*, Fay stopped in Milwaukee and enjoyed the city's famous beer. Despite her genteel appearance, she was fond of the city's trademark beer. She declared, "Why I have had my glass of beer after rehearsal for years!"[16] She showed her most serious side and confirmed the strength of her dramatic ability as Mary Tyrone in 1959 when she toured with the National Company's rendition of *A Long Day's Journey into Night*. When Fay did return to Hollywood for one last film, it was a triumphant swan song. Cast as an unsympathetic grandmother in the 1961 film *The Children's Hour*, she was nominated for Best Supporting Actress. Although she did not win, the acclaim she won for her part was an appropriate end to her career.

Once Fay retired from acting, she settled with her husband into a lovely house overlooking Malibu Beach. She owned an apartment complex, the Bon Arms, in Palm Springs. As she grew older, her ambitions rested more with family than with her career. "What I truly want is to be a grandmother," she said. "I want to be able to pick the little thing up myself. I don't want it placed in my lap...my son just says quietly, 'there's a lot of time, Mother.'"[17] Though she lacked grandchildren, she, like her characters on screen, was a loving and gentle woman to her direct and extended family. The words she spoke as Katharine Hepburn's aunt in *Woman of the Year* (1942) could have been her own: "Success is no fun unless you share it with someone."[18] Fay's great-nephew, Rick Cooney of Sacramento, California, fondly remembers his much-anticipated visits to see "Auntie Fay." When his family came to Palm Springs, Fay gave them a pleasant room at the Bon Arms. Mr. Cooney recalls that Fay spoke with an accent that one could mistake for British. "It wasn't put on at all. It was just the way she talked,"[19] he explained. Her sophisticated and refined way of speaking was as unfeigned as her natural elegance that shone through in even her most unglamorous roles.

When she was seventy-four, Fay succumbed to pneumonia. It is fitting that so admirable a lady as she was buried at Arlington National Cemetery alongside her husband.

At 7021 Hollywood Boulevard, visitors to Los Angeles will see Fay's star on the Walk of Fame. Tourists young and old might wonder who she was and question why a name they do not recognize has a spot on the Walk of Fame. But, whether or not her name is unknown today, there are few actresses more deserving of an honored place in Hollywood history than Fay Bainter. Her ability to touch audiences by capturing the most subtle of human emotions, whether they be in the form of drama or comedy, is as moving today as it was the first time she graced the stage.

FILMOGRAPHY

1961	*The Children's Hour*	Mrs. Amelia Tilford
1953	*The President's Lady*	Mrs. Donaldson
1951	*Close to My Heart*	Mrs. Morrow
1948	*June Bride*	Paula Winthrop
1948	*Give My Regards to Broadway*	Fay Norwick
1947	*The Secret Life of Walter Mitty*	Mrs. Eunice Mitty
1947	*Deep Valley*	Ellie Saul
1946	*The Virginian*	Mrs. Taylor
1946	*The Kid from Brooklyn*	Mrs. E. Winthrop LeMoyne
1945	*State Fair*	Melissa Frake
1944	*Three Is a Family*	Frances Whittaker
1944	*Dark Waters*	Aunt Emily
1944	*The Heavenly Body*	Margaret Sibyll
1943	*Cry 'Havoc'*	Captain Marsh
1943	*Salute to the Marines*	Jennie Bailey
1943	*Presenting Lily Mars*	Mrs. Thornway
1943	*The Human Comedy*	Mrs. Macauley
1942	*Journey for Margaret*	Trudy Strauss
1942	*Mrs. Wiggs of the Cabbage Patch*	Mrs. Elvira Wiggs
1942	*The War Against Mrs. Hadley*	Stella Hadley
1942	*Mister Gardenia Jones (documentary short)*	Emmy Jones
1942	*Woman of the Year*	Ellen Whitcomb
1941	*Babes on Broadway*	Miss 'Jonesy' Jones
1940	*Maryland*	Charlotte Danfield
1940	*A Bill of Divorcement*	Margaret 'Meg' Fairfield
1940	*Our Town*	Mrs. Gibbs
1940	*Young Tom Edison*	Mrs. Samuel 'Nancy' Edison
1939	*Our Neighbors — The Carters*	Ellen Carter
1939	*Daughters Courageous*	Nancy 'Nan' Masters
1939	*The Lady and the Mob*	Hattie Leonard
1939	*Yes, My Darling Daughter*	Annie Murray
1938	*The Shining Hour*	Hannah Linden
1938	*The Arkansas Traveler*	Mrs. Martha Allen
1938	*Mother Carey's Chickens*	Mrs. Margaret Carey

HOLLYWOOD REBEL
CHARLES BICKFORD

CHARLES BICKFORD CIRCA 1949. AUTHOR'S COLLECTION

"Personable, dynamic, sensitive, intelligent, generous, courageous, arrogant, cantankerous, talented, and successful."[1]

Such a string of disparate adjectives are seldom used to describe a single person. However, there was one man to whom all of the aforementioned qualities could be attributed: Charles Bickford. He was known in the 1940s through the 1960s as an intense screen presence with a robust frame, curly white hair, craggy features, and a gruff voice that commanded respect. Younger picture goers did not remember that the aged character actor had been in films since 1929, beginning as a fiery young redhead and gaining the distinction of being Hollywood's first "bad boy." However, his refusal to conform to the studio system kept him from reaching star status. Still, he has remained more enduring than many leading men of Hollywood's Golden Age. Whether he was the empathetic and wise priest in *The Song of Bernadette* (1943), the tough butler in *The Farmer's Daughter* (1947), or the loyal yet salty father of a deaf-mute daughter in *Johnny Belinda* (1948), Charles Bickford gave each role a vivid and authentic quality unequalled on screen.

Charles Bickford was born during the first minute of 1891 in Cambridge, Massachusetts. He was the fifth child in a family of seven children. According to Charles, he was "the spitting image" of his Grandpa Tom Woods with "a snub nose, blue eyes, and red blond hair."[2] His grandfather, a former sea captain, lived with the Bickford family throughout Charles's childhood and became the young boy's idol. "I never tired of listening to his stories of the sea. I began to develop a most colorful vocabulary…I tried to imitate his way of speaking, manner of walking. The results linger to this day,"[3] Charles explained. In his endeavors to imitate the ways of a world-wise sailor, Charles grew up to be the proverbial red-headed problem child. Like Tom Sawyer or Huck Finn, he spent his days playing hooky or cavorting with stray people and animals along the city's docks. He encountered not a few bullies in his adventures, most of whom taunted him for his as yet uncut red curls. But, before and after his curls were sheared, he seldom lost a fight. He developed a "formidable reputation"[4] that warded off all bullies except the very foolish or very brave. Charles's fighting spirit was never more troublesome than when his favorite boyhood companion, a mutt named Tige, was killed by a speeding streetcar. The nine-year-old Charles retaliated by taking his father's gun and shooting the streetcar conductor. The boy was only convicted with assault, but the experience shook his parents to such a degree that Charles decided to try his "damndest to be what they used to call 'a good boy.'"[5]

Being a good boy meant pursuing a higher education. Charles chose to attend MIT with a major in construction engineering. But, Charles admitted that when his grandfather died the year before he entered college, his "ambition died with him."[6] Charles abandoned the conventional life in favor of an existence as picaresque as Mark Twain's before him or Jack Kerouac's after him. He was first employed at a lumber camp at which he flexed his fighting skills and learned to cuss and drink. After this gig, he traveled to New York and was variously employed hauling beer kegs in trucks, selling hunting and fishing gear, or barking for the Chinatown bus. His most ambitious endeavor was to begin his own insect extermination business with his friend, but his lack of interest in the enterprise led to its rapid demise.[7] Heading West, he worked mining copper, harvesting wheat, and hauling freight. "I was living in the grand old days of the American tradition, the great days of free enterprise and opportunity...I was really and truly an American boy. Free. Proud. And Happy,"[8] Charles reflected in 1965.

Charles's travels ended when he hit the port of San Francisco. After entering a raunchy bar, he caught the attention of show girls employed there, who encouraged him to audition for their boss. He was hired as an actor there and began by performing a hilarious impersonation of an "outrageous fairy."[9] As he ventured into straight roles, he began to take his craft seriously and went to New York to study technique. He joined the legitimate theater when he became a member of the John Craig Stock Company. Still, he was not a full time actor; between engagements, he worked as a manual laborer. His sporadic employment was in part due to his own choosiness, for he refused roles in plays he considered sub par. "It set a pattern of independence of thought and action which has characterized my entire career,"[10] Charles stated.

Charles gave up digging ditches when he joined the Al Woods Casting Agency, which gave him regular work along Loew's vaudeville circuit. Of all his theater experience, he most enjoyed vaudeville, mostly because there he "found fewer sons-of-bitches than in any other theater group."[11] It was during Charles's years touring in stock and vaudeville that he met fellow thespian Beatrice Loring. They married in 1919 and remained so until his death in 1967. Their first child, Rex, was born in 1919 and a daughter, Doris, followed in 1924. Charles was better able to support his growing family after he made his first vaudeville hit in *Zander the Great,* co-starring future screwball comedienne Alice Brady. He filled the dry spell following an unsuccessful engagement at the Palace Theatre by staging a play of his own, *The Cyclone Lover.* The two-actor play starred only himself and his wife and ran just six weeks. After his show closed, he did what he would go on to do during every dry spell in his career: retreat into solitude. His place of choice was a cabin in Massachusetts with no telephones for eight miles.

Upon Charles's return to New York, he considered joining his brother in a new construction endeavor, but a call from his agent made him reconsider. In *Outside Looking In,* Charles won the role of Oklahoma Red, a part that would catapult him to Broadway stardom. He cited it as "the first real challenge of my ability as an actor." [12] Charles revealed his rebellious side when he refused to play the part in the intellectual manner the director demanded. He rehearsed the role each night at his hotel the way he intended to play it — savage and raw. On opening night, his method was a great success. The *New York Times* wrote that he gave the show "color" and was "the center of activity" [13] from the moment he appeared.

Charles's sense of loyalty to Broadway was so strong he refused a $50,000 role in the silent film *Beau Geste* (1926) as well as five subsequent contract offers in Hollywood. [14] But after his next play, *Gods of Lightening* (based on the Sacco-Vanzetti trial), flopped, Charles declared that his loyalty to Broadway "flopped with it." [15] Charles accepted Cecil B. DeMille's offer to star him in his new film, *Dynamite* (1929), in which he would portray a man on death row for a crime he did not commit. Despite the difficulties he would encounter in the film industry, Charles never regretted leaving Broadway.

At M-G-M, Charles's contract contained an unprecedented verbal clause giving him the right to approve his roles and pictures. However, given that the clause was verbal, the studio had no legal obligation to respect it. When Charles was given no more quality roles following *Dynamite,* he again retreated into solitude. He trekked through California's Death Valley and Trinity Alps with his old roadster and pet dog. He came back ready to work and fight for better scripts. His first assignment was a move in the right direction. He was to play Greta Garbo's lover in the actress' first talking picture, *Anna Christie* (1930). "It was not only a smashing success, it made motion picture history," [16] Charles explained. This made little difference to his career, for he was not among those praised in the film's notices. Nevertheless, Charles had become enough of a name at the box office so that Louis B. Mayer ordered the studio's spies to keep close watch on the tempestuous actor's behavior.

After Charles refused to give an interview, he was punished by being cast in four poorly scripted films, all of which put him in "unsuitable

Buddy Rogers type" roles. [17] He turned down the four parts offered to him over the course of six weeks. "They say I'm temperamental," Charles told the *Daily Boston Globe*, "but it isn't true. I merely want to play a role that fits me… I'd rather take less money and play fewer roles, as long as I don't have to play unsuitable characters." [18] Charles's contrariness gained notoriety about Hollywood and made him known variously as "The No

CHARLES BICKFORD AND KAY FRANCIS IN *PASSION FLOWER* (1930).
COURTESY OF JERRY MURBACH.

Man," "Hollywood's Bad Boy," and "Hollywood Rebel." Louis B. Mayer's less tactful nickname for his troublesome new star was "that god-damned red-headed Bolshevik." [19]

Mayer had more extreme expletives to throw at Charles after the actor refused to continue work on another film he deemed terrible: *The Sea Bat* (1930). When Mayer did not grant Charles's request to be released from his contract, Charles called the mogul "an ignoramus" and "a junk ped-dler." [20] This altercation finally ended Charles's contract, but the incident blacklisted him at every major Hollywood studio. "Overnight I was mirac-ulously transformed into box office poison. No longer was I a great actor. I had suddenly become a mediocre ham," [21] Charles explained. Charles attempted revenge by hiring a private detective to build a case against M-G-M, but there was no evidence found to incriminate the studio.

Charles turned to freelancing in independent productions and branching into various business enterprises. He set up an office across the street from the M-G-M administration building, erecting in seventy-five-foot letters his own name above the office's front. It was no coincidence that within a short time the M-G-M administration building moved to the opposite side of the studio property. Charles's office was much used as he funneled his energy into business. He operated a coconut plantation on an island he owned near Java, held a half-interest in a New England hog farm, a share in a pearling schooner, a stable and horses, and a gold mine. [22] As well as becoming a business man, the next ten years saw Charles finding work in films that were "passably good...or just plain lousy." [23] Among his better efforts in this ten-year period were as the surly Slim in *Of Mice and Men* (1939) and as a dock worker in the Cary Grant drama *Mr. Lucky* (1943).

Salvation for Charles's limping career came when Darryl Zanuck offered him a role in Shirley Temple's *The Littlest Rebel* (1935), followed by a long-term contract. Charles was ready to sign, but he needed to finish filming a low budget adventure picture, *East of Java* (1935), first. During filming, a lion used in the film went rogue and grabbed Charles by the neck, proceeding to drag him several feet. The nerves in his neck were severed and he lost a great deal of blood. Though his survival chances were ten to one, he recovered with miraculous speed. However, due to the severe scarring on his neck, leading man parts were no longer an option for him. With no 20th Century-Fox contract or prospects, Charles explained: "I again put my shoulder to the rock and pushed. And the rock seemed heavier and heavier during the next decade, and my career, though active, remained in comparative eclipse." [24] During this eclipse, Charles and his family relocated to their own private ranch, where he found the solitude and peace he craved.

The shadow over Charles's film career lifted when David O. Selznick gave him a supporting role as the sympathetic, philosophical Father Peyramale in *The Song of Bernadette* (1943). "After the premiere, I was newly discovered and literally overnight leaped into great demand as a character star," [25] Charles stated. He received an Oscar nomination for his performance; a second nomination came four years later. In his portrayal of the crusty butler, Clancy, who aids a young maid in her quest to run for Congress in the political satire *The Farmer's Daughter* (1947), Charles had the chance to show his comedic skills. He was honored for a third and final nomination in 1948 for what he called his favorite role, Black MacDonald, in *Johnny Belinda* (1948). Charles is at his best in the film, alternately showing comedy and pathos. It is difficult not to smile when the formerly reluctant and skeptical Black enthusiastically shows his sister the sign language motions for "butterfly." It is more difficult to hold in tears when he ultimately falls to his death in defense of his deaf-mute daughter.

Charles's chameleon-like ability to fit into any type of role made audiences believe he *was* any given character he portrayed on screen. He did not strive to create a career based on personality alone. He claimed that when young stars' "personality fades, they [stars] slip into obscurity." He ordered stars young and old to "stop trying to turn on personality and start acting — if they can."[26] Charles accepted his advancing age and did not miss leading man status. In fact, his years as a character star brought him more fanfare than his earlier years. The Ladies Senior League in San Francisco called him "not only magnetic and manly, but credible...he's the ideal example of the type of man the mature woman wishes to see on the screen."[27]

Charles continued to give exemplary performances into the 1950s and 1960s. As studio head Oliver Niles in *A Star Is Born* (1954), he creates a brusque yet human studio mogul that brings to mind the type of man Charles might have wished was his employer. His most moving performance of the 1960s was as the patient yet curmudgeonly florist Ellis Arneson in the haunting tale of two alcoholics, *Days of Wine and Roses* (1962). The audience feels compassion for the long suffering Arneson after his son-in-law destroys his entire hothouse stock in search of a hidden liquor bottle. He garners even greater compassion at the close of the film when, giving in to tears, he explains that he has lost his daughter to liquor and the seedy men with whom she steps out each night. Though it was an Oscar worthy performance, Charles received no nomination.

Into his old age, Charles continued to keep occupied with more than one career at a time. In addition to his other businesses, he ran his own delivery firm and a telephone exchange, both of which employed more than one hundred people.[28] However, growing business successes did not mean retirement from Hollywood. Though television, according to Charles "had taken the small picture audience away from the theater,"[29] he saw this as no reason why he should quit acting. "Retire? Why should I? There are things I want to do,"[30] he declared. Among the things he wanted to do was compose his memoirs. After he penned an autobiography and threw it in the ash can, his wife saved it and sent it to his publisher. A few days later, the publisher "called raving about the book."[31] The memoir, humorously titled *Bulls, Balls, Bicycles, and Actors*, is written in Charles's gruff yet likeable voice, mostly recounting his rebellions through the years. Apart from writing, Charles tested his talent in the new medium of television. He had no difficulty transitioning to the small screen and became a frequent guest star on programs, including *Playhouse 90* and *The Eleventh Hour*. He experienced a resurgence in popularity when, at age seventy-five, he starred as rancher John Grainger in NBC's western series *The Virginian*.

In November 1967, days after filming an episode of *The Virginian*, Charles died of a blood infection. His will stipulated that there be no services held, simply a cremation. [32]

Among the opening pages of Charles's autobiography, he wrote: "It's appropriate that I should have come in on the wings of a blizzard. I've been blowing up a storm ever since." [33] The storm Charles blew up with his fierce and uncompromising demand for quality scripts and appropriate characters may have provoked resentment among studio moguls. However, these attributes are what have kept him riveting to audiences for generations. His strength and toughness on screen is reassuring; those watching him feel they can trust him to see them through any hardship they may encounter. Charles's perseverance, self-reliance, and ability to stay true to himself personify the pillars on which America was founded.

"I was stubborn," Charles stated. "I refused to conform and fit into the setup. I got the impression early in life I was born into a jungle and the way to survive is fight." [34]

FILMOGRAPHY

1966	*A Big Hand for the Little Lady*	Benson Tropp
1964	*Della*	Hugh Stafford
1962	*Days of Wine and Roses*	Ellis Arnesen
1960	*The Unforgiven*	Zeb Rawlins
1958	*The Big Country*	Maj. Henry Terrill
1957	*Mister Cory*	Jeremiah Des Plains 'Biloxi' Caldwell
1956	*You Can't Run Away from It*	A.A. Andrews
1955	*The Court-Martial of Billy Mitchell*	Gen. Jimmy Guthrie
1955	*Not as a Stranger*	Dr. Dave W. Runkleman
1955	*Prince of Players*	Dave Prescott
1954	*A Star Is Born*	Oliver Niles
1953	*The Last Posse*	Sampson Drune
1951	*The Raging Tide*	Hamil Linder
1951	*Elopement*	Tom Reagan
1951	*Jim Thorpe — All-American*	Glenn S. 'Pop' Warner

1950	*Branded*	Mr. Lavery
1950	*Riding High*	J.L. Higgins
1950	*Guilty of Treason*	Joszef Cardinal Mindszenty
1949	*Whirlpool*	Lt. James Colton
1949	*Roseanna McCoy*	Devil Anse Hatfield
1948	*Command Decision*	Elmer Brockhurst
1948	*Johnny Belinda*	Black MacDonald
1948	*Four Faces West*	Pat Garrett
1948	*The Babe Ruth Story*	Brother Matthias
1947	*Brute Force*	Gallagher
1947	*The Woman on the Beach*	Tod
1947	*The Farmer's Daughter*	Joseph Clancy
1946	*Duel in the Sun*	Sam Pierce
1945	*Fallen Angel*	Mark Judd
1945	*Captain Eddie*	William Rickenbacker
1944	*Wing and a Prayer*	Capt. Waddell
1943	*The Song of Bernadette*	Father Peyramale
1943	*Mr. Lucky*	Hard Swede
1942	*Tarzan's New York Adventure*	Buck Rand
1942	*Reap the Wild Wind*	Bully Brown
1941	*Burma Convoy*	Cliff Weldon
1941	*Riders of Death Valley*	Wolf Reade
1940	*Queen of the Yukon*	Ace Rincon
1940	*South to Karanga*	Jeff Worthing
1940	*Girl from God's Country*	Bill Bogler
1939	*Thou Shalt Not Kill*	Rev. Chris Saunders
1939	*Of Mice and Men*	Slim
1939	*One Hour to Live*	Insp. Sid Brady
1939	*Mutiny in the Big House*	Father Joe Collins
1939	*Our Leading Citizen*	Shep Muir
1939	*Street of Missing Men*	Cash Darwin
1939	*Romance of the Redwoods*	Steve Blake
1939	*Stand Up and Fight*	Arnold
1938	*The Storm*	Bob 'Sparks' Roberts
1938	*Valley of the Giants*	Howard 'Steve' Fallon
1938	*Gangs of New York*	Rocky Thorpe/John Franklin
1937	*Daughter of Shanghai*	Otto Hartman
1937	*Night Club Scandal*	Det. Capt. McKinley
1937	*Thunder Trail*	Lee Tate
1937	*High, Wide, and Handsome*	Red Scanlon

1936	*The Plainsman*	John Lattimer
1936	*Pride of the Marines*	Steve Riley
1936	*Rose of the Rancho*	Joe Kincaid
1935	*East of Java*	Red Bowers
1935	*The Farmer Takes a Wife*	Jotham Klore
1935	*Under Pressure*	Nipper Moran
1935	*A Notorious Gentleman*	Kirk Arlen
1934	*A Wicked Woman*	Pat Naylor
1934	*Little Miss Marker*	Big Steve Halloway
1933	*Red Wagon*	Joe Prince
1933	*White Woman*	Ballister
1933	*This Day and Age*	Louis Garrett
1933	*Song of the Eagle*	Joe (Nails) Anderson
1933	*No Other Woman*	James 'Jim' Stanley
1932	*Vanity Street*	Brian
1932	*The Last Man*	Bannister
1932	*Thunder Below*	Walt
1932	*Scandal for Sale*	Jerry Strong
1932	*Panama Flo*	Dan McTeague
1931	*Men in Her Life*	Flashy Madden
1931	*The Pagan Lady*	Dingo Mike
1931	*The Squaw Man*	Cash Hawkins
1931	*East of Borneo*	Dr. Allan Clark *(Dr. Allan Randolph)*
1930	*Passion Flower*	Dan Wallace
1930	*River's End*	John Keith/Sgt. Connie Conniston
1930	*The Sea Bat*	Reverend Sims
1930	*Anna Christie*	Matt Burke
1929	*Hell's Heroes*	Robert 'Bob' Sangster
1929	*Dynamite*	Hagon 'Buddy' Derk
1929	*South Sea Rose*	Capt. Briggs

THE DAME
WITH A HEART OF GOLD
JOAN
BLONDELL

JOAN BLONDELL CIRCA 1935. COURTESY OF JERRY MURBACH

"Life is phony with baloney
From the start until it's done.
Gold or tatters, neither matters.
For the strife of life is fun!" [1]

So wrote Joan Blondell, the curvy and pert, wise-cracking gal with inimitable black-lashed, saucer eyes. Her career spanned decades and included over a hundred films, but she is best known for the fifty-two films she made in an eight-year period during the 1930s. [2] Her films of this decade established her as the quintessential gold digger, whether she be in the form of a "secretary, chorus girl, or gun moll." [3] Her definitive 1930s film was *Gold Diggers of 1933*. In the film, she performs the haunting finale, "The Forgotten Man," a tune that could have been the theme song of the Depression. Film historian Charles Higham wrote that Joan symbolized the 1930s just as "Joan Crawford in broad-shouldered mink on a fog-cloaked wharf in *Mildred Pierce* absolutely symbolizes the forties." [4] During this period, Joan frequently graduated to leading lady status, but she was more often given parts as the comedic sidekick to the decidedly less interesting starring actress. It was as a supporting actress that she kept her career alive into the 1970s. In middle age, she accepted her new status as character actress and was placed in roles as "madams, nannies, mystics, and matchmakers." [5] Like her characters on screen, she was adaptable to whatever role she was offered, whether it was "phony with baloney", "gold or tatters."

Joan Blondell was born on August 30, 1906 to seasoned vaudevillians Ed and Katie Blondell. As the cliché goes, she was born in a trunk *(indeed, her first crib was made from a prop trunk)*. She traveled the vaudeville circuits with her parents and siblings across the United States and as far as Australia. Because of the constant uprooting such traveling required, Joan made few friends and attended even fewer years of school. She grew up as a sensitive child with an affinity for animals that she would carry throughout her entire life. Biographer Matthew Kennedy wrote: "She avoided meat out of compassion for the animals she watched passing by from train windows." [6]

When Joan reached a legal working age, she decided to enroll in Texas State University's Teachers College. However, due to her sporadic schooling, she only lasted for one semester before flunking out. She then turned her attentions to the family business of performing. Her first efforts were not so much acting as parading her figure before beauty pageant judges. She won the 1924 Miss Dallas contest and finished fourth in the 1926 Miss

America contest in Atlantic City. Joy over her victory in the 1924 pageant was destroyed after she accepted a ride home from a man who proceeded to assault her on a deserted road. Joan jumped from the car to escape him but suffered painful ankle injuries. Ever perseverant, Joan recovered mentally and physically with firm determination to begin a career on Broadway.

Joan's diligence won her chorus roles in two Ziegfeld productions: *Rosalie* and the *Ziegfeld Follies of 1927*. When not employed in the theater, Joan worked the late shifts at a nearby library. One night after closing time, a trusting Joan unlocked the library door for a policeman. The policeman brutally raped her, slamming her to the floor with such force that she sustained injuries to her back from which she never fully recovered. After surviving two sexual attacks, it is amazing Joan was able to retain the motivation and energy to go on performing with a smile on her face. In her later years, Joan gave insight into how she was able to recover from such trauma: "I'm a great appreciator of good things. I try to forget the bad things. There's a lump inside you always, lumps of sorrow, griefs, and failures...but with a little effort, you can make them stay in the background." [7]

Joan was rewarded for her faith and optimism in 1929 when she landed leading roles in two shows. The first, *Maggie the Magnificent,* had her as bootlegger James Cagney's outspoken wife. A subsequent play, also with Cagney, *Penny Arcade,* garnered the attention of audience member Al Jolson. He proceeded to buy the rights to the show and sell them to Warner Bros. Warner Bros. with the stipulation that Joan and Cagney repeat their onstage roles in the film. Joan, along with her parents and siblings, relocated to California, where, for the remainder of the decade, she would be the family's breadwinner.

The play, renamed *Sinner's Holiday (1931)* for the screen, proved to Warner Bros. Warner Bros. that Joan and Cagney were a lucrative screen team. The two new stars were placed alongside each other in several films of varying genres, including *The Public Enemy (1931), Blonde Crazy (1931),* and *The Crowd Roars (1932).* Joan appeared in such a rapid succession of movies that she was often filming more than one at a time. Joan's new status as Warner Bros.' most exciting new star led to her being named one of the WAMPAS Baby Stars of 1931. Joan's brassy and imperturbable screen persona, coupled with her ability to remain feminine despite her outspoken and independent spirit, made her equally ideal for screwball comedies, backstage musicals, and cynical noir pictures.

Joan's popularity was in no small part due to the flattering camerawork by cinematographer George Barnes. Joan and Barnes' mutual attraction to each other resulted in an inopportune pregnancy. Though Joan wished to keep the child, Barnes prodded her into having an abortion. Joan pushed the unpleasantness of her personal life to the back of her mind as she continued performing memorable supporting roles in a number of notable films, including *Night Nurse (1931)*, *Three on a Match (1932)*, and *Gold Diggers of 1933 (1933)*. *Gold Diggers of 1933* was to be the first of her

JOAN BLONDELL AND JAMES CAGNEY IN *FOOTLIGHT PARADE* (1935). COURTESY OF JERRY MURBACH.

many pairings with screen team Dick Powell and Ruby Keeler. The film cemented her particular screen character and gave her many of the film's snappiest quips. In one scene, after a producer declares his show will be "all about the Depression," Joan replies: "We won't have to rehearse that!"[8] The film's success convinced Warner Bros. more than ever to discourage Joan from branching into different sorts of roles. Joan's lament of "I'm so sick of being the wisecracking, hail fellow well met, slap me on the back sort of baby!"[9] fell on deaf ears.

Joan could have fought harder for better roles and a higher salary, but she was more interested in making a home for herself. "I was never a career girl,[10]" Joan confessed after she and George Barnes married in 1933. As eager as Joan was to be a wife and mother, Barnes demanded she have abortions performed each time she found she was pregnant. Joan was not as outspoken as she was on screen and acquiesced each time. She put on a bright face in more bubbly Busby Berkeley musicals, including *Footlight Parade (1933)* with James Cagney and *Dames (1934)* with Dick Powell and Ruby Keeler. Joan's trademark acid tongue was put to its best use in the latter film, as shown when she kicks a conniving actress hopeful from her boss' office, exclaiming: "Outside countess! As long as they've got sidewalks, *you've* got a job!" [11]

Joan's ongoing proof that she was a moneymaker for Warner Bros. finally resulted in a raise to $2,000 a week. With this victory came another that was more important to her than any monetary gain: she was pregnant and this time, she refused an abortion. She gave birth to a son, Norman. Her marriage ended soon after the child's birth. Norman would never meet Barnes and would go through his entire childhood believing Joan's second husband, Dick Powell, was his actual father.

During the unraveling of her marriage to Barnes, Joan and her ubiquitous co-star, the boyish crooner Dick Powell, became romantically linked. They were married in 1936. Though Joan still continued with her career after her second marriage, she explained, "What meant most to me was getting home, and that's the truth. [12]" Joan continued playing the same fortune-hunting gals in films like *The King and the Chorus Girl (1937)* and *Gold Diggers of 1937 (1936)*. Warner Bros. kept her so busy that she was forced to perform during her pregnancy with her second child, Ellen, in 1939. Her growing stomach was obscured by coats or tables set conveniently in front of her.

The following year, Joan and Powell were both through with being typed in the same roles again and again. They both left their home studio with plans to freelance. Shortly after she left the studio, the years of overwork caught up with Joan and she was admitted to a hospital for nervous and physical exhaustion. During her recovery, she had the opportunity to be a traditional mom and relished every moment of it. She dutifully returned to the screen in 1941 to appear as Gail, a chipper ghost who helps timid businessman Cosmo Topper solve her murder in the final installment of the frothy Topper series, *Topper Returns*. After the completion of this film, Joan followed Dick to New York, where he was to appear in a Mike Todd show, *Beat the Band*.

While in New York, Joan and Powell attended the popular musical show *Best Foot Forward*. When they visited backstage after the play, the cast gazed at them, awestruck. Among the most awed was the petite, young dancer June Allyson. If Powell had not been busy noticing June, he may have seen that Mike Todd was busy noticing Joan. But neither Dick nor Joan would see Allyson or Todd for a long period afterward; instead, they became immersed in patriotic work for the USO. Joan went on a grueling tour, during which she was greatly lauded for lifting the spirits of thousands of servicemen.

Mike Todd lured Joan back to New York to star in his new show, *The Naked Genius*. Joan agreed against the wishes of Powell, who was not in favor of his wife portraying a stripper on stage. Joan proceeded to complete this play and another with Todd, *Something for the Boys*, despite her initial reservations about Todd's intentions towards her.

When Joan returned to Hollywood with her stage success to boost her, she was given an excellent supporting role in the Elia Kazan production of *A Tree Grows in Brooklyn (1945)*. Her part was that of the motherly, brash, and flamboyantly dressed Aunt Sissy who yearns for children, but, with each pregnancy, her babies are stillborn. The *New York Times* called Joan's performance "little short of wonderful." [13] Sissy was the first role to truly showcase Joan's depth of emotion, free as it was of her usual sarcastic barbs. Joan was nominated for Best Supporting Actress for her performance.

As praiseworthy as Joan's professional life was, her personal life was disintegrating. Dick Powell's overriding interest in business plus his increasing infatuation with June Allyson ended the seemingly idyllic Blondell/Powell union. The divorce devastated Norman and Ellen, marking the beginning of erratic behavior in Ellen that would later be diagnosed as manic depression. Upon Powell's death in 1963, Joan would openly admit she never should have divorced him.

Now a single mother, Joan could not afford to stop working. She took a supporting role in the Clark Gable picture *Adventure (1945)*, in which she is the typical sidekick to Greer Garson's less engaging character. As Joan's divorce was finalized, Mike Todd's wife conveniently died, thus spurring Todd to pursue Joan more aggressively. Joan accepted Todd's affection despite the concerns of friends, including Frances Marion. Marion warned her: "He eventually might kill your spirit, and that's the cruelest phase of a living death." [14]

Nevertheless, Joan and Todd were married in Las Vegas in 1947. The marriage began on a positive note with Joan starring in the noir classic *Nightmare Alley (1947)* and Todd purchasing them an elaborate twenty-two-acre estate close to Manhattan. However, Joan's happiness was short-lived as she quickly discovered that Todd could neither pay for the estate nor find a hit to produce. Still, he would not allow her to support the family. Joan's friends claimed he turned her into a "Jewish fishwife." [15] The children were often awakened by violent arguments between Joan and Todd. One argument became so heated that Norman's dog attacked Todd to protect Joan. Todd, in turn, murdered his stepson's pet.

A necessary separation followed in which Joan toured as the dramatic lead in *Come Back Little Sheba*. Upon her return, conditions in her marriage grew worse. After she caught Todd leering at Ellen's adolescent body, she packed her and her children's bags. She left in the middle of the night, drove to Nevada, and won her divorce.

Joan returned to Hollywood a plumper, sadder, but no less determined woman. She was not too proud to admit that she was no longer a cute chorus girl. "An actor's life is finally one of rejection...no matter how smoothly you've transferred yourself into character roles, rejection, depression, panic, hurt, bewilderment, even fury is 'your treat'," [16] Joan explained. Joan's beginnings as a character actress found her playing "fallen-faced dames." [17] Her first notable role was a fading star in 1951's *The Blue Veil*, a film that won her a second Oscar nomination. Despite this honor, Joan was largely marginalized in the city that she had once dominated. Her friend, Art Cohn, explained: "Few came to interview her anymore. Her name was in lower case." [18] Joan's loneliness only increased when Ellen went to live with Dick Powell and June Allyson on their ranch, Mandeville, and Norman pursued a life of his own.

Joan did not receive renewed notice from Hollywood until the mid-1950s. The roles she came to play were like grown-up versions of the tart-tongued secretaries she had portrayed in her youth. In the satirical *Will Success Spoil Rock Hunter? (1957)* she was Jayne Mansfield's unlucky-in-love personal assistant and in the Tracy/Hepburn film *Desk Set (1957)*, she was Hepburn's reliable pal and co-worker. No longer considered the beauty she once had been, Joan was often given such self-deprecating lines as the following from *Desk Set:*

> *I could tell from the way he was lookin' at me that if I were any other kind of girl, it would've been the beginning of a beautiful friendship.* [19]

Joan did not seem to mind if she was now typed as the *(often boozy)* woman without a man. "Who says it's tough to grow older!" she declared. "Not me!...let's face it — I'm plump, I'm getting bags under my eyes, but the parts keep getting better and better!" [20]

Joan spoke too soon, for following *Desk Set*, her career experienced a dry spell. During this time, she returned to Broadway in several flops including the depressing tale of an alcoholic, *The Rope Dancers*. However, she did gain a Tony award nomination for the play. Most often, she went home alone rather than attend after-show events. Her primary companions at this stage of her life were her pug dogs, Bridey Murphy and Fresh. "I loved those dogs with all my heart…they went everywhere with me," [21] she fondly claimed.

Joan remained active on the stage and in television despite the fact she was suffering from severe rheumatoid arthritis and ongoing pain from her past back injury. She performed in a tour of *Bye Bye Birdie* with a back brace under her costume and appeared on many television programs including *The Real McCoys* and *The Twilight Zone*. Joan's career saw a positive turn when she received a Golden Globe nomination for her portrayal of the flashy Lady Fingers in 1965's *The Cincinnati Kid*. At the same time, she rejoiced in becoming a grandmother to her children's newborn babies *(both of whom would call her 'Matey' rather than Grandma)*. Her change of fortune continued into 1967 when she was given a starring role in a new television series, *Here Comes the Brides*, a program with a plot not dissimilar to the classic musical *Seven Brides for Seven Brothers (1954)*. Joan received an Emmy nomination for her part. Her renewed luck abruptly ended when the show was cancelled, her dogs died, and Ellen was institutionalized.

Joan comforted herself with a new pet tabby cat named Shadow and transferred her attentions to writing. She penned a semi-autobiographical novel, *Center Door Fancy*, which followed the career of a vaudevillian from the circus to Broadway. The book proved to be popular and was selected as the Literary Guild's Book of the Month. Joan's love of literature seemed to be stronger for her lack of education; she spent as much as $150 a month on building her personal library. [22]

Though Joan's career and health were waning, she was a tireless trouper. She appeared in the John Cassavetes's film *Opening Night (1977)* and the Jon Voight boxing picture *The Champ (1979)*, despite the fact she had suffered from a stroke and been diagnosed with leukemia. Among her most enduring final roles was Vi, "a fast talking waitress with a heart of gold," in the musical *Grease (1978)*. "Just like being back at Warners in the good old days," [23] Joan declared.

Joan was forced to stop working when she suffered a second stroke and began to lose her vision. As her condition worsened, her children gathered at her hospital bedside. Ellen, who had been stabilized on lithium, asked her mother if she would rather die at home with her cats. Though Joan nodded "yes," her doctor would not allow her to be moved. She died on Christmas Day, 1979.

To filmgoers, Joan Blondell was the tough dame who could weather any setback and stand up to any man. Under her sarcastic exterior was a sensitivity that was betrayed by the slightest pout of her lips or expressive flutter of her eyes. On and off screen, she found love elusive, yet she failed to become hard or embittered. "I loved too intensely for it not to be painful when things went wrong," she said. "You have to have gone through pain to end with understanding and compassion for all people." [24] From her portrayals of pert and sassy gold diggers to plump and tipsy matrons, Joan gave humanity and compassion to the hardest of characters. Through "gold or tatters," she made "the strife of life fun" no matter how bleak her own life or the world seemed to be.

FILMOGRAPHY

1981	*The Woman Inside*	Aunt Coll
1979	*The Glove*	Mrs. Fitzgerald
1979	*The Champ*	Dolly Kenyon
1978	*Grease*	Vi
1977	*Opening Night*	Sarah Goode
1977	*The Baron*	
1976	*Won Ton Ton: The Dog Who Saved Hollywood*	Landlady
1971	*Support Your Local Gunfighter*	Jenny
1970	*The Phynx*	Ruby
1969	*Big Daddy*	
1968	*Kona Coast*	Kittibelle Lightfoot
1968	*Stay Away, Joe*	Glenda Callahan
1967	*Waterhole #3*	Lavinia
1966	*Ride Beyond Vengeance*	Mrs. Lavender
1965	*The Cincinnati Kid*	Lady Fingers
1964	*Advance to the Rear*	Easy Jenny
1957	*Will Success Spoil Rock Hunter?*	Violet
1957	*This Could Be the Night*	Crystal St. Clair
1957	*Desk Set*	Peg Costello
1957	*Lizzie*	Aunt Morgan
1956	*The Opposite Sex*	Edith
1951	*The Blue Veil*	Annie Rawlins
1950	*For Heaven's Sake*	Daphne Peters
1947	*Christmas Eve*	Ann Nelson
1947	*Nightmare Alley*	Zeena Krumbein
1947	*The Corpse Came C.O.D.*	Rosemary Durant

1945	*Adventure*	Helen Melohn
1945	*Don Juan Quilligan*	Marjorie Mossrock
1945	*A Tree Grows in Brooklyn*	Aunt Sissy
1943	*Cry 'Havoc'.*	Grace
1942	*Lady for a Night*	Jenny Blake
1941	*Three Girls About Town*	Hope Banner
1941	*Model Wife*	Joan Keating Chambers
1941	*Topper Returns*	Gail Richards
1940	*I Want a Divorce*	Geraldine 'Jerry' Brokaw
1940	*Two Girls on Broadway*	Molly Mahoney
1939	*The Amazing Mr. Williams*	Maxine Carroll
1939	*Good Girls Go to Paris*	Jenny Swanson
1939	*The Kid from Kokomo*	Doris Harvey
1939	*East Side of Heaven*	Mary Wilson
1939	*Off the Record*	Jane Morgan
1938	*There's Always a Woman*	Sally Reardon
1937	*Stand-In*	Lester Plum
1937	*The Perfect Specimen*	Mona Carter
1937	*Back in Circulation*	Timothea 'Timmy' Blake
1937	*The King and the Chorus Girl*	Miss Dorothy Ellis
1936	*Gold Diggers of 1937*	Norma Perry
1936	*Three Men on a Horse*	Mabel
1936	*Stage Struck*	Peggy Revere
1936	*Bullets or Ballots*	Lee Morgan
1936	*Sons o' Guns*	Yvonne
1936	*Colleen*	Minnie Hawkins
1935	*Miss Pacific Fleet*	Gloria Fay
1935	*We're in the Money*	Ginger Stewart
1935	*Broadway Gondolier*	Alice Hughes
1935	*Traveling Saleslady*	Angela Twitchell
1934	*Kansas City Princess*	Rosie Sturges
1934	*Dames*	Mabel Anderson
1934	*Smarty*	Vicki Wallace Thorpe
1934	*He Was Her Man*	Rose Lawrence
1934	*I've Got Your Number*	Marie Lawson
1933	*Convention City*	Nancy Lorraine
1933	*Havana Widows*	Mae Knight
1933	*Footlight Parade*	Nan Prescott
1933	*Goodbye Again*	Anne Rogers, Bixby's Secretary
1933	*Gold Diggers of 1933*	Carol

1933	*Blondie Johnson*	Blondie Johnson
1933	*Broadway Bad*	Tony Landers
1933	*Just Around the Corner (short)*	Mrs. Graham
1932	*Lawyer Man*	Olga Michaels
1932	*Central Park*	Dot
1932	*Three on a Match*	Mary Keaton, AKA Mary Bernard
1932	*Big City Blues*	Vida Fleet
1932	*Miss Pinkerton*	Nurse Adams, AKA Miss Pinkerton
1932	*Make Me a Star*	'Flips' Montague
1932	*The Famous Ferguson Case*	Maizie Dickson
1932	*The Crowd Roars*	Anne Scott
1932	*The Greeks Had a Word for Them*	Schatzi Sutro
1932	*Union Depot*	Ruth Collins
1931	*Blonde Crazy*	Anne Roberts
1931	*The Reckless Hour*	Myrtle Nichols
1931	*Night Nurse*	B. Maloney
1931	*Big Business Girl*	Pearl
1931	*My Past*	Marion Moore
1931	*The Public Enemy*	Mamie
1931	*God's Gift to Women*	Fifi
1931	*Illicit*	Helen 'Duckie' Childers
1931	*Millie*	Angie Wickerstaff
1931	*Other Men's Women*	Marie
1931	*How I Play Golf, by Bobby Jones* No. 10: 'Trouble Shots' *(short)*	Gallery Member *(uncredited)*
1930	*Sinners' Holiday*	Myrtle
1930	*The Office Wife*	Katherine Murdock
1930	*The Devil's Parade (short)*	
1930	*Broadway's Like That (short)*	Ruth's Pal
1930	*The Heart Breaker (short)*	

THE GENTLEMAN'S GENTLEMAN
ERIC BLORE

ERIC BLORE CIRCA 1936. AUTHOR'S COLLECTION.

"I frequently wonder what peculiar fascination butlers possess for the human imagination. Such cogitations are inspired by my own rather odd case. I find I am associated in the public mind with that calling."[1]

If ever an actor embodied the archetypal butler or other elite servant, it was Eric Blore. He became indistinguishable from the gentlemen's gentlemen he portrayed on screen, most memorably in five of the nine pictures in which Fred Astaire and Ginger Rogers appeared together. With his "elfish, long, straight nose," "squint eyed demeanor,"[2] and "sibilant voice,"[3] he was both sophistication and superciliousness personified. As such, he made those he served seem positively unpolished in comparison. He could have sprung from the pages of a P.G. Wodehouse "Jeeves" comic masterpiece. He is a butler who "glides" or "shimmers" in and out rooms seemingly without warning. He is not hesitant to give negative opinions of items his foppish master likes, such as a scarlet cummerbund or straw boater hat. The character's priceless brand of humor comes with the pedantic, polite manner in which he delivers his insults. Anyone who views Eric Blore's work would find it hard to deny that he more than possessed the irrepressible wit and humor of his fictional counterpart in literature.

Eric Blore was born on December 23, 1887 in London, England. With crispness that would become his trademark, he described the date as one "I have an annual cause to deplore, since I get no birthday presents so close to Christmas."[4] Eric was educated in private schools but, according to the actor, he "remained immune"[5] from their strictures. "There never was the slightest hope of following in the footsteps of my illustrious father, who had been an honors student at Trinity College,"[6] Eric stated. He further said that his father could read Greek and Latin "like you read the daily news." Eric did inherit his father's talent for language, but he used it for writing comedic sketches, not classical translations. In his brief time at college, Eric frustrated his father when he shirked schoolwork and instead funneled his energies into publishing his pithy jokes and stories in several well-respected English comics.[7] Eric quickly left school, claiming his presence there was "a profitless venture" that put "undue strain upon the professors."[8] His father helped him find work as an insurance agent for a time, but it was as "profitless" a venture as college had been. "I was consumed by an URGE," Eric declared. "Odd that a lad of no great industry should have had the potent driving power of an urge — to do fine things in the theater — wishing indeed to starve for the cause of drama."[9]

Eric's first substantial dramatic experience came when he joined G.P. Huntley on a tour of the Australian provinces. The play was entitled *The Merry Makers* and brought Eric beginner's luck. The aspiring actor won such laudations as: "Mr. Eric Blore was decidedly clever in his eccentric effusions. He sang 'There's a Sun Still Shining' and in a sneezing song, sneezed so naturally that he fairly brought down the house." [10] However, parallel to his success was failure. He performed in cheap music halls where patrons often showed their "displeasure at his singing by booing him off the stage." [11] Eric gained more pleasant stage experience when he joined the Liverpool Repertory Company. He appeared in a revue called *March Hairs*, which ran at the Empire Theatre, the most popular establishment in London. He found further good fortune when the show's lead fell ill and Eric was promoted to the part. He began to enjoy true success as both an actor and a writer at this stage in his career. He wrote an effective sketch for G.P. Huntley called "Burlington Arcadians" before, in Eric's words, World War I "brought a violent interlude to my acting career." [12] As a member of the Royal Air Force, he provided a welcome distraction from the violence of battle by writing a revue entitled "Welsh Wails." He produced the show with the aid of his fellow soldiers. It was such a hit that he was put in charge of a "concert unit" to entertain both troops and royalty, as proven when he had the honor of performing for King Edward. [13]

By the close of the war, Eric had risen to rank of commissioned officer and had also married a young woman named Violet Winter. The marriage would be a brief one; Eric married Violet in 1917, but by 1919 she had passed away. [14]

After his trying experiences in war and the loss of his wife, Eric claimed his urge to continue acting had begun to subside. "But the need for sustenance was still pressing," he stated. "So I turned to the musical stage, and fortune began to smile mildly upon me." [15] He found lucrative work both on stage and in the British cinema, most notably in Warren Baxter's screen adaptation of *The Great Gatsby* (1926). But it was the stage that kept him most occupied. Eric wrote his own book musical and organized a cooperative company to perform it. The revue, entitled *Ring Up*, led to Eric's first American engagement in *Little Miss Bluebeard*, which had a short run on Broadway in 1923 [16]. As he was enjoying success in his career, Eric also found success in his personal life. In 1926 he married Clara Mackin. They would have one son together, Eric Jr. [17]

Eric and his family remained in America after *Little Miss Bluebeard*, and he succeeded in bringing his unique brand of British humor to receptive audiences. He appeared almost exclusively in comedies such as *Mixed Doubles* (1927) and *Meet the Prince* (1928) but did prove his versatility in several mystery and dramas as well, namely *The Ghost Train* (1926) and *Give Me Yesterday* (1931). Though apt in all genres, audiences were most delighted with the array of basic comic characters he had been perfecting since his London stage days. His most popular characters were "leering-eyed English gentlemen" and "brusque/wise-acre butlers or waiters or other service providers," all performed with a "lock-jawed British accent." [18]

It was as a waiter that Eric became a star in his own right. The show was *The Gay Divorcee* (1928) and it would mark the beginning of his fruitful association with Fred Astaire. Eric's performance as a waiter exasperated with a customer's inability to remember what he was going to order was small, but it stood out enough to bring Eric to Hollywood's attention. In 1933, he again played a waiter in *Flying Down to Rio*. The film also starred Fred Astaire. Its success was quickly followed by a film rendition of *The Gay Divorcee* (1933) in which Eric reprised his stage role. The film marked the beginning of the best of Fred Astaire and Ginger Rogers' screen pairings and would also mark the beginning of Eric's finest screen work.

Top Hat (1935) and *Shall We Dance* (1937) best showcase Eric's ingenious comic ability. In *Top Hat*, he portrays Bates, character actor Edward Everett Horton's "invaluable manservant." Bates is nearly identical to Wodehouse's Jeeves. He is particularly effective in a scene with Fred Astaire (as Jerry). His ingratiating treatment of Jerry is all too clearly a means of revenge at his employer, Edward Everett Horton (as Horace), with whom he has just had a disagreement over an inelegant tie.

> BATES (taking Jerry's hat and coat): *Allow us to introduce ourselves, sir. We are Bates.*

> JERRY (amused): *And we are Jerry Travers.*

> BATES: *We'd like to compliment you on your taste in ties, sir.* (He gives a scathing look of judgment at Horace).

> JERRY: *Thank you, Bates.* (Bates leaves the room and Jerry turns to Horace) *They like me!* [19]

Though very much like the impeccable Jeeves in some ways, Eric brings his own unique zest to his archetypal gentleman's gentleman. A case in point is again in *Top Hat*. It is a scene in which Bates is speaking to an Italian policeman, calling him quite uncomplimentary names such as "nincompoop," all the while with an affable smile on his face. His expression of shock is priceless when the policeman (in English) tells Bates he is under arrest for insulting an officer. This bit of humor gives Eric's "gentleman's gentleman" a zanier, unexpected side than the more subtle and sagacious Jeeves. Ginger Rogers aptly concluded that Eric's "deadpan expressions were worth their weight in gold."[20]

In *Shall We Dance,* Eric bests even his performance in *Top Hat.* As the pompous Cecil Flintridge, floor manager of a hotel at which Astaire

ERIC BLORE AND ROBERT MONTGOMERY IN *PICCADILLY JIM* (1936).
AUTHOR'S COLLECTION.

and Rogers are staying, he never lacks in humor. He is hilarious as a fussbudget, fluttering back and forth as he tries to deduce whether or not Astaire and Rogers are actually married. At one point he lies down as a physical barrier against a door when he believes they are indeed unmarried and thus should not be in one another's rooms. Perhaps his most humorous scenes are those in which he is with Edward Everett Horton, with whom he was so effectively paired in *Top Hat.* Horton and Eric make a comic team arguably on par with Burns and Allen; indeed, their interplay is often not unlike that of a bickering married couple. The highlight of *Shall We Dance* is a scene in which Cecil (Eric) is mistakenly booked into prison and must call Jeffrey (Horton) to bail him out. Their conversation is a screwball masterpiece in exasperation, as evidenced in the following exchange:

JEFFREY BAIRD (picks up phone): *Hello?*

CECIL FLINTRIDGE: *Oh, hello, Jeffrey. Yes, are you there?*

JEFFREY BAIRD: *Of course I'm here.*

CECIL FLINTRIDGE: *Now don't shout at me — I'm in jail.*

JEFFREY BAIRD: *Well, that's all right; we don't need you.*

CECIL FLINTRIDGE: *I'm in jail for battery, and I want you to get me out. I'm at the Susquehannah Street Jail...Susquehannah! Susquehannah–S-U-S-Q-U-Q! Q! You know, the thing you play billiards with...Billiards! B-I-L-L-*

POLICEMAN AT JAIL: *What is this, a spelling bee?*

CECIL FLINTRIDGE: *Ahem. No, "L" for larynx. L-A-R-Y...N-No, not "M", N!... "N" as in neighbor! Neighbor, N-E-I-G-H-B — B! B! Bzzz. Bzzz. You know, the stinging insect! Insect! I-N-S-S! S, for symbol. S-Y...Y! Y!*

JEFFREY BAIRD: *Well, why? Don't ask me "why."*

CECIL FLINTRIDGE: *Look, Jeffrey. I'm in jail. W-wait a minute. What jail did you say this was?*

POLICEMAN AT JAIL: *Susquehannah Street Jail.*

CECIL FLINTRIDGE: *Thank you, indeed. Thank you very much. I'm in the Substi — The Subset — Jeffrey, listen closely...Do you know where the Oak Street Jail is? You do? Fine. I'll have them transfer me there in the morning!* [21]

As in *Top Hat*, Eric added his unique brand of madcap humor to an otherwise archetypal, pompous butler/elite servant role. His success in the Astaire/Rogers pictures led to him being cast as little else but butlers or valets for the rest of his career. His roles were almost indistinguishable from one another; he was Robert Montgomery's butler in *Piccadilly Jim* (1936), Warren Williams' valet in the *Lone Wolf* serial (1940-1947) , and

Monty Woolley's manservant in *Holy Matrimony* (1943). Eric earned both glowing and weary reviews from critics. One columnist proclaimed him "a pearl of…unlimited price" [22] while another quipped that if Eric appeared in another stereotyped butler role, "he might as well drop the 'l' in his last name." [23] Eric, too, admitted his mixed feelings about his identical roles. He claimed that they were so similar that on occasion he found he was speaking the right lines for the wrong picture or wearing the proper wardrobe at the wrong studio. [24]

Ultimately, Eric embraced his stereotype and developed a characteristically dry philosophy about it. When pondering the fascination butlers had on filmgoers' imagination, he reasoned: "Perhaps we are all social climbers at heart, and thus place the autocrat of the pantry on the place above the guardian of cravats and the humble dispenser of viands." [25] His only complaint regarding his role was not the stereotype but the required wardrobe. "Personally, I am no worshipper at the shrine of butlers," he said. "If anything, my feelings are tinged with resentment. Butlers invariably wear high stiff collars and my neck rebels at such confinement." [26] Eric confessed that he preferred the roles of valets and waiters, claiming they had "more dash" and "a superior zip." From his performances as the waiter in *The Gay Divorcee* and the valet in the *Lone Wolf* serial, one would find it difficult to argue this point.

Perhaps what makes Eric's portrayals of gentlemen's gentlemen so comically effective is their inaccuracy. Jean Marsh, star of *Upstairs, Downstairs* and descendant of a long line of servants, stated that Eric is not the perennial butler viewers profess him to be. "English butlers never look their masters in the face," she said. "All servants come from serfs. No matter how high a household they worked in, they were never haughty." [27] She went on to claim that servants would never knock on doors before entering a room. "They just walked in because no one paid any more attention to them than they would dogs," she declared. [28] It is impossible not to notice Eric when he enters a room on screen, so supercilious and arrogant is his manner. Undeniably, film audiences were, and still are, thankful that Eric did not strive to bring reality to his characterizations.

When not emoting onscreen, Eric was just as amusing in his personal life. When visiting Charles Bickford after the actor was injured by a lion during the filming of a motion picture, Eric said, "Don't blame it on the lion. Someone undoubtedly handed him the wrong script." [29] When not making such witticisms, Eric was an expert sportsman. He enjoyed swims, "a fast game of tennis," and golf. He once claimed the pressure of work "proved embarrassing for my golf" and went on to describe it in a pedantic way worthy of Wodehouse's Jeeves giving a monologue on a bit of "improving" literature: "Under the azure California sky, upon the peerless, sunlit green sand, it [golf] is a sport for kings and butlers. Often I feel myself in the throes of another urge — in this matchless golfing environment, to shatter 100." [30] Eric kept active not only in sports, but also in creative pursuits. He had never lost his fondness for the stage and took on multiple roles in the *Ziegfeld Follies of 1943*. It is a testament to the comedic standing he had achieved that one of the roles he essayed in the *Follies* was as himself. [31]

By the late 1940s, the screwball comedies that provided such a niche for pompous butlers and valets swiftly fell out of favor. Eric appeared in fewer and fewer films; his last notable appearance was as a shipboard doctor in Doris Day's film debut, *Romance on the High Seas* (1948). The best work in his latter career came when he superbly lent his voice to Mr. Toad in the animated *The Wind in the Willows* (1949). Eric retired in 1955, but his personal life was anything but dull. His son made the news when, in 1954, he had an argument with his wife and tore down a fence, tore off the steering wheel of his car, and tore up the furniture in his home. Eric Jr.'s marriage was annulled after only ten days. [32] Eric himself appeared in the news in no less shocking a way when, following a stroke in 1955, his death was prematurely announced. Eric employed a lawyer to sue the editor of the *New Yorker* for such misinformation, but the paper never had to print a retraction. In a twist of fate worthy of one of his madcap comedies, Eric passed away the night before the retraction was to be run. [33]

Eric Blore's name may not be immediately recognizable to the modern film viewer, but the irrepressible gentleman's gentleman character he created is firmly embedded in America's collective conscious. He entered films at the height of Jeeves' popularity in Britain and made the character his own in America. Through Eric, butlers and valets were not just nondescript figures entering and exiting rooms. Rather, he elevated the servant class to one above aristocrats, one capable of sophistication and witticisms made all the more humorous from the unexpectedness of their source. To see Eric in his best films with Fred Astaire and Ginger Rogers is to be transported to a bygone world of elegance and impeccable comedy, not a little aided by Eric's "delicious philosophies" and "quaint exasperations." One critic best described the actor when he wrote: "There never was anybody even remotely like Eric Blore before — there probably never will be again. No gentleman's gentleman…was ever so real — or so funny." [34]

FILMOGRAPHY

1955	*Bowery to Bagdad*	Genie of the Lamp
1950	*Fancy Pants*	Sir Wimbley
1949	*Love Happy*	Mackinaw
1949	*The Adventures of Ichabod and Mr. Toad*	Mr. Toad *(voice)*
1949	*The Wind in the Willows (short)*	J. Thaddeus Toad *(voice)*
1948	*Romance on the High Seas*	Ship's Doctor
1947	*The Lone Wolf in London*	Claudius Augustus Lucius Jamison
1947	*Winter Wonderland*	Luddington
1947	*The Lone Wolf in Mexico*	Jamison
1946	*Abie's Irish Rose*	Stubbins, Asst. Hotel Manager
1946	*The Notorious Lone Wolf*	Jameson
1945	*Kitty*	Dobson
1945	*Men in Her Diary*	Florist
1945	*Easy to Look at*	Billings
1945	*Penthouse Rhythm*	Ferdy Pelham, snitty critic
1945	*I Was a Criminal*	Obermueller, the Mayor
1944	*San Diego I Love You*	Nelson, Butler
1943	Caribbean Romance *(short)*	
1943	*Holy Matrimony*	Henry Leek
1943	*Passport to Suez*	Llewellyn Jameson
1943	*Submarine Base*	Spike, Morgan's aide
1943	*The Sky's the Limit*	Jackson, Phil's Butler *(uncredited)*
1943	*Heavenly Music (short)*	Mr. Frisbie, Public Relations
1943	*Forever and a Day*	Charles
1943	*One Dangerous Night*	Jamison
1943	*Happy Go Lucky*	Betsman
1942	*The Moon and Sixpence*	Capt. Nichols
1942	*Counter-Espionage*	Jamison
1941	*The Shanghai Gesture*	Caesar Hawkins
1941	*Sullivan's Travels*	Sullivan's Valet
1941	*Confirm or Deny*	Mr. Hobbs, Regency Hotel
1941	*Secrets of the Lone Wolf*	Jamison the Butler
1941	*New York Town*	Vivian
1941	*Three Girls About Town*	Charlemagne, looking for Charlie
1941	*Lady Scarface*	Mr. Hartford
1941	*Redhead*	Digby
1941	*Road to Zanzibar*	Charles Kimble

1941	*The Lone Wolf Takes a Chance* .... Jamison
1941	*The Lady Eve*.................................. Sir Alfred McGlennan Keith
1940	*The Lone Wolf Keeps a Date*.. Jamison
1940	*South of Suez*...................................... Harold 'Limey' Wemsley
1940	*Earl of Puddlestone*.. Horatio Bottomley
1940	*The Boys from Syracuse*.. Pinch
1940	*The Lone Wolf Meets a Lady*.. Jamison
1940	*'Til We Meet Again*..................................... Sir Harold Pinchard
1940	*The Lone Wolf Strikes* .... Jamison
1940	*The Man Who Wouldn't Talk* .... Horace Parker
1940	*Music in My Heart*... Griggs
1939	*$1000 a Touchdown*... Henry
1939	*Island of Lost Men* .... Herbert
1939	*A Gentleman's Gentleman* .... Heppelwhite
1938	*A Desperate Adventure*... Trump
1938	*Swiss Miss*.. Edward
1938	*Joy of Living*... Potter
1937	*Hitting a New High*...Cedric Cosmo,
	AKA Captain Braceridge Hemingway
1937	*Breakfast for Two* ....Butch, Blair's Valet
1937	*It's Love I'm After*...Digges
1937	*Shall We Dance*...................................... Cecil Flintridge
1937	*The Soldier and the Lady*.. Henry Blount
1937	*Quality Street*... Recruiting Sergeant
1936	*Smartest Girl in Town*..................... Lucius Philbean, Dick's Valet
1936	*Swing Time*.. Gordon
1936	*Piccadilly Jim*...Bayliss, Jim's Butler
1936	*The Ex-Mrs. Bradford*........................... Stokes, Bradford's Butler
1936	*Sons o' Guns*... Hobson
1936	*Two in the Dark* ....Edmund Fish
1935	*Seven Keys to Baldpate*............................Prof. Harrison Boulton
1935	*I Dream Too Much* ....Roger Briggs
1935	*To Beat the Band* .... Hawkins
1935	*I Live My Life*............................... Grove, Bentley's Butler
1935	*Diamond Jim*... Sampson Fox
1935	*Top Hat*.. Bates
1935	*Old Man Rhythm*...'Phil' Phillips
1935	*The Casino Murder Case* .... Currie, Vance's Butler
1935	*Folies Bergère de Paris*.. Francois
1935	*The Good Fairy* .... Dr. Metz

1934 *Limehouse Blues*.. Slummer *(uncredited)*
1934 *Behold My Wife*..Benson *(butler)*
1934 *The Gay Divorcee*.. The waiter
1933 *Flying Down to Rio*............ Mr. Butterbass, Asst. Hotel Manager
1931 *My Sin*.. Barfly
1931 *Tarnished Lady*...................... Jewelry Counter Clerk *(uncredited)*
1930 *Laughter*................... Party Guest in Angel Costume *(uncredited)*
1926 *The Great Gatsby* .... Lord Digby
1920 *A Night Out and a Day In (short)*...

AMERICA'S
SOFT SHOE MAN
RAY BOLGER

RAY BOLGER CIRCA 1941. COURTESY OF JERRY MURBACH.

He was slim, plain-faced, and inconspicuous. That is, until he donned a pair of dancing shoes. His soft-shoe transformed the quiet man into the object of every observer's attention. He seemed to have no bones at all, so elastic were his legs and liquid were his movements. He could do a series of falls and get up and do them over again. He was graceful in his clumsiness, yet he kept his audience in stitches with each rubber-faced expression of shock that accompanied his dizzying falls and spins. "Nobody danced the way he did,"[1] choreographer Michael Kidd asserted. Those who have seen Ray Bolger perform would doubtlessly agree. There are few who have not had the privilege of seeing his work; indeed, the phenomenal popularity of the classic musical *The Wizard of Oz* (1939) has introduced Ray's floppy-limbed, loveable Scarecrow to each new generation of filmgoers. Though *Oz* would mark Ray's zenith in film, he was never long off the screen or stage, lending his inimitable blend of pantomime and dance to musicals from the 1930s through the 1980s. The dancer was invariably lauded as "a swell gent"[2] by family and co-stars, always remaining modest despite his considerable successes. It is his complete lack of formal dance or dramatic training that makes him so unpretentious and accessible to adults and children alike. "He was never given the status he deserved, but he was never bothered by it," a colleague remarked. "He truly enjoyed what he did best — dancing, singing, and acting."[3]

Raymond Wallace Bolger was born in 1904 in Boston, Massachusetts. "We were Boston Irish," Ray described his family. "Dorcester Irish, to be exact. I grew up in an Irish-Jewish neighborhood and spoke pretty good Yiddish."[4] As a child, he was judged to be one of the best dressed boys in his neighborhood. However, his dapper Buster Brown suits with high collars made him the target of bullies. But, according to one of Ray's boyhood friends, "He was good-natured and took this [bullying] lightly."[5] Ray had more sobering matters to consider than his peers' approval of his dress. The son of a housepainter, Ray's life was dominated by poverty when his father fell ill and could no longer support the family. To survive, Ray kept a busy schedule of work in the afternoon and school in the morning. "Ray was always a lonely boy," his mother said. "When he was in high school, he got on the hockey team and played whenever the boss of the store he was working in would let him off. He didn't know many people because he was on a job when he wasn't in school."[6]

Ray assuaged his loneliness through the theater. He spent his precious free time watching his idols, Jack Buchanan and Fred Stone (Stone coincidentally originated the role of the Scarecrow in the stage version of *The*

Wizard of Oz). It was when watching Stone perform that Ray decided he wanted to follow in the dancer's footsteps. "Up until then, the theater had nothing to do with me. That moment in the theater changed that," [7] Ray stated. He gained experience in dramatics, landing roles in school productions of *Merchant of Venice* and *Father Rabbit.* But his success in acting did not translate to social success. He was a male wallflower at proms and recalled that, "I was so skinny and homely no girls would go out with me." [8] An ex-vaudevillian gave the awkward boy some dance lessons to break down his inhibitions, and suddenly he "had no problem getting dates." As Stone's performance in the theater had filled Ray with ambition toward the stage, the dancing lessons gave him an expanded vision for his future. "I decided that if wanted to be success in life, I had to learn to dance," [9] Ray said.

To earn money for dance lessons, Ray worked as everything from a bank messenger to a vacuum cleaner salesman. In the halls of one his places of employment, Ray allegedly could not help dancing. Though his jigs led Ray's employer to fire him for being undignified, they caught the attention of ballet instructor Senia Russakoff. Russakoff offered the young man his first chance in show business. In return for being the ballet instructor's bookkeeper, Ray could have lessons and a place to sleep in Russakoff's office. Ray made his stage debut at Boston's Grand Opera House, where he did a series of dances ranging from a mazurka, an interpretive dance of a "Chinese dope fiend," [10] a ballet, to an adagio that had Ray dressed in tails. [11] His efforts garnered a positive reception, and he no longer had to take any jobs outside of the theatrical world. He appeared at local revues and then joined Phil Spitainy's orchestra. His time with the orchestra, as well as his time with a repertory company in 1924, gave him valuable experience in vaudeville. It was during Ray's time on vaudeville that he met Gwen Rickard, "a California college girl who didn't know a thing about show business." [12] They married in 1929 and would remain so until Ray's death.

His and Gwen's meeting coincided with Ray's Broadway debut in *The Merry World,* a musical revue that premiered in 1926. In 1931, Ray enjoyed more substantial stage time in *George White's Scandals,* succeeded by another hit show, *Life Begins at 8:30,* in which he appeared in three comical sketches. Ray was just as apt a comedian off stage, as evidenced when, during a performance of *Life Begins at 8:30,* a small fire broke out on the theater roof. Ray reportedly helped to keep the crowd calm by performing an impromptu tap dance saying, "You can't walk out on me!" [13]

It was in 1936 that Ray's fate as a Broadway star was sealed. The show that made this possible was a Rodgers and Hart revue entitled *On Your Toes*. Ray was featured in the exhausting dance number "Slaughter on Tenth Avenue" about a gangster and his moll. The number would later be recreated by Gene Kelly and Vera-Ellen in a sober, noir style in the 1948 film *Words and Music*. But in Ray's shoes, it was comedy routine. It was vigorously cheered and heralded as the show's most celebrated act. His success in *On Your Toes* "entranced Hollywood missionaries"[14] who thought Ray's unusual technique would translate well in the flurry of musicals that flooded the 1930s.

Upon arriving in Hollywood, Ray enjoyed the life of a film star while waiting for M-G-M executives to give him his first assignment. "Ray was enchanted with the fact that he had a real house for the first time since he was a child," Gwen said. "He never tired of walking out of the front door on to the green grass."[15] Ray's awe also extended to his work environment, where he had an insatiable interest about the technical aspects of talking pictures. He had appeared in a bit part in one silent film, *Carrie of the Chorus* (1926), and admitted that, "I don't know about pictures — I can tell them nothing…it is foolish for anyone like me to go to Hollywood without having the great humility."[16] Ray gained many friends among cameraman and grips through his modesty and sincere curiosity about all aspects of the new medium in which he found himself. It was the beginning of his reputation as being one of the "nicest guys" in show business.[17]

In 1935 M-G-M assigned Ray his first film role, and it was an appropriate one: imitating Jack Donahue. The film was *The Great Ziegfeld*, and Ray stole the show from even his best co-star, Fanny Brice. He dances to "She's a Follies Girl" and ingeniously blends pantomime, comedy, and soft shoe. The most memorable moment of the skit finds Ray holding a split for over thirty seconds. He then slowly raises himself up by his heels, only to slide down again and do it all over. The flabbergasted expression on his face is hilarious, as if he does not know what his legs are doing and they are acting of their own volition. He becomes even more flustered as he spins across the stage, running into the backdrop curtain and gazing about as if he is lost. The uproarious routine was well-received by critics and earned him the laudation of being a new eccentric dance phenomenon. Ray would appear in more films in quick succession, but oddly enough he did not dance in them. Rather, he lent only his comedic touch to two Nelson Eddy films, *Rosalie* (1937) and *Sweethearts* (1938). He is particularly effective in the former film as aviator Eddy's friend who gets himself into no end of trouble in his efforts to impress his girlfriend, even if it means flying a plane when he has not the first idea of how to navigate it.

Ray's early films were pleasant, but they did not provide adequate showcases in which to blend his comedic, musical, and dancing talents. It was not until 1939 that Ray found his ideal showcase: *The Wizard of Oz*. M-G-M assigned Ray the role of the Tin Man, but Ray campaigned for the Scarecrow. While the Tin Man is stiff-jointed, the Scarecrow is floppy and boneless, ideal for Ray "Rubber-legs" Bolger. Indeed, his style was perfectly matched to the Scarecrow's gait in L. Frank Baum's novel. Baum wrote that the straw man "fell at full length on the hard bricks" of the yellow road and had Dorothy "pick him up and set him upon his feet again, while he joined her in laughing merrily at his own mishap." [18]

Ray's campaigning won him the role and he became the Scarecrow. Like Baum's Scarecrow, he elicited much merry laughter with his comedic as well as dancing talents. Though purportedly a children's film, adults could appreciate some of his quips such as "Some people without brains do an awful lot of talking!" [19] while juveniles could get laughs out of his slapstick falls and bounces on the Yellow Brick Road. When Dorothy whispers "I think I'll miss you most all" to the Scarecrow at the film's close, audiences cannot help but agree.

On the set of *The Wizard of Oz*, Ray's colleagues would discover that he seemed to have truly been awarded a brain by a wizard. He could most often be found engrossed in one of the hundreds of tomes he kept in a studio behind his home. He listed his favorite authors as Maupassant, Boccaccio, and Balzac. Ray avidly studied foreign languages as well, namely German and French. He filled out his knowledge of language with a course in phonetics he found time to take. "If I were ten or twenty years younger and was told I couldn't go into show business, I would spend my entire life in the literary world," [20] Ray declared. Ray's intellectualism set him apart from his co-stars, Bert Lahr and Jack Haley, but he was not as much the loner as he professed to be. One young extra remarked that, "Mr. Bolger was always the first to make us laugh, and always helped others out when we had trouble with our scripts...or our dance routines... He was like a big brother who was always there for everyone." [21]

Ray's extraordinary success as the Scarecrow would not be fully realized until the movie became a staple on television each year. As such, Ray continued to be underused in mediocre musicals such as *Sunny* (1941) and *Four Jacks and a Jill* (1942). He turned his energies back to the stage and found success in the Broadway revue *Keep Off the Grass* in 1940, followed with *By Jupiter* in 1942. He also spent some time performing with Harry

James's band. In the midst of his busy work schedule, Ray made time to contribute to the war effort. He performed in the USO and enlivened many a G.I.'s day with his humorous dance routines. Nurse Lieutenant Carolyn Brown recalled his effect on the soldiers: "You have watched Ray Bolger dance but until you have seen him just back from the front lines, tired, hungry, wearing soiled clothes and dancing in a pair of ill-fitting

RAY BOLGER WITH PAUL HARTMAN AND ANNA NEAGLE IN *SUNNY* (1941).
COURTESY OF JERRY MURBACH.

G.I. shoes…you have never seen him at his best. The boys simply adore him…the morale went up and the evening ended with everyone around the piano…having a marvelous time singing old American songs." [22]

Ray continued to boost Americans' morale after the war, lightening the country's spirits in his return to film. He was reunited with Judy Garland in *The Harvey Girls* (1946) in which he gave a memorable performance as a blacksmith afraid of horses. He performs a side-splitting tap dance routine in the film, ending with a clumsy attempt to waltz with a short-tempered Marjorie Main. In 1948 he found a role that would rival the Scarecrow in popularity: as Charley Wykeham in *Where's Charley?*, the musical remake of the play *Charley's Aunt*. He portrays a man masquerading as his friend's aunt from Brazil when the woman, who is supposed to act as chaperone for Charley and his friends when they are with their girls, fails to materialize. The hilarious show also gave Ray a song that would become one of Broadway's most beloved hits, "Once in Love with Amy." The show ran for two years and when revived in 1951, ran for another six months. As Ray had done on the set of *Oz,* he left warm memories with those on the set of *Where's Charley?* A young cast member recalled him as the most "kind and gentle creature around" who would "profusely apologize if he so much as sneezed on someone by accident...He loved children, and would always be tweaking a nose or pulling pennies out of your ear, sometimes trying to teach you how to work your legs like he did (because all of us youngsters would beg so much). He was a doll." [23] Ray himself told one fan of the 1952 film adaptation of the film, "Oh, my dear, I'm so pleased. That was my favorite film." [24]Critics of the film had just as favorable a view of it and claimed Ray had "the run of the picture." [25] However, they did express a wish that "something original could be made for his dancing feet." [26]

Ray had the same wish. After appearing as none other than Jack Donahue in a film about dancer Marilyn Miller, *Look for the Silver Lining* (1949), his stage and film work came more slowly and was less satisfying. Television work kept Ray most active in the 1950s. He landed his own situation comedy entitled *Where's Raymond?* The show revolved around the life of a hoofer with a penchant for arriving to his performances seconds before the curtain rises. The show ran from 1953-1955. Ray longed to return to the legitimate stage, but as times and tastes changed away from zany tap dances and nostalgic musical comedies, he found it more difficult to find a vehicle that would give audiences what they expected from him while remaining up-to-date. With no ideal productions presenting themselves, Ray devoted his time to philanthropy. He performed for countless charity shows and in 1971, toured twenty cities giving lectures on everything from good citizenship to his *Oz* experiences. By the 1970s *Oz* had reintroduced Ray to a whole new generation of audiences and its legacy alone kept Ray more than busy. He even began planning to create a theme park called "Wizardland." When asked if he tired of being identified solely with the Scarecrow, Ray shook his head and said, "To be bothered by this would be a sin and to be disrespectful to the role would be a sin." [27]

Ray gained further prominence among new generations of audiences through his frequent guest appearances on popular television shows. His best remembered performances were as the swinging grandfather on *The Partridge Family* and in a memorable advertisement for Dr. Pepper in which the geriatric Ray proved to be rubber-legged as ever in a lively dance. He kept spry by rehearsing for two hours daily and exercising for fifteen minutes before each routine. "Old age never killed anybody. They died because their hearts stopped," Ray stated. "Instead of growing old mentally I seem to be growing younger." [28] The tireless entertainer continued to stay young at heart well into the 1980s; what would ultimately be his final performance was in the television sitcom *Diff'rent Strokes* in 1984.

Shortly after his final television appearance, he suffered a fall from a stage that resulted in the need for an artificial hip. His doctor told him he could no longer dance but Ray took the news with his usual good-nature. "I'm eighty, and how much more dancing do I want to do?" he asked. In 1987 Ray was the final of the *Oz* quartet to pass away. He joined his three friends when he succumbed to cancer at age eighty-three.

Ray's death in no way diminished his presence in film history. Today, through his *Oz* legacy Ray is arguably better known than he was in his own time. However, few know the name behind the Scarecrow and have little to no knowledge of the comic and dancing genius from dozens of other stage and film productions. Ray's dancing may not have been a hidden talent, but in life he was man possessive of many. He was highly intellectual and had a modesty not seen in many big name Broadway and film stars. "He was never unkind to a single soul," [29] a colleague claimed. Though the modest, shy Ray many times professed a wish to be in a field other than entertainment he was truly best suited to his chosen profession. The words he speaks about show business as Jack Donahue in *Look for the Silver Lining* could have been spoken by Ray himself:

> *Why should you want to do anything else? I don't. The only reason everybody in the world isn't doing what we're doing is because they don't know how. It's a wonderful way to live and a wonderful way to make your exit…If I had my wish, that's the way I'd want to have it happen, at the end of a tap dance.* [30]

FILMOGRAPHY

1982	*Annie*	Radio Sound Effects Man *(uncredited)*
1979	*The Runner Stumbles*	Monsignor Nicholson
1979	*Just You and Me, Kid*	Tom
1966	*The Daydreamer*	The Pieman
1961	*Babes in Toyland*	Barnaby
1952	*April in Paris*	S. 'Sam' Winthrop Putnam

1952	*Where's Charley?*	Charley Wykeham
1949	*Look for the Silver Lining*	Jack Donahue
1946	*The Harvey Girls*	Chris Maule
1943	*Forever and a Day*	Sentry *(scenes deleted)*
1942	*Four Jacks and a Jill*	Nifty Sullivan
1941	*Sunny*	Bunny Billings
1939	*The Wizard of Oz*	Hunk / The Scarecrow
1938	*Sweethearts*	Hans
1938	*The Girl of the Golden West*	Happy Moore *(scenes deleted)*
1937	*Rosalie*	Bill Delroy
1935	*The Great Ziegfeld*	Himself
1926	*Carrie of the Chorus: The Berth Mark*	Banker

THE MOTHER NEXT DOOR
BEULAH BONDI

BEULAH BONDI IN *MR. SOFT TOUCH* (1949). AUTHOR'S COLLECTION.

"I started as a character actor and I've always been a character actor, and I've never played myself yet." [1]

Beulah Bondi could not have been more correct when she spoke these words. One of the most ubiquitous and recognizable faces of the silver screen, she was a small and dainty yet sharp-featured woman with a salt and pepper colored bun at the nape of her neck. She not only became audiences' favorite "kindly and long suffering mother" but also their favorite "intolerable old harridan." [2] However, in her personal life, Beulah was neither a mother nor an old harridan. Rather, she was an independent, sometimes outspoken woman who could also claim titles of everything from world traveler to doctor of law. Unlike the matrons she portrayed on screen though she was, she never complained about her minor, uniform roles. Even if it was the twentieth time she portrayed a mother who had little else to do but look concerned, Beulah would unaffectedly declare, "I'm very cooperative, and if you'll just tell me exactly what you want, I'll always try to do it." [3] For over sixty years, Beulah Bondi did the parts that were asked of her. However, she made them unpredictable by bringing her own unique brand of warmth and shrewdness to even the mildest of matrons.

Beulah was born on May 3, 1888 to Abraham and Eva Bondy in Chicago. As a toddler, she moved with her family to Valparaiso, Indiana, where her mother returned to college to pursue a Bachelor's degree in theater arts. Eva became an acting teacher after graduation. In the 1890s, it was quite unusual for a woman to return to school. Eva would pass her resilience and flouting of convention to Beulah, not to mention her love of the theater. Beulah recalled her earliest memories as those of her mother "play acting" and teaching her to recite instead of saying a prayer before bed each night. [4] The girl first stepped before an audience when she was nine years old, essaying the lead in *Little Lord Fauntleroy* at the Valparaiso Memorial Opera House. Eva was as ambitious to make her daughter a career woman as she had been to make herself one. It was she who had secured Beulah the lead when the child initially hired for the role fell ill. Eva tirelessly rehearsed with her daughter and by opening night, the girl had not only memorized all forty-seven pages of her own part, but everyone else's part as well. [5]

Beulah further followed in her mother's footsteps when she attended Valparaiso University to earn a B.A. of her own. She gravitated toward the school's theatricals and played a debutante in one production called *An American Citizen*. She was also active writing poetry and scripts for the school's plays.

After receiving a B.A. and later an M.A. in Oratory, Beulah signed with Stuart Walker, head of one of the best established repertory companies of the era. Beulah toured with the company for two years before she reached New York and made her Broadway debut in 1919. Though only twenty-seven years old at the time, her portrayal of a seventy-year old servant in the play was so effective that it neatly typed her in roles of women older than herself. She made her legitimate Broadway debut six years later in *One of the Family.* The show ran for an impressive 238 performances, followed by *Saturday's Children,* which ran for 376 performances. However, it was not until 1929 that Beulah could call herself a full-fledged star. The play responsible for sealing her success was *Street Scene,* in which she again played an elderly woman. When the play was bought by Samuel Goldwyn two years later, he wanted Beulah to reprise her stage role on screen. Beulah accepted, but refused to sign the seven-year contract Goldwyn offered. The seemingly soft-spoken, petite actress must have turned many studio heads by asserting such independence. She later claimed her decision to "tear up a contract from Sam Goldwyn"[6] prevented her from being cast in roles more befitting a younger actress and thus outside her forte. Beulah sincerely preferred playing older women and, contrary to other mature actresses, she added years to her age instead of shaving them off. She kept people guessing about her age even after she died; the date of her birth varied by as much as four years. "Age is just a number,"[7] became Beulah's pet advice to fellow actresses.

Without a binding contract, Beulah was free to select her own parts without being forced into unpalatable roles. Though she briefly returned to Broadway between 1931 and 1933, the plays were flops. For the next fifty years she would devote herself to motion pictures. She was a welcome addition to the film industry, for her gentle, pleasant voice and subtle acting manner were well-suited to talkies. Beulah proved that she was her own best agent by appearing in almost invariably grade A movies. The reason for the lack of mediocre programmers on her filmography is best described by the actress herself: "When an actor is out of work, it's tempting to take any job for the money. But an old quotation used to come to me, 'Don't sell your birthright for a mess of pottage.' I don't think I ever did."[8] Indeed, with top-notch pictures like Joan Crawford's *Rain* (1932), Marie Dressler's *Christopher Bean* (1933), and Greta Garbo's *The Painted Veil* (1934) no one could say she appeared in any messes of pottage.

The year of 1936 would usher in the most successful decade of Beulah's career. Over the next ten years, she would not only appear in her most memorable roles but also earn two Academy Award nominations. The new category of Best Supporting Actress seemed to be made for her. In 1936, she was nominated for her role as the sharp-tongued but wise wife of Andrew Jackson in *The Gorgeous Hussy*. Though Beulah lost to Gale Sondergaard in *Anthony Adverse*, her role in *The Gorgeous Hussy* maintains a special place on her filmography not only for earning her a nomination, but

BEULAH BONDI WITH JAMES STEWART IN OF *HUMAN HEARTS* (1938).
AUTHOR'S COLLECTION.

for marking the first time she and James Stewart, her most oft-repeated co-star, appeared together on screen. Two years later, Beulah would earn another Academy Award nomination playing James Stewart's self -sacrificing mother in the Civil War period piece *Of Human Hearts* (1938).

Though Fay Bainter won over Beulah at 1938's Academy Awards, this did nothing to diminish Beulah as filmdom's first choice in any mother/grandmother part available. Among those who counted Beulah as "first choice" was James Stewart. He is quoted as saying that he always, "had a sort of respect and love for her. I started treating her just as I did my own mother."[9] Beulah offered Stewart equal praise, declaring him her favorite onscreen son. "Nobody can play his mother but me,"[10] she later stated. She did not exaggerate; they would ultimately appear in five films together. "I don't think we ever really discussed our scenes," Beulah recalled, "There was always a natural relationship."[11] Just as Stewart stood for all-American young manhood in the years of the Depression and World War II, Beulah became synonymous with all-American motherhood.

Beulah never better reflected America than in Leo McCarey's masterful drama *Make Way for Tomorrow* (1937). The film dealt with an issue virtually unknown to the screen: the displaced elderly. Beulah donned a gray wig and portrayed Lucy, a woman near seventy years old who, because of the Depression, is forced to separate from her husband and lodge with one of their grown children. Beulah makes herself both irritating and sympathetic in the film; her performance gives the film its realism and depth. Viewers cannot help but find her intrusive and garrulous in a scene when her daughter-in-law is trying to teach a class on card playing; at the same time, viewers cannot help but feel on the verge of tears when Lucy discovers her son is considering sending her to an old folks' home. Beulah is especially poignant in a scene with her granddaughter, Rhoda, after the girl tells her to "face facts." Lucy replies with a calmness that makes her words all the more affecting:

> *Oh, Rhoda! When you're seventeen and the world's beautiful, facing facts is just as slick fun as dancing or going to parties, but when you're seventy...well, you don't care about dancing. You don't think about parties anymore, and about the only fun you have left is pretending that there ain't any facts to face, so would you mind if I just went on pretending?*[12]

It is surprising that Beulah was not nominated for another Academy Award for her portrayal of Lucy. Nevertheless, she went on without complaint, taking supporting roles even after proving herself such a capable leading actress in *Make Way for Tomorrow*. She was not one to dwell on what she could have been or could be. She once replied, when asked about her favorite role, "It has always been the one I was playing at the moment that I liked best."[13] She effectively appeared in such films as *Our Town* (1940), *Penny Serenade* (1941), and *The Snake Pit* (1948). She proved her versatility in the latter film by playing not a kind-faced matron but an inmate at a mental asylum. Though she took enough roles completely out of her niche to keep audiences eager to see what she would do next, the ever humble Beulah would be the last one to admit this. "We, the character actresses, are sort of the mortar between bricks," she said. "I never had any ides of stealing a scene or being better than anyone else. The idea is to make the whole thing look perfect with cooperation."[14]

Perhaps no other film shows better cooperation than *It's a Wonderful Life* (1946), arguably the movie for which Beulah is best remembered. The cast included some of the best character actors in the business, including Thomas Mitchell, H.B. Warner, and Henry Travers. And, of course, James Stewart played Beulah's son. The cast has such a natural rapport on screen that film viewers feel as if they are looking through the keyhole of the home of a true American family. Beulah's portrayal of Mrs. Bailey allows her to show both roles she did best: kindly mother and old harridan, the former in George's real life, the latter in his dark vision of what the world would be like without him. She is both subtly humorous and touching as the knowing Mrs. Bailey, engaging her son in such banter as:

MRS. BAILEY (speaking of George's girl, Mary): *Why, she lights up like a firefly whenever you're around. Besides, Sam Wainwright [George's rival] is off in New York, and you're here in Bedford Falls.*

GEORGE: *And all's fair in love and war, right?*

MRS. BAILEY: *Well, I don't know about war...*

GEORGE (laughing and hugging her): *Mother, you know I can see right through you — right to your back collar button... trying to get rid of me, huh?*

MRS. BAILEY: *Uh-huh.*[15]

Beulah is equally convincing as the hardened "Ma Bailey" in George's dystopia, caustically telling him he belongs in an insane asylum and slamming the door in his face when he cries, "Mother, don't you know me?"

Though *It's a Wonderful Life* would mark the end of Beulah's most memorable period in Hollywood, she remained no less busy over the course of the next two decades. She turned increasingly toward the new medium of television for work and appeared in episodes of *Alfred Hitchcock Presents* (1955), *Route 66* (1961), and *Wagon Train* (1961). In films, she continued to play either tough women or soft matronly characters. She was a perseverant, pharisaic mother in Robert Mitchum's gritty *Track of the Cat* (1954), but between 1961 and 1963, she portrayed matrons in the decidedly more lightweight *Tammy* films. Her appearance in *Tammy and the Doctor* (1963) would be her final film appearance.

Though her work was less frequent, Beulah was anything but unoccupied. She became a bona fide jet setter in the United States and abroad. She found a desert retreat in Victorville, Yucca Loma, and also enjoyed vacationing on Colorado dude ranches and fishing at Yellowstone Park. Even when well into her eighties, Beulah remained unfazed at the incredulous stares she received when she spoke of a proposed trip to say, Taiwan, as casually as she would propose going on a trip to so innocuous a location as Akron, Ohio. "Oh yes, I travel a great deal," she told an interviewer in 1976. "I motored to Alaska last summer, and last year I spent Christmas with friends in Lima, Peru. I've traveled from the Antarctic to northern Norway and circled the globe a couple of times. I love to visit ancient civilizations." [16] Though she had lofty scholastic credentials behind her, Beulah remained keenly interested in expanding her education through travel and literature. In her home, she had collected a voluminous number of books since 1944 on all subjects, including ancient civilizations.

"I believe Africa is my favorite continent," she said. "Although I also like the Middle East. It's always nice to go back to places and see them again." [17]

When not traveling, Beulah was happy being a homebody. She enjoyed doing her own grocery shopping despite the fact she had a cook. She treated her cook, whom she described as "a real southern mammy from West Virginia," as an invaluable friend. As adventurous as Beulah was in travel, her palate and daily routines were simple and homespun. She once confided that she liked her dinner at midday, and often had hot cereal at night.

Perhaps Beulah's love for both travel and the home life stemmed from the fact that she no longer wished to be part of an industry she no longer recognized. She claimed that the "blight of sex shops and massage parlors"[18] that had sullied Los Angeles was now too much reflected on screen. She disapproved of nudity and the explicit violence in hard crime films that had become so ubiquitous by the 1970s. "We all know what life is, but it is too awful to advertise it in that way," Beulah said in 1977. "I go to films to learn. Good acting, good writing, good directing, all the technical part is what I learn from."[19]

Beulah proved she had never stopped learning and perfecting her craft when she made what would be her final appearance on any screen, big or little. In a 1976 two-hour special entitled *The Pony Cart* on the hit television show *The Waltons*, Beulah portrayed a strong-spirited mountain woman who refuses a government order to leave her land. Ironically, Beulah had been offered the part of Grandma Walton on the series, but her friend Ellen Corby took it upon Beulah's rejection. Beulah's work on the show earned her an Emmy, a well-deserved award for her sixty-plus-year career. Upon receiving her award, Beulah meekly stood on stage and murmured, "My, isn't this wonderful. This is truly a bonus."[20] She received another "bonus" in 1978 when her alma mater, Valparaiso University, made her an honorary doctor of law.

Beulah remained lively and vital into her nineties and seemed not to feel her age. "I have too much to do and too active a life,"[21] she stated. Perhaps it was because she always played a woman older than herself that her age never seemed to catch up with her; but, in 1981, it finally did. After tripping over her cat, Beulah sustained severe injuries including several broken ribs. She died of pulmonary complications at ninety-two years old.

Wise mother or outspoken, irascible matron on screen, world traveler or average little old lady next door off screen, Beulah Bondi was not a predictable woman. True, she was typed in predictable roles in her films, but to each one she brought a sincerity and effortlessness that made even the smallest role seem fresh and worthy of mention. She could be equally convincing as poor women and rich women, modern women and old-fashioned women. Beulah herself best explained why she was so adept at portraying matriarchs from all walks of life, and why she remains so familiar and endearing to each new generation of film viewers: "What distinguishes the real actor from the pseudo is the passionate desire to know what is going on in the hearts and minds of people."[22]

FILMOGRAPHY

1963	*Tammy and the Doctor*	Annie Call
1961	*Tammy Tell Me True*	Mrs. Annie Call
1959	*A Summer Place*	Mrs. Emily Hamilton Hamble
1959	*The Big Fisherman*	Hannah
1957	*The Unholy Wife*	Emma Hochen
1956	*Back from Eternity*	Martha Spangler
1954	*Track of the Cat*	Ma Bridges
1953	*Latin Lovers*	Analyst
1952	*Lone Star*	Minniver Bryan
1950	*The Furies*	Mrs. Anaheim
1950	*The Baron of Arizona*	Loma Morales
1949	*Reign of Terror*	Grandma Blanchard
1949	*Mr. Soft Touch*	Mrs. Hangale
1949	*The Life of Riley*	Miss Martha Bogle
1948	*So Dear to My Heart*	Granny Kincaid
1948	*The Snake Pit*	Mrs. Greer
1948	*The Sainted Sisters*	Hester Rivercomb
1947	*High Conquest*	Clara Kingsley
1946	*It's a Wonderful Life*	Ma Bailey
1946	*Sister Kenny*	Mary Kenny
1946	*Breakfast in Hollywood*	Mrs. Annie Reed
1945	*Back to Bataan*	Bertha Barnes
1945	*The Southerner*	Granny Tucker
1944	*And Now Tomorrow*	Aunt Em
1944	*The Very Thought of You*	Mrs. Harriet Wheeler
1944	*Our Hearts Were Young and Gay*	Miss Horn
1944	*I Love a Soldier*	Etta Lane
1944	*She's a Soldier Too*	Agatha Kittredge
1943	*Watch on the Rhine*	Anise
1943	*Tonight We Raid Calais*	Mme. Bonnard
1941	*One Foot in Heaven*	Mrs. Lydia Sandow
1941	*The Shepherd of the Hills*	Aunt Mollie
1941	*Penny Serenade*	Miss Oliver
1940	*The Captain Is a Lady*	Angie Peabody
1940	*Our Town*	Mrs. Webb
1940	*Remember the Night*	Mrs. Sargent
1939	*Mr. Smith Goes to Washington*	Ma Smith
1939	*The Under-Pup*	Miss Thornton

1939	*On Borrowed Time*	Nellie Northrup–Granny
1938	*The Sisters*	Rose Elliott
1938	*Vivacious Lady*	Mrs. Martha Morgan
1938	*Of Human Hearts*	Mary Wilkins
1938	*The Buccaneer*	Aunt Charlotte
1937	*Make Way for Tomorrow*	Lucy Cooper
1937	*Maid of Salem*	Abigail Goode
1936	*The Gorgeous Hussy*	Rachel Jackson
1936	*Hearts Divided*	Madame Letizia
1936	*The Case Against Mrs. Ames*	Mrs. Livingston Ames
1936	*The Moon's Our Home*	Mrs. Boyce Medford
1936	*The Trail of the Lonesome Pine*	Melissa
1936	*The Invisible Ray*	Lady Arabella Stevens
1935	*Bad Boy*	Mrs. Larkin
1935	*The Good Fairy*	Dr. Schultz
1934	*Ready for Love*	Mrs. Burke
1934	*The Painted Veil*	Frau Koerber (scenes deleted)
1934	*Finishing School*	Miss Van Alstyne
1934	*Registered Nurse*	Nurse McKenna
1934	*Two Alone*	Mrs. Slag
1933	*Christopher Bean*	Mrs. Hannah Haggett
1933	*The Stranger's Return*	Beatrice
1932	*Rain*	Mrs. Alfred Davidson
1931	*Arrowsmith*	Mrs. Tozer (uncredited)
1931	*Street Scene*	Emma Jones

MORE THAN
A GOOD WITCH
BILLIE BURKE

BILLIE BURKE CIRCA 1941. COURTESY OF JERRY MURBACH.

"Her hair was a rich red in color and fell in flowing ringlets over her shoulders. Her dress was pure white but her eyes were blue, and they looked kindly upon the little girl." [1]

These words by L. Frank Baum describe Glinda, the beautiful, if a bit flighty, good witch of the North who has enchanted filmgoers for decades in *The Wizard of Oz* (1939). However, the words could just as well describe the woman behind Glinda. She was a talented character actress of whom modern audiences have likely never heard, but who in her day was the darling of Broadway and hailed as the most photographed woman in the world. Who was she? Her name was Billie Burke.

Billie was born on August 6, 1884 to Blanche and Billy Burke in Washington, D.C. Her father was a famous clown with the Barnum and Bailey circus, instilling from an early age a gift for comedy in his daughter. Her ambitious mother pushed Billie toward the theater, though Billie was a shy child with a small voice seemingly unfit for the stage. Considering that Billie did not want to be an actress as a girl, it is all the more amazing to consider how quickly she catapulted to fame in England, where her father had established his own touring company. Initially, it was only her striking beauty and long red hair that attracted the attention of theater managers. But after being coached by luminary of the British theater Sir Charles Hawtrey, Billie established herself as not only one of England's most beautiful actresses, but one of its most gifted. Hawtrey himself, a hard to please man, told her she was going to be "a fine comedienne" [2] who would make her mark in straight comedy.

By 1907, Billie had enjoyed three successful plays in a row and succeeded in attracting the attention of John Drew in America. She was promptly cast as his leading lady in *My Wife*. Audiences' responses to her in America were even more enthusiastic than those in Britain. She exuded an effervescent charm on stage that made her like a female Peter Pan. America immediately embraced her ageless quality, for it was a young country and loved youth. Following her successful U.S. stage debut, Billie's pictures began to cover shop windows; her name began to appear on everything from silver spoons and lace collars to bouncy hair pieces the same color as her own copper curls. Her name even became part of the Edwardian vernacular; to "billieburke" meant to behave adorably. [3]

At this point in her life, Billie was alternately described as "the most wild and alluring witch that ever went about stirring up trouble" and "what a perfect lady should be, Victorian style…a Dresden figurine." [4] Witch or porcelain doll? Whatever Billie was, men fawned over her. Somerset Maugham kept her portrait prominently displayed in his home,

Mark Twain invited her to dinner and sent her red roses, the Marquis of Anglesey followed her from England to Washington, spurring rumors that he and the young actress were engaged.

Billie admitted that she grew complacent with her success. She enjoyed being admired, petted, and given such exquisite gowns to wear on stage that the costumes elicited gasps from men and women alike. However, by

BILLIE BURKE CIRCA 1912. COURTESY OF JERRY MURBACH.

1914, Billie was almost thirty and was tiring of playing roles that required little else but for her to giggle and bob her curls about. She wanted to try her hand at drama and prove she was not just like the fluffy young ladies she portrayed on stage. In an interview she gave during this period, she expressed her feelings about her type casting: "When you are on the stage you are not yourself — you are somebody else. When you go home you forget all about that someone else." [5]

Billie was given her chance at a dramatic role in a Somerset Maugham play entitled *The Land of Promise.* Unfortunately, the show proved to be one of Billie's rare flops. In it, she wore no decadent clothing, she provided no laughter. Audiences were not ready for a mature Billie Burke.

As if to save her from the rut in which she found herself, legendary Broadway producer Florenz Ziegfeld entered her life. "It seemed he danced me into a glimmering world of swirling emotion, a new country full of awe and delight," [6] Billie wrote of Ziegfeld. They did not wait long to marry. On April 11, 1914 they eloped and moved to a massive estate on Hastings upon Hudson, which became the perfect locale in which to raise their daughter, Patricia, when she was born in 1916. Billie and Ziegfeld became predecessors to Scott and Zelda Fitzgerald, the first couple of Jazz Age. They had no less than five Rolls Royces, their own island off of Canada, a menagerie of animals including an elephant and two tiger cubs, and a miniature replica of Mount Vernon as a playhouse for Patricia. But their life was not all luxurious fantasy. Rather, Billie found that married life cast her in the type of heavy dramatic role that had so eluded her on stage. Within the first year of marriage, she discovered that her husband was unfaithful to her with more than one of the girls he glorified in his shows. She also found that he had no money sense. He consistently spent more than he earned and lost what he earned at the gambling tables. No trace of the giggly, fluffy-headed girl on stage was evident when Billie alternately fell into depressions and jealous rages at her husband. She sobbed, tore down curtains, and threw diamond bracelets Ziegfeld offered as peace offerings across the room.

Yet, Billie loved him. Now a mature woman, a friend described her as a realist able to hold "up a cynical glass to inspect [the world] at close range." [7] Ziegfeld always came home to his family at night; whatever flirtations he had were superficial and not serious threats. Billie recognized this and learned to overlook her husband's faults, thus developing a steel spine that enabled her to maintain a steady home base for herself, her husband, and especially Patricia. She called her childhood an "abnormally happy" [8] one.

During the 1910s Ziegfeld starred Billie in several shows to let her exercise her range of acting abilities, among them *Annie Dear* and *Caesar's Wife*. However, these productions failed and nowhere near matched the successes of his Follies. Silent film was the rage at this time, and Ziegfeld encouraged Billie to be a part of it. She starred in her first film, *Peggy*, in 1916 and went on to be one of the silent screen's most popular stars in a serial Ziegfeld put together for her titled *Gloria's Romance*. By 1922, Billie was named Queen of the Movies in a New York popularity poll.

Despite Billie's success in Hollywood, she missed her home in New York and feared her work was becoming a detriment to her marriage. Also, silent film was restrictive for her as an actress accustomed to expressing herself with her voice. She returned to New York to further pursue her stage career and maintain her family life. Billie proved that motherhood, marriage, and her time away from the stage had not diminished her abilities, but instead had added new dimensions to them. Never did she prove her new depth more than in sophisticated shows like Booth Tarkington's *The Intimate Strangers* and Noël Coward's *The Marquise*. Reviewers hailed her as having, "out of space...acquired a repose and a dignity that she used not to have." [9] At the same time Billie was enjoying a comeback, Ziegfeld was enjoying his greatest success with the musical *Show Boat*.

Both Billie and Ziegfeld's fortunes fell with the crash of 1929. Ziegfeld admitted to Billie he was ruined. The great showman's health began to deteriorate as fast as his fortune. Billie's deep love for Ziegfeld was very evident when he died in 1932. She fell into despair, claiming that "for the first time I was on my own." [10] Though the Ziegfelds had appeared to have no monetary woes, after Ziegfeld's death, Billie was left to cope with insurmountable debts. She was forced to shutter their estate and move to a modest bungalow in Hollywood.

"Everything is so muddled now," she wrote. "It's very hard for me to get a hold of things." [11]

However, the endurance she had developed in her marriage carried her through this difficult transition in her life. She would certainly need resilience in the new world she was entering in Hollywood: talking pictures. It was a completely new medium to her and one in which she, as a middle-aged woman, had a far more difficult time than younger actresses.

"I should have returned to Broadway," Billie later said. "I know I could have found good plays...But New York with all its associations was unthinkable. My immediate concern was to look after my daughter...I did what I had to do at that moment, and who can say doing that is ever wrong?" [12]

Audiences had all but forgotten the woman who was once the sweetheart of the silent screen. Billie happily took supporting character roles; she knew she was no longer the leading lady she had been on Broadway.

"I have no time to pout by the fireplace about how marvelous I think I used to be," she stated. [13]

Filmgoers have been thanking her ever since for not pouting by the

BILLIE BURKE, FAR RIGHT, WITH CAST OF *DINNER AT EIGHT* (1933).
COURTESY OF JERRY MURBACH.

fireplace and for instead embracing her comedic talent. Interestingly, Billie's first two roles were heavy dramatic ones in movies about marital strife: *A Bill of Divorcement* (1932) and *Christopher Strong* (1933). It was not until her third film, *Dinner at Eight* (1933), that she brilliantly blended comedy and drama to create the type of character role she would make her own. She portrayed Millicent Jordan, a woman whose main worry in life is finding an equal number of men and women to invite to her highbrow dinner party — until she finds that her husband's business has crashed. Even in scenes with screen divas Marie Dressler and Jean Harlow, it is Billie who grabs the audience's attention and laughter. In one scene, after hearing her daughter complain of a quarrel with her fiancé and her husband lament of his own ailments, Billie launches into the most memorable monologue she gave in her eighty-plus films. Millicent Jordan, is "half out of her mind" from the series of seemingly earth-shattering disasters that have befallen her plans for her dinner party, including having to order crab meat in place of aspic and having to find a new butler at the last moment.

> MILLICENT: *I've had the most ghastly day anybody ever had!...* *They [the Ferncliffes, her guests of honor] call up at this hour, the miserable Cockneys, to say they've gone to Florida* — Florida! *And who can I get at this hour? Nobody! I've got eight people for dinner...eight people isn't a dinner!... I'm the one who ought to be in bed, I'm the one who's in trouble. You don't know what trouble is, either of you!* [14]

Over the next two decades Billie played roles similar to Millicent Jordan, thus creating her own unique, unforgettable character: a scatterbrained, flibbertigibbet society matron who steals every scene in which she appears. Sir Charles Hawtrey had certainly been correct in predicting that she would leave her mark as a fine comedienne. Among her most memorable "flibbertigibbets" are Topper's wife in the three-part *Topper* films (1937-1941) and Emily Kilbourne, a wealthy matron with a penchant for taking in tramps and reforming them by employing them as her chauffeurs in the screwball comedy *Merrily We Live* (1938). Audiences in the 1930s and today are sure to get giggles as they watch Ms. Kilbourne, blithely oblivious, insult herself through a hilarious exchange between her and her daughter:

> EMILY: *My mother always said children should be seen and not heard.*

> DAUGHTER: *Yes, but your mother was smarter than my mother.*

> EMILY: *Yes, I know she was darling.* [15]

For her performance in *Merrily We Live*, Billie earned a Best Supporting Actress Academy Award nomination. Although she did not win, she continued to receive steady work in supporting roles, including her most famous role as Glinda in *The Wizard of Oz* (1939), which she would long claim to be her favorite one, as it most reminded her of parts she essayed on stage in her youth.

With a steady income, Billie was secure enough to settle into a modest two-story house in Brentwood, California that resembled a London cottage. It was a far cry from the lavish estate she had once enjoyed, but, inside, the cottage was packed with mementoes of her halcyon days. Billie did not always relish being a character actress, although she admitted that "many a woman has lost out because she insisted on playing the ingénue when she should have played the mother, often the more rewarding part." [16]

Even more rewarding in Billie's life was her new role as grandmother. She was an indulgent and loving one, but could also be old-fashioned when she made sure her little granddaughters learned proper lady-like behavior. When she was not spending time with her family, she plunged into new diet or exercise trends that perhaps aided in keeping her looking at least ten years younger than she was. She was not a complete vegetarian, but her meat intake was greatly reduced as she ingested mainly vegetables and fruits. On weekends, she attended the Christian Science Church in Beverly Hills along with fellow character actress Charlotte Greenwood. [17]

However, no amount of activity could dispel her growing feelings of depression and loneliness. She often regretted never remarrying, especially as her work offers slowed to almost nothing. In 1947, she claimed to be "in a daze, to put it mildly." [18] Her daze was not improved by her lack of success with her own radio show in 1944 or her failed attempt at returning to Broadway with the unsuccessful *Mrs. January and Mr. Ex.* Throughout the late 1940s and 1950s, Billie appeared in small-scale theater productions and performed ever-smaller roles in increasingly unmemorable films, including *Small Town Girl* (1953) and *And Baby Makes Three* (1949). Billie knew the roles were beneath her talents as an actress and yearned for roles that presented a positive challenge

"...I could do better parts better, for those were the roles that I was trained in — the gay but intelligent, well-written, funny but believable roles that I had [on Broadway]...I should like to attempt to make those interesting young women grow up," [19] Billie stated.

Billie was better able to express herself through the pen rather than the screen when she became an author in 1948. Billie's dwindling income was supplemented by royalties from her memoirs, the first of which she penned in 1948. *With a Feather on My Nose* proved to be a modest success, due mostly to her candid recounts of her life that were refreshingly honest and unaffected. She followed up two years later with a quasi-memoir called *With Powder on My Nose* that was mostly her advice on health and etiquette. Both books are charming and remain readable to this day.

Billie remained active until 1960 when she appeared in her last film, the John Ford Western *Sergeant Rutledge*. After this film, she admitted that "acting was not fun anymore." [20] She retired to her little cottage, surrounded by her memories of the past. She spent her days attending to her orange tabby cat, Tommy, and her rose garden. Billie died on May 16, 1970 of natural causes. The great director, George Cukor, spoke at her funeral at the request of Billie's daughter. It was indeed the end of two eras when Billie died, signifying as she did the golden age of the theater and film. There are few actresses who have created such distinct personalities on stage, in film, and in her personal life as Billie did.

Billie Burke was truly a multi-faceted woman of unexpected depth both on and off screen. She had a temper to match her red hair; she had courage and wit to see her through the most trying of situations in her work and personal life. But whether modern audiences know her name or not, they will at least always recognize her as the ageless Witch of the North, a good fairy who, in Billie's own words, "has only to wave her wand and the world is changed." [21]

FILMOGRAPHY

1960	*Sergeant Rutledge*	Mrs. Cordelia Fosgate
1959	*The Young Philadelphians*	Mrs. J. Arthur Allen, Owner, Allen Oil Co.
1953	*Small Town Girl*	Mrs. Livingston
1951	*Father's Little Dividend*	Doris Dunstan
1951	*Three Husbands*	Mrs. Jenny Bard Whittaker
1950	*Father of the Bride*	Doris Dunstan
1950	*The Boy from Indiana*	Zelda Bagley
1949	*And Baby Makes Three*	Mrs. Marvin Fletcher
1949	*The Barkleys of Broadway*	Mrs. Livingston Belney
1948	*Billie Gets Her Man (short)*	
1948	*Silly Billy (short)*	Billie
1946	*The Bachelor's Daughters*	Molly Burns
1946	*Breakfast in Hollywood*	Mrs. Frances Cartwright
1945	*The Cheaters*	Mrs. James C. Pidgeon
1945	*Swing Out, Sister*	Jessica Mariman
1943	*Gildersleeve on Broadway*	Mrs. Laura Chandler
1943	*You're a Lucky Fellow, Mr. Smith*	Aunt Harriet Crandall
1943	*So's Your Uncle*	Minerva
1943	*Hi Diddle Diddle*	Liza Prescott

1942	*Girl Trouble*	Mrs. Rowland
1942	*They All Kissed the Bride*	Mrs. Drew
1942	*In This Our Life*	Lavinia Timberlake
1942	*What's Cookin'?*	Agatha Courtney
1942	*The Man Who Came to Dinner*	Mrs. Ernest Stanley
1941	*One Night in Lisbon*	Catherine Enfilden
1941	*Topper Returns*	Mrs. Clara Topper
1941	*The Wild Man of Borneo*	Bernice Marshall, Boardinghouse Keeper
1940	*Hullabaloo*	Penny Merriweather
1940	*Dulcy*	Eleanor Forbes
1940	*The Captain Is a Lady*	Blossy Stort
1940	*Irene*	Mrs. Herman Vincent
1940	*And One Was Beautiful*	Mrs. Julia Lattimer
1940	*The Ghost Comes Home*	Cora Adams
1939	*Remember?*	Mrs. Louise Bronson
1939	*Eternally Yours*	Aunt Abby
1939	*The Wizard of Oz*	Glinda
1939	*Bridal Suite*	Mrs. Lillian McGill
1939	*Zenobia*	Mrs. Bessie Tibbett
1938	*Topper Takes a Trip*	Mrs. Clara Topper
1938	*The Young in Heart*	Marmy Carleton
1938	*Merrily We Live*	Mrs. Emily Kilbourne
1938	*Everybody Sing*	Diana Bellaire
1937	*Navy Blue and Gold*	Mrs. Alyce Gates
1937	*The Bride Wore Red*	Contessa di Meina
1937	*Topper*	Mrs. Clara Topper
1937	*Parnell*	Miss Clara Wood
1936	*Craig's Wife*	Mrs. Frazier
1936	*Piccadilly Jim*	Eugenia Willis, Nesta's Sister
1936	*My American Wife*	Mrs. Robert Cantillon
1935	*Splendor*	Clarissa
1935	*A Feather in Her Hat*	Julia Trent Anders
1935	*She Couldn't Take It*	Mrs. Daniel Van Dyke
1935	*Doubting Thomas*	Paula Brown
1935	*Becky Sharp*	Lady Bareacres
1935	*After Office Hours*	Mrs. Norwood
1935	*Society Doctor*	Mrs. Crane
1934	*Forsaking All Others*	Aunt Paula
1934	*We're Rich Again*	Mrs. Linda Page

1934	*Finishing School*	Mrs. Helen Crawford Radcliff
1934	*Where Sinners Meet*	Eustasia
1933	*Only Yesterday*	Julia Warren
1933	*Dinner at Eight*	Millicent Jordan
1933	*Christopher Strong*	Lady Elaine Strong
1932	*A Bill of Divorcement*	Meg Fairfield
1921	*The Education of Elizabeth*	Elizabeth Banks
1920	*The Frisky Mrs. Johnson*	Belle Johnson
1920	*Away Goes Prudence*	Prudence Thorne
1919	*Wanted: A Husband*	Amanda Darcy Cole
1919	*Sadie Love*	Sadie Love
1919	*The Misleading Widow*	Betty Taradine
1919	*Good Gracious, Annabelle*	Annabelle Leigh
1918	*The Make-Believe Wife*	Phyllis Ashbrook
1918	*In Pursuit of Polly*	Polly Marsden
1918	*Let's Get a Divorce*	Mme. Cyprienne Marcey
1918	*Eve's Daughter*	Irene Simpson-Bates
1917	*The Land of Promise*	Nora Marsh
1917	*Arms and the Girl*	Ruth Sherwood
1917	*The Mysterious Miss Terry*	Mavis Terry
1916	*Gloria's Romance*	Gloria Stafford *(as Miss Billie Burke)*
1916	*Peggy*	Peggy Cameron

THE PIXILATED MATRON
SPRING BYINGTON

SPRING BYINGTON CIRCA 1950. AUTHOR'S COLLECTION.

"There are two types of bird brains...Type A...will say anything that comes into her head...Type B...everything she says follows logically. She's always true to herself. I love to play that type." [1]

So spoke Spring Byington who, though she portrayed an endless array of addled matriarchs, aunts, and town gossips, was the furthest thing from a bird brain one could be. Unlike fellow character actresses Billie Burke (the Type A brand of bird-brain) and Fay Bainter (whose matriarchs stressed subtle wit and common sense over humor), Spring brought a unique flavor of zaniness and whimsy to her homey matrons. One biographer aptly described her with the string of adjectives, "sunny, sparkling, flowery, energetic...eternally cheerful...wonderfully old-fashioned." [2] At the same time, her characters were more outspoken and almost tomboyish in comparison to her daintier contemporaries, Burke and Bainter. Off screen, Spring was not only as physically energetic as her onscreen persona, but also intellectually. Indeed, she possessed a remarkable love of learning and a disarming intelligence in male-dominated areas such as science and aviation. It is Spring's blend of cheer, zaniness, warmth, and unexpected intelligence that has endeared her to audiences as a woman everybody would want as their mother or confidante.

Spring Byington was born in Colorado Springs. Depending on the source, her birth year is 1886, 1890, or 1893. Most sources agree it was October 17, 1886. Spring later admitted one method she used for retaining her ever-youthful persona was "Clean living — and lie about your age." [3] At an early age, Spring's intellectual curiosity was fostered by her parents. Her father, Edwin, was a well-respected professor and superintendent of schools in Colorado. According to Spring, her mother, Helene, "had little to keep her occupied, [so] she went down to the college with my father and took pre-medical courses just for fun." [4] After Edwin unexpectedly died when Spring was four years old, her mother did not cease her medical studies. Rather, she was able to pursue them by sending Spring to live with relatives in Denver and sending Spring's sister to live with grandparents in Ontario, Canada. [5] Spring, a virtual orphan, later described her childhood as a lonely one. Though she, her sister, and mother were reunited when Helene graduated in 1896 and returned to Denver, her mother was often occupied with maintaining her medical practice with fellow female doctor Mary Ford.

Spring assuaged her loneliness by continuous activity in summer stock theatrics. She put together her own theatrical company before she graduated, which toured mining camps in Colorado Springs. [6] Spring's ambition was boundless in both theatrics and scholastics; she graduated

from high school two years early at age sixteen. No sooner had she graduated when her mother fell ill, forcing Spring to earn her own living. She
quickly found work with a stock company for $125 a week. Rather than
let her sudden change in circumstances overwhelm her, Spring, with a
sunny smile, described her three years in stock company as "experiences
in playing that money can't buy." [7]

When her mother died, Spring used her inheritance to move from
Denver to pursue a theatrical career in New York. [8] But before Spring
could establish herself in the big city, her stock company took a tour to
Buenos Aires. At twenty years old, she married the company's manager, Roy
Chandler. She had two daughters, Lois and Phyllis, who spent their first
three years of life in Spain. Along with perfecting her mothering and acting
skills, Spring further sharpened her mind by teaching herself Spanish. She
became fluent in the language in a relatively short amount of time. [9]

After eight years, Spring's marriage faltered. She and Chandler
divorced, and she returned to New York with her children. Because her
stock company work forced her to tour the country, Spring temporarily
placed her daughters with friends. The years 1919 to 1924 saw Spring
appear in over thirty plays, ranging from the Hawaiian-themed *Birds of
Paradise* to well-established playwright Clare Kummar's *Rollo's Wild Oats*.
Her roles rarely put her above bit or supporting parts until 1924, when
the leading lady fell ill and Spring was called upon to take her place as
"a vapid matron" in a production of *Beggar on Horseback*. [10] A George S.
Kaufman play, it was such a success that it ran on Broadway and on tour
off and on between 1924 and 1935. Spring further established herself in
grade A productions such as *Once in a Lifetime* (another Kaufman play)
and *When Ladies Meet* (in a role she reprised on the screen in 1941). In
1929 she garnered particularly enthusiastic notices for her performance
in *Be Your Age*. As a grandmother who, through a lab experiment, is reju-
venated as an attractive matron, one reviewer declared that she brought
to the play "moments of gayety and spontaneity" through her "exuberant
performance." [11] By the early 1930s, Spring had made a name for herself
as "one of the most prominent stock actresses in America." [12]

It was a great loss to the stage when, in 1933, she left the footlights
for Hollywood to play not a vapid matron, but the epitome of homey
matriarchs: the warm yet steel-spined Marmee in *Little Women* (1933).
Ever drawn to innovation and modernity, Spring was fascinated by movie
making and never returned to Broadway. She picked up where she left
off on stage, playing supporting roles in A pictures such as *Mutiny on the
Bounty* (1935) *Ah, Wilderness* (1935), *Dodsworth* (1936), and *Theodora Goes*

Wild (1936). Her roles invariably cast her as an addled mother or other female relation, a town gossip, or a flighty eccentric. In 1936, Spring became permanently identified as Hollywood's favorite mother figure when she was cast as the indulgent and complacent, yet ever light-hearted mom in the Jones family series. The series provided Mickey Rooney's popular Andy Hardy family serial with stiff competition, producing seventeen installments between 1936 and 1940. Incidentally, Spring appeared in the first Hardy film, *A Family Affair* (1937), but she was replaced by Fay Holden.

Between Jones pictures, Spring received what was arguably the best role of her screen career: Penny Sycamore, mother of the loveable screwball family in the Kaufman-Hart play *You Can't Take It with You* (1938). Penny allowed Spring to meld her maternal character with her talent at zany comedy. Penny was a bit like Spring herself: intensely interested in learning and trying new things. She lives her life on the spur of the moment. A case in point is when a typewriter is mistakenly delivered to her door and she decides to become a writer. A classic moment of Spring's self-described "Type B bird brain" is reflected in this exchange between Penny and her father, Grandfather Vanderhof, portrayed by Lionel Barrymore:

GRANDFATHER: *Penny, why don't you write a play about —ism mania?*

PENNY: *Ism mania?*

GRANDFATHER: *Yeah, sure, you know, communism, fascism, voodooism, everybody's got an ism these days.*

PENNY: *Oh.* (laughs) *I thought it was some sort of itch or something…I know! Maybe Cynthia [the heroine in her play set in a monastery] can have an ism in the monastery!* [13]

Also priceless is the childlike excitement on Spring's face when, in another scene, she delightedly discovers a gun hidden under a policeman's trouser cuff and exclaims, "Look Grandpa, G-men!" Spring's flawless portrayal of Penny is among the best in the screwball comedies of the 1930s. She was nominated for an Academy Award, but lost to Fay Bainter in *Jezebel* (1938).

Off screen, Spring was as lively as her pixilated onscreen persona. She "adored clothes and was always smartly attired. She had many hobbies, among them inventing things. One of her inventions was a button on a hat to preserve her hair-do when going to bed at night."[14] She also tried her hand at painting watercolors. But her inventiveness was not limited to art and gadgets; in 1937 she invented a new alimony plan. "Alimony has become a racket," she stated. She went on to bemoan how women who were married only a month received the same alimony as women married thirty years would receive. "It is not only providing thousands of undeserving ex-wives with a comfortable living, but it has been twisted into a weapon by which women vent their hatred on men they once loved."[15] Her idea reflects how independent-minded she was; she further proved her self-reliance by never seeking alimony or remarrying. Because she was so content without male companionships or suitors to speak of, rumor had it that she was more than just friends with fellow actresses Marjorie Main[16] and Maude Adams.[17]

As the 1940s dawned, Spring continued to bring as much freshness and unpredictability to her screen roles as she did to her private life. Though past fifty, she proved to be no less chic and feminine in *The Devil and Mrs. Jones* (1941) as a flirtatious salesclerk. At the same time, she could not have been more motherly and old-fashioned in *Meet John Doe* (1941) and *The Vanishing Virginian* (1942). Among her most delightful performances in the 1940s were in two Judy Garland vehicles: *Presenting Lily Mars* (1943) as Garland's forever cheerful, hat maker mom, and *In the Good Old Summertime* (1949), as Garland's no-nonsense but romantic co-worker in a music shop. The highlight of the latter film is Spring's affectionate but argumentative exchanges with her fiancé (the portly, loveable S.Z. "Cuddles" Sakall). She is hilarious when she uses his own pet expression of frustration to vent at him: "Dumkopf!"

The year 1950 brought Spring what she would come to call her favorite role, that of Louisa in a film of the same name. Louisa is an aging woman being wooed by two bachelors, portrayed by Edmund Gwen and Charles Coburn. The story was a love triangle, but Spring loved the fact that it avoided the cliché by being a *geriatric* triangle. "I liked the role because it was gay and flippant," Spring said. Louisa was "an older woman with young ideas."[18] Her performance earned her a Golden Globe nomination, but she lost to Judy Holliday in *Born Yesterday* (1950). Though she did not win the award, her role of Louisa ultimately led to Spring's greatest triumph: television.

Spring was not the first stage and/or screen actress who turned to television when roles for a woman of her age became scarce. Spring spent no time lamenting the fact that scripts were not coming to her as fast as they used to. Instead, she funneled her energy into first radio and then television as mother-in-law Lily Ruskin in the *December Bride* series. Lily was not dissimilar to Louisa; she "thought young" and was, according to Spring, "a kid all the way." All of Spring's screen characters came together in Lily. At one moment she can be a gossip, blithely declaring over the phone that a friend "eloped to Las Vegas with her druggist!

SPRING BYINGTON WITH EDMUND GWEN ON THE LEFT AND CHARLES COBURN ON THE RIGHT IN *LOUISA* (1950). AUTHOR'S COLLECTION.

I'm sure she'll be very happy!" The next moment, she can be the madcap eccentric, jitterbugging with a beatnik in black horn-rimmed glasses. Finally, she can be the homey matriarch, growing sentimental over a grandfather clock that has been in the family for generations ("That's half its charm!" she defends the clock when it makes unholy racket every fifteen minutes). [19] But what made the role, like "Louisa," completely against stereotype, was the fact that instead of being the typical meddling mother-in-law, Lily was a pleasure to all those around her. "Our stories on *December Bride* are human though funny, or is it funny though human?" [20] she said.

Spring's performance on the television show further endeared her not only to older audiences who knew her from film, but to younger generations who now relied on the modern invention of television for their entertainment. Her warm voice and kind face made her like a member of these viewers' families, so much that she was stopped on the street by fans that openly said hello and chatted for a few minutes with her like they would an old friend. "They tell me their problems and joys. We discuss their children and grandchildren and more…it's a funny, happy thing. When we part I don't believe they can actually decide whether I'm really Spring — or Lily!" [21] Spring said. The show lasted until 1959, making it the longest running comedy program to star a female. Spring would later call Lily the "truly-shared fulfillment of my career" [22]

Spring proved to be just as wise a mother-in-law in real life as on screen. Indeed, through Lily viewers can glimpse what type of a mother Spring was to her daughters. "I never drop in on them unexpectedly," she said of her daughters and their husbands. "I try to keep my lip buttoned and let them talk over their problems." However, she did admit that because "the most wonderful moments in living are those we share with loving family," she tended to visit one of her daughters (who lived only three blocks away) a bit too often. "One of my daughters lives in Santa Barbara," she said and added with a smile that this daughter was "safer." [23]

Now at the peak of her career, Spring had reached an age when most would be in retirement. When asked her secret to staying young, Spring said part of it was "keeping in touch with the times," adding that if one did not, he was "as a dead as a dodo." [24] Her pet peeve was the expression, "as I always say." "When you hear yourself say that, it is time you thought of something new," she said. [25] Perhaps Spring's true secret to staying young was that she never ceased developing her mind. She was not only an avid student of gerontology, but of metaphysics and science fiction. Her favorite novel was George Orwell's *1984*. She allegedly surprised her co-stars on *December Bride* with her knowledge of Earth's satellites and star constellations as well. The tireless actress took flying lessons in 1955 and a few years later vacationed to South America. While there, she acquired a small coffee plantation and decided to learn Portuguese to improve her communication skills while overseeing the land. She listened to a condition record before she slept each night and became as fluent at the language as she had at Spanish years before. [26]

"As soon as you think you have all the knowledge in the world, then you really are old," [27] Spring philosophized.

When *December Bride* concluded its run in 1959, the ageless Spring still had no intention of retiring. "Working helps keep you young. Especially if you don't have a job when you don't do exactly what you have done today. Constant change is essential," [28] she reasoned. Spring found "constant change" in the genres and mediums in which she appeared between 1960 and 1968. She was in Western television series such as *Laramie* and *Kentucky Jones* but also performed in light sitcoms like *I Dream of Jeannie* and *The Flying Nun*. She also returned to the screen in 1960 to portray Doris Day's mother in *Please Don't Eat the Daisies*.

As indomitable as Spring was in spirit, when she reached her seventies, even she could not maintain the pace of youth. She spent her final decade in a "cool, whitewashed villa." [29] Though her life was quiet, one can be assured she kept busy painting watercolors, reading the tomes lining her walls, and assessing the constellations above the Hollywood hills surrounding her home. She died of cancer in 1971 at the age of eighty-five. Considering her fascination with innovation and new ideas, it is fitting that she donated her body to science.

"I may never be a celebrated actress, but what good is it to play the part of a neurotic murderess and get an Academy Award if everyone is afraid of you?" [30] Spring once asked. "Fame can be such a lonely business when it is unshared."

Spring did, and continues, to share her fame with audiences; her screen presence, as ageless as the woman herself, shows no signs of fading.

FILMOGRAPHY

1960	*Please Don't Eat the Daisies*	Suzie Robinson
1954	*The Rocket Man*	Justice Amelia Brown
1952	*Because You're Mine*	Mrs. Montville
1952	*No Room for the Groom*	Mama Kingshead
1951	*Bannerline*	Mrs. Loomis
1951	*Angels in the Outfield*	Sister Edwitha
1951	*According to Mrs. Hoyle*	Mrs. Hoyle
1950	*Walk Softly, Stranger*	Mrs. Brentman
1950	*Devil's Doorway*	Mrs. Masters
1950	*The Skipper Surprised His Wife*	Agnes Thorndyke
1950	*Louisa*	Louisa Norton
1950	*Please Believe Me*	Mrs. Milwright
1950	*The Reformer and the Redhead*	Kathy's Mother (voice, uncredited)
1949	*The Big Wheel*	Mary Coy
1949	*In the Good Old Summertime*	Nellie Burke
1948	*B.F.'s Daughter*	Gladys Fulton
1947	*It Had to Be You*	Mrs. Martha Stafford

1947	*Cynthia*	Carrie Jannings
1947	*Singapore*	Mrs. Bellows
1947	*Living in a Big Way*	Mrs. Minerva Alsop Morgan
1947	*Little Mister Jim*	Mrs. Starwell
1947	*My Brother Talks to Horses*	Mrs. 'Ma' Penrose
1946	*Faithful in My Fashion*	Miss Mary Swanson
1946	*Dragonwyck*	Magda
1946	*A Letter for Evie*	Mrs. McPherson
1946	*Meet Me on Broadway*	Sylvia Kane Storm
1945	*Captain Eddie*	Mrs. Frost
1945	*Thrill of a Romance*	Nona Glenn
1945	*Salty O'Rourke*	Mrs. Brooks
1945	*The Enchanted Cottage*	Violet Price
1944	*I'll Be Seeing You*	Mrs. Marshall
1944	*Reward Unlimited (short)*	Peggy's Mother
1944	*The Heavenly Body*	Nancy Potter
1943	*Heaven Can Wait*	Bertha Van Cleve
1943	*Presenting Lily Mars*	Mrs. Mars
1942	*The War Against Mrs. Hadley*	Cecilia Talbot
1942	*The Affairs of Martha*	Sophia Sommerfield
1942	*Rings on Her Fingers*	Mrs. Maybelle Worthington
1942	*Roxie Hart*	Mary Sunshine
1942	*The Vanishing Virginian*	Rosa Yancey
1941	*When Ladies Meet*	Bridget 'Bridgie' Drake
1941	*Ellery Queen and the Perfect Crime*	Carlotta Emerson
1941	*Meet John Doe*	Mrs. Mitchell
1941	*The Devil and Miss Jones*	Elizabeth Ellis
1941	*Arkansas Judge*	Mary Shoemaker
1940	*Lucky Partners*	Aunt Lucy
1940	*My Love Came Back*	Mrs. Clara Malette
1940	*On Their Own*	Mrs. John Jones
1940	*Young as You Feel*	Mrs. John Jones
1940	*The Blue Bird*	Mummy Tyl
1940	*Laddie*	Mrs. Stanton
1939	*A Child Is Born*	Mrs. Mamie West
1939	*Too Busy to Work*	Mrs. John Jones
1939	*Quick Millions*	Mrs. John Jones
1939	*Chicken Wagon Family*	Josephine Fippany
1939	*The Jones Family in Hollywood*	Mrs. John Jones
1939	*The Story of Alexander Graham Bell*	Mrs. Hubbard

1939	*Everybody's Baby*	Mrs. John Jones
1938	*Down on the Farm*	Mrs. John Jones
1938	*You Can't Take It with You*	Penny Sycamore
1938	*Safety in Numbers*	Mrs. John Jones
1938	*A Trip to Paris*	Mrs. John Jones
1938	*Jezebel*	Mrs. Kendrick
1938	*Love on a Budget*	Mrs. Louise Jones
1938	*Penrod and His Twin Brother*	Mrs. Schofield
1938	*The Buccaneer*	Dolly Madison
1937	*The Jones Family in Borrowing Trouble*	Mrs. John Jones
1937	*It's Love I'm After*	Aunt Ella
1937	*Hot Water*	Mrs. John Jones
1937	*Hotel Haywire*	Mrs. Parkhouse
1937	*The Road Back*	Ernst's Mother
1937	*Big Business*	Mrs. John Jones
1937	*A Family Affair*	Mrs. Emily Hardy
1937	*Penrod and Sam*	Mrs. Laura Schofield
1937	*Clarence*	Mrs. Wheeler
1937	*Green Light*	Mrs. Dexter
1937	*Off to the Races*	Mrs. John Jones
1936	*Theodora Goes Wild*	Rebecca Perry
1936	*The Charge of the Light Brigade*	Lady Octavia Warrenton
1936	*The Girl on the Front Page*	Mrs. Langford
1936	*Dodsworth*	Matey Pearson
1936	*Stage Struck*	Mrs. Randall
1936	*Back to Nature*	Mrs. Louise Jones
1936	*Palm Springs*	Aunt Letty
1936	*Educating Father*	Mrs. John Jones
1936	*Every Saturday Night*	Mrs. Evers
1936	*The Voice of Bugle Ann*	Ma Davis
1935	*The Great Impersonation*	Duchess Caroline
1935	*Broadway Hostess*	Mrs. Duncan-Griswald-Wembly-Smythe
1935	*Ah, Wilderness!*	Essie Miller
1935	*Mutiny on the Bounty*	Mrs. Byam
1935	*Way Down East*	Mrs. Louisa Bartlett
1935	*Orchids to You*	Alice Draper
1935	*Love Me Forever*	Clara Fields
1935	*Werewolf of London*	Miss Ettie Coombes
1933	*Little Women*	Marmee
1930	*Papa's Slay Ride (short)*	Mama

"DAMN THE TORPEDOES, FULL SPEED AHEAD!"
CHARLES COBURN

CHARLES COBURN, CIRCA 1944. AUTHOR'S COLLECTION.

"He has the rather special sort of face a monocle requires, a certain paternal austerity, a benign aloofness — in short, the countenance of a man well fed upon a rich tradition." [1]

The monocled man described above is the beloved player of endearing scalawags and fun-loving septuagenarians, Charles Coburn. The portly Mr. Coburn was indeed well fed, not only with fine Southern cooking, but with the rich tradition of the theater. He is better known for his film work, with his most famous roles being the wealthy matchmaker Benjamin Dingle in *The More the Merrier* (1943) and the skirt-chasing diamond tycoon Lord Beekman in *Gentlemen Prefer Blondes* (1953). However, he spent the bulk of his career as a Broadway wit and a touring Shakespearean actor. Charles was not of a privileged upbringing despite his talent for performing the classics. He taught himself all he knew through diligent apprenticeship which gave him a thorough understanding of the inner and outer workings of the theater. It is the mix of heartiness and refinement in Charles Coburn that makes him, in the words of his 1961 obituary, "as polished as the monocle he wore" and possess a dignity "as real as his ever present cigar." [2] Charles's frequent comedy roles plus his penchant for living like a swinger half his age seems as if it would diminish his dignity, but he defied all stereotypes and created an air of nobility in whatever situation he found himself on and off screen.

Born June 19, 1877 in Macon, Georgia, Charles Coburn spent the majority of his childhood in Savannah, the quintessential town of southern charm and hospitality. His parents, Emma and Moses Coburn, were, as Charles later said, "devotees of the theater." [3] His mother read him stories of theater folk rather than nursery rhymes, a tradition that was the seed of Charles's interest in show business. "The glamour and excitement of their [actors'] lives intrigued me and I wanted to be like them," [4] he explained. Though his father had in interest in drama as well and was a devoted theatergoer, he warned Charles to stay far from the neighboring burlesque shows or he might see something too mature for his young eyes. "Of course when I got old enough, I went right in, and sure enough I saw something I shouldn't — my father!" [5] Charles later recalled. Whether or not this is true, it was an oft-repeated anecdote by Charles, whose fondness for a good yarn overrode his fondness for complete honesty.

Charles entered the world of theater at age thirteen when he acquired a position as a program boy at the Savannah Theater. He was eventually promoted to usher. The Savannah Theater was a prestigious and elegant structure possessing the glamour that so intrigued Charles. Many of the theater's most prominent actors played there, including Ellen Terry, Mrs. Fiske, Otis Skinner, and Maxine Elliot. Charles met these actors in person during his two years as "the youngest entrepreneur in the country."[6] At the tender age of seventeen, Charles was managing the theater himself. However, his true ambition was to be on the stage rather than behind it. "I joined a stock company...I thought I wanted to be a comic opera comedian. I could sing and dance a bit,"[7] Charles explained. Charles flexed his opera talents in amateur productions, including *The Mikado*, but his desire for opera stardom withered after he first played Shakespeare. Charles's ambition to be a serious Shakespearean actor led him to leave Savannah for New York. During his first few years of struggling to gain a foothold in the big city, he took odd jobs such as a utility man and an advance agent. For a brief period, he had the unlikely position as a member of "the greatest bicycle racing team of all time"[8] in New York.

When Charles became established on Broadway, he happily never engaged in bicycling or any purposeful exercise for the rest of his life. He made his Broadway debut in 1901 in *Up York State* and appeared in several more shows between engagements with Shakespearean touring companies. In 1906, he met fellow stock actress Ivah Wills, who was his leading lady in *As You Like It*. The two married after the show closed and then proceeded to form their own theater company. Though much of their company's work was in touring productions performed at universities, they did establish the Coburn Theater on West 63rd Street in New York. The Coburn Theater was not solely a producer of Shakespeare. The majority of the shows in which Ivah and Charles produced and performed were originals, the first being *The Yellow Jacket* in 1916. True fortune came in 1918 when Charles acquired the rights to a play no one else wanted. *The Better Ole'* was an English comedy telling of an infantryman who intercepts a spy's plan to destroy a bridge and is inadvertently arrested as a traitor. The show had been a smash hit in London and became equally as successful with Charles as star and producer. It ran for two years and established Charles and Ivah as one of Broadway's brightest leading couples.

Charles and Ivah performed in over twenty plays until 1937, a year that marked what Charles would later call "the lowest ebb" in his life. His wife, partner, and leading lady died suddenly. "I was lost. There seemed nothing left, nothing to live for,"[9] Charles stated.

A new direction for Charles's life came in the form of a film offer from M-G-M. The movie, *Of Human Hearts* (1938), was a Civil War tearjerker starring James Stewart, in which Charles plays a philosophical alcoholic doctor, Charles Shingle. Charles discovered that he did indeed have something to live for once he entered Hollywood. "The movies gave me a new lease on life. I was happy and content," [10] he recalled in 1950. Charles quickly became one of the most ubiquitous old gentlemen in film. His earliest roles cast him most often as a priggish father or tough businessman rather than the young-at-heart swingers he would later essay. In romantic comedies like *Vivacious Lady* (1938) and *Bachelor Mother* (1939), he was the dramatic rather than the comic element of each film. In *Kings Row* (1942), he was a sinister doctor who performed debilitating operations on his unwitting patients. However, the early 1940s saw his roles begin to sway toward more light-hearted fare. In 1941, Charles was nominated for his first Academy Award for *The Devil and Miss Jones*. He portrayed John Merrick , the boss of a department store who goes undercover as an employee in an attempt to break up union activity. The role blended the stuffy businessman persona with his dignified comic style. More roles in this vein followed, including one as Barbara Stanwyck's shifty father in *The Lady Eve* (1941) and one as Uncle Stanley in the Kaufman and Hart farce *George Washington Slept Here* (1942). Charles's trickster character is among the most hilarious in the latter film. Though he is a self-purported millionaire, he confesses that he is penniless but keeps up the illusion that he is wealthy so that his relations and friends will give him royal treatment. His lovable, if sometimes deceptive, characters were most often dandified by the monocle Charles had begun to wear for an eye deficiency.

Charles spent the early 1940s not only perfecting his screen persona but also instructing amateur stage actors. He mourned the state of modern amateur shows and felt it his duty to save them. "The hope of the legitimate theater are the amateurs," [11] he declared. Charles's first love was the theater, and his enthusiasm was contagious to those he taught. However, he did not discourage his pupils from experimenting with new methods or styles. He followed the same principal in his own acting. "A man must be careful not to start repeating himself," he said. "So I would like to do something I have never done before in the theater — anything fresh, bright, and new." [12]

Though Charles did not perform on stage in the 1940s, his films offered him "fresh, bright, and new" characters to portray. The mischievous old gentleman he had created on screen was perfectly honed in his best screen performance as Benjamin Dingle in the classic World War II screwball comedy *The More the Merrier* (1943). In the film, he is a retired millionaire in Washington D.C. during a housing shortage. He rents half of career girl Jean Arthur's apartment and then rents out half of his half to Mr. Carter, an eligible young man portrayed by Joel McCrea. Despite Arthur's protests, McCrea stays and Charles surreptitiously plays Cupid. In matters of love and in the way one lives one's life, he declares that his motto is: "Damn the torpedoes, full speed ahead!" The same motto could be applied to Charles and the way he chose to live despite his age or obstacles and tragedies that befell him. Like Dingle, Charles did not see himself as an elderly man unable to participate fully in life. One scene in the film particularly shows Dingle's wry humor and lack of fear concerning death:

> [Dingle and Carter are reading a newspaper on the rooftop]
> BENJAMIN DINGLE: *Hand me that section, will you? I want to see if anyone I know is being mourned today.* [13]

Charles won the Best Supporting Actor Oscar in 1944. At the ceremony, he was "visibly affected as he accepted the shining statuette." [14]

Charles was at the height of his popularity and had a salary to prove it. At $75,000 a picture, he was among the highest paid character actors in Hollywood. He was quoted as saying he would like to see the 16th Amendment (which instated income tax) repealed. [15] Despite income tax, Charles still brought home large sums as he found little trouble finding roles. He was known for his reliability and was seldom known to forget a line or delay production. Charles remained successful although he never signed a long-term contract with any studio. He valued his freedom too much to do so. In 1946, he was offered a plum role as Dean Stockwell's alcoholic, trouble-making, and leprechaun-like grandfather in *The Green Years*. He was nominated for a second Academy Award for his performance. Soon after, he was cast in what he would later call his favorite film, *Louisa* (1950). In the film, he and Edmund Gwen portray two bachelors competing for Spring Byington's love. Even after completing forty-eight pictures, he still declared he found making a movie "interesting." [16]

As interesting as he found filmmaking, Charles's pursuits extended past the movie camera. He enjoyed discussing Republicanism and Shakespeare with his fellow actors at the Masquers Club. During the Red Scare in the late 1940s and early 1950s, he became vice president of the Motion Picture Alliance for the Protection of American Ideals. Charles may have been conservative in his politics, but he lived like a bohemian. He looked the part, too, when he donned his pet hat, a blue beret. He spent eight months a year in Hollywood but he still considered New York his place of residence. The apartment in which he and Ivah had resided in Gramercy Park remained under his ownership. He stated that none of the antiques and theater props in the space he could "sell for a nickel"[17] and thus, he had no intention of parting with them. He may have been attached to the past, but he did not intend to be complacent. He learned to drive at age

CHARLES COBURN WITH PIPER LAURIE, ROCK HUDSON, AND GIGI PERREAU IN *HAS ANYBODY SEEN MY GAL?* (1952). AUTHOR'S COLLECTION.

seventy, but developed a deeper love for a different mode of transportation: horses. By 1953, he had a stable of trotters and pacers, some of which brought him monetary returns in races. Yet, his love for the animals was not purely mercenary. "A horse is different from a woman," he said. "You can't buy his affection, and he always remembers you."[18]

When not at the stables or in New York, Charles engaged in his favorite vices: liquor, cigars, poker, and gin rummy. His easygoing demeanor was tested in 1951 when he and a number of his friends were fined fifteen dollars each for breaking the gambling laws of California. Charles indignantly told the papers that "if a law is a bad one, it is not observed, and certainly that is a bad law...it permits law officers to enter private homes without a warrant."[19] Charles received a pile of consolatory letters, including ones from a bishop and a Supreme Court judge who called the invasion of poker players' rights "an outrage." The incident in no way slowed Charles's pace; he was often out until the early morning hours, doing the cha-cha or the jitterbug. "Don't overindulge in anything; my single exception is dancing," [20] he said. Often, the showgirls with whom he danced could not keep up with his energy.

Charles showed his fondness for beautiful women and dancing in 1953 in his best role of the decade, as the flirty diamond tycoon Lord Beekman in *Gentlemen Prefer Blondes* (1953). After working with his co-stars Marilyn Monroe and Jane Russell, he declared he "felt ten years younger." [21] Charles's interest in youth grew as his age advanced, but he felt this interest had a positive effect on his work. "I have always made it a habit to watch young people," he said. "That's the best way to find out how people are living and thinking." [22] Perhaps it was studying young people that made Charles turn almost solely to the young generation's medium: television. For the bulk of the mid to late 1950s, Charles's acting was on the small screen in weekly programs, including *Ford Television Theater, The Red Skelton Show,* and *Kraft Television.*

Charles, feeling as lively as a man half his age at eighty-one, married a woman of forty in 1959. Widow and mother of two, Winifred Natzka was a former New York opera singer to whom Charles had been a constant companion for two months before the wedding. They married in Las Vegas and, according to reporters, Charles whispered to his nervous bride: "Calm down, I'm not going to bite you — at least not very hard." [23] Charles and Winifred's unlikely marriage was a happy one for the two short years they were together. He continued to make appearances on the big and small screen with his most notable later film roles being Hippocrates in *The Story of Mankind* (1957) and Benjamin Franklin in *John Paul Jones* (1959).

As Charles entered his eighties, he wrote a will that reflected no fear of his inevitable end. He stipulated that there be no hymns sung and no Bible passages read at his memorial. "All who come to my funeral come with smiling faces and joy in their hearts," [24] he wrote. Though he was ailing, he joined an Indianapolis production of *You Can't Take It with You* for a six-day run. He then returned to New York for a throat operation. Shortly after the procedure, he died of a heart attack at age eighty-four. His body was cremated and his ashes were scattered together with Ivah Wills' along New York's Mohawk Trail around the base of Edwin Booth's statue in Gramercy Park.

Charles Coburn fit into no category but his own. He lived like a man half his age and his mind remained sharper than the most distinguished professor's. He was equally adept at the classical acting style and the contemporary; his versatility of style was apparent in his breadth of roles that ranged from those that were villainous to comical to avuncular. He once stated that "I have no morals and do not moralize."[25] It is this lack of condescension and judgment that made Charles beloved by young and old audiences, audiences who only wished they could enjoy themselves half as much he seemed to. Charles's recipe for living a full life was identical to that of Benjamin Dingle's in *The More the Merrier:*

> *There are two kinds of people — those who don't do what they want to do, so they write down in a diary about what they haven't done, and those who are too busy to write about it because they're out doing it!* [26]

FILMOGRAPHY

1959	*John Paul Jones*	Benjamin Franklin
1959	*A Stranger in My Arms*	Vance Beasley
1959	*The Remarkable Mr. Pennypacker*	Grampa Pennypacker
1957	*The Story of Mankind*	Hippocrates
1957	*How to Murder a Rich Uncle*	Uncle George
1957	*Town on Trial*	Dr. John Fenner
1956	*Around the World in Eighty Days*	Steamship Company Clerk
1956	*The Power and the Prize*	Guy Eliot
1955	*How to Be Very, Very Popular*	Dr. Tweed
1954	*The Long Wait*	Gardiner
1954	*The Rocket Man*	Mayor Ed Johnson
1953	*Gentlemen Prefer Blondes*	Sir Francis 'Piggy' Beekman
1953	*Trouble Along the Way*	Father Matthew William Burke
1952	*Monkey Business*	Mr. Oliver Oxley
1952	*Has Anybody Seen My Gal*	Samuel Fulton / John Smith
1951	*The Highwayman*	Lord Walters
1950	*Mr. Music*	Alex Conway
1950	*Peggy*	Professor 'Brooks' Brookfield
1950	*Louisa*	Abel Burnside
1949	*Everybody Does It*	Major Blair *(Doris's father)*
1949	*The Gal Who Took the West*	Gen. Michael O'Hara
1949	*The Doctor and the Girl*	Dr. John Corday
1949	*Yes Sir That's My Baby*	Professor Jason Hartley
1949	*Impact*	Lt. Quincy
1948	*Green Grass of Wyoming*	Beaver Greenway

1948	*B.F.'s Daughter*	Burton F. 'B.F.' Fulton
1947	*The Paradine Case*	Sir Simon Flaquer
1947	*Lured*	Inspector Harley Temple
1946	*The Green Years*	Alexander Gow
1946	*Colonel Effingham's Raid*	Col. Will Seaborn Effingham
1945	*Shady Lady*	Col. John Appleby
1945	*Over 21*	Robert Drexel Gow
1945	*Rhapsody in Blue*	Max Dreyfus
1945	*A Royal Scandal*	Chancellor Nicolai Iiyitch
1944	*Together Again*	Jonathan Crandall Sr
1944	*The Impatient Years*	William Smith
1944	*Wilson*	Professor Henry Holmes
1944	*Knickerbocker Holiday*	Peter Stuyvesant
1943	*My Kingdom for a Cook*	Rudyard Morley
1943	*Princess O'Rourke*	Holman–Maria's Uncle
1943	*Heaven Can Wait*	Hugo Van Cleve
1943	*The Constant Nymph*	Charles Creighton
1943	*The More the Merrier*	Benjamin Dingle
1943	*Forever and a Day*	Sir William *(scenes deleted)*
1942	*George Washington Slept Here*	Uncle Stanley J. Menninger
1942	*In This Our Life*	William Fitzroy
1942	*Kings Row*	Dr. Henry Gordon
1941	*H.M. Pulham, Esq.*	John Pulham
1941	*Unexpected Uncle*	Seton Mansley aka Alfred Crane
1941	*Our Wife*	Professor Drake
1941	*The Devil and Miss Jones*	John P. Merrick
1941	*The Lady Eve*	'Colonel' Harrington
1940	*Three Faces West*	Dr. Karl Braun
1940	*The Captain Is a Lady*	Captain Abe Peabody
1940	*Florian*	Dr. Johannes Hofer
1940	*Edison, the Man*	General Powell
1940	*Road to Singapore*	Joshua Mallon IV
1939	*In Name Only*	Richard Walker
1939	*Stanley and Livingstone*	Lord Tyce
1939	*Bachelor Mother*	J. B. Merlin
1939	*The Story of Alexander Graham Bell*	Gardner Hubbard
1939	*Made for Each Other*	Judge Joseph M. Doolittle
1939	*Idiot's Delight*	Dr. Hugo Waldersee
1938	*Lord Jeff*	Captain Briggs
1938	*Yellow Jack*	Dr. Finlay

THE FEARLESS ARISTOCRAT
GLADYS COOPER

GLADYS COOPER CIRCA 1942. AUTHOR'S COLLECTION.

"With her firm chin and wide nostrils, she strode through life brushing obstacles from her path, her eyes on the horizon, an intolerant and rather gallant figure." [1]

The figure of which British authoress Daphne DuMaurier speaks is actress of the stage and screen, Dame Gladys Cooper. She is known to filmgoers as a thin-lipped and snobbish old woman, every bit as intolerant as DuMaurier describes. However similar the acid-tongued Gladys was to her onscreen characters, she could just as easily be a contradiction of herself. Her stage co-star, Betsy Von Furstenberg, had a different view of Gladys: "She had enormous deep blue eyes full of intelligence and ready for mischief, for Gladys at her most dignified was never above a giggle." [2] In film, Gladys rarely strayed from playing the woman DuMaurier describes, but in her private life she was a balance of both prim grand dame and fun-loving woman. Though she is best known as Bette Davis' heartless mother in *Now, Voyager* (1942) and as the brutally honest society matron Mrs. Higgins in *My Fair Lady* (1964), in Edwardian times Gladys was known as Britain's most beautiful stage actress. She did not weep over her lost beauty or star status; rather, she kept her eyes straight ahead and trooped into whatever character roles Hollywood had to offer. On screen and off, Gladys was a Darwinian study in survival of the fittest, with Gladys being the fittest. [3]

Gladys Constance Cooper was born to Charles and Mabel Cooper on December 18, 1888. She was raised in Chiswick, an upper middle class neighborhood of London. Gladys was the oldest of three children, and, growing up, she seemed to know this well. Her sister Doris recalled: "She was a show-off child, but very good, and totally without nerves of any kind...she...would never tolerate fools gladly...she was frightfully bossy and expected immense obedience from those around her — curiously enough, she usually got it, too." [4] Though Gladys preferred the outdoors, she modeled for postcard photographs at her mother's urging. By age twelve, she became "the most photographed little girl in London." [5] Gladys also sought parts in school plays, but she professed she had "no real idea of going on the stage." [6]

After graduating high school, Gladys's aimlessness led her back to the stage. Her first role was touring in the 1905 musical *Bluebell in Fairyland*. Her debut led to another role in the 1906 Billie Burke play *The Belle of Mayfair*. She did not initially care for the stage, but she still accepted an offer from George Edwardes to join his company at the Gaiety in 1907, a theater specializing in musical repertory. Gladys made her first appearance in the chorus of *The Girls of Gottenberg*.

In the Gaiety audience was twenty-six-year-old Boer War veteran Herbert Buckmaster. It was no wonder that Buckmaster noticed Gladys above the other chorus girls. By this time, she had a virtual monopoly on the Mssrs. Foulsham and Banfield photography studio to sit for their postcards; thus, her face was known throughout all of Britain. Being accustomed to getting what she wanted, Gladys eloped with Buckmaster against her father's wishes. Mr. Cooper did not speak to her for an entire year after the marriage. However, when Gladys became a mother in 1910 to a baby girl, the Coopers were proud grandparents.

Intolerant of illness and weakness of any kind, Gladys did not allow herself to be inactive for long after her first pregnancy. She soon acquired a role in the 1911 production of *The Importance of Being Earnest* and, in that show, won the best reviews of her career thus far. However, she truly matured as an actress after her first meeting with director and actor Gerald DuMaurier in 1913. Under DuMaurier's tutelage, she learned a naturalistic acting style. Though Gladys was thriving on stage, she made one brief venture into moving pictures to star in the Famous Players' production *The Eleventh Commandment* (1913). She would later describe her early experiences in silent film with a less than enthusiastic reflection: "I have seldom been so miserable." [7] She returned immediately to the stage and made a huge hit in 1916's *My Lady's Dress.*

With the coming of World War I, Gladys's popularity was reaching its height. According to her *New York Times* obituary, "hers was the most popular pinup picture...and Tommies carried it in their battle tunics." [8] During the war years, Gladys gave birth to her second child, John. Again, she only paused for a moment before returning to the stage in J.M. Barrie's *The Real Thing at Last.* While Gladys's husband was at war, it was rumored that she engaged in affairs with air ace Gustav Hamel and her frequent co-star Dennis Eadie. Without naming names, the *London Mail* criticized Gladys, declaring she "was never really happily wed, which was entirely her own fault, inasmuch as she rushed to the registry office against the advice of all." [9] The article intimated that a divorce was eminent. Gladys, with her gray eyes at their most piercing and her jaw set firm, filed a libel suit against the paper and won $6,000 damages. Though the newspaper had been presumptuous in its divorce intimation, there was tremendous strain growing in Gladys and Buckmaster's marriage. "After the war, she had made an entirely new set of friends. I had the done the same," [10] Buckmaster stated. The couple was shortly thereafter divorced in 1921.

Gladys had indeed become a major social presence. Her rise in eminence came in 1916 when she began to work almost exclusively at the prestigious London Playhouse. She was the primary leading lady for such luminaries as Somerset Maugham and Noël Coward. Her plays became so profitable that the Playhouse manager, Frank Curzon, invited Gladys to partner with him in running the theater. Gladys's sprawling home in Surrey became the main gathering place for her social set, which included the Barrymores, Irving Berlin, Rudolph Valentino, Groucho Marx, the King of Greece, the Marquis of Queensberg, and the Welsh Valentino, Ivor Novello. [11] With Novello, she co-starred in several more silent films including *The Bohemian Girl* (1922) and *Bonnie Prince Charlie* (1923). When not entertaining actors, writers, or royalty, she enjoyed the company of her estate's menagerie, which included dogs, cats, flying bats, a pony, and a monkey. [12]

Somerset Maugham later spoke of Gladys in her peak years with a mixture of awe and judgment. "I have a notion that her beauty has been at once her greatest asset and her greatest handicap: an asset because she could never have gone on the stage without it…a handicap because… there is a certain coldness in perfect beauty…if Miss Cooper has succeeded in overcoming the handicap…I ascribe it to her great common sense and to industry." [13] Gladys's industry won her the lead in a Pinero play popularized by the prominent actress Mrs. Patrick Campbell: *The Second Mrs. Tanqueray* (1922). Maugham declared the play saw Gladys turn "from an indifferent actress to an extremely competent one." [14] After a second hit, *The Last of Mrs. Cheyney,* Frank Curzon died and left Gladys with sole management of the Playhouse. Gladys not only managed the Playhouse but also had her own line of beauty products (which she did not use). She possessed a unique position of leadership for a woman in her times and proved her competence as her own manager in selecting a hugely successful Maugham play for her first venture, *The Letter.*

In 1927, near the end of *The Letter*'s two-year run, Gladys met a divorced, upper-class businessman ten years her junior, Sir Neville Pearson. The couple was married within the year. However, she remained like an independent single woman as she pressed on in her career, starring in another Maugham drama, *The Sacred Flame,* and in the coveted role of Peter in *Peter Pan.*

Gladys was forced to turn her attentions to her personal life in 1928 when, at the age of thirty-six, she was surprised to find she was pregnant with a second daughter. Her son, John, was also a matter of concern as he was reacting badly to having a stepfather. The union between Sir Neville and Gladys was not a matter of felicity to them either, as they found they had little in common.

By the early 1930s, Gladys was in her forties and was already being considered a symbol of the 1920s rather than contemporary times. As early as 1932, Gladys was beginning to have difficulty remembering her lines. Her grandson would later write that it was "considered an endearing eccentricity, since most of her latter plays had forgettable dialogue." [15] The Playhouse was in financial straits, and Gladys shut its doors in 1933. As was her nature, she shed no tears over this seeming step back in her career. "Getting on was her philosophy," [16] her grandson, Sheridan Morley, explained.

"Getting on" meant pursuing both Broadway and motion pictures. Gladys found a small role in the George Arliss period piece *The Iron Duke* (1934), but the film gave her no further incentive to become a film star. More successful was her venture into American theater. With her friend, Raymond Massey, she starred in *The Shining Hour*. The show was well-received, and Gladys was quite impressed with the Continent. "In New York, audiences are more keenly alive in their relationship to the theater — they are liberal...and like to experiment. In London...people seem to prefer old situations...and old jokes," [17] she stated.

Also playing on Broadway was *Mary of Scotland* starring a British actor, Philip Merivale. He was two years Gladys's elder and the father of four children. According to Merivale's son, Jack: "Philip was stunned by Gladys and was to remain so until the end of his days." [18] Gladys divorced Pearson in 1936, married Merivale, and decided to relocate to the United States.

Though the union with Merivale seemed an ideal way for the spouses to boost each others' careers, they were bankrupt after two years. Merivale and Gladys financed their own productions of Shakespearean plays on Broadway and in Britain with themselves as the stars. However, given their lack of Shakespearean training, the shows were dismal flops. They were forced to return to contemporary drawing room comedy with a profitable return to Broadway in *Spring Meeting*. After the run of this show, Merivale went on tour with a new one and Gladys scavenged for what work she could find. Help came from Gerald DuMaurier's daughter, Daphne, whose best-selling novel, *Rebecca*, was being filmed for the screen by Alfred Hitchcock. Gladys was cast in the role of Maxim DeWinter's tomboyish and blunt sister, Beatrice.

Gladys made a home in California and found her niche in the large population of British actors turned Hollywood stars. As in England, her home became the gathering place for the British acting crowd. Among her most frequent guests were Nigel Bruce, C. Aubrey Smith,

Basil Rathbone, Herbert Marshall, Vivien Leigh, Laurence Olivier, and David Niven. "I came out here for a two-week visit and stayed twenty-six years," [19] Gladys declared in 1966. Most appealing to her was the California sun, of which she took full advantage. "She didn't pamper her looks or avoid the sun," Betsy Von Furstenberg said in 1971. "But the lines she had didn't mar her beauty a bit — it was strong and the sun and wind suited it." [20] While in the sun, Gladys set about making her seaside home her own. She planted a garden, picked oranges from her trees to make marmalade, and added on to the menagerie she had brought with her from Britain. "I don't think she ever really wanted to go on making films...all she really wanted to do was work in that garden of hers," [21] her stepson, Jack, later said.

As pleased as Gladys was with her new home, she was less pleased with her appearance on screen. After her first viewing of *Rebecca* (1940), she stated: "I really looked quite terrible...a strange hunchback creature in an ill-fitting tweed suit out of whose mouth [came] such a frightful grating noise...no wonder nobody else want[ed] to hire me!" [22] Not being the beauty she was once was, Gladys's choice of roles was narrow. Once she began to acquire steady work, she was typed as an upper-crust and often unsympathetic snob. She appeared in *Kitty Foyle* (1940) and *That Hamilton Woman* (1941) before landing the role that would put her in the top ranks of Hollywood's character actors. As Bette Davis' septuagenarian mother in the classic melodrama, *Now, Voyager,* Gladys's intolerant nature was expanded and exaggerated to create a truly wicked old woman. In the film's opening scene, Mrs. Vale (Gladys) is among the first people the audience sees, and immediately, she makes herself known as the villain. In an unflinching and cold voice, she tells her daughter's psychiatrist:

> *This girl — 'a child of my old age' I always called her...her father passed on soon after she was born, my ugly duckling...I've kept her close by me always. When she was young, foolish, I made decisions for her, always the right decisions. One would think a child would wish to repay her mother's love and kindness.* [23]

Gladys received an Oscar nomination for her performance, but lost to newcomer Teresa Wright in *Mrs. Miniver* (1942). However, a nomination was enough to make casting directors take notice. She appeared in many low-budget or mediocre films including *Mr. Lucky* (1943) and *Princess O'Rourke* (1943) before winning her next Oscar-nominated role as the stone-faced and secretly envious Sister Marie Vauzous in *The Song of Bernadette* (1943). The audience has the rare opportunity to see her lose her composure as she openly weeps during a confession to God.

Though Gladys again lost the Oscar, she began to appear in higher-caliber period pieces including *The White Cliffs of Dover* (1945) and *Mrs. Parkington* (1945). In *The Pirate* (1948), she stepped out of type and por-trayed a woman closer to her own age, Judy Garland's flighty Aunt Inez.

Gladys's performances remained exemplary despite the personal trag-edies she suffered in 1946. After her husband, Philip, died of heart failure, her grandson wrote that it was "no doubt the greatest sadness of her long life." [24] The same year, Gladys's son, John, suffered a nervous breakdown and was soon thereafter admitted to Bellevue.

After these heartbreaks, Gladys felt she needed to "get on." She returned to England and made a spectacular comeback to the stage in Noël Coward's 1951 play, *Relative Values*. Five years later, she was a hit in *The Chalk Garden* in London and later on Broadway. Gladys resurged in Hollywood in a film adaptation of Noel Coward's *Separate Tables* (1958), which featured an all British cast. Co-star Wendy Hiller remarked that Gladys "warmed as she grew older." [25] Though Gladys admitted she was a "difficult person to live with," she, in her son-in-law, Robert Hardy's, words, "adored other people and enjoyed them." [26]

Gladys remained in Hollywood for several years after *Separate Tables*, primarily to perform in television. She was effective as an old woman attempting to keep the Angel of Death (played by Robert Redford, at her request) from crossing through her door in a *Twilight Zone* episode. Also while in America, she made her final Broadway appearance in 1962's *A Passage to India*. However, the role of her later career that truly immortal-ized her was as Mrs. Higgins in the Academy Award winning musical *My Fair Lady* (1964). She is at her most intolerant and hypercritical when she laments to Professor Higgins (Rex Harrison):

> *Henry! What a disagreeable surprise!...You'll offend all my friends. The moment they meet you, I'll never see them again. Besides, you're not even dressed for Ascot.* [27]

Though Gladys was again nominated without winning an Oscar for her performance, she, in the words of director George Cukor, "remained a Queen in her own right." [28]

As well-received as Gladys was in America, she permanently relocated to England to co-star in David Niven's British television program *The*

Rogues. But, Gladys was growing less interested in performing and more interested in her animals, garden, and grandchildren. Daphne DuMaurier remembered that near the end of her life "they [her grandchildren] were then what mattered to her far above anything she'd ever done on stage."[29] Though she was made Dame Gladys Cooper in 1967, the title of grandmother was her true glory.

GLADYS COOPER IN FOREGROUND WITH AUDREY HEPBURN AND REX HARRISON TO HER LEFT IN *MY FAIR LADY* **(1964).** COURTESY OF JERRY MURBACH.

Despite her waning interest in the theater, Gladys's loyalty and tireless work ethic prompted her to temporarily take over her former part in a 1971 Broadway revival of *The Chalk Garden*. During the run of the show Gladys became visibly ill with viral pneumonia. "I've played on stage with cracked ribs and when I was miscarrying...in those days they called me the iron lady. Now I have alas proved that even iron can crack," [30] she declared. Gladys died on November 17, 1971. Along Shaftesbury Avenue in London, the lights outside each theater were dimmed in her honor.

Gladys's passing represented the end of a genteel society that, though old-fashioned, audiences then and now find themselves wishing still existed. She once bemoaned the state of the theater, asking if there were "no morals, no standards, no faith" [31] left in the world. But as long as Gladys graced the stage and screen, there were sure to be morals, standards, and faith present. On her headstone under her name is engraved a most appropriate epitaph: "Unafraid." [32] Gladys remained unafraid of what convention dictated she do as a woman or as an aging actress. She never fell into what she called "the depth of filth and obscenity" [33] on the modern stage and screen, for she believed she was always correct in her judgment. And, when viewing her effective performances that still endure today, it is difficult to argue her belief.

FILMOGRAPHY

Year	Title	Role
1969	*A Nice Girl Like Me*	Aunt Mary
1967	*The Happiest Millionaire*	Aunt Mary
1964	*My Fair Lady*	Mrs. Higgins
1963	*The List of Adrian Messenger*	Mrs. Karoudjian
1958	*Separate Tables*	Mrs. Railton-Bell
1955	*The Man Who Loved Redheads*	Caroline, Lady Binfield
1952	*At Sword's Point*	Queen Anne
1951	*Thunder on the Hill*	Mother Superior
1949	*Madame Bovary*	Mme. Dupuis
1949	*The Secret Garden*	Mrs. Medlock
1948	*Homecoming*	Mrs. Kirby
1948	*The Pirate*	Aunt Inez
1947	*The Bishop's Wife*	Mrs. Hamilton
1947	*Green Dolphin Street*	Sophie Patourel
1946	*The Cockeyed Miracle*	Amy Griggs
1946	*Beware of Pity*	Mrs. Klara Condor
1946	*The Green Years*	Grandma Leckie

1945	*Love Letters*	Beatrice Remington
1945	*The Valley of Decision*	Clarissa Scott
1944	*Mrs. Parkington*	Alice–Dutchess de Brancourt
1944	*The White Cliffs of Dover*	Lady Jean Ashwood
1943	*The Song of Bernadette*	Sister Marie Therese Vauzous
1943	*Princess O'Rourke*	Miss Haskell
1943	*Mr. Lucky*	Captain Veronica Steadman
1943	*Forever and a Day*	Mrs. Barringer
1942	*Now, Voyager*	Mrs. Henry Vale
1942	*Eagle Squadron*	Aunt Emmeline
1942	*This Above All*	Iris Cathaway
1941	*The Gay Falcon*	Maxine Wood
1941	*A Yank in the R.A.F.*	Mrs. Pillby *(scenes deleted)*
1941	*The Black Cat*	Myrna Hartley
1941	*That Hamilton Woman*	Lady Frances Nelson
1940	*Kitty Foyle: The Natural History of a Woman*	Mrs. Strafford
1940	*Rebecca*	Beatrice Lacy
1934	*The Iron Duke*	Duchess d'Angouleme
1923	*Bonnie Prince Charlie*	Flora MacDonald
1922	*The Bohemian Girl*	Arlene Arnheim
1920	*Unmarried*	
1917	*Masks and Faces*	Mabel Vane
1917	*My Lady's Dress*	The Wife
1917	*The Sorrows of Satan*	Lady Sybil Elton
1916	*The Real Thing at Last (short)*	American Witch
1914	*Danny Donovan, the Gentleman Cracksman*	Mrs. Ashworth
1913	*The Eleventh Commandment (short)*	Edith

OLD FAITHFUL
HARRY DAVENPORT

HARRY DAVENPORT CIRCA 1941. AUTHOR'S COLLECTION.

There are actors who audiences cannot imagine were ever young. Their baggy, grandfatherly eyes, thinning white hair, and gentle, wise voices remain constant in spite of changing times or tastes. Such an actor was Harry Davenport. Having entered Hollywood at age sixty-nine, filmgoers knew him only as an elderly man. Over the course of his 116 film career, Harry portrayed forthright doctors, judges, fathers, and grandfathers, all of whom, despite their blunt way of speaking, carried within them a youthful streak evidenced by their wry jokes or unexpected giggles. Though he was strictly a supporting film actor, Harry spent the bulk of his career as a leading man on stage. However, over the course of his thirteen years in film, he became more widely known and recognized than he ever had during his nearly sixty years on stage. On screen Harry gave viewers the impression he had always been there and always would be, so faithful was his constant presence.

Harry Davenport's life began in 1866, a quarter century before the advent of moving pictures. He was raised in Philadelphia by Edward Davenport and Fanny Vining. Both parents came from families rich in theatrical history, with Edward's father being respected actor E.L. Davenport and Fanny counting among her descendants the well-known 18th century Irish actor, Jack Johnson. [1] Of the nine children born to Fanny and Edward (Harry being the youngest), the majority entered show business. Harry's career began at age five when he appeared at the Chestnut Street Theatre in Philadelphia as Damon's son in *Damon and Pythias*. His earnings amounted to $1.95, in coins. The young boy, not knowing what to do with such a fortune, set the coins aside. Despite financial hardships later in his life, Harry would never part with his first coins. He retained them in a safe deposit box until the end of his life, declaring with a sentimental grin: "A million dollars couldn't purchase these." [2]

Harry's theater engagements arrived steadily as he continued playing children's parts until he was thirteen. It was not until he finished high school that he graduated to mature roles. He left his beloved Pennsylvania home to brave the West, where he worked for four years in a stock company at San Francisco's Alcazar Theatre. [3] However, because California was predominantly composed of farmland, Harry found few opportunities to further his career there. He returned to the East and appeared in various theatricals, though none were yet on Broadway. It was not until 1893 that his fortunes changed. He met and married actress Alice Shepard, who was two years his senior. Soon after, he received his first Broadway engagement in a musical comedy called *The Voyage of Suzette*. He was quite adept at musicals, which is surprising given his later fame for strictly dramatic roles. Harry's good fortune extended into his personal life as his first child, Dorothy, was born in 1895. However, the marriage with Alice Shepard only survived one more year, ending in divorce in 1896.

Harry did not remain single for long. The same year of the divorce, he married another actress, Phyllis Rankin. Though she was nine years his junior, she and Harry had been friends since childhood. Harry's family grew over the next fifteen years as Phyllis gave birth to three children: Kate, Ned, and Fanny Ann. All of the Davenport children would later enter show business of their own volition.

Like Harry, Phyllis came from a theatrical family. It was Harry's marriage to Phyllis that catapulted him to top-rate productions. In a business that relies greatly on connections to attain career advancement, marriage to Phyllis was judicious. Her sisters, Doris and Gladys, were married into the royal family of theater: the Barrymores (Doris was married to Lionel while Gladys was wedded to the Barrymores' cousin, Sidney Drew). [4] Phyllis and Harry became a dynamic stage duo. Their first appearance together was in *The Belle of New York*, in which they sang "When We Are Married." Harry and Phyllis continued to be musical stars in *The Rounders* and *The Liberty Belles*. In a solo venture, Harry proved his dramatic abilities when he appeared beside Ethel Barrymore in *A Country Mouse*. He was equally successful in comedy when he received positive reviews for 1900's *Tom Pinch*, a play based on Charles Dickens's *Martin Chuzzlewit*. The *New York Times* wrote: "Harry Davenport is a tipsy officer who is sometimes droll and never offensive." [5] Harry's talent at droll comedy would later be pleasing in film, though his musical talents were sadly lost in the medium.

Aside from his family and acting, Harry spent a great deal of energy in bettering the harsh conditions under which he and his fellow actors worked. At this point in history, actors received no days off for holidays, paid for their own costumes, endured dressing rooms that were either stifling or ice cold and that possessed no proper restrooms. [6] Harry began his fight against the producers' mismanagement of actors by creating a small, but ultimately ineffective group, called the White Rats. It was not until 1913 when he joined forces with Eddie Foy and 112 other actors that the cause gained any recognition. The actors formed the Actors Equity Association, a group that would not truly make meaningful progress until 1919 when they joined the American Federation of Labor.

Because conditions in the theater were displeasing for Harry, he decided to try the fledgling film industry. In 1914, studios were largely based in New York. Harry joined Vitagraph, but did not receive any lucrative assignments until 1918 when he appeared as Mr. Jarr in a series of eighteen comedy shorts that followed the domestic travails of the Jarr family. Aside from performing in moving pictures, Harry also directed ten feature films between 1915-1917, among them the Marie Dressler film *Tillie Wakes Up* (1917) and *A Woman Alone* (1917) with Alice Brady. However, he restricted most of his activity to being in front of rather than behind the camera. The only silent film of Harry's known to exist

HARRY DAVENPORT CIRCA 1900. AUTHOR'S COLLECTION.

is the 1921 Harold Lloyd short *Among Those Present*, in which Harry has an uncredited cameo. He would remain absent from the screen for nine years following the Lloyd film.

Despite unrest in the theater, it still remained Harry's preferred place of work. He found much satisfaction in his return to the stage as he and Phyllis made their biggest hit yet in 1918's *Lightenin'*, which ran for 1,291 performances. [7] The Davenports continued to appear in a succession of popular shows and earned enough to purchase their own home in Pennsylvania. The property they settled on was a converted 1827 tavern they called Old Brick. They accented its vintage look with their antique collection, including Harry's pet collection of cigarette holders.

Harry's dedication to his home and family was reflected in his beliefs concerning the need for wholesome entertainment. In 1922, he spoke at the Harrison Place Methodist Episcopal Church in Brooklyn on the subject of "clean plays." His lecture was so convincing that Reverend Harry Dwight Miller "declared that the so-called ban of the church upon the theatre had driven 1000s of young people from its fold" and that "they should all see a number of 'clean, wholesome' plays," many of which included Harry's. [8] Harry set as positive a role model on stage as he later would on screen.

As revered as Harry was, his string of hits ended with *Topaze* in 1930. The Crash of 1929 crippled the theater's success, subsequently forcing the Davenports to search for alternate means of income. Old Brick became the site of their new enterprises. Harry spent many afternoons picking strawberries on the property while Phyllis turned them into preserves. The jam was so well received in New York that Harry hired a few boys to help pick the berries, offering each of them a bicycle as reward. Phyllis also opened Old Brick to the public and converted its parlor into a tea room. [9] To further supplement the family's income, Harry did venture into a few Hollywood pictures in the early 1930s although his home base remained Old Brick. Among his early efforts were 1931's *My Sin* with Tallulah Bankhead (in which he plays an oil company president) and 1933's *Get That Venus* with Jean Arthur (in which he plays Arthur's father).

The quaint life the Davenports led during the early 1930s came to an abrupt end when Phyllis became ill and died in 1934. Harry had seemingly lost everything — his career, his wife — and now, he gave up his home to relocate to the West Coast. Like his resilient, determined characters on screen, Harry set out to begin on a new career despite the fact he was advancing in years. He arrived in Hollywood in a jalopy and lived with his son Ned until he found steady employment.

As dire as the employment situation was in the Depression, the film industry remained relatively unaffected. Studios produced a picture a week, all of which provided no shortage of bit parts for character actors. Harry made it known he was available and quickly found work in many mediocre films. He gained a higher degree of respect when he appeared as an Army chief of staff in his first A picture, *The Life of Emile Zola* (1937). He took a comic, as well as musical, turn in the Gary Cooper romance *The Cowboy and the Lady* (1938). He is hilarious in a scene when, before his stiff-collared brother, he begins singing and dancing to the jazzy tune "A Tisket, a Tasket," advising his brother to loosen his hold over his niece's social life. Next, Harry portrayed his oft-repeated role of a judge in Frank Capra's Best Picture winner *You Can't Take It with You* (1938), the Kaufman-Hart story of the eccentric Sycamore family. Harry is at his most lovable as he tosses a donation into the collection plate the family's friends have put together to pay for the Sycamores' fine — even though he is supposed to be against them because they *did* break the law. Lionel Barrymore, Harry's co-star in the picture, claimed Harry "gave everybody a lesson every time he stepped on a stage or before a camera." [10] Child actor Mickey Kuhn, with whom Harry co-starred in *Juarez* (1939), concurred with Barrymore: "He was a very kind and courteous gentleman, not to mention his invaluable teaching skills for a young performer, as I was then." [11]

Harry received arguably his best role in 1939 as Dr. Meade in the legendary film *Gone With the Wind*. Dr. Meade is all at once comical and harsh, tipsy and sober. But, throughout the film, he remains a faithful presence. Dr. Mead's comical and stern sides are well mixed in this exchange with Scarlett O'Hara's aunt Pittypat:

> DR. MEADE (to Scarlett): *Now you've got to listen to me, you must stay here!*

> AUNT PITTYPAT: *Without a chaperone, Dr. Meade? It's simply isn't done!*

> DR. MEADE: *Good heavens, woman! This is a war, not a garden party!* [12]

Harry was beloved on the set of film, as proved when his co-stars presented him with his own, inscribed actor's chair in celebration of his 69th year as an actor.

As well-liked as Harry was, he did have moments of impatience towards his fellow actors. During the filming of *Lucky Partners* (1940) (in which he again plays a judge), he lost his temper with Ronald Colman, who could not remember his lines. He stormed from the set, declaring "I'm through!" Only after director Lewis Milestone talked with him and shared a few jokes did Harry's good humor return. [13]

Harry's conscientiousness towards an acting work ethic carried into his beliefs for being a good citizen. During World War II, Harry and his daughter, Kate, worked at the Hollywood Canteen, where Harry was not too proud to work as a busboy. [14] It was during the war years that Harry received many of his most memorable roles, all of which fostered models of upstanding citizenship. Most of his films of the early 1940s have since become classics: *Foreign Correspondent* (1940), *Kings Row* (1942), and *The Ox-Bow Incident* (1943).

However, it was 1944's *Meet Me in St. Louis* (the top-grossing film that year) that gave him one of the most substantial roles of his career. In it, Harry even sings two lines of the title song, harkening back to his days in Broadway musicals. He portrays Grandpa Prophater, a young at heart old man with twelve guns in his room and a collection of eccentric hats, with his favorite being a red fez with a blue tassel dangling down the side. He is at times as devilishly sly as Tom Sawyer, teasing his grandchildren about their beaus or scheming with them on how best to wreak havoc on Halloween. Throughout the film, he exhibits a deadpan humor, as shown in this exchange between him and his onscreen daughter, Mary Astor, and granddaughter, Joan Carroll.

> MRS. SMITH: *Now remember, not a word of this to your papa. You know how he plagues the girls about their beaus.*

> AGNES SMITH: *Everybody knows but Papa?*

> GRANDPA: *Your papa's not supposed to know. It's enough that we're letting him work hard every day to support the whole family. He can't have everything.* [15]

The likeable presence Harry added to *Meet Me in St. Louis* warmed many more films of the 1940s including *Courage of Lassie* (1946), *The Bachelor and the Bobby Soxer* (1947), and *Little Women* (1949). On screen and off, he was well-liked by children, especially Margaret O'Brien in *Meet Me in St. Louis*. She later called him a "great talent" [16] who enhanced the atmosphere on the set. His own child, Ann, was appreciative to him for supporting her in her new venture. She managed The Actors Hobby Market, a unique shop selling "products of the idle hours of show people." Actors donated handiwork including knit scarves or handmade and painted tables and chairs. Harry gave cigarette holders. Ann explained: "Most of the customers who wander in here seem to be baffled. But nearly all of them are amazed that actors can do something besides act." [17]

Harry was the first to agree that being active in work as well as hobbies was the key to longevity. In 1949, at the age of 83, Harry spoke against complacency in his usual forthright manner: "I hate to see men of my age sit down as if their lives were ended and accept a dole. An old man must show that he knows his job and is no loafer. If he can do that they can take their pension money and buy daisies with it." [18] Besides work, Harry's other recipe for a long life was to drink two bottles of ale with dinner each night.

Maintaining his tireless pace, Harry next went into Frank Capra's film about horse racing, *Riding High* (1950). As production on the film wrapped in summer 1949, he was already in talks for another film that would begin production in two weeks. Only hours before he was struck with a fatal heart attack, he had been on the telephone with his agent inquiring about the role.

During his seventy-eight years in show business, Harry was beloved by generations of play and moviegoers. About him was an air of trustworthiness that seemed to invite those around him to confide in or seek comfort from him. He was at once young and old, whimsical and wise. His characters onscreen were people audiences felt they knew — or wished they had in their lives. The words of his character Colonel Skeffington in *Kings Row* (1942) best describes his legacy:

When [he] passes, how much passes with [him]! A whole way of life, a way of gentleness and honor and dignity. These things are going, and they may never come back to this world. [19]

FILMOGRAPHY

1950	*Riding High*	Johnson
1949	*Tell It to the Judge*	Judge MacKenzie Meredith
1949	*That Forsyte Woman*	Old Jolyon Forsyte
1949	*Little Women*	Dr. Barnes
1949	*Down to the Sea in Ships*	Benjamin Harris
1948	*The Decision of Christopher Blake*	Courtroom Attendant

1948	*For the Love of Mary*	Justice Peabody
1948	*That Lady in Ermine*	Luigi
1948	*Man from Texas*	'Pop' Hickey *(bank president)*
1948	*Three Daring Daughters*	Dr. Cannon
1947	*The Fabulous Texan*	Rev. Baker
1947	*That Hagen Girl*	Judge A. Merrivale
1947	*The Bachelor and the Bobby-Soxer*	Thaddeus
1947	*Keeper of the Bees*	Michael Worthington
1947	*Sport of Kings*	Maj. Denning
1947	*Stallion Road*	Dr. Stevens
1947	*The Farmer's Daughter*	Dr. Matthew Sulven
1946	*A Boy and His Dog (short)*	Squire Jim Kirby
1946	*Lady Luck*	Judge Martin
1946	*Three Wise Fools*	The Ancient
1946	*Faithful in My Fashion*	Great Grandpa
1946	*G.I. War Brides*	Grandpa Giles
1946	*Courage of Lassie*	Judge Payson
1946	*A Boy, a Girl and a Dog*	Gramps
1946	*Claudia and David*	Dr. Harry
1945	*Adventure*	Dr. Ashlon
1945	*Pardon My Past*	Grandpa Pemberton
1945	*The Enchanted Forest*	Old John
1945	*Too Young to Know*	Judge Boller
1945	*She Wouldn't Say Yes*	Albert
1945	*This Love of Ours*	Dr. Wilkerson
1945	*The Thin Man Goes Home*	Dr. Bertram Charles
1944	*Music for Millions*	Doctor
1944	*Meet Me in St. Louis*	Grandpa Prophater
1944	*The Impatient Years*	Minister
1944	*Kismet*	Agha
1943	*Jack London*	Prof. Hilliard
1943	*Government Girl*	Senator MacVickers
1943	*Gangway for Tomorrow*	Fred Taylor
1943	*Princess O'Rourke*	Supreme Court Judge
1943	*Headin' for God's Country*	Clem Adams
1943	*We've Never Been Licked*	Pop Lambert
1943	*The Ox-Bow Incident*	Arthur Davies
1943	*Shantytown*	'Doc' Herndon
1943	*The Amazing Mrs. Holliday*	Commodore Thomas Spencer Holliday

1938	*The Higgins Family*	Grandpa William Jordan
1938	*The First Hundred Years*	Uncle Dawson
1938	*Reckless Living*	'General' Jeff
1938	*Gold Is Where You Find It*	Dr. 'Doc' Parsons
1938	*Saleslady*	Miles Cannon
1938	*Man-Proof*	Hitch-Hiking Old Man *(uncredited)*
1937	*Wells Fargo*	Ingalls–Banker
1937	*First Lady*	Charles
1937	*The Great Garrick*	Innkeeper of Turk's Head *(uncredited)*
1937	*The Perfect Specimen*	Carl Carter
1937	*Radio Patrol*	John P. Adams, inventor *(Chapter 1)*
1937	*Fit for a King*	Archduke Julio
1937	*Mr. Dodd Takes the Air*	Doc Jeremiah George Quinn
1937	*The Life of Emile Zola*	Chief of Staff
1937	*White Bondage*	Pop Craig
1937	*They Won't Forget*	Confederate Veteran
1937	*Fly Away Baby*	Col. Higgam
1937	*Armored Car*	Pop Logan
1937	*As Good as Married*	Jessup
1937	*Mountain Justice*	Printer *(scenes deleted)*
1937	*Maytime*	Opera Director *(uncredited)*
1937	*Her Husband's Secretary*	Dan Kingdon
1937	*Paradise Express*	Jed Carson
1937	*Under Southern Stars (short)*	Party Guest
1937	*Under Cover of Night*	Dr. Reed
1936	*King of Hockey*	Tom McKenna
1936	*Four Days' Wonder*	Ticket Agent
1936	*Three Men on a Horse*	Williams
1936	*Legion of Terror*	Senator Morton *(uncredited)*
1936	*The Case of the Black Cat*	Peter Laxter
1935	*The Scoundrel*	Slezack
1933	*Get That Venus*	Mr. Rendleby
1932	*The Wiser Sex*	Rolfe's defense attorney *(uncredited)*
1932	*The Campus Mystery (short)*	Dean Perry
1931	*His Woman*	Customs Inspector
1931	*My Sin*	Roger Metcalf
1930	*Her Unborn Child*	Dr. Remington
1921	*Among Those Present (short)*	*(uncredited)*
1919	*She's Everywhere (short)*	
1919	*Dawn*	Daniel Burton

1919	*A Girl at Bay*... Frank Galt
1919	*The Unknown Quantity*................................Septimus Kinsolving
1917	*The Planter*.. Short
1917	*Sowers and Reapers* .... Henry Ainsworth
1916	*The Heart of a Fool (short)* ....
1916	*The Father of Her Child (short)* ....
1916	*The Wheel of the Law*....................................John Daniels
1916	*Fashion and Fury (short)* ....
1916	*One Night*...
1915	*Mrs. Jarr and the Society Circus (short)* ....Mr. Jarr
1915	*Mr. Jarr and the Visiting Firemen (short)* ....Mr. Jarr
1915	*Mr. Jarr and Circumstantial Evidence (short)* ....Mr. Jarr
1915	*Mr. Jarr's Big Vacation (short)*............................Mr. Jarr
1915	*Mr. Jarr and Gertrude's Beaux (short)*...................Mr. Jarr
1915	*Mr. Jarr and the Captive Maiden (short)* ....Mr. Jarr
1915	*Mr. Jarr and Love's Young Dream (short)*...........Mr. Jarr
1915	*Philanthropic Tommy (short)*................................. Mr. Moreland
1915	*Mr. Jarr and the Ladies' Cup (short)*....................Mr. Jarr
1915	*Mrs. Jarr and the Beauty Treatment (short)*..........Mr. Jarr
1915	*Mrs. Jarr's Auction Bridge (short)*........................Mr. Jarr
1915	*Mr. Jarr Visits His Home Town (short)* ....Mr. Jarr
1915	*Mr. Jarr and the Dachshund (short)*....................Mr. Jarr
1915	*The Jarrs Visit Arcadia (short)*............................Mr. Jarr
1915	*The Closing of the Circuit (short)* ....Mary's Father
1915	*Mr. Jarr's Magnetic Friend (short)* ....Mr. Jarr
1915	*Mr. Jarr Takes a Night Off (short)*......................Mr. Jarr
1915	*Mr. Jarr and the Lady Reformer (short)* ....Mr. Jarr
1915	*Mr. Jarr Brings Home a Turkey (short)*...............Mr. Jarr
1915	*The Jarr Family Discovers Harlem (short)* ....Mr. Jarr
1914	*C.O.D.* .... C.O. Darlington
1914	*The Professional Scape Goat (short)*..................................
1914	*Rainy, the Lion Killer (short)*....................... Jack Brown
1914	*Fogg's Millions (short)* ....
1914	*The Accomplished Mrs. Thompson (short)*........................
1914	*Too Many Husbands (short)*...

THE SENTIMENTAL
WISE GUY
JAMES
GLEASON

JAMES GLEASON IN *THE PLOT THICKENS* (1936). AUTHOR'S COLLECTION.

He was a man of slight build with sunken cheeks, a pointed chin, and deep eyes that could change from burning to glimmering in the course of one second. He was best known for his tough guy, hard-boiled characters that could come in the form of prizefight trainers, detectives, Army sergeants, fathers, or cab drivers. The nasal and rapid New York slang that was his trademark was indecipherable to anyone but an American — and even Americans could become lost at times listening to him. His name was James Gleason, one of the most popular character actors from the 1930s through the 1950s. Best known as Max Corkle the boxing trainer in *Here Comes Mr. Jordan* (1941), James also showed his talent as the wiseacre milkman in *The Clock* (1945) and as Sylvester the ice skating cab driver in *The Bishop's Wife* (1947). Off screen, he was a decidedly ordinary man. He fought for his country three times and exemplified good citizenship through his generosity to others, tireless work ethic, and devotion to his son and his wife, to whom he was married for 32 years. James Gleason's unpretentious speech, forthright personality, and loyalty to family made him relatable to Americans of all classes and ages.

James Gleason was born on May 23, 1882 in New York City in a theatrical boarding house. His parents and extended family were troupers long before he set foot on the stage as a young man. His father, William, worked as a stage director for noted producer Charles Frohman before forming his own stock company. It is interesting to note that before William ventured into acting, he worked as a prizefighter. He could not have known that his son would later gain fame on Broadway portraying a prizefighter's trainer. James's mother, Mina Crolius, began acting at the age of fifteen. [1] When Mina and William married and became parents, their new baby son was brought up in the family business. James made his stage debut at two months old when he was bundled in Mina's arms in the play *Clouds*. Five years later, William produced a play, *Stricken Blind*, which put James in a more substantial part.

James toured as a child actor for a few years until his parents decided he needed formal schooling. He attended the Friends Seminary in New York, but continued making stage appearances on school holidays. Aside from theatrical work, James earned pocket money as a messenger boy, printer's devil, an assistant in an electrical store, and as an elevator boy. [2] His varied upbringing left little doubt that he was a street smart kid, amazingly self-sufficient by the time he was a teenager.

When William and Mina relocated to Oakland, California to operate their own theater, James went with them. However, he did not pursue a great deal more of formal schooling. At age sixteen, he enlisted in the

Army at the outbreak of the Spanish-American War. He spent three years fighting in the Philippines before discharging. It was during his first military service that James learned a portion of the slang he would later make his trademark. In 1941, the *New York Times* remarked that "Gleason is…a master of…hard-bitten words [that] are barked from the corner of a wry mouth. Partly this is because during the Spanish-American War he was put in a regiment where you either talked out the side of your mouth or had your own private war on your hands."[3] James survived the war and became a tougher and more mature man, but he returned to acting immediately after his discharge. He joined the Bishop Players in San Francisco for a time before moving to his parents' theater, the Liberty, in Oakland.

During his time in Oakland, James met Lucile Webster, a young actress in his father's company. Lucile was the opposite of James in appearance; she was plump and merry while he was scrawny and dour. The couple nevertheless clicked and went on to become one of the most prolific couples in show business. After marrying in 1905, they toured in vaudeville before joining a stock company in Portland, Oregon. In 1909, they had their only child, Russell, who would take up the family business of acting early in his life. James and Lucile returned to New York when James won a role in his first Broadway show, *Pretty Miss Smith*. Shortly after the show's run, James once more was compelled to serve in the military during the Mexican border campaign. In 1918, James again put his career on hold to serve as an intelligence officer in World War I.

As was the case with his first military discharge, James returned immediately to acting after each stint in service. His first part after World War I was in the Broadway production *Five Million*. He soon became as much a fixture on the stage as he later would be on screen, but the unreliability of theater managers booking shows often left him out of work. In 1925, James and his friend Richard Taber sat down to dinner together to concoct a way to have steady work with no undependable managers on which to rely. They decided to create a play of their own that would guarantee life-long parts to all members of the cast and crew.[4]

The comically titled *Is Zat So?* was the end result of James and Taber's discussion. The play tells the story of a boxer and his manager (James) who are employed by a wealthy young man to work undercover as his valet and butler. On the sly, James and the fighter teach the rich young man to box, a skill the young man wishes to learn so that he can reveal the crooked dealings of his brother-in-law, even if it means a fight. In the end, the boxer stands in for the rich young man in a fight and ultimately unmasks the dishonesty of the brother-in-law. *Is Zat So?* utilized

James's knowledge of the many varieties of slang, all of which he said "were worthy of study." He further quipped: "Americans speak English only on certain sections of 5th and Park Avenue." Though James acquired many fans due to the success of his show, one woman approached him back stage with the offer to coach him in proper speech. James surprised her by answering in "suave and impeccable English," thus making the woman flee with embarrassment. [5] Despite a lack of formal education, James was articulate in his speech, as demonstrated in this statement to the *New York Times:* "There is no national slang…it is almost necessary for the playwright to learn slang if he learns to understand human nature." [6]

Understanding human nature is perhaps the key reason James's performance so clicked with audiences, even those not familiar with New Yorkese. *Is Zat So?* grossed more than one million dollars over its three-year run. [7] It was backed by such luminaries as Earle Booth and Fanny Brice (who owned 50% of the production). [8] James's success with *Is Zat So?* led him to write many more shows including *The Fall Guy* (which used crook slang, what James called "the common language of New York City" [9]), *The Shannons of Broadway, Rain or Shine,* and *Puffy.*

No matter how hard-boiled a character James portrayed, he declared that "I wouldn't want my character to do anything I myself won't do." [10] In *The Shannons of Broadway,* written primarily as a showcase for Lucile and James to do together, the couple portrayed characters not unlike themselves. They quarrel but are "kind and generous and soft" [11] at the same time. Lucile and James fueled each others' creativity and consequently did most of their work together. One *New York Times* reporter stated: "Give the Gleasons a good cook and comfortable dining room chairs and they'll turn out a good play." [12] Most often, James's ideas came over his and Lucile's oft-repeated dinner of steak and mashed potatoes. If his ideas were "too zany," Lucile "drenched them with cold water…and tempered the idea." [13] One zany and generous idea Lucile did not temper was James's plan to write in at least a dozen parts in his play *Puffy* that would give employment to out-of-work, elderly actors.

As thriving as he was on Broadway, James accepted an offer from Republic Studios in 1927. He signed the first four-way contract ever on record, giving him the option to work as a writer, producer, actor, or director. [14] Early in his career, he attempted to adapt his stage successes to the screen, including a 1929 adaptation of *The Shannons of Broadway* in which he and Lucile starred, and *Rain or Shine* (1930). More notable were James's efforts in writing. He co-authored the screenplay to *The Broadway Melody* (1929), the first talking film to win Best

Picture. Among his other collaborations were *What a Widow!* (1930), *The Swellhead* (1930), and a Janet Gaynor film in which he also co-starred as a hotdog vendor, *Change of Heart* (1934). He became a familiar face to audiences as he began receiving more and more acting work in such films as *Puttin' on the Ritz* (1931) and *A Free Soul* (1931), both starring Norma Shearer and Clark Gable. However, it was a mystery serial produced from 1932 to 1937, collectively called the Hildegard Withers series, that typed James as the tough and streetwise character he repeated throughout his career. As Police Inspector Oscar Piper, he made a comic partner for the pompous, upper crust Hildegard, played by the inimitable Edna May Oliver.

The entire Gleason family was accepted by Hollywood: Lucile found steady work in character parts and Russell won a role as the young German soldier, Mueller, in the prestigious World War I film *All Quiet on the Western Front* (1930). The Gleasons became one of Hollywood's most beloved families when they co-starred together in a series of seven domestic comedy films from 1936 to 1940, beginning with *The Higgins Family* (1936).

Despite the fact that he had been trained on Broadway, James felt an immediate loyalty to Hollywood. He came to its defense when high-brow New York playwright Moss Hart declared that films should be moved to New York if they were to be of better quality. "The trouble with New Yorkers like Moss is that they think the world is bounded by the Battery and the Harlem River...I'll tell you why the movies are in California. Because within two and a half hours' drive, I can take you to backgrounds for any picture you can imagine. We've got everything here," [15] James declared.

Hollywood loved the Gleasons as much as they loved Hollywood. In 1931, when James and Lucile celebrated their silver wedding anniversary, Beverly Hills experienced major traffic congestion from the sheer number of people attending the celebration. Industry elites including Marie Dressler, Robert Montgomery, and Gloria Swanson, were among the guests. Their twenty-five year marriage was an exception to the norm in Hollywood; consequently, they were asked what their secret was. Lucile admitted that she and James were opposites in many ways — James loved golf and polo and Lucile abhorred any exercise — but that she retained her marriage because of this philosophy: "Don't marry a man expecting to change him...have a hobby...treat marriage and your career with equal seriousness." [16] James's words on marriage are equally insightful and reveal the fighting spirit he so effectively communicated onscreen: "Don't come home without a joke to tell…never let the sun go down on your wrath… fight it out if it takes all night…treat your wife as a partner." [17] It is no wonder the Gleasons' union was called the Pride of Hollywood.

Once the 1940s began, Lucile's roles became fewer and Russell left pictures to join the Army. However, the decade marked the acme of James's career. The *New York Times* reported in 1959 that James "most

JAMES GLEASON ON FAR RIGHT WITH WALTER BRENNAN, IRVING BACON, GARY COOPER AND BARBARA STANWYCK IN *MEET JOHN DOE* (1941). COURTESY OF JERRY MURBACH.

often played the role of the colorful functionary in the slangy American vein — the detective, the Army sergeant, or the sidekick." [18]He was at his slangy best in his Oscar-nominated performance as boxing manager Pop Corkle in *Here Comes Mr. Jordan* (1941). The film's most comic moments occur when a bewildered Pop is speaking to the invisible heavenly host, Mr. Jordan, unaware he is being observed by the befuddled owner of the house in which he is visiting. Pop is as skeptical as everybody else around him, but, at the same time, his innate belief in something greater than himself gives him trust and faith that make him a likable and relatable character. There was no shortage of plum roles for the bulk of the 1940s, with James appearing in such films as *A Guy Named Joe* (1943), *Arsenic and Old Lace* (1944), and *A Tree Grows in Brooklyn* (1945).

Arguably the best of James's films from the mid-forties is *The Clock* (1945), a Vincent Minnelli story of a GI, his girl, and their whirlwind courtship. James plays Al, a milkman who gives the young couple a midnight ride home. James is obviously in his element in the New York City setting, displaying his fast-paced, urban dialect to its fullest extent. It is difficult not to chuckle as he engages in an argument with an unseen announcer heard over the radio of his milk truck.

> RADIO ANNOUNCER: *And now for another request, this one from Nellie Green.*

> AL: *Nellie Green! That dame again! Ha ho! Discrimination there! Get a load of what she wants now...*

> ANNOUNCER: *"How am I to know?"...*

> AL: *Wouldn't she ask for that? How do you like that?... That's the second request in two weeks he's had of hers. What's this gettin' to be? A Miss Nellie Green private program?...I've had a request in now for three months. Do they get it? No. Miss Nellie Green? Yeah!* [19]

The most rewarding scenes in the film are those when James and Lucile appear together as husband and wife. Watching them is like having a private view into the Gleason home. One exchange is so natural it does not seem scripted in the least:

> AL: *I think you can find out as much about a person in a minute as in a lifetime. You know what she was doing the first time I saw her? Flipping butter cakes in Charles's window. And the minute I laid eyes on her, I knew she was for me.*

> LUCILE: *And it took three weeks for him to get up the courage to come in! Then he had to bring his uncle with him.*

> AL: *It wasn't my uncle, it was my cousin!* [20]

As positive as James's professional life was, his personal life was tarnished with tragedy. On Christmas night in 1945, Russell fell from the fourth floor of a hotel window and died at the age of thirty-six. It was never determined whether the fall was a suicide or an accident. "My son was a soldier and of that I am proud. He died a soldier and that is what his mother and I always will remember,"[21] James told the press. Two years later, James again experienced a severe loss with the death of Lucile.

With no family left, James devoted himself to his career. Much of his later work consisted of unmemorable features, including a quasi-sequel to *Here Comes Mr. Jordan* called *Down to Earth* (1947), but there were numerous notable performances as well. In the Christmas classic *The Bishop's Wife* (1947), James stole the show as the wise-cracking cab driver, Sylvester, who discovers his faith in humanity when he is taught to ice-skate by angelic messenger Cary Grant. In a dramatic turn, James co-starred in the Charles Laughton-directed suspense film *The Night of the Hunter* (1955), as a boozy boathouse keeper who helps two children escape from their murderous stepfather.

James did not noticeably slow his pace until 1958 when his chronic asthma flared and incapacitated him for the next year. On April 13, 1959, after he was hospitalized at the Motion Picture Country House Hospital, James passed away at age seventy-two.

The *New York Times*, in summarizing James's career wrote that within the "limited panel" of types he portrayed, he "managed to provoke an amazingly wide range of humor and insights with his dour and deadpan dismay."[22] As a student of human nature James knew how to move an audience whether it was through laughter or tears. He may have seemed a cliché — the hard-boiled wise guy with a soft heart — but he was not playing a stock character: he was playing himself. As one journalist wrote in a 1941 profile of James: "Gleason is Irish and he believes in sentiment. Every time he's for keeping in the heart stuff and throwing out material that is simply smart."[23]

FILMOGRAPHY

1958	*Money, Women and Guns*	Henry Devers
1958	*The Last Hurrah*	'Cuke' Gillen
1958	*Once Upon a Horse…*	Postmaster
1958	*Rock-a-Bye Baby*	Doc Simpkins
1958	*Man or Gun*	Sheriff Jim Jackson
1958	*The Female Animal*	Tom Maloney
1957	*I Man in the Shadow*	Hank James
1957	*Loving You*	Carl Meade
1957	*Spring Reunion*	Mr. 'Collie' Collyer *(as Jimmy Gleason)*
1956	*Star in the Dust*	Orval Jones

1955	*The Girl Rush*	Ether Ferguson
1955	*The Night of the Hunter*	Birdie Steptoe
1954	*Suddenly*	Pete 'Pop' Benson
1954	*Hollywood Thrill-Makers*	Risky Russell
1953	*Forever Female*	Eddie Woods
1952	*What Price Glory*	Gen. Cokely
1952	*The Story of Will Rogers*	Bert Lynn
1952	*We're Not Married!*	Duffy
1951	*I'll See You in My Dreams*	Fred Thompson
1951	*Come Fill the Cup*	Charley Dolan
1951	*Joe Palooka in Triple Cross*	Knobby Walsh
1951	*Two Gals and a Guy*	Max Howard
1950	*Joe Palooka in the Squared Circle*	Knobby Walsh
1950	*The Jackpot*	Harry Summers
1950	*Riding High*	Racing Secretary
1950	*The Yellow Cab Man*	Mickey Corkins
1950	*Screen Snapshots 2856: It Was Only Yesterday (short)*	Commentator
1950	*Key to the City*	Sergeant Hogan
1949	*Miss Grant Takes Richmond*	Timothy P. Gleason
1949	*Take One False Step*	Captain Gledhill
1949	*The Life of Riley*	Gillis
1949	*Bad Boy*	Chief
1948	*When My Baby Smiles at Me*	Lefty Moore
1948	*The Return of October*	Uncle Willie Ramsey
1948	*The Dude Goes West*	Sam Briggs
1948	*Smart Woman*	Sam Corkle
1947	*Tycoon*	Pop Mathews
1947	*The Bishop's Wife*	Sylvester
1947	*Down to Earth*	Max Corkle
1947	*The Homestretch*	Doc Kilborne
1946	*Lady Luck*	Sacramento Sam
1946	*Home, Sweet Homicide*	Sgt. O'Hare
1946	*The Well-Groomed Bride*	Capt. Hornby
1946	*The Hoodlum Saint*	Snarp
1945	*Captain Eddie*	Tom Clark
1945	*The Clock*	Al Henry
1945	*A Tree Grows in Brooklyn*	McGarrity
1945	*This Man's Navy*	Jimmy Shannon
1944	*The Keys of the Kingdom*	Rev. Dr. Wilbur Fiske
1944	*Arsenic and Old Lace*	Lt. Rooney

1944	*Once Upon a Time*	McGillicuddy aka The Moke
1943	*A Guy Named Joe*	'Nails' Kilpatrick
1943	*Crash Dive*	Chief Mike 'Mac' McDonnell
1942	*Manila Calling*	Tim O'Rourke
1942	*Tales of Manhattan*	Joe
1942	*Footlight Serenade*	Bruce McKay
1942	*The Falcon Takes Over*	Inspector Mike O'Hara
1942	*My Gal Sal*	Pat Hawley
1942	*A Date with the Falcon*	Inspector Michael 'Mike' O'Hara
1942	*Hay Foot*	Colonel J. A. Barkley
1941	*Babes on Broadway*	Thornton Reed, Theatrical Producer
1941	*Nine Lives Are Not Enough*	Sgt. Sam Daniels
1941	*Tanks a Million*	Col. 'Spitfire' Barkley
1941	*Here Comes Mr. Jordan*	Max Corkle
1941	*Affectionately Yours*	'Chet' Phillips
1941	*Meet John Doe*	Henry Connell
1940	*Earl of Puddlestone*	Joe Higgins
1940	*Grandpa Goes to Town*	Joe Higgins
1939	*Money to Burn*	Joe Higgins
1939	*The Covered Trailer*	Joe Higgins
1939	*On Your Toes*	Phil Dolan Sr.
1939	*Should Husbands Work?*	Joe Higgins
1939	*My Wife's Relatives*	Joe Higgins
1938	*Army Girl*	Sgt. 'Three Star' Hennessy
1938	*The Higgins Family*	Joe Higgins
1937	*Manhattan Merry-Go-Round*	Danny The Duck
1937	*Forty Naughty Girls*	Inspector Oscar Piper
1936	*The Plot Thickens*	Oscar Piper
1936	*The Big Game*	George Scott
1936	*Don't Turn 'em Loose*	Detective Daniels
1936	*Yours for the Asking*	Saratoga
1936	*The Ex-Mrs. Bradford*	Inspector Corrigan
1936	*Murder on a Bridle Path*	Police Insp. Oscar Piper
1935	*We're Only Human*	Detective Danny Walsh
1935	*Hot Tip*	Jimmy McGill
1935	*West Point of the Air*	Joe 'Bags'
1935	*Murder on a Honeymoon*	Inspector Oscar Piper
1935	*Helldorado*	Sam Barnes
1934	*Murder on the Blackboard*	Inspector Oscar Piper
1934	*Change of Heart*	Hot Dog Vendor *(uncredited)*

1934	*Orders Is Orders*	Ed Waggermeyer
1934	*Search for Beauty*	Dan Healy
1934	*The Meanest Gal in Town*	Duke Slater
1933	*Hoop-La*	Jerry
1933	*Gleason's New Deal (short)*	
1933	*Mister Mugg (short)*	
1933	*Alias the Professor (short)*	
1933	*Clear All Wires!*	Lefty Williams
1933	*Rock-a-Bye Cowboy (short)*	Jimmy
1933	*Billion Dollar Scandal*	Ratsy Harris
1932	*Lights Out (short)*	
1932	*A Hockey Hick (short)*	
1932	*The Devil Is Driving*	'Beef' Evans
1932	*Penguin Pool Murder*	Police Inspector Oscar Piper
1932	*Always Kickin' (short)*	
1932	*Yoo-Hoo (short)*	
1932	*The All-American*	Chick Knipe
1932	*The Crooked Circle*	Arthur Crimmer
1932	*Off His Base (short)*	Picture in Opening Credits *(credit only)*
1932	*Blondie of the Follies*	Pa McClune
1932	*High Hats and Low Brows (short)*	Danny Ruff
1932	*Lady and Gent*	Pin Streaver
1932	*Fast Companions*	Silk Henley
1932	*Stealin' Home (short)*	
1932	*Rule 'Em and Weep (short)*	Spike Mc Gorey
1932	*Battle Royal (short)*	
1931	*Doomed to Win (short)*	
1931	*Suicide Fleet*	'Skeets' O'Riley
1931	*Slow Poison (short)*	
1931	*The Big Gamble*	Fred 'Squint' Dugan
1931	*Where Canaries Sing Bass (short)*	
1931	*Sweepstakes*	Sleepy Jones
1931	*A Free Soul*	Eddie
1931	*It's a Wise Child*	Cool Kelly
1931	*Beyond Victory*	Pvt. Jim 'KP' Mobley
1930	*Big Money*	Tom
1930	*Her Man*	Steve
1930	*The Matrimonial Bed*	Gustave Corton
1930	*Dumbbells in Ermine*	Mike
1930	*The Swellhead*	Johnny Trump

1930	*Puttin' on the Ritz*	James 'Jimmy' Tierney
1930	*Don't Believe It (short)*	
1929	*The Shannons of Broadway*	Mickey Shannon
1929	*Fairways and Foul (short)*	Husband
1929	*Oh, Yeah!*	Dusty
1929	*The Garden of Eatin' (short)*	
1929	*Meet the Missus (short)*	
1929	*The Broadway Melody*	Music Publisher *(uncredited)*
1928	*The Count of Ten*	The Manager
1922	*Polly of the Follies*	Paul Gordon

MORE THAN
A WICKED WITCH
MARGARET
HAMILTON

MARGARET HAMILTON IN THE BROADWAY SHOW *GOLDILOCKS* (1959).
AUTHOR'S COLLECTION.

Margaret Hamilton received ten fan letters a week forty years after her most productive years as a character actress had ended. Most actresses, who, in the majority of their films played bit parts, would not receive even one fan letter a week after such a passage of time. Margaret might have been in that same category of forgotten bit players had it not been for one role that immortalized her forever: the Wicked Witch of the West in *The Wizard of Oz* (1939). Margaret, a naturally generous, witty, and warm woman, admitted that she did most often play "really mean, awful people."[1] But, her fans saw through these characterizations and often told her she was not "nearly as nasty" as she seemed in the movies."[2] She appeared in a variety of roles including a litigious member of a school board in *Babes in Arms* (1939), a judgmental yet humorous Ladies League member in *My Little Chickadee* (1940), and, in her senior years, the lovable storekeeper Cora on Maxwell House commercials. Margaret called her less "nasty" characters women with "hearts of gold and corsets of steel."[3] This description is more indicative of the true Margaret Hamilton. She was a woman dedicated to family, the welfare of animals, and the education of children. She retained "a corset of steel" throughout a career not without obstacles — the primary obstacle being the inability to dissociate herself from the Wicked Witch. "It's not the part I'd most like to be known for, but I don't mind,"[4] she resolved in the last years of her life.

The part in which Margaret was often cast, a schoolteacher, was a role she was destined for early in life. Born in 1902 in Cleveland, Ohio, Margaret grew up receiving the most proper education. Despite the strictness of her schooling, Margaret developed a vivid imagination and found escape in the pages of her favorite book, *The Wizard of Oz*. Stage struck from the start, she gave her first performance at age six in a neighborhood production of *Sleeping Beauty*. However, she was Sleeping Beauty rather than the Wicked Witch in this production. "That was…the last time, if I may say, that I ever played a beauty of any kind,"[5] Margaret wryly said in the 1980s. When Margaret reached adolescence, she was sent to Hathaway Brown School for Girls in Shaker Heights, Ohio. There, Margaret participated in campus productions. She was typecast before she ever entered Hollywood, filling parts such as elderly Englishwomen and spinsters. Her enjoyment of her stage work led her to abandon her decision to become a kindergarten teacher in favor of pursuing a Broadway career. But, Margaret's mother insisted she learn how to earn a reliable living before "fooling around with the theater."[6]

Margaret obediently earned her teaching degree and did not return to her acting ambition until several years afterward. Her mother died, and, while caring for her widowed father, she taught day school in Cleveland before opening her own nursery school. She later said being a kindergarten teacher was good training for her acting: "Teaching kindergarten and acting are very close because you have to entertain the same audience

MARGARET HAMILTON AND ANNE SHIRLEY IN *CHATTERBOX* (1936).
AUTHOR'S COLLECTION.

for a long time."[7] Margaret was entertaining theater audiences as well as children; she joined the Cleveland Playhouse and filled character parts in its shows. In 1931, while she was working as a teacher, she married Paul Meserve. However, the marriage became troubled as Margaret began to further consider acting as her primary career. Given that her marriage was in jeopardy and her acting ambitions had the potential of failing, Margaret was grateful to have obtained an education. "Whenever I talk to aspiring actresses and actors, I always say the first thing is to know how to do something else so you can get your clothes cleaned and have your hair done once in a while,"[8] she later declared.

Margaret risked having to clean her own clothes and do her own hair when she traveled to New York to pursue legitimate stage work.

She landed her first Broadway role in *Another Language* portraying a waspish relation to the leading lady. When M-G-M bought the rights to the show in 1933, Margaret went to Hollywood to costar in the film adaptation starring Robert Montgomery and Helen Hayes. Margaret appeared in a few small films until 1935 when she returned to Broadway in *The Farmer Takes a Wife* with Henry Fonda and Margaret Sullavan. As usual, she was a small-town woman with a stiff collar and a sharp tongue. She returned to Hollywood for the film adaptation and remained in the city for ten years before returning to Broadway in 1944. She fit easily into 1930s Hollywood, an era in which stock character performers were in high demand to flesh out lesser productions as well as substantial ones.

In 1936, Margaret was at her busiest, appearing in five films as well as giving birth to her son, Hamilton. Many of her early roles were uncredited cameos, but they were usually among the most memorable scenes in the films. In *Saratoga* (1937), she was a homely woman on a train duped into buying beauty products from a shrewd salesman. In *These Three* (1937), she was a strict housemaid who is the only one courageous enough to discipline the house's vindictive daughter. One of her most famous roles was in the screwball classic *Nothing Sacred* (1937). In the film she portrays the owner of a drugstore, unhappy that her little city has been thrown into the spotlight after a local woman's false claim to be dying of radium poisoning has made her a national model of bravery. When leading man Fredric March (as a journalist from New York), arrives in the small town and stops in the drugstore, Margaret does not rise to greet him but remains rooted in her rocking chair with her knitting.

MARCH: *Good morning sister.* (Margaret says nothing, only scowls) *You in charge here?*

MARGARET: *Yep.*

MARCH: *I've been wandering through your fascinating metropolis for an hour. May I sit down here?*

MARGARET: *Nope.*

MARCH: *I guess you misunderstood me.*

MARGARET: *Nope.*

She does not say more than monosyllables until she gives him her harsh opinion of New York newspapermen and their tendency to disturb the peace of her small town. After her spiel, March sarcastically asks:

MARCH: *What do I owe you?*

MARGARET: *Well, you've tookin' up my time.* [9]

March then hands her a coin and she accepts it, and returns to rocking in her chair with her knitting.

The essence of this character was repeated in most of Margaret's subsequent roles. She became one of Hollywood's most oft-used character actresses whenever a New England spinster, schoolmarm, or Christian Ladies League type was needed.

In 1938, after Margaret's place in Hollywood was secure, she and her husband divorced, leaving her to raise her toddler son alone. "It simply didn't work out," Margaret explained when asked about her marriage. "But we separated on good terms and didn't just hang on. I think that kind of marriage can hurt a growing child...children are so observant." [10] To ensure she would always have enough time to spend with her son, Margaret went through her career without ever signing contracts. Thus, her income never rose above $1,000 a week. Her reasons for failing to sign a contract were twofold: she feared it would imprison her in minuscule roles of the same type. "Got those kinds of parts anyway," [11] Margaret sighed in a 1980s interview. Though she was not under contract to any one studio, the majority of her roles were for M-G-M.

M-G-M gave Margaret roles in two of its most popular pictures of 1939: *The Wizard of Oz* and *Babes in Arms*. In the latter film, a classic Mickey Rooney-Judy Garland backstage musical, Margaret is a member of the Board of Education on a mission to send the children of travelling vaudevillians to a state boarding school. The villainous role was only training for the Wicked Witch of the West. Originally, M-G-M planned to make the Witch a glamorous one like the Wicked Queen in *Snow White and the Seven Dwarves* (1937). However, the writers decided to be more true to the book. L. Frank Baum's book describes the Witch as even homelier than Margaret was made up to be in the film: "She had but one eye, yet that was as powerful as a telescope." [12] Despite the uncomfortable make-up needed for the part, Margaret was enthusiastic to be given not one but two parts in the adaptation of her favorite book. Margaret found Miss Gulch to be more darkly comical than villainous, explaining that she was "funny in her audacity and in her feeling of being appalled at the simplest things."[13] She had more fun playing the Witch, for Miss Gulch was "like a hundred other parts I'd done."[14] Margaret preferred the Witch because, according to the actress, the Witch "enjoyed every minute of what she was doing."[15] However, Margaret feared that the Witch would be too frightening for young audiences and alienate her from the children of whom she was so fond. This was true to a certain extent, but, the fright she induced in children was one born from excitement, much like the enjoyable fear youngsters experience while trick or treating on Halloween.

Though Margaret's role in the film was an important one, she was not treated importantly on the set. Her dressing room was so dingy and barren that she would often use co-star Billie Burke's dressing room to eat lunch in if Burke was absent. Burke, who filled the part of Glinda the Good Witch and who was the widow of the legendary producer Florenz Ziegfeld, had a plush dressing room in hues of pink and blue. When Burke injured her ankle during rehearsal, she was rushed away in an ambulance and was mentioned in the newspaper the following day. Margaret suffered much more severe injuries during filming, but she received no such sympathy, perhaps due to her lower star status. When filming her Munchkinland sequence where she appears and disappears in a cloud of smoke, Margaret's hands and face were badly burnt. She recovered at home with an iron constitution, refusing to sue the studio "for the very simple reason that I wanted to work again."[16] When she did return, she refused to perform in another risky the sequence in which she spells out "Surrender Dorothy" while riding on a smoke spewing broomstick. "I have a little boy and I'm his sole support,"[17] she explained.

The perils Margaret experienced while being the Wicked Witch were well worth it when considering the fame it brought her. However, it did cement her as a witch forever in audiences' memories. "That's downgrading me,"[18] Margaret said in 1977. She refused to reprise the role of the Wicked Witch in 1973, though it would have earned her a hefty sum. "I just don't want to spoil the magic. Little children's minds can't cope with seeing a mean witch alive again,"[19] Margaret explained.

The Wicked Witch marked the apex of Margaret's career, but she still had many juicy roles following it that are too often forgotten. In the classic W.C. Fields and Mae West comedy *My Little Chickadee* (1940), Margaret is excellent as a touchy townswoman intent on keeping Mae West out of the community. She stepped out of her harridan type roles in 1948 in Frank Capra's political comedy-drama *State of the Union* (1948). As Norah the maid, she displays her comedic talents when she develops an obvious crush on Van Johnson. Each time she enters a room, she grins and bats her eyelashes as if she were a young girl. The 1940s also saw Margaret return to her training as an educator. She served on the Beverly Hills Board of Education from 1948 to 1951 and taught Sunday school.

As settled as Margaret was in Hollywood, she ventured to Broadway twice in the 1940s. First, she appeared in *Outrageous Fortune* (1944) and second in *The Men We Marry* (1948). She relocated to Gramercy Park in New York in the early 1950s and appeared in many Broadway shows during this decade and into the 1960s, including a revival of *Our Town* in 1969 and tours of *Show Boat* and *Oklahoma*. Because of her new location in New York, she also took the ready opportunities the East Coast presented in television and radio. She was the voice behind Emily Tipp on cartoon commercials for Tip-Top bread and made a number of guest appearances on weekly programs. She came as close as ever to returning to her role as the Wicked Witch when she played Morticia Addams' mother on *The Addams Family*. In radio, she had a recurring role on *The Couple Next Door* and the soap opera *The Secret Storm*, in which she was the housekeeper, Katie. In 1959, Margaret used her years of experience playing servants and housekeepers to stage her own one-woman show entitled *Ham's Hash*. [20] Like the working-class characters she portrayed in her show and on screen, Margaret lived an unpretentious life. Rather than take a taxi or private train car to visit her sister in New Jersey, she took the bus. [21]

Margaret did not fade into obscurity even as the era of the Vietnam War and gratuitous entertainment came into vogue. New generations of young people came to know and love her as the yearly television broadcast of *The Wizard of Oz* became one of childhood's rites of passage. However, Margaret found a new screen image for herself as Cora, the homespun storekeeper, on Maxwell House commercials from 1974-1979. Her agent, Mike Thomas, noted that "She drinks loads of coffee...she never stops. You just can't catch up with her. She's always on her broom." [22] The tireless Margaret also spent her time volunteering at government hospitals cheering up Vietnam veterans or speaking for the Friends of Animals. She was active in the campaign against the tuna industry for needlessly murdering porpoises caught in nets meant for tuna. "Everyone one on earth — man, woman, and plant — must have an opportunity to enjoy our planet," [23] she declared. Margaret's modern thinking concerning animal rights proved her to be anything but the antiquated woman she often portrayed in film.

Margaret's activities slowed in the 1980s as her age finally began to show. "I've lost four inches in height...from slipped discs. Maybe I'm melting,"[24] she joked. In 1983, Margaret made her first public appearance in over two years to present an award to Mildred Natwick at the National Film Society ceremony. Though the honorees that night included such luminaries as James Cagney and Leonard Bernstein, Margaret received the most impressive ovation when she stepped on the stage. "I thought I had an award,"[25] she laughed in surprise. After the applause subsided, Margaret revealed the reason for her lack of public appearances in the past two years: she was losing her memory.

As her health continued to fail in the next two years, Margaret still retained her wit. She quipped to her agent, "I hope that when I die, someone has the presence of mind to say 'ding dong the witch is really dead'."[26] When she did pass away in her sleep in 1985, there were no feelings but ones of sorrow for the death of a woman who was anything but a witch.

It is a testament to the talent of Margaret Hamilton that, despite the fact she appeared on the screen for less than ten minutes in *The Wizard of Oz*, she is imprinted on the memories of all the generations of children who have seen the film. The majority of her roles required less than ten minutes of screen time; some were mere walk-on parts. Yet, when her body of work is taken collectively, her parts seem not at all insignificant. Whether she was a severe townswoman, cranky maid, or prim school teacher she, television and radio writer Cynthia Lowry wrote, played "these unsavory creatures with a twinkle of humor."[27] This twinkle of humor even shone through the green mask and pointy chin of the Wicked Witch. Though Glinda the Good Witch stated that only bad witches are ugly, Margaret Hamilton was indeed a good witch despite her lack of beauty.

FILMOGRAPHY

1974	*Journey Back to Oz*	Aunt Em *(voice)*
1971	*The Anderson Tapes*	Miss Kaler
1970	*Brewster McCloud*	Daphne Heap
1969	*Angel in My Pocket*	Rhoda
1967	*Rosie!*	Mae
1966	*The Daydreamer*	Mrs. Klopplebobbler
1962	*Paradise Alley*	Mrs. Nicholson
1962	*The Good Years*	
1951	*People Will Talk*	Miss Sarah Pickett–Housekeeper *(uncredited)*

1951	*Comin' Round the Mountain*	Aunt Huddy
1950	*Riding High*	Edna
1950	*Wabash Avenue*	Tillie Hutch
1950	*The Great Plane Robbery*	Mrs. Judd
1949	*The Beautiful Blonde from Bashful Bend*	Mrs. Elvira O'Toole *(uncredited)*
1949	*The Red Pony*	Teacher
1949	*The Sun Comes Up*	Mrs. Golightly
1948	*Bungalow 13*	Mrs. Theresa Appleby
1948	*Texas, Brooklyn & Heaven*	Ruby Cheever
1948	*State of the Union*	Norah
1948	*Reaching from Heaven*	Sophia Manley aka Sophie
1947	*Driftwood*	Essie Keenan
1947	*Pet Peeves (short)*	
1947	*Dishonored Lady*	Mrs. Geiger
1947	*The Sin of Harold Diddlebock*	Flora
1946	*Faithful in My Fashion*	Miss Applegate
1946	*Janie Gets Married*	Mrs. Angles
1945	*George White's Scandals*	Clarabelle Evans
1944	*Guest in the House*	Hilda, the Maid
1943	*Johnny Come Lately*	Myrtle Ferguson
1943	*The Ox-Bow Incident*	Mrs. Larch *(uncredited)*
1943	*City Without Men*	Dora
1942	*The Affairs of Martha*	Guinevere
1942	*Meet the Stewarts*	Willametta
1942	*Twin Beds*	Norah
1941	*The Gay Vagabond*	Agatha Badger
1941	*Play Girl*	Josie
1940	*The Invisible Woman*	Mrs. Jackson
1940	*I'm Nobody's Sweetheart Now*	Mrs. Thriffie
1940	*The Villain Still Pursued Her*	Mrs. Wilson
1940	*My Little Chickadee*	Mrs. Gideon
1939	*Main Street Lawyer*	Lucy, Boggs' Housekeeper
1939	*Babes in Arms*	Martha Steele
1939	*The Angels Wash Their Faces*	Miss Hannaberry
1939	*The Wizard of Oz*	Miss Gulch / The Wicked Witch of the West
1938	*Stablemates*	Beulah Flanders
1938	*Breaking the Ice*	Mrs. Small
1938	*Four's a Crowd*	Amy, Dillingwell's Housekeeper

1938 *Mother Carey's Chickens* .... Mrs. Pauline Fuller
1938 *A Slight Case of Murder*.. Mrs. Cagle
1938 *The Adventures of Tom Sawyer*.................................. Mrs. Harper
1937 *Nothing Sacred*... Drugstore Lady
1937 *I'll Take Romance* .... Margot
1937 *Saratoga*...Maizie *(uncredited)*
1937 *Mountain Justice* .... Phoebe Lamb
1937 *The Good Old Soak*... Minnie
1937 *When's Your Birthday?* .... Mossy–the Maid
1937 *You Only Live Once*... Hester
1936 *Laughing at Trouble* .... Lizzie Beadle
1936 *The Witness Chair*...............Miss Grace Franklin, the Bookkeeper
1936 *The Moon's Our Home*... Mitty Simpson
1936 *These Three*.. Agatha
1936 *Chatterbox*...Emily 'Tippie' Tipton
1935 *Way Down East* ....Martha Perkins
1935 *The Farmer Takes a Wife*... Lucy Gurget
1934 *Broadway Bill* .... Edna
1934 *By Your Leave* .... Whiffen
1934 *There's Always Tomorrow*.. Ella
1934 *Hat, Coat, and Glove*...................................... Madame Du Barry
1933 *Another Language* ....Helen Hallam

"OH DEAR!"
EDWARD EVERETT HORTON

EDWARD EVERETT HORTON CIRCA 1938. COURTESY OF JERRY MURBACH.

"Oh dear!"

If ever an actor has been associated with an oft-spoken line, it is Edward Everett Horton. Viewers of classic film are doubtlessly familiar with the veteran character actor whose performances linger in their minds long after those of the leading players have faded. Edward is among the most comical supporting players from the 1930s and 1940s, even more than the bemused Frank Morgan or the deadpan Roland Young. He is most remembered for his appearances in three of Fred Astaire and Ginger Rogers' best films, in which he provided comic relief in his inimitable way. Edward's obituary in 1970 adequately described him: "…he was virtually an acting technique. A spindly six-footer with an expression of genteel timidity, his trademarks were an air of fluttery anxiety in the face of crisis and his sly, mischievous grin…he played almost any role that called for a display of confusion, panic, or disintegration in the face of adversity." [1] To illustrate his characters' impending panic, he created an extended version of the double-take. He would smile and nod agreeably after an event occurred before allowing his face to suddenly fall into a grim and worried expression when realization of his predicament hit. Judging from the nervous wrecks he portrayed on screen, one would be surprised to learn that the actor was actually a contented and calm man at peace with his lot in life. In the prime of his career, he declared: "I have my own little kingdom. I do the scavenger parts no one else wants and get well paid for it." [2]

Edward Everett Horton was born in Brooklyn, New York on March 18, 1886. He inherited a love of the written word from his father, Edward Everett Sr., who worked as a compositor for the *New York Times*. Edward later said, "My father was a hero worshipper and named all his children after famous men…he was named for Edward Everett, the great orator who was an ambassador to England." [3] Edward's parents brought him and his siblings to the theater often and saw to it that their children had no shortage of life experience. Edward explained: "I was the oldest son and my father always wanted me to see interesting events." [4] These events included Edward witnessing the unveiling of Grant's tomb when he was three years old and cheering for Admiral Dewey and Theodore Roosevelt during a parade after the Spanish American War. Perhaps because of his exposure to excitement, Edward was a restless student despite his inner love of learning. He was asked to leave Oberlin College in Ohio after he climbed to the top of the school tower and threw a dummy from it, making it appear as if he himself had jumped. The school administrators found his boyish prank without comic value. Edward transferred to Columbia University, where he said he "had the idea of becoming a professor." However, after some friends convinced him to audition for the campus play, he declared: "That did it!...I had nothing — no looks, no voice, no clothes. All I had was this burning desire to be an actor." [5]

With a new career path clear in his mind, Edward found a job as a walk-on in a Gilbert and Sullivan stock troupe on Staten Island. He worked his way up to Broadway by 1910 when he appeared in his first success, *The Mikado*. He acted in one more, less popular, show called *Elevating a Husband* before he found that Broadway did not offer him steady enough employment. He decided to take up with a variety of traveling stock companies, one of which was managed by Thomas Wilkes in California. It was Wilkes who first cast Edward in the "nervous Nelly" type of character in the plays *Clarence* and *The Nervous Wreck*. Edward would feel affection for stock companies and theater folk for the rest of his life and often stated he preferred the stage to the screen. As he built a name for himself, Edward faced the problem of just *what* to call himself. He began as Eddie Horton, but decided to use his nineteen-letter full name after he saw a marquis at a Los Angeles theater reading: Eddie Horton at the Organ. His decision was solidified after he, a man who did not even own an automobile, opened his door to find a traffic policeman on his doorstep with a ticket for speeding. Nothing Edward could say would convince the policeman he had the wrong Ed Horton. According to a newspaper article from 1934, "he decided finally there was slight risk of mistaken identity if he used his complete cognomen." [6]

It was in California with Wilkes's stock company that Edward decided to try the movies. At the age of thirty-six in 1922, he appeared in his first film, *Too Much Business*. He received a more substantial part as Clara Bow's uncle in *Helen's Babies* (1924) but was back to a smaller role in a subsequent sophisticated M-G-M film *La Boheme* (1926). He starred in numerous short films, some of which were produced by legendary comedian Harold Lloyd. Edward's early career shows that he had not yet developed the Horton persona audiences know today. He appeared in a variety of different parts, including that of the romantic lead in the short film *Taxi! Taxi!* (1927) and the role of a World War I veteran wooing a society girl in *The Whole Town's Talking* (1926). No matter what character he portrayed on screen, he gained favor with the public. He was quickly making more money than he ever thought possible. Still, he was unhappy with the silent film medium and sighed: "How I longed to talk!" [7] In 1926, he found an outlet for his love of the stage. He became manager of the Majestic Theater and the Hollywood Playhouse.

At the height of the silent era when decadent lifestyle was a rite of passage for silent stars, Edward decided to buy a plot of land in Encino and
build an estate. With his brother and mother, he bought four acres in an
area that was "little more than cow pastures and walnut groves." [8] Hedda
Hopper wrote that "the original four acres were owned by a bootlegger
who was going to jail the next day, so the Hortons got them for $7,500."
[9] As the real estate values soared in the San Fernando Valley, Edward
expanded his property until it reached manorial status. The estate included
a 28x34 music room, banquet room, and private tennis court. His home
became the site of elaborate dinner parties where the table would cover
the entire length of the dining room, an eight-piece orchestra would
play on the balcony, and guests would spend the night and breakfast
with champagne. Edward dubbed his estate "Belly Acres." He began to
stock its interior with precious antiques as his income continued to rise.
"You can't pass up wonderful things just because you have no place to
put them," [10] he stated. When not entertaining, he spent afternoons in
the garden reading with his English sheepdogs and collies lying at his
feet. According to a 1931 article, Edward's "pet diversion is the study of
Baconian Theory, about which he has many ideas, and he is the owner of a
library of relevant volumes. His ranch house is well stocked with antiques,
mostly early American pieces, and he owns rugs, paintings, and literary
treasures of great value." [11]

Edward had no trouble funding his expensive hobbies. He was among
the most in demand supporting players of the 1930s. "The phone never
stopped ringing," [12] he stated. The coming of talkies only fueled his success as most of his comedy came from his repartee with co-stars. He was
earning up to $7,000 a week at the height of his popularity. By the 1930s,
he had honed his screen character and had found his niche in intelligent
drawing room comedies.

"I found my métier by examining the traits of ten of my nearest friends,"
Edward explained. "One of them was a pill swallower…another man
was lazy…still another suffered from timidity…and was deadly afraid
of women…It struck me that a combination of several of these types,
slightly exaggerated and broadened, would make an excellent comedy
screen personality." [13]

Edward's status allowed him to appear in virtually all high caliber
pictures. He was Kay Francis' luckless suitor in *Trouble in Paradise* (1932)
and a fussy reporter in *The Front Page* (1931). He played many different
types of parts — counts, judges, a marquis, the Mad Hatter, and a butler
impersonating his master, to name a few. Although he had not graduated

from Columbia or pursued his idea of becoming a professor, he convincingly played one in the Katharine Hepburn film *Holiday* (1938) and in the Frank Capra classic *Lost Horizon* (1937). No matter if he was a count or a professor, each character he portrayed had the Edward Everett Horton personality. In a 1951 interview, Edward admitted he was "conceited, long-winded, and apt to be too fond of his own humor." Yet, the reason people found him so funny was because, as he said: "I remind them of someone they know. Somebody who probably annoys them considerably, but for whom they really have an affection — a husband, for instance." [14] In grade A pictures or mediocre programmers, Edward was invariably singled out as the high point of each film. In the obscure Cary Grant film *Ladies Should Listen* (1934), Rob Wagner of *Script* magazine wrote: "Edward Everett Horton clicks in every scene. Did you ever stop to think that Eddie Horton is one of the few actors who is exactly the same in both private life and on screen — amusing and charming?" [15] Ginger Rogers agreed with this statement and wrote glowingly in her memoir: "I am always asked if someone is just as he or she seems to be in the movies. In this case, Horton was exactly the same as he appeared on screen. He loved comedy and behaved in a comical manner all the time...we couldn't take our eyes off him, for fear of missing the topper to whatever he was doing." [16]

Edward's show-stopping comedy is most remembered because of three of his best films, which incidentally star Ginger Rogers: *The Gay Divorcee* (1934), *Top Hat* (1935), and *Shall We Dance?* (1937). Arguably, he outshines the leading players, Rogers and Fred Astaire, in the scenes he shares with them.

In each Astaire-Rogers film, he portrays a nervous, weak-willed man who is gullible and argumentative at the same time. Edward's best scenes are with British character actor Eric Blore. If ever there was an unsung comedy duo, it is Horton and Blore. Film historian Eve Golden likens their onscreen dynamic to that of a "bickering couple." [17] The following exchange from *The Gay Divorcee*, in which Blore is a waiter and Edward is Ginger Rogers' lawyer, is an example of their comic banter:

WAITER: *Pardon, you, uh, rang sir?*

EDWARD: *Who me? Well, my dear fellow, what is there to ring with?*

WAITER: *Pardon sir, that's just a figure of speech.*

EDWARD: *Oh, oh. Uh, well bring me a, let me have a...there, there. You see? Your figure of speech has made me forget entirely what I wanted!* [18]

Edward continued to delight audiences in the 1940s, playing a hapless heavenly messenger in *Here Comes Mr. Jordan* (1941), a worried hus-

EDWARD EVERETT HORTON, JOSEPHINE HULL, AND JEAN ADAIR IN *ARSENIC AND OLD LACE* **(1944).** COURTESY OF JERRY MURBACH.

band in *The Gang's All Here* (1943), and a frazzled asylum director in the madcap comedy *Arsenic and Old Lace* (1944). Although the 1940s started off strong for Edward, his film career was all but over by decade's end. The high-society comedies so popular in the 1930s had waned in favor of more relatable films with domestic settings to match the growing baby boom following the end of World War II. In 1947, Edward co-starred in two ill-fated films. The first was a disappointing follow-up to *Here Comes Mr. Jordan* called *Down to Earth* (1947) and the second was a Lucille Ball comedy about a man peddling a baldness cure called *Her Husband's Affairs* (1947). Edward recalled: "After I finished it [the film], the phone didn't ring." [19]

Edward was undaunted by his fizzling screen career. He took the opportunity to return to the place he loved most: the stage. The play that would support him until the end of his life was *Springtime for Henry*, a one-set, four-character play by Ben Levy that was a "tale of a reformed gay blade and the problems of mismatched lovers." [20] Edward had first played in the show in 1932 after he had met Levy and decided to see if the play could pay the lease on the ailing Hollywood Playhouse he managed. "There were six weeks left on the lease...Henry paid all the bills!" [21] For the next four decades, Henry Dewlip was Edward's character. He would play the role more than 1500 times in his lifetime. As Edward aged, the script was altered to accommodate him. Edward started in 1963: "You're never too old for the part of Henry...also, I can't imagine anyone else playing the part." [22] When Edward brought the part to Broadway for the first time in 1951, he expressed some opening night jitters. He told the *New York Times*, "If they [critics] say I'm not funny, I shan't be too concerned...but if they say I'm too old for the part, that'll really hurt." [23] Edward need not have worried; he was a hit. Despite his absence from the screen for four years, audiences had not forgotten him. "People may come out of curiosity about me," he claimed. "But they stay out of contentment with the play." [24]

Aside from theater Edward also became known on the small screen. He made memorable guest appearances on *I Love Lucy* and *Batman* and narrated the "Fractured Fairy Tales" segments of the children's program *Rocky and His Friends*. He only made a brief return to the big screen for a cameo in *It's Mad, Mad, Mad, Mad World* (1963) and a supporting part as a magazine editor in *Sex and the Single Girl* (1964).

Edward settled into his senior years with dignity. Although a lifelong bachelor, he was never without friends. He remained a closeted homosexual throughout his life, carrying on a discreet partnership with actor Gavin Gordon for several years. This side of Edward's life has remained obscure and he left virtually no record of his relationship with Gordon. He never lived alone: his sister and two brothers lived with him in their later years and his mother lived with him until her death at age 101. Longevity seemed to run in the Horton family. Edward remained active until the end of his life. He played tennis and walked a mile to the post office each morning. He stated: "I take care of myself. I'm anxious to keep working. I love work!" [25]

The seemingly ageless actor succumbed to cancer and died at his home in 1970. Edward was posthumously honored when the city of Los Angeles renamed a portion of the dead end street on which he had lived "Edward Everett Horton Lane." Today, in the words of the *New York Times*, Edward's "persimmon face, crowbeak nose, and scissor lips" [26] are still sure to bring a smile to the faces of even the most cynical audiences. Like Harold Lloyd and Buster Keaton before him, he brought an endearing likeability to his bumbling and timid characters. Yet, Edward Everett Horton managed to create his own special brand of befuddled humor no one could duplicate.

FILMOGRAPHY

1971	*Cold Turkey*	Hiram C. Grayson
1969	*2000 Years Later*	Evermore
1967	*The Perils of Pauline*	Caspar Coleman
1964	*Sex and the Single Girl*	The Chief
1963	*It's a Mad Mad Mad Mad World*	Mr. Dinckler
1963	*One Got Fat (short)*	Narrator *(voice)*
1961	*Pocketful of Miracles*	Hudgins
1957	*The Story of Mankind*	Sir Walter Raleigh
1947	*Her Husband's Affairs*	J.B. Cruikshank
1947	*Down to Earth*	Messenger 7013
1947	*The Ghost Goes Wild*	Eric *(Monte's butler)*
1946	*Earl Carroll Sketchbook*	Dr. Milo Edwards
1946	*Faithful in My Fashion*	Hiram Dilworthy
1946	*Cinderella Jones*	Keating
1945	*Lady on a Train*	Mr. Haskell
1945	*Steppin' in Society*	Judge Avery Webster
1944	*The Town Went Wild*	Everett Conway
1944	*Brazil*	Everett St. John Everett
1944	*San Diego I Love You*	Philip McCooley
1944	*Arsenic and Old Lace*	Mr. Witherspoon
1944	*Summer Storm*	Count 'Piggy' Volsky
1944	*Her Primitive Man*	Orrin
1943	*The Gang's All Here*	Peyton Potter
1943	*Thank Your Lucky Stars*	Farnsworth
1943	*Forever and a Day*	Sir Anthony Trimble-Pomfret
1942	*Springtime in the Rockies*	McTavish
1942	*I Married an Angel*	Peter
1942	*The Magnificent Dope*	Horace Hunter
1941	*The Body Disappears*	Prof. Reginald X. Shotesbury
1941	*Weekend for Three*	Fred Stonebraker
1941	*Here Comes Mr. Jordan*	Messenger 7013
1941	*Bachelor Daddy*	Joseph Smith

1941	*Sunny*...Henry Bates
1941	*Ziegfeld Girl* .... Noble Sage
1941	*You're the One*.. Death Valley Joe Frink
1939	*That's Right–You're Wrong* .... Tom Village, a Screenwriter
1939	*The Amazing Mr. Forrest*... Treadwell
1939	*Paris Honeymoon*... Ernest Figg
1938	*Little Tough Guys in Society*..Oliver
1938	*Holiday* .... Professor Nick Potter
1938	*College Swing*...Hubert Dash
1938	*Bluebeard's Eighth Wife*......................The Marquis De Loiselle
1937	*Hitting a New High*... Lucius B. Blynn
1937	*The Great Garrick*.. Tubby
1937	*The Perfect Specimen* .... Mr. Grattan
1937	*Angel*... Graham
1937	*Danger: Love at Work*.................................... Howard Rogers
1937	*Wild Money* .... P.E. Dodd
1937	*Shall We Dance*...Jeffrey Baird
1937	*Oh, Doctor*.................................... Edward J. Billop
1937	*The King and the Chorus Girl* .... Count Humbert Evel Bruger
1937	*Lost Horizon* .... Lovett
1936	*Let's Make a Million* ....Harrison Gentry
1936	*The Man in the Mirror* ....Jeremy Dilke
1936	*Hearts Divided*.....................................Senator John Hathaway
1936	*Nobody's Fool* ....Will Wright
1936	*The Singing Kid*..................................... Davenport Rogers
1936	*Her Master's Voice*... Ned Farrar
1935	*Your Uncle Dudley*.....................................Dudley Dixon
1935	*His Night Out* .... Homer B. Bitts
1935	*The Private Secretary* .... Rev. Robert Spalding
1935	*Little Big Shot*.. Mortimer Thompson
1935	*Top Hat* .... Horace Hardwick
1935	*Going Highbrow* .... Augie Winterspoon
1935	*In Caliente* .... Harold Brandon
1935	*$10 Raise* .... Hubert T. Wilkins
1935	*The Devil Is a Woman*......................Gov. Don Paquito 'Paquitito'
1935	*The Night Is Young*...Baron Szereny
1935	*Biography of a Bachelor Girl*......................Leander 'Bunny' Nolan
1934	*The Gay Divorcee*.......................................Egbert 'Pinky' Fitzgerald
1934	*The Merry Widow* ....Ambassador Popoff
1934	*Ladies Should Listen*.. Paul Vernet

1934	*Kiss and Make-Up*	Marcel Caron
1934	*The Woman in Command*	Sebastian Marvello
1934	*Smarty*	Vernon Thorpe
1934	*Sing and Like It*	Adam Frink–Producer
1934	*Uncertain Lady*	Elliot Crane
1934	*Success at Any Price*	Harry Fisher
1934	*The Poor Rich*	Albert Stuyvesant Spottiswood
1934	*All the King's Horses*	Count Josef 'Peppi' von Schlapstaat
1934	*Easy to Love*	Eric Schulte
1933	*Design for Living*	Max Plunkett
1933	*Alice in Wonderland*	Mad Hatter
1933	*The Way to Love*	Prof. Gaston Bibi
1933	*It's a Boy*	Dudley Leake
1933	*Professional Sweetheart*	Reporter *(uncredited)*
1933	*A Bedtime Story*	Victor Dubois
1932	*Trouble in Paradise*	François Filiba
1932	*Roar of the Dragon*	Busby
1932	*– But the Flesh Is Weak*	Sir George Kelvin
1931	*The Great Junction Hotel (short)*	The Groom
1931	*The Age for Love*	Horace Keats
1931	*Smart Woman*	Billy Ross
1931	*Six Cylinder Love*	Monty Winston
1931	*The Front Page*	Roy V. Bensinger
1931	*Lonely Wives*	Richard 'Dickie' Smith / Felix, the Great Zero
1930	*Reaching for the Moon*	Roger, the Valet
1930	*Kiss Me Again*	René
1930	*Once a Gentleman*	Oliver
1930	*Holiday*	Nick Potter
1930	*Wide Open*	Simon Haldane
1930	*Take the Heir*	Smithers
1929	*The Aviator*	Robert Street
1929	*Good Medicine (short)*	
1929	*The Sap*	The Sap
1929	*Prince Gabby (short)*	
1929	*The Hottentot*	Sam Harrington
1929	*Trusting Wives (short)*	
1929	*The Right Bed (short)*	
1929	*/I Sonny Boy*	Crandall Thorpe
1929	*Ask Dad (short)*	Dad
1929	*The Eligible Mr. Bangs (short)*	Mr. Bangs

1928   *Call Again (short)* ....
1928   *Vacation Waves (short)* .... Eddie Davis
1928   *The Terror* ....Ferdinand Fane
1928   *Lights of New York* .... Extra *(uncredited)*
1928   *Scrambled Weddings (short)* ....
1928   *I Horse Shy (short)* ....
1928   *Miss Information (short)* ....
1928   *Behind the Counter (short)* ....
1928   *Dad's Choice (short)* .... Eddie
1927   *Find the King (short)* ....
1927   *No Publicity (short)* ....
1927   *Taxi! Taxi!* .... Peter Whitby
1926   *The Whole Town's Talking* .... Chester Binney
1926   *Poker Faces* ....The hero
1926   *The Nutcracker (short)* .... Horatio Slipaway
1926   *La bohème* .... Colline
1925   *The Business of Love* ....
1925   *Marry Me* .... John Smith #2
1925   *Beggar on Horseback* .... Neil McRae
1924   *Helen's Babies* ....Uncle Harry
1924   *The Man Who Fights Alone* .... Bob Alten
1924   *Try and Get It* .... Glenn Collins *(as Edward Horton)*
1924   *Flapper Wives* .... Vincent Platt *(as Edward Horton)*
1923   *To the Ladies* .... Leonard Beebe *(as Edward Horton)*
1923   *The Vow of Vengeance* ....
1923   *Ruggles of Red Gap* .... Ruggles *(as Edward Horton)*
1922   *A Front Page Story* .... Rodney Marvin *(as Edward Horton)*
1922   *The Ladder Jinx* .... Arthur Barnes *(as Edward Horton)*
1922   *Too Much Business* ....John Henry Jackson *(as Edward Horton)*

THE HIGH PRIESTESS OF
THE BOURGEOISIES
PATSY KELLY

PATSY KELLY CIRCA 1937. COURTESY OF JERRY MURBACH.

With the maturing process of sound in film during the 1930s, there was a blossoming of many different genres of humor. Each genre gave performers, formerly confined to silent comedy, the chance to display their talents in their respective brand of humor. Cary Grant and Carole Lombard had an edge in screwball, Katharine Hepburn and William Powell were the forerunners in high comedy, and adult low comedy was ruled by Wallace Beery and Marie Dressler. However, after Dressler's death, there was a gaping hole left in adult low comedy, not to mention a lack of a female comedienne to represent the proletariat. The gap was filled to a great extent by one hearty and nasal voiced comedienne: Patsy Kelly. In 1935, journalist Mollie Merrick described Patsy as "the natural guy who shoves her hat to the back of her head and kicks off her high heeled shoes when everyone else is putting on another layer of powder and rouging the lips for the tenth time." [1] Patsy, a plain Irish tomboy, began in Hal Roach slapstick shorts and moved into adult low comedies and screwball. Much of her work has not stood the test of time, but many of her films have become classics of their genre. No matter what the quality of any given film in Pasty's repertoire, her work provides a delightful view into the era when Depression-stricken audiences wanted nothing more than a good chuckle. Patsy's wisecracking common sense, incredulous frown, arched brow, and lack of glamour gave her an unpretentiousness on screen that made her, as Mollie Merrick put it, "the High Priestess of the Bourgeoisies." [2]

Patsy Kelly was born on January 2, 1910 under the name Sarah Veronica Rose. Raised in Brooklyn and Manhattan by her Irish immigrant parents (her father worked as a policeman in Manhattan), Patsy grew up playing on the streets with neighborhood boys. Somehow, she gained the nickname "Patsy" and her Christian name was all but forgotten. "I guess I was kind of a tomboy. In grade school I played baseball on the boys' team," [3] Patsy recalled years later. Patsy's preoccupation with playing outdoors as well as her penchant for catching rides on the backs of fire engines prompted one fire chief to advise Mrs. Kelly to keep her daughter inside. The best way to keep Patsy from mischief, in Mrs. Kelly's opinion, was to send her to dancing school.

"When I was six, they gave me dancing lessons to keep me off the streets of New York. I always wanted to be a fireman — and I still do," [4] Patsy sighed in 1967. Though Mr. Kelly favored having Patsy learn Irish jigs, she showed a talent for tap dancing after a few classes at Jack Blue's school. Among her classmates was future tap queen Ruby Keeler. Even with such competition, Patsy was a star pupil and, by age twelve, was teaching the younger pupils their dance steps. Patsy's brother joined her in learning dance at the urging of popular vaudevillian Frank Fay. Fay further advised Patsy and her brother to concoct a vaudeville act. After he sat in on their act, he decided he wanted only Patsy to join him in his act.

Fay employed Patsy to act as a stooge as well as a dancer. Fay and Patsy's act, which was included in the 1927 show *Harry Delmar's Revels,* was a hit both at the Palace and on a national tour. "I started at the top and worked my way down," Patsy later reflected on her stellar beginning in show business. Her promising start came on hard terms, though. "Fay was a great wit...but he could be cruel," [5] Patsy explained. Fay grew overly fond of his sixteen-year-old protégée and once asked her to marry him. When Patsy declined, she found that she was out of work two weeks later. Despite this setback, Patsy's career did not stall. Her old friend, Ruby Keeler, brought her to the attention of the prestigious Broadway producer Charles Dillingham. Dillingham hired her to appear in *Three Cheers,* starring Will Rogers. The show was a hit, partly due to Patsy's comical duet with Andrew Tombes called "Because You're Beautiful." Her success continued in 1929 when she won another musical comedy part in *Earl Carroll's Sketch Book* and later in *Earl Carroll's Vanities.* In 1931, she further proved her stage presence when she co-starred with the legendary Al Jolson in *Wonder Bar,* "the theatrical event of the year." [6]

It was during the run of the Jolson show that Vitaphone approached Patsy with the offer to co-star in the comedy short *The Grand Dame* (1931). Patsy accepted the offer but was not immediately converted to the movies. "I always thought of New York as my home," [7] Patsy said. Working in pictures revealed a dormant shyness she did not often show. In 1937, Ruth White explained that "despite her happy-go-lucky attitude, Patsy is a shy person...she suffered...because there was no audience to tell her she was doing all right." [8] New York audiences continued to assure her she was doing well as she was well received in her first starring role in *Flying Colors,* co-starring Clifton Webb and Buddy and Vilma Ebsen. Patsy's second brush with Hollywood came during the run of this show when producer Hal Roach offered her a contract to costar in a series of short films with Thelma Todd. Patsy was hesitant, but she accepted. She, with her frizzy black hair, pug nose, weak chin and "sassy growl and shameless loud mouth shenanigans," [9] was not quite the stereotypical Hollywood star.

Though dubious, it would be ten years before Patsy would return to New York. Her first short, *Beauty and the Bus* (1933), had her playing "a clumsy cluck," [10] a role she would repeat in most of her shorts for Roach.

"When I first arrived at Roach, I thought they had me mixed up with Toto the clown…when I had to hang by my teeth from an airplane and have an elephant on my stomach, I drew the line. 'Get a stunt girl,' I said," [11] Patsy later recalled. After Patsy settled into Roach Studios, she found that she enjoyed working in pictures. She quickly became a favorite among her peers, particularly Thelma Todd, with whom she co-starred in over a dozen shorts in 1933 alone. "Those were the happiest days I had in pictures," Patsy said in 1937. "I have made more money since, but the fun Thelma and I had making those silly two-reel comedies is something that comes only once in a lifetime. Thelma was better than any tonic and taught me a lot about comedy" [12] Aside from Todd, Patsy was learning skills from stars such as Zazu Pitts and Laurel and Hardy. Forty years later, she reflected that "I laughed from the time I arrived at the studio until I left at night. I was ashamed to take a paycheck." [13]

Patsy's entry into full-length films may not have come with as many laughs backstage, but her own spontaneous brand of humor brought just as many laughs to the audience. Her first part was a studio extra in Marion Davies' swan song, *Going Hollywood* (1933). She appeared in two more small roles in 1934 until she received her first substantial role as Jean Harlow's man hungry and spunky girlfriend in *The Girl from Missouri* (1934). Her homely appearance only adds to the film's comic value as she pursues every man she sees from butlers to valets to vacationing millionaires. "If you can't afford to tip 'em, you have to be polite!" [14] Patsy, as Kitty Lennihan, quips to Jean Harlow.

Patsy's ascending career was nearly destroyed when she was involved in a serious automobile accident in 1934. Her friend, Gene Malin, accidentally backed off of Venice Pier and into the ocean. Malin drowned, but Patsy miraculously survived. Four years later, she recalled the accident with a philosophical air: "I overheard a jury of grave-faced doctors nodding their heads over my supposedly unconscious body. They were giving me a maximum of ten years to live. Maybe they're right. When I heard that scientific verdict, I was plenty scared. But I pulled myself together and said, 'Kelly, there's only one way to beat this rap: don't worry — and have fun out of the remaining years'." [15] Patsy did indeed have fun in the subsequent years. She enjoyed her wealth and spent not a little of it on fine foods. Eventually, she was sent to a sanitarium to lose fifty pounds; however, the diet did not stick. "Look," she said in 1937, slapping her thighs, "I might get those down an inch or so by dieting, but what fun is there in not eating what you want to eat?" [16] Patsy spent her leisure time attending the theater, often seeing eight or ten movies a week. At other times, she spent evenings playing penny roulette on Redondo Beach rather than attending chic Hollywood parties. This did not mean she was not popular in Hollywood; it was the contrary, as proved by columnist Ruth White's observation: "Wherever you find a laughing group on a sound stage, you will find Patsy in the center of it. She's everybody's friend, as kindly to the prop boys as she is with the most famous stars." [17]

PATSY KELLY WITH MARION DAVIES IN *PAGE MISS GLORY* **(1935).** COURTESY OF JERRY MURBACH.

Patsy continued to please audiences as she churned out more shorts with Thelma Todd as well as more feature films, including *Every Night at Eight* (1935) and *Thanks a Million* (1935), in which she had a singing role. Her fruitful partnership with Todd ended in 1935 when Todd was found dead under mysterious circumstances in her garage. Though Patsy was devastated by the loss, her energy on screen gave no indication of it. In 1936, she appeared in a quick succession of films including *Private Number* and *Sing, Baby, Sing*. Among her most memorable films was 1936's *Pigskin Parade* in which she is football coach Jack Haley's tough and outspoken wife who knows more about football than he does. She played the masculine role of a prizefighter's trainer in *Kelly the Second* and the more feminine role of Walter Winchell's secretary in *Wake Up and Live* (1937). In 1938, she portrayed a frazzled maid in her first A picture, the screwball classic *Merrily We Live*. Biographer Charles Stumpf described the reason for her widespread popularity thus: "Kelly's homely but loveable mug...became a favorite with millions of moviegoers...frequently cast as a sassy maid with her cap askew, she never let up with the wisecracks and smart aleck antics."[18] Patsy played another maid with her cap askew in the final installment of Hal Roach's popular *Topper* series, *Topper Returns* (1941). Patsy was cast as a maid so often throughout her career on the stage and screen that she later joked she played maid's roles simply "because I had a maid's costume that fit. They didn't have to get me a new outfit. They lent it from one studio to another."[19]

As well-liked as Patsy was in the 1930s, the waning popularity of the screwball comedy in the 1940s slowed her career considerably. Her acting, so much a part of early talkies with its stagy, vaudevillian style, was already becoming outdated. She soon found she no longer had the funds to which she had become accustomed. "I lived very well — too well, I guess," she said in 1959. "I didn't save a dime. Oh well. I have no regrets."[20] Her lack of regret extended into her confirmed status as an unmarried woman. "I was in love once a long time ago, but he was killed in the war," Patsy laconically explained, "Besides, I'm the world's worst cook. I've always said, 'I can't do this to a man'."[21] With no husband to fall back on, Patsy persevered in her work and returned to New York to appear in stock productions of *My Sister Eileen* and *On the Town*.

In her most affluent period, Patsy had been known for her generosity; she gave money to everyone from close friends to extras to prop people at the studio. When her fortunes reversed, Patsy accepted friend Tallulah Bankhead's, generosity. In 1952, Bankhead invited her penniless friend to live with her and also secured her a guest spot on her television show, *All Star Revue*. Bankhead next booked a nightclub tour through Las Vegas and asked Patsy to accompany her. In an ironic twist, Patsy acted as Bankhead's personal maid during the tour. She continued with her new position as lady's maid into 1955 when Bankhead toured in *High Time*. Patsy apparently did not mind and did the work without complaint, so loyal was she to her friend. Because Patsy never married, there is speculation that she and Bankhead were more than friends or employer and employee. However, there is no evidence to support that they were romantically involved. [22]

After seventeen years off screen, Patsy parted ways with Bankhead and returned to Hollywood. Her comeback role was, not surprisingly, as a maid in the Doris Day comedy *Please Don't Eat the Daisies* (1959). "When you're hungry, it doesn't matter how big the part is. You just want to go back to work," [23] she told journalist Bob Thomas. Another part came the same year in *The Crowded Sky* (1959) as well as guest roles in television. She took what roles she could get; among the best known films of her later career is *Rosemary's Baby* (1968), in which she played an overweight babysitter. "I never really appreciated California. I've changed. California never looked so good to me," [24] Patsy declared.

Patsy's luck changed in 1970 when old friend Ruby Keeler helped her win the part of Pauline, the maid, in a Broadway revival of the 1925 hit *No, No Nanette*. Patsy became the star of the show, receiving standing ovations each time the curtain rose. Critic Earl Wilson wrote that "of all the stars named Kelly — and there have been Gene, Grace, Al, and Nancy — none is greater than Patsy, who, for a year and a half, has been making audiences roar as she plays a clumsy, lumpy, and rebellious maid servant." [25] Patsy nearly fainted when she won the Tony Award for Best Supporting Actress in 1971. She again found a home on Broadway when she next was cast as Debbie Reynolds' mother in a revival of *Irene*.

Despite her success in New York, Patsy returned to Hollywood for more television and film work. She became known to a new generation of filmgoers when she appeared in two Walt Disney films, *Freaky Friday* (1976) and *North Street Irregulars*(1979). In the former she was an exasperated housekeeper while in the latter she was a livid housewife seeking revenge on a crooked group of gamblers. She insisted on performing her own stunt work in the film and, while riding the back of a motorcycle, fractured three ribs and pinched a nerve in her back. It was an unceremonious end to her screen career. Her final stint in show business was a nightclub act with comedienne Jean Kean.

The seemingly indestructible Patsy's boundless energy ended after she was partially paralyzed by a stroke in 1980. The following year she succumbed to bronchial pneumonia. Unlike some of her peers from Hollywood's golden age, Patsy did not die in obscurity.

Ruth White once articulated why Patsy endured in audiences' minds to such an extent: "This jolly picture thief…makes picture work such play that not until the film is previewed do her co-stars realize she has stolen the show."[26] Patsy most reflected the bygone days of vaudeville and screwball comedy, but her playful humor and barbs appealed to filmgoers across the decades. Because she did not take herself too seriously and made her work "play," she was never too proud to portray an undignified sidekick or homely maid servant. She possessed a contagious vigor and innate perception of everyday laughter, and, through this vigor and perception, made the commonplace genuinely humorous.

FILMOGRAPHY

Year	Title	Role
1979	*The North Avenue Irregulars*	Rose
1976	*Freaky Friday*	Mrs. Schmauss
1968	*Rosemary's Baby*	Laura-Louise
1967	*C'mon, Let's Live a Little*	Mrs. Fitts
1966	*The Ghost in the Invisible Bikini*	Myrtle Forbush
1964	*The Naked Kiss*	Mac, Head Nurse
1960	*The Crowded Sky*	Gertrude Ross
1947	*Paramount Pacemaker: Babies, They're Wonderful (short)*	
1943	*Danger! Women at Work*	Terry Olsen
1943	*My Son, the Hero*	Gerty Rosenthal
1943	*Ladies' Day*	Hazel Jones
1942	*In Old California*	Helga
1942	*Sing Your Worries Away*	Bebe McGuire
1941	*Playmates*	Lulu Monahan
1941	*Broadway Limited*	Patsy
1941	*Topper Returns*	Emily–Maid
1941	*Road Show*	Jinx
1940	*Hit Parade of 1941*	Judy Abbott
1939	*The Gorilla*	Kitty–the Maid
1938	*The Cowboy and the Lady*	Katie Callahan
1938	*There Goes My Heart*	Peggy O'Brien
1938	*Merrily We Live*	Etta
1937	*Wake Up and Live*	Patsy Kane

1937	*Ever Since Eve*	Sadie Day, aka Susie Wilson
1937	*Pick a Star*	Nellie Moore
1937	*Nobody's Baby*	Kitty Reilly
1936	*Pan Handlers (short)*	
1936	*Pigskin Parade*	Bessie Winters
1936	*Sing, Baby, Sing*	Fitz
1936	*Kelly the Second*	Molly Patricia Kelly
1936	*Private Number*	Gracie
1936	*Hill-Tillies (short)*	Patsy
1936	*At Sea Ashore (short)*	Patsy Kelly
1936	*All-American Toothache (short)*	Patricia Veronica Kelly
1935	*Top Flat (short)*	Patsy Kelly
1935	*Hot Money (short)*	Miss Patsy Kelly
1935	*Thanks a Million*	Phoebe Mason
1935	*Twin Triplets (short)*	
1935	*Slightly Static (short)*	Patsy
1935	*Page Miss Glory*	Betty
1935	*Every Night at Eight*	Daphne O'Connor
1935	*The Misses Stooge (short)*	Patsy Kelly
1935	*Go Into Your Dance*	Irma 'Toledo' Knight
1935	*The Tin Man (short)*	Miss Kelly
1935	*Sing, Sister, Sing (short)*	Patsy
1935	*Treasure Blues (short)*	
1934	*Bum Voyage (short)*	Patsy
1934	*Done in Oil (short)*	Patsy Kelly aka Fifi aka Magnolia
1934	*Transatlantic Merry-Go-Round*	Patsy Clarke
1934	*Opened by Mistake (short)*	Patsy
1934	*The Party's Over*	Mabel
1934	*The Girl from Missouri*	Kitty Lennihan
1934	*One Horse Farmers (short)*	
1934	*Three Chumps Ahead (short)*	Patricia 'Patsy' Kelly
1934	*I'll Be Suing You (short)*	Miss Kelly
1934	*Maid in Hollywood (short)*	Patsy
1934	*Roamin' Vandals (short)*	
1934	*Soup and Fish (short)*	Miss Patsy Kelly
1934	*The Countess of Monte Cristo*	Mimi
1934	*Babes in the Goods (short)*	Patsy Kelly
1933	*Air Fright (short)*	Patsy
1933	*Going Hollywood*	Jill Barker
1933	*Backs to Nature (short)*	Patsy

1933 *Beauty and the Bus (short)* ....Patsy
1931 *The Grand Dame (short)* .... Peggy O'Rourke
1929 *A Single Man* .... Undetermined Role *(uncredited, unconfirmed)*

THE ECCENTRIC HARRIDAN
ELSA LANCHESTER

ELSA LANCHESTER IN *NAUGHTY MARIETTA* **(1935).**
COURTESY OF JERRY MURBACH.

"Don't be afraid of Elsa if you find her too honest and she seems bitchy. She's really, you know, very nice inside."[1]

So testified actor Charles Laughton in reference to a woman who also happened to be his wife, Elsa Lanchester. Her appearance matched his description; outwardly, her popping eyes and red hair, which in the words of critic Kevin Kelly "looks like a fright wig but isn't,"[2] concealed the witty, intellectual woman behind them. However, both mens' statements ideally reflect the Elsa audiences grew to know during the actress's over forty-year career. She could be "bitchy" in her roles as "eccentric spinsters, maiden aunts, and harridans in general,"[3] yet in her next part, she could be a wide-eyed maid, timid artist, or what became her most recognizable role, the bride in *The Bride of Frankenstein* (1935). Crone, soft-spoken matron, or monster, Elsa's characters never failed to be unique and colorful. The reason Elsa's portrayals remained fresh was because they were so varied. This was no accident; Elsa specifically selected her parts based not on their size, but their level of interest and relation to the plot. One reviewer best summarized Elsa's effect when he noted, "She can be tender and spine-chilling, too."[4]

Elsa entered the world as Elizabeth Lanchester Sullivan in Lewisham, London on October 20, 1902. Her name was already notorious before she was born, thanks to her mother. Edith Lanchester's name had become ubiquitous in London newspapers after her family committed her to a mental institution for living, unmarried, with James Sullivan, the man who would be Elsa's father. Her parents became no less surrounded by controversy when her daughter was born. They were active in the Social Democratic Federation and did not believe in any institution, marriage included. Elsa thrived in her unconventional upbringing and admitted, "I found it rather glamorous to be a bastard."[5] Elsa's taste for the spotlight, whether it was positive or negative, grew as she reached puberty. By age ten, she had the ambition to be a classical dancer. In only a year, she was already well on her way to becoming one, for she had enrolled in Isadora Duncan's Bellevue School in Paris. She gained enough skills under Duncan's tutelage to return to England as a dance instructor. At age thirteen, she landed her first teaching job. In return for her services, the school gave her food, board, and education. She stayed with this work for two years before going freelance. Elsa needed little of her training as a classical dancer for her first stage performance. She debuted behind the footlights as a snake dancer, a job Elsa thought sordid and wished to rise above.

Elsa did indeed rise in prestige, becoming an entrepreneur of sorts. She created not only a Children's Theater, but also a club called the Cave of

Harmony that she described as "a scantily decorated fire trap for which they could not obtain a liquor license." [6] As unglamorous as she made the Cave appear, it became the haunt of such luminaries as Aldous Huxley, H.G. Wells, and James Whale. Elsa's associations with artists were what led her into her various jobs as a nude model for painters, photographers, and sculptors. Perhaps her most unusual job was acting as co-respondent for men wishing to obtain divorces. Elsa cheerfully called it her first real acting experience. "I was never bored with my part in the little drama," [7] she said.

Elsa gained true dramatic experience as the 1920s progressed, proving her versatility in a variety of plays. She was cast as Larva opposite a young Claude Rains in *The Insect Play* and in *Beggar's Opera*, she sang and danced. She was most popular in the area of song as audiences relished her bawdy ditties and dances. However, the royal family was not among her fans. They walked out of the Midnight Follies at London's Metropole when she sang "Please Sell No More Drink to My Father." [8] One of Elsa's more admiring audience members was a fleshy young man named Charles Laughton. He declared he had long dreamt of meeting her after they briefly crossed paths on the set of a 1927 play, *Mr. Prohack.* [9] The shy, rotund actor and the loud, petite redhead made an odd couple, but they married and would remain so until Laughton's death.

After honeymooning in Europe, the newlyweds both secured roles in the C.S. Forster play *Payment Deferred.* When it played in London, it was a great enough success to be brought to Broadway. The Laughtons travelled to America and quickly caught the attention of Hollywood. Though Elsa had made her film debut in a 1927 British film, *One of the Best,* it was not until 1933 when M-G-M offered her and Laughton contracts that she considered herself a film actress. The Laughtons became recognizable nationwide when they acted together in *The Private Life of Henry VIII* (1933) with Charles as the king and Elsa as Anne of Cleves. This marked the first of many roles in which Elsa would take advantage of being "unbeautiful." She explained that she did her best to "look like hell in order to keep Henry VIII at arm's length." [10] Though Laughton won an Oscar for his performance, Elsa did not fare as well. She had played her ugly bit too well; she received few more film offers. Yet, she did not let this fact distress her. "I find good looking people are boring," [11] she asserted. She left the United States and returned to England, where she threw herself into Shakespearean productions at the Old Vic Theater.

Elsa's appearance was not the sole reason for her return to England; her marriage had already become troubled. Laughton had confided to her that he was homosexual. Though she had told him it did not matter to her, it hurt her and they became more distant following his confession. But outwardly, it still appeared they were a successful couple to be coveted. Elsa finally received some more film roles, small though they were, in *Naughty Marietta* (1935) and *David Copperfield* (1934), while Charles was flush with the success of *Mutiny on the Bounty* (1935). Elsa acted as the perfect wife, content to be the supporting actress to her husband. She told journalists the secret of a happy Hollywood union was to not "let the wife be more famous than the husband. It's a different story when only one mate is an actor, for then the other has his own field in which to be successful." [12] As much as Elsa tried to let Charles "be more famous," she became a worthy rival for the spotlight in what would be her big film break, as both Mary Shelley and the bride in the *Bride of Frankenstein* (1935). Directed by an old frequenter of the Cave of Harmony, James Whale, the film allowed Elsa to showcase her versatility. As the soft-spoken Shelley, she was sweet and modest; as the hissing Bride with a monolith of hair standing atop her head, she was terrifying and surreal. The role made her an icon overnight. Even without the wild hair, Elsa was now recognized on the street. Though she would never be able to get away from being "the Bride," Elsa acknowledged that the part gave her confirmation that she had not "turned into a type that looks like everybody else." [13]

Elsa's film success did not convert her into a full-time motion picture actress; the stage was still her preferred medium. With Charles, she returned to England, where they played Peter and Captain Hook in a production of *Peter Pan*. Elsa had the honor of being the last actress to be personally chosen by J.M. Barrie to play Peter. While in England, Elsa rejoined the intelligentsia when she began attending meetings of the Bloomsbury Group, an association of writers, painters, and artists. She would miss this company upon her return to Hollywood. She and Charles had bought an isolated home in the La Brea hills, and Elsa's main source of company came from felines who found their way to her doorstep. Elsa's trouble was finding a fine balance between too little togetherness and too much togetherness. She confessed to hating crowds of more than ten or twelve and avoided ladies' lunches because too many women together "sound like a zoo." [14]

Not a little of her loneliness also came from the fact that she and Charles had grown further estranged despite appearing together in four more films, *Rembrandt* (1936), *The Beachcomber* (1937), *Tales of Manhattan* (1942), and *The Big Clock* (1947). Her best role of the mid-1940s was not in a picture with Charles; it was as Ida Lupino's mad sister in *Ladies in Retirement* (1946). She is so secure and confident in her insanity that she manages to make those around her seem to be the crazy ones. But she received few more opportunities to flex her versatility. For the majority of the 1940s, she portrayed an assortment maids and schoolteachers, most notably in *The Spiral Staircase* (1945), *The Secret Garden* (1947) and *The Bishop's Wife* (1948). "Movies don't provide a career for a freak like I am. I'm offered spinster and schoolteacher roles by the dozen, but I don't want that,"[15] Elsa remarked.

Elsa found what she wanted when she again returned to the stage. It was with a theatrical group stemming from Yale University called the Turnabout Players. The Turnabout became her pet project and as long as she was a member, loneliness was not an issue. The group gave her a perfect venue to do what she did best: British songs riddled with double entendres. "I've been told that I can make anything sound a lot worse than it is," she joked.[16] In 1949, Hollywood finally validated the inexhaustible Elsa for her considerable acting abilities when she was nominated for an Academy Award. It was for her role as Amelia Potts, a frumpy, flibberti-gibbet artist of religious paintings in *Come to the Stable*. Though she did not win the coveted statuette, the nomination proved that film audiences loved Elsa best as a slightly daft matron. For this reason, she would play little else for the rest of her screen career. *Come to the Stable* would mark a highpoint that Elsa would not again see until nearly a decade later.

The 1950s found Elsa in a depression that not even the Turnabout could lift. "I was lonely, and ambition had left me," Elsa wrote. The bulk of her work was now on the small screen. She made appearances on such shows as *Alfred Hitchcock Presents*, *I Love Lucy*, and various anthology series. Elsa's ambition came back near the end of the decade from the most unlikely place: Charles Laughton. In 1958, she appeared alongside her husband for the last time on screen in the outstanding courtroom drama *Witness for the Prosecution*. Charles portrays Sir Wilfred, an irascible lawyer with a bad heart and a taste for drink. Elsa is Miss Plimsoll, his chatterbox nurse. Elsa earned her moniker of "laugh insurance" in the scenes in which she and Charles battle over his post-heart attack treatment. He can barely restrain himself from strangling her as she patronizes him in a lilting voice:

Teeny weeny flight of steps, Sir Wilfrid, we mustn't forget we've had a teeny weeny heart attack.[17]

She provides plenty of entertainment in the courtroom scenes as well, distracting proceedings as she whispers to Sir Wilfrid from the specta-tors box to take his heart pills. Perhaps her most effective moment in the picture is when, at the close of the film, she hands Sir Wilfrid a thermos of what he has been telling her is hot cocoa. She nonchalantly says,

Sir Wilfrid, you've forgotten your brandy! [18]

Elsa received her second Academy Award nomination for her performance and received several more substantial roles following it, namely as a fluttery witch in *Bell, Book, and Candle* (1958). *Witness for the Prosecution* led not only to a renewed relationship with Charles, but to what would

ELSA LANCHESTER AND CHARLES LAUGHTON IN *WITNESS FOR THE PROSECUTION* (1958). COURTESY OF JERRY MURBACH.

be the zenith of her career. It came in the form of a one-woman show Charles himself produced for her as a thank you for help she had given him during a production of *King Lear* in England. Part of the show's appeal was that Elsa made it different each night; thus, audiences did not know quite what to expect from performance to performance. "Whether she is rattling off a naughty ballad she used to sing in nightclubs or relating the sad, sad story of a wayward Spanish girl, she is always flawlessly in character," [19] Arthur Gelb of the *New York Times* wrote. The show was an enormous success and lasted for nearly two years in New York and on the road.

Just as Elsa and Charles's relationship was mending, Charles fell ill. His sickness so affected Elsa that she had a difficult time going on stage each night. He went downhill fast and succumbed to a heart attack in 1962. She admitted that after his passing, she "was like a child — all focus gone." [20] But idleness and despondency were not in Elsa's true character. She declared that she must work "at almost anything." She did indeed work in "almost anything," namely as what she called "old bags." Perhaps her most unforgettable "old bag" was Mrs. McDougall in Disney's charming *That Darn Cat!* (1964). Mrs. McDougal is the quintessential meddlesome battle ax who will stop at nothing to eavesdrop. One of the most humorous scenes is when her husband, Wilbur, calls the police on his wife to teach her a lesson and tells the officers she is a transvestite peeping through windows. It is understandable that Mrs. McDougal returns home from jail the next day full of vengeance for her husband. As in *Witness for the Prosecution*, Elsa leaves the audience laughing in the last scene in the film:

MRS. MCDOUGAL (to the policemen that just brought her home): *You might as well wait for me, it'll save time. I'm going into the house to murder someone* (as she starts to walk to the house) *Oh, Wilbur, don't try to hide. Come out and take your medicine like a man. Wilbur!*
[Wilbur MacDougall, as he hears her voice, grabs his cap and quickly runs away] [21]

It is ironic that the same lady who sang such ditties as "Song for a Shuttered Parlor" in her one-woman show was now a favorite regular of family-friendly Disney pictures. She followed *That Darn Cat!* with *Mary Poppins* (1964) and appeared in an episode of Disney's *Wonderful World of Color* in 1969. What made her humor so refreshing in films that could otherwise be overly cute was that she did not strain to be funny. "If you don't start out playing an eccentric or a nut, you can turn all sorts of things — particularly small things — into surprise and comedy…if I do something not quite in character, even drink a glass of port or hiccough — it is likely to seem funny." [22]

Elsa kept busy from the 1960s through the 1970s, again turning to television for much of her employment. Some of her best work was as the witty school principal on *The John Forsythe Show* (1965-66). She appeared on the big screen again in *Willard* (1971) and in the star-studded *Murder by Death* in 1976. Her final film was a Robby Benson picture entitled *Die Laughing* (1980). Though she had retired from film, Elsa kept herself active. She penned a memoir in 1983 called *Elsa Lanchester — Herself* which gave a candid image of her bohemian early years and her marriage to Charles. She provided a glimpse of her film career as well, summing it up with the philosophy that it was defined by "large parts in lousy pictures and small parts in good pictures."[23] It is fortuitous that she wrote her memoirs when she did. In 1987, shortly after its publication, she died of bronchial pneumonia.

Elsa Lanchester appeared in over one hundred films. Many of her parts were uncredited or little more than walk-ons. It is a testament to her charisma and talent that she managed to become such an icon through a few great roles. She may have often portrayed homebody matrons or maids on screen, but in life she was *avante garde*. She was an intellectual, a bohemian, and unapologetically candid in an era when candor was considered unbecoming to a woman. She once said she never liked doing the same thing twice on stage; in life she applied the same principle. She could enthrall audiences with a performance of Shakespeare or double up patrons with a risque song and dance routine. Though her training was in classical dance and theater, it is for "doubling up" audiences that she is best remembered. Indeed, critics complimented her most when she acted as "a wonderfully daft woman" and "an eccentric clown."[24] Elsa would likely have preferred to be remembered this way. "I'm happiest when I'm making people laugh," she said. "Happiness makes me feel smooth — you feel all smoothed out if you're happy."[25] Her happiness must be contagious; it would be a difficult feat to frown when watching this red-haired imp perform.

FILMOGRAPHY

1980	*Die Laughing*	Sophie
1976	*Murder by Death*	Jessica Marbles
1973	*Arnold*	Hester
1973	*Terror in the Wax Museum*	Julia Hawthorn
1971	*Willard*	Henrietta Stiles
1969	*Me, Natalie*	Miss Dennison
1969	*Rascal*	Mrs. Satterfield
1968	*Blackbeard's Ghost*	Emily Stowecroft
1967	*Easy Come, Easy Go*	Madame Neherina
1965	*That Darn Cat!*	Mrs. William MacDougall
1964	*Pajama Party*	Aunt Wendy
1964	*Mary Poppins*	Katie Nanna
1964	*Honeymoon Hotel*	Chambermaid

1958	*Bell Book and Candle*	Aunt Queenie Holroyd
1957	*Witness for the Prosecution*	Miss Plimsoll
1955	*The Glass Slipper*	Widow Sonder
1954	*3 Ring Circus*	The Bearded Lady
1954	*Hell's Half Acre*	Lida O'Reilly
1953	*The Girls of Pleasure Island*	Thelma
1952	*Androcles and the Lion*	Megaera
1952	*Les Miserables*	Madame Magloire
1952	*Dreamboat*	Dr. Mathilda Coffey
1950	*Frenchie*	Countess
1950	*The Petty Girl*	Dr. Crutcher
1950	*Mystery Street*	Mrs. Smerrling
1950	*Buccaneer's Girl*	Mme. Brizar
1949	*The Inspector General*	Maria
1949	*Come to the Stable*	Amelia Potts
1949	*The Secret Garden*	Martha
1948	*The Big Clock*	Louise Patterson
1947	*The Bishop's Wife*	Matilda
1947	*Northwest Outpost*	Princess 'Tanya' Tatiana
1946	*The Razor's Edge*	Miss Keith
1945	*The Spiral Staircase*	Mrs. Oates
1944	*Passport to Destiny*	Ella Muggins
1943	*Lassie Come Home*	Mrs. Carraclough
1943	*Thumbs Up*	Emma Finch
1943	*Forever and a Day*	Mamie
1942	*Tales of Manhattan*	Elsa *(Mrs Charles)* Smith
1942	*Son of Fury: The Story of Benjamin Blake*	Bristol Isabel
1941	*Ladies in Retirement*	Emily Creed
1938	*The Beachcomber*	Martha Jones
1936	*Rembrandt*	Hendrickje Stoffels
1936	*Miss Bracegirdle Does Her Duty (short)*	Millicent Bracegirdle
1935	*The Ghost Goes West*	Miss Shepperton
1935	*Bride of Frankenstein*	Mary Wollstonecraft Shelley / The Monster's Bride
1935	*Naughty Marietta*	Madame d'Annard
1935	*David Copperfield*	Clickett
1934	*The Private Life of Don Juan*	Maid (uncredited)
1933	*The Private Life of Henry VIII...*	Anne of Cleves, The Fourth Wife
1931	*The Officer's Mess*	Cora Melville
1931	*The Love Habit*	Mathilde

1931 *The Stronger Sex* ....Thompson
1931 *Potiphar's Wife* ....Therese
1930 *Ashes (short)* .... Girl
1929 Mr. Smith Wakes Up *(short)*...
1928 *The Tonic (short)* .... Elsa
1928 *Daydreams (short)* ....Elsa/Heroine in Dream Sequence
1928 *Blue Bottles (short)* .... Elsa
1928 *The Constant Nymph* ....Lady
1927 *One of the Best*...Kitty
1925 *The Scarlet Woman: An Ecclesiastical Melodrama (short)*.................
                                                              Beatrice de Carolle

STEAM
IN HER KETTLE
MARJORIE
MAIN

MARJORIE MAIN IN *THE WISTFUL WIDOW OF WAGON GAP* (1947).
COURTESY OF JERRY MURBACH.

Her disheveled gray hair was always out of place. Her clothes were frumpy and seldom matched. She spoke in a raspy Hoosier twang. In the hundred plus motion pictures in which she appeared, she was outspoken, irascible, and her humor was raucous. Her name was Marjorie Main, and it is doubtful she was ever anyone's idea of a movie idol. But somehow she rose to become a star in her own right; indeed, many critics heralded her as Marie Dressler's successor. Today Marjorie is identified almost solely by her portrayal of the "gravel-voiced but loveable hillbilly farm wife"[1] in the ten *Ma and Pa Kettle* films produced between 1947 and 1957. However, whether it was in one of her many B pictures or one of her many A pictures, she proved to be an actress of unexpected versatility and depth. She could be just as convincing as a hillbilly, a surly maid, a tough leader of a group of Old West outlaws, or a soft-hearted mother waiting for her son to come home from the warfront. Outwardly, Marjorie and Ma Kettle seemed to be "cut from the same homey cloth."[2] Inwardly, Marjorie was a shy, humble woman at home with her eccentricities that, in the words of one columnist, gave her an air of mystery akin to Garbo's.[3]

Marjorie began life as Marybelle Tomlinson on a farm near Acton, Indiana on February 24, 1890. She was the daughter of an extremely strict minister for the Church of Christ. She was descended from a long line of moralists; her grandmother was even one of the founders of the Women's Christian Temperance Union (WCTU).[4] The stage appealed to Marjorie as a child, but her father disapproved of dramatics. Consequently, Marjorie lived a rather Spartan life with none of the glamour one would expect of an aspiring actress. She later recalled that when she went to boarding school as a young girl "my mother would give me a number of dresses. I would wear just one of them until it was worn out."[5] Even as a child, Marjorie was one of a kind. She wanted to be an actress, but she did not care one whit about beauty. "Mother tried to get me into other clothes," Marjorie confessed. "She said I should dress to please others."[6] Clothing choices aside, Marjorie did nothing but please others as she grew up. Yet, at the same time, she surreptitiously pleased herself as well. "I got my first dramatic training under the guise of elocution," she said. "A term which covered a multitude of sinful things in my youth."[7] She made her stage debut in grammar school giving a reading of a sentimental ballad about a seedy cowboy who finds redemption. Apparently her recitation left the audience "in buckets of tears."[8] She gained more stage experience singing hymns for visiting clergymen.

When she reached young adulthood, Marjorie attended Franklin College but transferred to the Hamilton School of Dramatic Expression shortly afterward. Still adhering to her mother's advice to please others, she told her father she was attending Hamilton to become a teacher. What she did not tell him was that she wanted to be an *acting* teacher. She effectively taught drama for a year before entering vaudeville. She joined the Chautauqua circuit, one of the best touring companies in rural America during the World War I period. Allegedly "even preachers approved" of the company.[9] She received an offer to play in Shakespearean productions with the touring company and won the blessing of her father to accept. Nevertheless, she changed her name to Marjorie Main to avoid embarrassing her family [10]. She both acted and sang between acts with the Chautauqua circuit, two talents she would later blend ingeniously in her best films.

It was while working with the Chautauqua circuit that Marjorie met the man who was to be her husband. He was Dr. Stanley Krebs, a psychiatrist and former minister who wrote and lectured about applied psychology. Though Stanley was nearly twenty years Marjorie's senior, the unconventional pair married in 1921. Marjorie became interested in "mediums and table thumpings" through Stanley, who lectured that such things were "80% humbug" and "the extra 12% was inexplicable." [11] She gave up acting for the next several years and instead traveled with her husband and helped him with his work. When not traveling, the couple settled in New York, and, with Stanley's approval, Marjorie tried her luck on Broadway. She proved to be successful and acted with such luminaries as W.C. Fields and John Barrymore. [12] She once played Mae West's mother despite the fact that she was only a year older than West.

Though 1935 brought Marjorie much professional success, it was a tragic year for the actress. Losing her husband was an event that would be devastating for Marjorie yet would ultimately lead to her establishment as, in the words of one critic, one of the rare "consistently good actresses" [13] in show business. Marjorie was appearing in a gritty play entitled *Dead End* at the time of Stanley's passing, and according to one of her friends, "I think her grief for her husband added to her performance." [14] Marjorie herself explained her husband's effect on her work best: "Doctor was a creative man. We didn't need anyone else. We had each other. When he died I used to pour out my sorrow to the audience night after night…" [15] Her grief led not only to an added depth and genuineness in her professional life, but also to a spiritual awakening in her personal one. When Stanley died, he apparently left his wife "with a sentence only she knew." [16] Forever afterward, Marjorie grew keenly interested in Spiritualism, "trying to get some departed spirit to repeat that sentence to her." [17] She even began attending séances and she often had "conversations" with Stanley before doing a scene. It was only after she finished her silent talks with her husband that she would let the director know she was ready to continue. [18]

Marjorie's breakthrough performance in *Dead End* led to more substantial roles, supporting though they remained. Hollywood agents began to take notice of the scratchy-voiced, loud character they saw on stage

MARJORIE MAIN AND CLARK GABLE IN *HONKY TONK* (1941). COURTESY OF JERRY MURBACH.

and promptly asked her to reprise her stage roles in screen adaptations. In the screen version of *Dead End* (1937), she played Humphrey Bogart's spurning mother to much acclaim. The scene in which she slaps his face and calls him, "Ya yella dirty dog!" is now considered a classic moment in film history. Just as classic is Marjorie's performance as "a wise cracking ranch proprietor" in *The Women* (1939), which had been her final Broadway play. Despite her plain appearance, she manages to upstage her glamorous co-stars Norma Shearer, Joan Crawford, and Paulette Goddard. One critic noted that: "Her tongue-in-cheek attitude toward the pampered darlings who came to Reno for their divorces was one of the highlights, both in the stage play and in the movie." [19] Marjorie's no-nonsense, "tongue in cheek" persona led her to be cast in two types of roles: the surly maid or the mother of tough guy types. Though many of her films were low-budget and unexceptional, she always gave exceptional performances in each and proved that she was more than simple comic relief or a stock mother-type character. One reviewer aptly described her ability to elevate otherwise predictable films, such as 1938's *Romance of the Limberlost:* "Miss Main's part calls for overdoing the severity of a hard-beaten, miserly aunt but she is a strong personality and gives a forceful though restrained performance."[20]

No films better showcased Marjorie's strong personality than two spectacular musicals she made under M-G-M contract. In the first, *Meet Me in St. Louis* (1944), she portrays Katie, the hot-tempered maid of the Smith family. She prevents the picture from being unrealistic and overly sentimental with her acerbic quips. She offers such memorable lines as, "My sister's having trouble with her husband…him being a man."[21] Another unforgettable moment is when, after the eldest brother and sister in the Smith family find they have to be each other's's escorts to a Christmas ball, Katie declares, "And you'll have the best time of anybody! You won't have to be polite to each other!"[22] Though Marjorie does not sing in this musical, in *The Harvey Girls* (1946), she both sings and offers hilarious dialogue. Particularly memorable is a scene at a fancy-dress ball where she sings directions of how to dance a waltz to a group of cowboys. It is hilarious to see her making ungraceful, wide to and fro motions and shouting, "Then ya go right, then ya go left!,"[23] all the while convinced she is bringing gentility and grace to the rough-around-the-edges cowboys.

By the late 1940s, Marjorie was popular enough with audiences to be given her own film serial. She had already proved herself worthy of the title "the new Marie Dressler" as Wallace Beery's female foil in *Barnacle Bill* (1941), but it was after her performance as the outspoken hillbilly Ma Kettle in 1947's *The Egg and I* that she created her own signature brand of comedy. She had shown herself capable of drama when she portrayed a blind woman in *Shepherd of the Hills* (1941), but her performance as Ma Kettle was so enduring in audiences' minds that they could not accept her as anything but a raucous, blunt woman. It is little wonder that she won an Academy Award nomination for her work. Marjorie's performance is so natural and seemingly effortless that it's almost graceful when she clears a table by knocking dirty dishes from it with one sweep of her arm or serves a chicken by tearing it with her hands rather than going through the trouble of using a knife and fork. She would reprise her role every year for the next decade in a series of *Ma and Pa Kettle* films. She provided the biggest laughs in the films, often by calling one of her over dozen children by the wrong name (a running joke in the ten films) or having a hilarious exchange with them such as the following one from 1952's *Ma and Pa Kettle Go to the Fair*:

MA KETTLE: *Graduate high school one week, go to work the next. Ain't you ever gonna take a vacation?*

ROSIE KETTLE: *Ma, what did I tell you about "ain't"? Now listen, I "am not" taking a vacation, you "are not" taking a vacation, we "are not" taking a vacation, get it?*

MA KETTLE: *Yep, ain't nobody taking a vacation.* [24]

When asked to explain *Ma and Pa Kettle's* phenomenal popularity, Marjorie reasoned, "They're cheaply made, many of them done by inexperienced writers...They came in at the tail end of a lot of these arty pictures at Universal that weren't making any money..." [25] Marjorie further called the *Ma and Pa Kettle* series "nice and corny," just what Americans craved after the postwar slough of realistic, gritty noir films. "Ma is real to me, the kind of woman you feel you could go and visit in the country," Marjorie commented. "And no hayseed. They tried to get that in, but I'd always say no." [26] The genuineness Marjorie brought to her role in no small way added to the film series' success. Because she was raised in a rural environment, she had a unique knowledge of rural folks and knew what they would and would not do...or approve of. Just as she kept Ma Kettle realistic, she kept the films' scripts up to the same high standards. She once refused to do a scene in which her onscreen husband, Percy Kilbride, loses his pants after being butted by a goat. A staunch teetotaler, she also refused to do a scene that required her to be tipsy. A similar incident had taken place during filming of *The Harvey Girls* when she refused to take a bite out of an apple a prop man had disinfected with alcohol. [27] "I've always taken a stand for clean scripts," [28] she declared, and she was true to her word.

Marjorie became a sort of poster-girl for good, clean fun, so much so that her biggest fans were priests and choir boys (a fact that would undoubtedly win her father's approval). Once when her car stalled on the side of the highway, it was a group of choirboys who pulled over to help her. "I wouldn't have stopped but the kids recognized you," the driver told her. [29]

By the 1950s, Marjorie had established herself as much a character off screen as on. Aside from her high moral standards (in itself an eccentricity in Hollywood), she also had high standards for hygiene. She allegedly wore white gloves and a surgical mask at times to avoid contamination. [30] Her Spiritualism also continued to set her apart. She took it seriously; after a medium told her to eat plenty of corn bread, she ate it every day in the studio cafeteria. She ate the majority of her meals in cafeterias and usually rode the bus to work though she had ample money to avoid both. Her thriftiness was also reflected in her clothes. In 1957, she was named "the worst dressed woman" in Hollywood. Marjorie was unaffected by the title and even stated, "They should have put me first on the list." [31] She offered a bit of homespun philosophy instead, arguing that, "If you can't please people without dressing up then what are you? Your real friends love you for what you are, not for what you wear." [32] Marjorie had no need for fancy dresses; she preferred staying at home, tending her roses, planting herbs, avocado trees, and lilies. One columnist described her modest existence as "living alone in a middle class neighborhood, doing her own cooking, and housekeeping and sitting up evenings to enjoy her old movies on television." [33]

Contrary to her very audible bark onscreen, off screen Marjorie was quiet and spoke falteringly, often lapsing into meditative silences. Her friend, Spec McClure, described this unexpected nature of "Ma Kettle": "Marjorie used to be as mysterious as Greta Garbo. She's never gone out a lot nor seen many people, because crowds make her nervous. She enjoys being alone, because she's interested in metaphysics and is capable of much meditation." [34] Marjorie was all the more mysterious and intriguing when, in 1954, she announced she was taking a tour of Europe. "I'm not an educated woman, but I have a hungry mind," [35] she explained. Though she did enjoy soaking in the foreign cultures, she did not leave her shyness behind. "A friend's going with me — a socialite. If we find ourselves at some high-toned place like Buckingham Palace, I'll just push her in ahead of me," [36] she stated. When Marjorie returned home from her trip, she told newspapers that she still liked her own cooking better than anything she tried in Europe. [37] Marjorie's simplicity and the earthiness she maintained despite money, travel, and fame truly made her more like a female Will Rogers than another Marie Dressler.

As the 1960s dawned, Marjorie increasingly spent more time at home. She had been slowly decreasing her workload since 1948 following a spell of ill health. Her roles in films were becoming frustratingly small, and minuscule as they were, they were often lost on the cutting room floor.

Marjorie did win acclaim in even her smallest roles, as evidenced by a Golden Globe nomination she received for her performance as a Quaker widow in *Friendly Persuasion* (1954). After her final film, *The Kettles on Old Macdonald's Farm* (1957), she retired from the big screen. She continued working sporadically on television and appeared in episodes of such shows as *Perry Mason* and *Wagon Train*. But Marjorie was tired. "It might be fun to just do nothing after working all your life," she said. [38] By the 1970s, Marjorie had retired from show business, but she did not "just do nothing." She made public appearances in the annual Hollywood Christmas parade and attended the 1974 premiere of *That's Entertainment*, a revue of her former home studio, M-G-M. She also did philanthropic work, donating most of her paychecks to the support of a school. Director George Sidney called her "a great lady," [39] and he was making no understatement.

Marjorie's indomitable and vital spirit was overpowered by lung cancer in 1975. She was eighty-five years old. She was buried beside her husband at the Forest Lawn cemetery in Hollywood.

Marjorie Main was no glamour queen; her acting was not revolutionary or highbrow. She lived simply and acted simply in her films, and audiences loved her all the more for it. Marjorie could be called as "nice and corny" as the *Ma and Pa Kettle* films for which she was best known, but it is her "corniness" that has endeared her to filmgoers for generations. As folksy, outspoken, and rowdy as she was in film, she was equally humble, self-deprecating, and generous in life. She was a complex woman of unexpected interests, eccentricities, and phobias. Most simply put, she was human, and audiences never for a moment forgot this when watching her on screen. As near to rarefied film stardom she ever became was when she bought herself a blue Thunderbird and stated with a gentle chuckle, "I think I'll put 'M.M.' on the door. Ha! People will think it's Marilyn Monroe." [40]

FILMOGRAPHY

Year	Film	Role
1957	*The Kettles on Old MacDonald's Farm*	Phoebe 'Ma' Kettle
1956	*Friendly Persuasion*	The Widow Hudspeth
1956	*The Kettles in the Ozarks*	Ma Kettle
1955	*Ma and Pa Kettle at Waikiki*	Phoebe 'Ma' Kettle
1954	*Ricochet Romance*	Pansy Jones
1954	*Ma and Pa Kettle at Home*	Phoebe 'Ma' Kettle
1954	*Rose Marie*	Lady Jane Dunstock
1953	*The Long, Long Trailer*	Mrs. Hittaway
1953	*Fast Company*	Ma Parkson

1953	*Ma and Pa Kettle on Vacation*	Phoebe 'Ma' Kettle
1952	*Ma and Pa Kettle at the Fair*	Phoebe 'Ma' Kettle
1952	*The Belle of New York*	Mrs. Phineas Hill
1951	*It's a Big Country*	Mrs. Wrenley
1951	*The Law and the Lady*	Julia Wortin
1951	*Ma and Pa Kettle Back on the Farm*	Phoebe 'Ma' Kettle
1951	*Mr. Imperium*	Mrs. Cabot
1951	*A Letter from a Soldier (short)*	Mrs. Wrenley
1950	*Mrs. O'Malley and Mr. Malone*	Harriet 'Hattie' O'Malley
1950	*Summer Stock*	Esme
1950	*Ma and Pa Kettle Go to Town*	Phoebe 'Ma' Kettle
1949	*Big Jack*	Flapjack Kate
1949	*Ma and Pa Kettle*	Phoebe 'Ma' Kettle
1948	*Feudin', Fussin' and A-Fightin'*	Maribel Mathews
1947	*The Wistful Widow of Wagon Gap*	Widow Hawkins
1947	*The Egg and I*	Phoebe 'Ma' Kettle
1946	*The Show-Off*	Mrs. Fisher
1946	*Undercurrent*	Lucy
1946	*Bad Bascomb*	Abbey Hanks
1946	*The Harvey Girls*	Sonora Cassidy
1945	*Murder, He Says*	Mamie Fleagle Smithers Johnson
1944	*Gentle Annie*	Annie Goss
1944	*Meet Me in St. Louis*	Katie–Maid
1944	*Rationing*	Iris Tuttle
1943	*Johnny Come Lately*	'Gashouse' Mary
1943	*Heaven Can Wait*	Mrs. Strable
1942	*Tennessee Johnson*	Mrs. Maude Fisher
1942	*Tish*	Miss Letitia 'Tish' Carberry
1942	*Jackass Mail*	Clementine 'Tina' Tucker
1942	*The Affairs of Martha*	Mrs. McKissick
1942	*We Were Dancing*	Judge Sidney Hawkes
1942	*The Bugle Sounds*	Susie 'Suz'
1941	*Honky Tonk*	Mrs. Varner
1941	*The Shepherd of the Hills*	Granny Becky
1941	*A Woman's Face*	Emma Kristiansdotter
1941	*Barnacle Bill*	Marge Cavendish
1941	*The Trial of Mary Dugan*	Mrs. Collins
1941	*The Wild Man of Borneo*	Irma, the Cook
1940	*Wyoming*	Mehitabel
1940	*The Captain Is a Lady*	Sarah May Willett

1940	*Susan and God* ....Mary Maloney
1940	*Turnabout* ....Nora–the Cook
1940	*Dark Command*.......................... Mrs. Cantrell, aka Mrs. Adams
1940	*Women Without Names*.................... Mrs. Lowery–Prison Matron
1940	*I Take This Woman*... Gertie
1939	*Two Thoroughbreds*..............................Hildegarde 'Hildy' Carey
1939	*Another Thin Man*.. Mrs. Dolley, Landlord, Chesterfield Apartments
1939	*The Women* ....Lucy
1939	*The Angels Wash Their Faces* ....Mrs. Arkelian
1939	*They Shall Have Music* ....Mrs. Miller
1939	*Lucky Night* .... Mrs. Briggs
1938	*There Goes My Heart* ....Fireless Cooker Customer *(uncredited)*
1938	*Girls' School*.......................... Miss Honore Armstrong
1938	*Too Hot to Handle* ....Miss Kitty Wayne
1938	*Under the Big Top* .... Sara Post
1938	*Little Tough Guy* .... Mrs. Boylan
1938	*Prison Farm* ....Matron Brand
1938	*Romance of the Limberlost* ....Nora
1938	*Three Comrades*....................... Old Woman by Phone *(uncredited)*
1938	*Test Pilot*..Landlady
1938	*King of the Newsboys* ....Mrs. Stephens *(uncredited)*
1938	*Penitentiary* .... Miss Katie Mathews *(uncredited)*
1938	*City Girl*.................................... Mrs. Ward *(uncredited)*
1937	*The Shadow*...................................... Hannah Gillespie
1937	*Boy of the Streets*...........................Mrs. Mary Brennan
1937	*The Wrong Road* ....Martha Foster
1937	*The Man Who Cried Wolf*....................................Amelia Bradley
1937	*Dead End*.. Mrs. Martin
1937	*Stella Dallas*... Mrs. Martin
1937	*Love in a Bungalow* ....Miss Emma Bisbee
1934	*Music in the Air*.. Anna
1934	*Crime Without Passion* . Backstage Wardrobe Woman *(uncredited)*
1934	*Art Trouble (short)*......Woman Who Sits on Painting *(uncredited)*
1933	*New Deal Rhythm (short)*.......Delegate from Arizona *(uncredited)*
1932	*Hot Saturday*............................... Gossip in Window *(uncredited)*
1932	*Broken Lullaby*..............Frau Schmidt–Townswoman *(uncredited)*
1931	*A House Divided* .... Townswoman at Wedding *(uncredited)*
1929	*Harry Fox and His Six American Beauties (short)* .... Statler Hotel Beauty *(uncredited)*

BITTER WITH THE SWEET
HATTIE McDANIEL

HATTIE MCDANIEL IN *GONE WITH THE WIND* (1939).
AUTHOR'S COLLECTION.

She was called an inadvertent reformer, a woman who paved the way for all future generations of her race. Indeed, in reading the history of black entertainers, one would find Hattie McDaniel's name as the forerunner in numerous categories. She was the first black entertainer to sing over the airwaves, to win an Academy Award, and to have a radio program intended for general audiences. Hattie virtually changed audiences' perceptions of the black community through her sassy, confident portrayals of women in supposedly servile positions such as Mammy in *Gone With the Wind* (1939) or Beulah on her radio show of the same name. Before Hattie, blacks were often used solely for comic relief in entertainment. Hattie did provide comedy, but her humor was not at her own expense. What made Hattie so popular on and off screen was that she met everyone "on the basis of equality," both "high and low, black and white." [1]However, not everyone saw Hattie as a reformer. She would nearly lose her career and life because of the unceasing criticism she received from those of her own race for playing maids and servants in her films. But Hattie more than rose above her subservient positions onscreen. In the words of journalist Monica L. Haynes, Hattie "imbu[ed] them with dignity and the kind of common sense the heroes or heroines seemed to lack." [2]

Hattie was born on June 10, 1895 in Denver, Colorado. From birth she was unique; of her thirteen siblings, half of whom died, she survived. Her father, Henry, was born into slavery but gained freedom after fighting for the Union Army. He then joined a minstrel group but would later find a calling to be a minister. He met Susan, Hattie's mother, when she was a member of the female chorus with his minstrel group. Her parents' love of music and closeness to their faith would be instilled in Hattie throughout her childhood. "He [Hattie's father] told me, 'Hattie, always stay close to God, and you will have enthusiasm in your heart. That enthusiasm added to the natural charm that God gave you will bring opportunity and friends to you. Of course, my father overestimated me." [3] Hattie was too modest; in reality, she did find a wealth of friends and opportunities through her charm and enthusiasm. Her teachers recalled that she was "full of rhythm," had "outstanding dramatic ability" and an "ever present sense of humor." [4] She did not know the word discrimination as she grew up. On the contrary, those who knew her remembered her as a take charge type of girl from the start. Her best friend in school was a white girl, and year after year Hattie was in demand for school plays and activities (many of which she organized). When Hattie joined her church's choir, she found she had a talent not only at acting but in singing. She allegedly sang so continuously that her mother "bribed her into silence with spare change." [5] When not vocalizing, Hattie taught herself modern dances like the cakewalk and wing dance.

Hattie's talents would prove a great advantage as she grew toward adulthood. Henry's work was unreliable and the family would move more than ten times by the time Hattie finished school. At the age of thirteen, Hattie earned her first bit of income performing in a minstrel show and overnight was heralded "Denver's favorite soubrette." [6] She found equal success performing in a decidedly different venue: the WCTU. Hattie's tear-jerking recitation of a poem entitled "Convict Joe" earned her a gold medal. Hattie knew she wanted to be an entertainer after winning this honor and yearned to join the minstrel company her father had formed with her brother, Otis. Against her mother's wishes, Hattie did not complete high school in order to become a full time actress. She performed with various stock companies along the West Coast, but her budding career was swiftly put on hold when her brother died and her father's minstrel group disintegrated. Hattie took any job she could get cooking, cleaning, and washing to help her family. But working menial jobs did not stop the perseverant Hattie from pursuing her dream. She landed a job with the George Morrison Orchestra and his Melody Hounds, a band that, rather than lampoon black culture, celebrated it. Hattie was even given the chance to write and sing her own songs for the show. She became the show's major draw. Critics spotlighted her unique way of dancing with "a hop, skip, and a jump...on stage while keeping up her vocal stunts." [7]

Between performances with Morrison's Orchestra Hattie met and married a young man named George Langford. Their marriage lasted only two years; in 1924, George was killed by gunfire. It is unclear what events led to the murder. Hattie masked her sorrow through her work. Her efforts were rewarded in 1924 when she made the phenomenal accomplishment of being the first black singer to be heard over the radio. The enthusiastic response her performance received opened the door to the famed Orpheum Circuit and Pantages Theater, but her rising fame came to an abrupt halt with the Crash of 1929. Suddenly no jobs were forthcoming, and the closest Hattie came to show business was as a ladies room attendant at the Club Madrid in Milwaukee, Wisconsin. Hattie found opportunity wherever she was, and the Club was no exception. While in the washroom, she would conspicuously sing along to the dance tunes the band played outside. The club's owner noticed her and liked what he heard. He hired Hattie to sing with the band and soon, according to a fellow singer at the club, "People were coming out just to hear Hattie sing." [8]

Milwaukee was not big enough for a woman of Hattie's talents; she soon set her eyes on Hollywood. In 1931, she arrived in Los Angeles with a rabbit's foot and $20 in her purse. [9] While searching for work in entertainment, Hattie returned to the job of maid and had to borrow money for car fare to her first interviews. On one particular interview for the radio show *The Optimist Do-Nuts*, Hattie arrived at the studio wearing an evening gown. "Look breezy and people will think you are," [10] a friend had advised her. Hattie's "breezy" dress won her the job and a nickname that immediately distinguished her on the airwaves: "Hi-Hat Hattie." [11] "Hi-Hat Hattie" turned her small role into a big opportunity and did not take long to become a hit with the show's listeners.

Hattie's rabbit foot must have brought her much luck not only in radio, but also in film. She was becoming ubiquitous in that medium, appearing (though uncredited) in fifteen films between 1932 and 1934. Among her most notable unbilled performances were as Mae West's manicurist in *I'm No Angel* (1933) and as Marlene Dietrich's maid in *Blonde Venus* (1932). She first saw her name in film credits in *Judge Priest* (1935), a delightful Will Rogers vehicle. Hattie won over her audience in a scene when she does a duet of "My Old Kentucky Home, Good Night" with Rogers, showing off her musical as well as acting talents. The film also gave her an opportunity to write and perform a tune written by herself entitled "Aunt Dilsey's Song." At the same time Hattie was enjoying her first success in film, she married Howard Hickam. Their marriage would not endure, but no record exists as to when and why their divorce took place. [12]

Though Hattie's film roles were growing larger, they seldom strayed from those of maids and servants. Nevertheless, she filled them with such charisma that even her briefest appearance was memorable. Documentarian Madison Lacey describes the progression of Hattie's film career: "She'd have a walk-on and walk-off part, then she had lines. As the lines built, she had a character." [13] Among her best characters was Queenie, the cook in *Show Boat* (1936). In this film, she again showed her musical talent to good advantage singing arguably the best song in the picture, "Can't Help Lovin' Dat Man of Mine." Though she invariably played servants, Hattie made her characters anything but servile. In *Alice Adams* (1935), she is a confident, outspoken maid and in *The Mad Miss Manton* (1938), she throws water in Henry Fonda's face. Hattie held no qualms about her "inferior" roles. She philosophized, "Hell, I'd rather play a maid than be one." [14] Hattie had come far from her past working as maids and bathroom attendants; now, she found among her greatest fans Clark Gable, Bette Davis, Katharine Hepburn, Edward Arnold, and

Joan Crawford. She found allies in Hollywood's black community as well and counted among her best friends Eddie "Rochester" Anderson, Louise Beavers, Ethel Waters, and Lillian Randolph. [15]

By 1936 Hattie had become so well-established that producer David O. Selznick was creating roles specifically for her. Though he did not create one role that seemed to have been written just for Hattie, he produced

EVELYN VENABLE AND SHIRLEY TEMPLE WITH HATTIE MCDANIEL IN *THE LITTLE COLONEL* **(1935).** COURTESY OF JERRY MURBACH.

the film in which it was featured: *Gone With the Wind*. After receiving the role of Mammy in the Civil War epic, Hattie read the novel upon which it was based three times before stepping in front of the cameras. Her dedication and feel for the role showed so much on screen that for the rest of her life Hattie and Mammy were one in the same in viewer's minds. Hattie was like Mammy in many aspects; even her description in Margaret Mitchell's novel brings Hattie to mind: "…her code of conduct and her sense of pride were as high or higher than those of her owners." [16] Mammy is the rock that holds the Tara plantation together after Mrs. O'Hara dies and Mr. O'Hara becomes incoherent with grief and alcohol. Hattie creates a character who is a servant in name only; she is the real boss, and she knows it. Whether she is unapologetically uttering "It ain't fittin', it just ain't fittin'" about the manner in which Rhett Butler is raising his and Scarlett's child or telling Scarlett (intentions of flattering her mistress's vanity nonexistent) that she would never see a sixteen-inch waist again after bearing a child, Mammy is a woman to be reckoned with. The scene that most critics agree ultimately won her an Academy Award is when she hysterically confides to Melanie Wilkes (Olivia De Havilland) about the disintegration of Rhett and Scarlett's marriage following the death of their daughter. It is difficult not to shed tears in the face of the raw emotion she shows in this scene.

Hattie's groundbreaking triumph in winning Best Supporting Actress of 1939 received an unprecedented ovation. One observer wrote of the audience's response: "The ovation that [Hattie] received will go down in history as one of the greatest ever accorded any performer in the annals of the industry. Stars stood and cheered, bringing tears to Hattie's eyes." [17] Hattie's acceptance speech was as moving as the audience's ovation. She declared that she hoped her win would be an inspiration to black youth that would encourage them to "aim high and work hard, and take the bitter with the sweet." [18]

The aftermath of Hattie's star-making role of Mammy would bring her plenty of sweetness, but all too much bitterness as well. The sweet came in the form of being awarded a certificate of merit from Eleanor Roosevelt for being "an outstanding member of the colored race in entertainment. [19]" She also married again to a wealthy land speculator who gifted her ten acres in Montana at their wedding. However, they made their home in a fifteen-room mansion in an area of Hollywood called "Sugar Top." [20] Hattie continued to be a true "outstanding member" of the entertainment community through her contributions to the war effort. She worked to organize a school in Los Angeles for illiterate black soldiers and was captain of the Women's Volunteer Service. She also headed the black Hollywood Victory Committee and held meetings at her home. Hattie was a philanthropist in other areas, too; she gave young actors and actresses room and board at her mansion and donated to organizations such as the Jewish Home for the Aged and the Braille Institute.[21] Hattie's philosophy of "It's not how much can I spare, it's how much have I?"[22] endeared her to everyone she met, black and white. Journalist Norman Vincent Peale did a posthumous piece on Hattie appropriately titled "Confident Living" and described her effect on those around her: "I watched...the people of Hollywood gathering about her. She had something to transmit to them that drew them. She exuded vibrancy; she was alive to her fingertips. They loved her for it and so did all who knew her."[23]

Hattie continued to exude vibrancy on the screen as well. She helped boost morale in the patriotic home front story of *Since You Went Away* (1944), starring Claudette Colbert and Shirley Temple. The film gave Hattie another role as a servant, but as was now customary with Hattie, she made the role into one of an independent-minded woman one could easily forget was supposed to be a servant. She is both heart-warming and hilarious as Fidelia, a maid who chooses to stay with the family who employed her even after they have to let her go due to financial straits. She offers quips comical in their straight forwardness, such as one she exchanges with a retired General boarding with the family:

COLONEL WILLIAM G. SMOLLETT: *By the way, Fidelia, just what was the experimentation you referred to in connection with this cake?*

FIDELIA: *I tried something new. I bought it.*[24]

When not making the audience laugh as Fidelia, she moved them with her unexpected moments of candor. Her most touching scene is when a friend of her employer's family (of whom she disapproves for painting pin-up girl posters for the Navy) presents her with a dignified, elegant sketch of herself. She begins to cry and declares, "That's how I always wanted to look!" She is forever afterward friends with the artist; she, like him, is a much more complex and deep a person than her/his occupation would suggest. Hattie's performance won her a second nomination for Best Supporting Actress.

As the 1940s drew to a close, bitterness began to overshadow Hattie's sweet victories. In 1944, she thought she was pregnant only to find her swelling and weight gain was due to diabetes and heart problems. She became severely depressed and began to question her faith, uttering that "the old man upstairs has deserted me." [25] Film offers became scarce as well. This was largely due to the vehement backlash against "Mammyism" by the NAACP. Walter White, head of the organization, believed Hattie was helping perpetuate the belief that slaves had been content and that her portrayals of maids and servants were keeping blacks from rising to higher positions in America. "What do you want me to do?" she asked. "Play a glamour girl and sit on Clark Gable's knee?" [26] What the NAACP was ignoring were Hattie's strides in the Civil Rights movement. It was she who was responsible for insisting upon the omission of the word "nigger" from the script of *Gone With the Wind*. It was she who, in 1945, battled all the way to the Supreme Court to keep her and her black neighbors from being forced from their homes by wealthy white property owners. White's militant activism had him placed on the black list by House UnAmerican Activities Committee, and despite Hattie's patriotism, her mere association with White landed her on the black list as well.

Blacklisted, Hattie's film career waned and she was forced to turn to radio. However, instead of hurting her career, radio gave her a long-deserved niche as a leading lady. Though she was still a servant in the show, she, as the title character, Beulah, was the focus. *Beulah*'s phenomenal popularity even dampened White's criticisms. Hattie refused to speak in dialect for the show, which brought it a dignity despite its being tagged as a "comic soap opera." [27] Hattie gave plenty of laughs, especially through her ongoing relationship with her shiftless boyfriend. She created catchphrases such as "Love dat man!" and, after their arguments, "On the con-positively-trary!" The show gained fifteen million listeners by 1948, most of them white. "I live the part...I feel I really am Beulah," [28] Hattie stated.

Despite her groundbreaking success on the airwaves, Hattie was struggling with severe depression in her personal life. Her marriage crumbled when her husband told her he was bisexual. She continued to receive criticism from those of her own race about her roles and she began to withdraw from even her best friends. She confessed that she was not happy and "never really have been." [29] Adding to her depression was the fact that, due to a heart attack, she could not accept the role of Beulah on television. To assuage her sadness, Hattie went on spending sprees, threw lavish parties, and turned to drugs and alcohol. But no distraction helped. "Hell can't be anything worse than what I'm living through," [30] she said. At her lowest ebb she took an overdose of sleeping pills, but a friend found her and she was saved.

Strangely, Hattie's brush with death revived her spirits. She declared that she was happy living as a single woman in a bungalow for one, tending to her mementoes, and continuing to play Beulah on the air. Hattie's new neighbors recalled her sitting on her porch every morning "no matter what the weather" and greeting everyone with "Hello there, good morning!" [31] Even after she suffered a stroke and was diagnosed with breast cancer, Hattie found strength to attend the dedication of the Motion Picture Country home in 1952. She would find herself at this hospital as her cancer weakened her. She received thousands of get well cards from fans, white and black, who saw her as a member of their family after listening to her everyday over the radio. It is fitting that theirs were the last words Hattie read before she died at fifty-seven years old, for they affirmed how much her public loved her despite the many criticisms she had received in past years. Her funeral was befitting a queen, with 125 limousines and two vans to carry the flowers stars and fans had sent in her honor. "Hattie is as alive as ever," friend Ruby Goodwin remarked. "... it is impossible to live in the shadow of such a vibrant personality...and think that such a nebulous thing as stopping a heartbeat could suddenly annihilate anything or anyone as indestructible as Hattie McDaniel." [32]

Hattie McDaniel can be called the first black celebrity. In being so, she was indeed a reformer, breaking long held barriers between whites and blacks. She was even laid to rest at Rosedale Cemetery, succeeding in being the first black individual to ever be buried there. Though her critics called her roles subservient or caricatures, she brought a sincerity, warmth, and individuality to them that stood in defiance to any evidence of inferiority they could have implied. Hattie never acknowledged her role in changing the place of blacks in America; rather, she humbly said of her performances, "I did my best, and God did the rest." [33]

FILMOGRAPHY

1949	*The Big Wheel*	Minnie *(as Hattie McDaniels)*
1948	*Family Honeymoon*	Phyllis
1948	*Mickey*	Bertha
1947	*The Flame*	Celia
1946	*Song of the South*	Aunt Tempy
1946	*Never Say Goodbye*	Cozy
1946	*Margie*	Cynthia
1946	*Janie Gets Married*	April
1944	*Hi, Beautiful*	Millie

1944	*Three Is a Family*	Maid
1944	*Janie*	April, Conway's Maid
1944	*Since You Went Away*	Fidelia
1943	*Thank Your Lucky Stars*	Gossip in 'Ice Cold Katie' Number
1943	*Johnny Come Lately*	Aida
1942	*George Washington Slept Here*	Hester, the Fullers' Maid
1942	*In This Our Life*	Minerva Clay
1942	*The Male Animal*	Cleota
1941	*They Died with Their Boots On*	Callie
1941	*Affectionately Yours*	Cynthia, Sue's Cook
1941	*The Great Lie*	Violet
1940	*Maryland*	Aunt Carrie
1939	*Gone with the Wind*	Mammy–House Servant
1939	*Zenobia*	Dehlia *(as Hattie McDaniels)*
1939	*Everybody's Baby*	Hattie
1938	*The Shining Hour*	Belvedere
1938	*The Mad Miss Manton*	Hilda *(as Hattie McDaniels)*
1938	*Carefree*	Hattie *(uncredited)*
1938	*The Shopworn Angel*	Martha
1938	*Vivacious Lady*	Hattie, Maid at Prom Dance *(uncredited)*
1938	*Battle of Broadway*	Agatha
1937	*True Confession*	Ella
1937	*Quick Money*	Hattie, Tompkins' Maid *(uncredited)*
1937	*45 Fathers*	Beulah
1937	*Nothing Sacred*	Mrs. Walker *(uncredited)*
1937	*Merry Go Round of 1938*	Maid
1937	*Over the Goal*	Hannah *(as Hattie McDaniels)*
1937	*Sky Racket*	Jenny *(as Hattie McDaniels)*
1937	*Stella Dallas*	Edna, Maid #2 *(uncredited)*
1937	*Saratoga*	Rosetta Washington *(as Hattie McDaniels)*
1937	*The Wildcatter*	Pearl *(uncredited)*
1937	*The Crime Nobody Saw*	Ambrosia
1937	*Don't Tell the Wife*	Mamie, Nancy's Maid *(uncredited)*
1937	*All Scarlet*	Abby
1937	*Mississippi Moods*	
1936	*Reunion*	Sadie
1936	*Can This Be Dixie?*	Lizzie
1936	*Libeled Lady*	Maid in Grand Plaza Hall *(uncredited)*
1936	*Valiant Is the Word for Carrie*	Ellen Belle *(as Hattie McDaniels)*
1936	*Star for a Night*	Hattie

1936	*Postal Inspector*	Deborah *(uncredited)*
1936	*High Tension*	Hattie
1936	*The Bride Walks Out*	Mamie–Carolyn's maid *(as Hattie McDaniels)*
1936	*Show Boat*	Queenie
1936	*Arbor Day (short)*	Buckwheat's mother
1936	*Gentle Julia*	Kitty Silvers
1936	*The Singing Kid*	Maid *(uncredited)*
1936	*The First Baby*	Dora
1936	*Next Time We Love*	Hanna *(uncredited)*
1935	*We're Only Human*	Molly, Martin's Maid *(uncredited)*
1935	*Another Face*	Nellie, Sheila's Maid *(uncredited)*
1935	*Music Is Magic*	Amanda *(as Hattie McDaniels)*
1935	*Harmony Lane*	Liza, the Cook *(uncredited)*
1935	*Murder by Television*	Isabella–the Cook
1935	*Alice Adams*	Malena Burns, Maid Serving Dinner *(as Hattie McDaniels)*
1935	*China Seas*	Isabel McCarthy, Dolly's Maid *(uncredited)*
1935	*The Four Star Boarder (short)*	Maid *(uncredited)*
1935	*Wig-Wag (short)*	Cook *(uncredited)*
1935	*Traveling Saleslady*	Martha Smith *(uncredited)*
1935	*Transient Lady*	Servant *(uncredited)*
1935	*The Little Colonel*	Becky *('Mom Beck')* Porter
1935	*Okay Toots! (short)*	Maid *(as Hattie McDaniels)*
1935	*Anniversary Trouble (short)*	Mandy, the maid
1934	*The Chases of Pimple Street (short)*	Hattie, Gertrude's Maid *(uncredited)*
1934	*Little Men*	Asia *(uncredited)*
1934	*Babbitt*	Rosalie, the Maid *(uncredited)*
1934	*Fate's Fathead (short)*	Mandy, the Maid *(as Hattie McDaniels)*
1934	*Lost in the Stratosphere*	Ida Johnson *(as Hattie McDaniels)*
1934	*Flirtation (uncredited)*	
1934	*Judge Priest*	Aunt Dilsey *(as Hattie McDaniels)*
1934	*King Kelly of the U.S.A.*	Black Narcissus Mop Buyer *(uncredited)*
1934	*Operator 13*	Annie *(a Cook) (uncredited)*
1934	*Merry Wives of Reno*	Bunny's Maid *(uncredited)*
1934	*Mickey's Rescue (short)*	Maid *(uncredited)*
1933	*Goodbye Love*	Edna the Maid *(uncredited)*
1933	*I'm No Angel*	Tira's Maid-Manicurist *(uncredited)*

THE NO NONSENSE
NITWIT
UNA MERKEL

UNA MERKEL CIRCA 1937. COURTESY OF JERRY MURBACH.

Before Marilyn Monroe was immortalized as the ubiquitous "dumb blonde" in film, another woman was synonymous with the archetype. Her name was Una Merkel. Though her Kewpie doll face, "fluttery mannerisms and high-pitched drawl" [1] were considered more comical than glamorous, she, like Monroe, exuded a charming naiveté on screen. It allowed her to deliver lines that could remain innocent because she seemed so genuinely oblivious to their suggestive double-meanings. However, unlike Monroe, Una never rose to leading lady status. In the words of one columnist, she was "always the bridesmaid, never the bride." [2] Rather, she was the sidekick to such beauties as Jean Harlow and Carole Lombard who managed to dispense good advice in the midst of her daffy moments. Though they earned her fame, Una called her endless succession of "nitwit" roles hard to tolerate. Thus, throughout her career, she remained torn between loving her work and yearning to live a domestic life free of stardust. The seemingly pert little blonde on screen was a humble girl who never saw herself as the celebrity she could have been, as proved when she philosophized, "I always tell them, 'When you can't give 'em looks, give 'em laughs.'" [3]

Una acquired her distinctive drawl as a child growing up in the southern town of Covington, Kentucky. Born on December 10, 1903 as Una Kohnfelder, her colorful childhood was one befitting a comic actress. Her father was a traveling salesman who sold calendars, Lifesavers, and a bottled drink called Cherry Smash. "This made me very popular at school," [4] Una commented. Until she was nine years old, she and her mother traveled across the South with Mr. Merkel — in a horse and buggy. [5] Una's upbringing made her the modest woman she would grow to be; she later remarked she was raised to be seen and not heard, "And I'm still all for it." [6] However, she found her chance to be seen and heard when she took ballet and elocution lessons (incidentally taught to her by Tyrone Power's mother). The lessons gave her a taste of being on the stage and she gained a strong appetite for it. When Una was fifteen, she and her family left Covington for New York, the ideal locale to begin a theater career. "I decided I didn't want to go to school anymore, that I wanted to be an actress," she stated. [7] As ambitious as she was, Una remarked that she knew she was not beautiful and lacked self confidence, two potential handicaps for a performer. "But my family encouraged me and I was enthusiastic!" [8] she said. Una attended a dramatic school but real luck was hers when director D.W. Griffith noticed her resemblance to Lillian Gish. Her resemblance was strong enough for Una to be used as Gish's double in long shots of her films, including *The Wind* (1928), *Way*

Down East (1920), and *World's Shadows*. [9] "I thought I owned the town, even though the picture was never filmed," [10] Una wryly commented in reference to the third film.

Her lack of conspicuous screen presence did little to dampen her ambition. Una made the rounds of casting offices and was rewarded for her perseverance. She made her Broadway debut in a production entitled *Two By Two*. However, she only spoke two lines in the play and spoke even less in her next one, *The Poor Nut*. But when someone told her she resembled the ingénue who was leaving a successful show (with the unfortunate title of *Pigs*) playing across the street, Una leapt at the chance to replace her. She went to see the show's producer herself. With the complete candor and lack of pretense that would characterize her both on screen and off for the rest of her life, she told the producer she was underage, had no real dramatic experience, and wanted a job badly. "You're the first person who ever came here and told me the truth and I rather like it," the producer told her. [11] Others must have "liked it," too, for following *Pigs*, Una had no lack of work on stage. Her most notable appearance was opposite Helen Hayes in *Coquette*, the play that would later be adapted into Mary Pickford's first talking picture. Una's performance in *Coquette* was enough to catch Joseph Schenk's attention at United Artists. He gave Una her first substantial screen role as Ann Rutledge in *Abraham Lincoln* (1930), starring Walter Huston. While Una was enjoying such success in her career, she found time to fall in love and marry aviation engineer Ronald Burla. Allegedly, Burla did not "give a whoop about the movies." [12]

Una's film career did not start slowly. She made up to twelve films a year between 1932 and 1938. Like many stock players in the studio system, Una was tested in any and every genre before studio heads decided what was to be her forte. She was Sam Spade's secretary in the original *The Maltese Falcon* (1931), little orphan Sally in *Daddy Long Legs* (1931), and Harold Lloyd's reluctant love interest in *The Cat's Paw* (1934). It was in *42nd Street* (1932) that she best showcased what would become her niche: the nit wit. With her hair dyed peroxide blonde, she was the not-too-bright showgirl supporting Ginger Rogers and Ruby Keeler. She was able to show off her musical talents in the film as well, namely in the "Shuffle Off to Buffalo" number. Her success in *42nd Street* led her to be cast in more top notch musicals: *Born to Dance* (1936) and *Broadway Melody of 1936* (1936). Though she sang only briefly in the former and not at all in the latter film, they further molded her typical screen character as the silly, wisecracking, but good-hearted girlfriend to leading ladies. Among her most memorable roles is as Sally in Jean Harlow's *Red-Headed Woman*

(1932). She plays a girl not unlike herself: humble and realistic. She brings Harlow down to earth in exchanges such as:

SALLY: *You're gonna marry Albert?*

LILLIAN 'LIL': *No, Gaerste.*

SALLY: *In love with Gaerste?*

LILLIAN 'LIL': *No, Albert. Besides, I always did wanna learn French.*

SALLY: *Oh, why don't you get yourself a laundryman and learn Chinese?* [13]

Because Una was often the comic relief in a film, her leading men complemented her humor. "I never had a really romantic type of lover," Una once lamented. She became the girl who never got her man, or when she did, her dissatisfaction toward him was all too clear. She was paired twice with the short and zany actor Sid Silvers. In her hilarious intimidations of his milquetoast character, she is anything but threatening with her high-pitched drawl and perky blonde looks.

In 1937, Una got her chance to rival leading ladies where glamour was concerned. The movie was *Saratoga*. Though best remembered as Jean Harlow's final film, it allowed Una to "kiss Clark Gable and marry Frank Morgan" and wear "twenty-four different costumes, three negligees and nine suits, all designed by Dolly Tree." [14] Finally, Una did not portray Harlow's pal in the picture. Rather, she was the ditzy, and much younger, wife of tycoon Frank Morgan. She romanticized her role as letting her be, "weird, mysterious, hypnotic." [15]

However, it was still as a screwball comedienne that she won most acclaim. Una got the biggest laughs of her career in the role for which she is arguably best known. In *Destry Rides Again* (1939), she plays Lily Belle, the woman who is saloon girl Frenchy's (Marlene Dietrich) adversary in an all-out "cat fight." Una recalled during the filming of the now classic scene that she was wearing soft shoes, but Dietrich was wearing heels. "She stomped on my feet so hard my toes still hurt," [16] she said. But Una was not one to complain. She forever seemed to see herself as a guest in film land. She addressed her co-stars formally by their surnames, as if she was not their colleague but their underling. "I was always scared to death to ask for a job. And that's the reason I get the kinds of parts I have," [17] she explained. "I've played a lot of comedy parts...which were pretty hard to swallow. But when you take a role you must believe in it, force yourself to believe in it, and do your best." [18]

Una did indeed do her best working twelve to fourteen hours a day as one of Hollywood's busiest comediennes. However, in her rare leisure

UNA MERKEL WITH JUNE KNIGHT IN *BROADWAY MELODY OF 1936* (1936).
COURTESY OF JERRY MURBACH.

moments, Una strove for a normal life of domesticity. She once confessed to the *Boston Globe*, "I wish I were my grandmother" because, though the elder woman had to wash, bake, iron, raise thirteen children, and run a spinning wheel, at least she was able to "stay home for meals." [19] Nothing showed Una's value of family and tradition more than the fact that her parents lived with her for her entire life. One columnist aptly described the Merkels as "madly reminiscent of the Sycamore" family in the Kaufman-Hart farce *You Can't Take It with You*. "Papa Arno Merkel... makes a hobby of traveling...just picks a spot on a map at random and goes there. Bessie, the mother, works tirelessly at her stamp collection. Burla [Una's husband] himself collects coins. Una reads voraciously. Another member of the family is a trained nurse who came there seven years ago and somebody was sick so she just stayed." [20]

Una's family was not as whimsical as journalists' depictions led readers to believe. Perhaps Una so yearned for domesticity because she never knew stability as a child or as a woman. In 1945, Una further lost stability when her mother slashed her wrists and turned on the gas in the apartment she and Una shared. Mrs. Merkel died, but the gas almost killed Una as well. Strangely, Mrs. Merkel's suicide note was not addressed to Una, but to Richard Burla. "Be good to her," Mrs. Merkel wrote. "She has had so many rotten deals in this world." [21] Despite Mrs. Merkel's note, Una and Burla's marriage was already in trouble. In 1947, they divorced.

Simultaneous to her personal tragedies, Una's film career took a precipitous downturn. "I always played sort of nitwit, dizzy roles," she observed. "As I got older, I got tired of playing dizzy telephone operators. Then the movies weren't doing dizzy telephone operators anymore." [22] With her type of character no longer in vogue, Una went from playing leading ladies' pals to playing their mothers. She appeared in inconsequential roles in fluffy musicals throughout the 1950s, most notably in the Debbie Reynolds picture *I Love Melvin* (1953) and in a Jane Powell vehicle, *Rich, Young, and Pretty* (1951). The bulk of her work was now in television programs such as *Schlitz Playhouse* and *Studio One*.

It was Una's return to the stage that revealed she was far from forgotten, obscure as her roles had become. However, it took another brush with death to prove it. While touring in a production of *Come Back Little Sheba* in 1952, Una took an overdose of sleeping pills. She went into a coma so severe that her doctor "could not determine her chance of survival." [23] Miraculously, she survived. Though the press speculated that it was her personal tragedies and career setbacks that had led to her suicide attempt, Una insisted: "It was all a terrible mistake. I was ill, but not despondent...I had gotten a cold, so I thought the best thing to do was to go to bed and get a rest...The next thing I knew, I woke up in the hospital." [24] Ironically, Una's "suicide attempt" was just what she needed to boost her career. It brought her back into the public eye and proved she still had an enthusiastic fan base. "I had never realized how many friends I had. I heard from boys in Korea. I got letters from men who had seen me in the last war...I had a lively letter from a bus driver in England, who included bits of poetry," [25] Una explained. She also received a letter from a minister whose wife paid the actress a visit. "Now we are good friends!" [26] Una declared. She continued to be amazed at the outpouring of attention she enjoyed not just through letters, but in public. "People stop me on the street to say hello," Una said. "Truck drivers yell, 'Hi ya Una, what ya doing now?' I guess they speak to me because I was always the girl next door, the one you could go to with all your troubles." [27]

In 1956, Una was validated not only by fans of her past work but by critics of her present work. She landed a role in a play entitled *The Ponder Heart*, described by Brooks Atkinson as "a comedy of rural manners" based on a Eudora Welty novel. Una earned some of the best notices of her career as Mrs. Ponder. "Una Merkel brings into the play the selfless affection that made the novel so pleasant and refreshing," Atkinson wrote. She won a Tony Award for her efforts. Her film career had taken an upswing as well. She received substantial roles as Debbie Reynolds' mother in *The Mating Game* (1959) and as Hayley Mills' housekeeper in *The Parent Trap* (1961). It was in 1961 that Una won a role that would bring her in film the acclaim *The Ponder Heart* had brought her on stage. The film was a Tennessee Williams work entitled *Summer and Smoke* (1961). Una played Geraldine Page's mother, "the selfish, childish, tyrannical victim of a nervous breakdown, a simple yet devious kleptomaniac." [28] Because the part was decidedly against the "girl next door," amusing types she was long known for playing, Una had to campaign for it. She claimed to have written the producer several letters championing herself. When the man finally called her, she stated: "I was in his office before he hung up the phone." [29] It is a testament to her ambition and resilience that she maintained such youthful ambition at a time when many would consider retiring. Her vitality must have shone through on screen, for she earned an Academy Award nomination for her performance. As much as she had championed herself for the role, she was still modesty personified. When she heard the news of her nomination, Una responded, "Are you sure?" [30]

Though she lost the Academy Award to Rita Moreno, the nomination was validation enough for Una. After *Summer and Smoke* (1961), she let more time to pass between pictures and stage work. She spent more time on herself, writing poetry and traveling on sightseeing tours with her father. An unexpected bequest from an aunt also gave her the financial security that allowed her to relax. But she had been working since she was fifteen and was unaccustomed to leisure. She declared she would like to "work again if something good came up." [31] Not much good did come up; following *Summer and Smoke* she only appeared in three films. What would ultimately be her final movie was a mediocre Elvis Presley vehicle, *Spinout* (1966). Her last role was bit part, an anticlimactic swan song to a career of over a hundred pictures.

As late as 1978, Una professed she could not feel her age. But in 1986, her age caught up with her. She died at eighty-two. Even in death, Una shunned the customary movie star treatment. She chose to be buried beside her parents in Covington, Kentucky rather than Forest Lawn, the final resting place of most celebrities.

Una Merkel may seem like an anachronism in any era but the 1930s. In the screwball comedies and snappy musicals of that era, her simultaneously sensible and nonsensical barbs and bits of advice were perfectly suitable. But, beneath the silly blonde on screen, Una projected a grit and sincerity that never goes out of fashion. She thumbed her nose at rejection with comebacks that could make the most adamant jeerer look at her afresh and believe that, like Marilyn Monroe once famously said as bubble-head Lorelei Lee, she could be "smart when it was important." It is this under-lying intelligence and sensitivity that endears Una so to film viewers and makes her more the girl next door than women who played similar wise-cracking, "girlfriend" roles, namely Joan Blondell or Patsy Kelly. In life, Una *was* the girl next door. Her friends "did not include many actors" and, even when she was at M-G-M, she professed to "know very few people at the studio." [32] It was her ever present humility and distance from the movie star façade that never made her feel she was not above playing the roles audiences loved — nitwits and pals. She remained as awed of movie stars as her audiences, leading her to confide with her characteristic lack of pretense:

"I never could believe that I was really in the movie business." [33]

FILMOGRAPHY

1966	Spinout	Violet Ranley
1964	A Tiger Walks	Mrs. Watkins
1963	Summer Magic	Mariah Popham
1961	Summer and Smoke	Mrs. Winemiller
1961	The Parent Trap	Verbena
1959	The Mating Game	Ma Larkin
1958	The Girl Most Likely	Mother
1957	The Fuzzy Pink Nightgown	Bertha
1956	Bundle of Joy	Mrs. Dugan
1956	The Kettles in the Ozarks	Miss Bedelia Baines
1955	The Kentuckian	Sophie Wakefield
1952	The Merry Widow	Kitty Riley
1952	With a Song in My Heart	Sister Marie
1951	Golden Girl	Mary Ann Crabtree
1951	A Millionaire for Christy	Patsy Clifford
1951	Rich, Young and Pretty	Glynnie

1950	*Emergency Wedding*	Emma–Nurse/Receptionist
1950	*My Blue Heaven*	Miss Irma Gilbert
1950	*Kill the Umpire*	Betty Johnson
1948	*Man from Texas*	Widow Weeks
1948	*The Bride Goes Wild*	Miss Doberly
1947	*It's a Joke, Son!*	Mrs. Magnolia Claghorn
1944	*Sweethearts of the U.S.A.*	Patsy Wilkins
1944	*To Heir Is Human (short)*	Una
1943	*Quack Service (short)*	
1943	*This Is the Army*	Rose Dibble
1942	*Twin Beds*	Lydia
1942	*The Mad Doctor of Market Street*	Aunt Margaret Wentworth
1941	*Cracked Nuts*	Sharon Knight
1941	*Road to Zanzibar*	Julia Quimby
1941	*Double Date*	Aunt Elsie Kirkland
1940	*The Bank Dick*	Myrtle Sousè
1940	*Sandy Gets Her Man*	Nan Clark
1940	*Comin' Round the Mountain*	Belinda Watters
1939	*Destry Rides Again*	Lily Belle
1939	*On Borrowed Time*	Marcia Giles
1939	*Some Like It Hot*	Flo Saunders
1939	*Four Girls in White*	Gertie Robbins
1937	*True Confession*	Daisy McClure
1937	*Checkers*	Mamie Appleby
1937	*Saratoga*	Fritzi
1937	*The Good Old Soak*	Nellie
1937	*Don't Tell the Wife*	Nancy Dorsey
1936	*Born to Dance*	Jenny Saks
1936	*We Went to College*	Susan Standish
1936	*Speed*	Josephine 'Jo' Sanderson
1936	*Riffraff*	Lil
1935	*It's in the Air*	Alice Lane Churchill
1935	*Broadway Melody of 1936*	Kitty Corbett
1935	*Murder in the Fleet*	'Toots' Timmons
1935	*Baby Face Harrington*	Millie Harrington
1935	*One New York Night*	Phoebe
1935	*The Night Is Young*	Fanni Kerner
1935	*Biography of a Bachelor Girl*	Slade Kinnicott
1934	*Evelyn Prentice*	Amy Drexel
1934	*The Merry Widow*	Queen Dolores

1934	*Have a Heart*	Joan O'Day
1934	*Bulldog Drummond Strikes Back*	Gwen
1934	*The Cat's-Paw*	Pat Pratt
1934	*Paris Interlude*	Cassie Bond
1934	*Murder in the Private Car*	Georgia Latham
1934	*This Side of Heaven*	Birdie
1933	*The Women in His Life*	Miss 'Simmy' Simmons
1933	*Day of Reckoning*	Mamie
1933	*Bombshell*	Mac
1933	*Menu (short)*	Mrs. Omsk *(uncredited)*
1933	*Broadway to Hollywood*	Flirt in Audience *(uncredited)*
1933	*Beauty for Sale*	Carol Merrick
1933	*Her First Mate*	Hattie
1933	*Midnight Mary*	Bunny 'Bun'
1933	*Reunion in Vienna*	Ilsa Hinrich
1933	*42nd Street*	Lorraine Fleming
1933	*Clear All Wires!*	Dolly Winslow
1933	*The Secret of Madame Blanche*	Ella
1933	*Whistling in the Dark*	Toby Van Buren
1932	*Men Are Such Fools*	Molly
1932	*They Call It Sin*	Dixie Dare
1932	*Red-Headed Woman*	Sally
1932	*Huddle*	Thelma
1932	*Man Wanted*	Ruth 'Ruthie' Holman
1932	*The Impatient Maiden*	Betty Merrick
1932	*She Wanted a Millionaire*	Mary Taylor
1931	*Private Lives*	Sibyl Chase
1931	*The Secret Witness*	Lois Martin
1931	*Wicked*	June
1931	*The Bargain*	Etta
1931	*Daddy Long Legs*	Sally McBride
1931	*The Maltese Falcon*	Effie Perine
1931	*Six Cylinder Love*	Margaret Rogers
1931	*All Women are Bad*	Tallulah Hope
1931	*Command Performance*	Princess Katerina
1930	*The Bat Whispers*	Dale Van Gorder
1930	*The Eyes of the World*	Sybil
1930	*Abraham Lincoln*	Ann Rutledge
1924	*The Fifth Horseman*	Dorothy
1923	*Love's Old Sweet Song (short)*	

THE TIPSY PHILOSOPHER
THOMAS MITCHELL

THOMAS MITCHELL CIRCA 1923. COURTESY OF JERRY MURBACH.

An elfin-faced, pudgy Irishman with a fondness for drink is among the most cliché of caricatures. However, no matter how many times Thomas Mitchell played this sort of character, he brought a spontaneity and naturalness to it that made his every performance stand out in the audience's memory. Today, Thomas is best remembered for his roles as the boozy Doc Boone in *Stagecoach* (1939), the tipsy Gerald O'Hara in *Gone With the Wind* (1939), and the scatter-brained Uncle Billy in *It's a Wonderful Life* (1946). In each of these films, he creates characters of unexpected depth that combine unique humor and pathos to win viewers' hearts. When describing Thomas Mitchell, his friend, author Thomas Mann, summed him up in one ideal adjective: "earthy." [1] On and off screen, Thomas's lack of pretentions made him the supporting actor's equivalent of the everyman leading player James Stewart came to symbolize. Thomas's own words best explain his philosophy for acting: "You've always got to act with the enthusiasm of an amateur. That goes for technique, too. Some of our actors get so bound up in the art of acting, the technique, they forget to be human." [2] At no point in Thomas Mitchell's prestigious forty-eight year career did audiences ever forget he was human.

Thomas Mitchell was born on July 11, 1892 in Elizabeth, New Jersey to Irish immigrants James and Mary Mitchell. He was one among the Mitchells' seven children. His father worked as a newspaperman, a profession both Thomas's older brother and he would later pursue. When Thomas graduated from high school, he became a cub reporter and worked for publications all over the East Coast, including Washington D.C., Newark, Baltimore, and Pittsburgh. [3] While on assignment with the *Elizabeth Journal* in New Jersey, Thomas was asked to report on one of Woodrow Wilson's presidential campaign speeches. Because he was required to do on-the-spot reporting, Thomas took up a post with his typewriter on the theater wing of the stage on which Wilson was speaking. Wilson's unrehearsed speech is said to have been the worst he ever gave, but Thomas typed every word on his typewriter, including the numerous pauses and "ums" the candidate spoke. When a flustered and stiff Wilson left the stage, he paused beside Thomas, who was pounding out the last of the speech, and whacked the back of the machine. With a red face, the future president cried: "I bet *you're* a Republican!" [4] Such a humorous anecdote plays like a scene one might expect to see in one of Thomas's later films, many of which were set in newspaper offices. Indeed, Thomas's years as a reporter gave him valuable life experiences that helped him to become a more versatile actor.

As much as Thomas loved to write, journalism was not the medium he wished to further pursue. In his free time, he penned skits that he performed in local stock companies. Thomas abandoned reporting altogether in 1913 when he decided acting was the career for which he was best suited. He made his first stage appearance the same year at Madison Square Garden, playing Trinculo in *The Tempest*.[5] His success in this Shakespeare play caught the attention of Broadway actor Charles Coburn, who subsequently invited Thomas to join his Shakespearean company, the Coburn Players. Thomas spent the next two years with Coburn, performing at various universities and colleges.

During this time, Thomas met Anne Brewer and married her in 1916. Little is known about their courtship and marriage except that it did result in Thomas's only child, Anne. The same year of Thomas's marriage, he appeared in his first original Broadway play, *Under Sentence*. For the next ten years, he appeared in eight more plays as well as one silent short film in 1923 called *Six Cylinder Love*. However, Thomas did not yet seriously consider Hollywood. In 1926, he took to the typewriter again to co-write with Floyd Dell an original show titled *Glory, Hallelujah*.

However, it was not until Thomas and Dell penned their next show in 1929 that Thomas attained his biggest success to date. The play, called *The Little Accident*, was adapted from a short story by Dell. The play told the story of a man who, as *The Pittsburgh Press* wrote, "sewed some wild oats in Boston…and…on the eve of his marriage is summoned to Chicago to see the baby presented by the girl he met in Boston."[6] The mother wishes to adopt out the child, but the father disagrees and proceeds to kidnap the baby to care for it himself. In the end, the mother and father marry and raise the baby together. The story is more familiarly known as *Casanova Brown*, the title it was given when it was adapted for the screen in 1944 as a Gary Cooper vehicle.

Co-starring with Thomas was a young actress named Rachel Hartzell. Despite their approximately twenty-year age difference, Thomas caught Rachel's eye as much as she did his. Three years later, she told the *Boston Daily Globe* that she had first seen Thomas on stage when she was five years old. Speaking to Thomas during the interview, she said: "I did love your laced boots…and I did think you were pretty noble."[7] Undoubtedly, Thomas's wife did not approve of the flirtation. Although the date of their divorce is not clear, it is known that Thomas and Anne's marriage ended sometime before 1932.

Rachel Hartzell's admiration for her talented leading man could not have been discouraged when Thomas went on to win the Megrue Prize in 1929 for *The Little Accident*. An award offered by the Dramatist's Guild, the Megrue bestowed a playwright $500 for presenting a play that "makes the audience a little brighter and a little more cheered up when it leaves than when it came in."[8]

Thomas's career continued to be on the ascendant as he was chosen to be Spencer Tracy's replacement in *The Last Mile* when Tracy left for Hollywood. He was simultaneously at work with Dell on another play called *Cloudy with Showers*. The show seemed written expressly with Rachel Hartzell in mind. The plot revolved around a modern college girl who suggests that she and her professor (Thomas), with whom she is smitten, get to "know each other" before marrying.[9] The edgy, sophisticated comedy was a hit. Heywood Broun wrote in *The Pittsburgh Press* that "Mitchell as the harassed, embarrassed young professor gave a performance which stamped him as a finished actor. The role is not an easy one and calls for subtlety and restraint. Thomas Mitchell has both."[10]

As successful as Thomas was on Broadway, he was lured to Hollywood as so many theater actors were during the transition from silents to talkies. Stage actors were in high demand as producers sought performers whose voices would transfer well to the screen. Thomas's first film was a promising start. He co-starred alongside Rosalind Russell in the well-regarded 1936 adaptation of the play *Craig's Wife*. However, he did not gain widespread acclaim until the following year when he appeared in the Frank Capra classic *Lost Horizon* (1937). Playing the banker/embezzler Henry Barnard, his confident and outspoken portrayal was a humorous contrast to co-star Edward Everett Horton's meek and anxious character. The year 1937 also brought Thomas his first Oscar nomination for his performance as the drunken Dr. Kersaint in John Ford's *The Hurricane* (1937).[11] The role of Dr. Kersaint contributed in part to the typecasting Thomas was to experience in his oft-repeated roles as alcoholics.

The final glory of 1937 for Thomas was his marriage to Rachel Hartzell. The match was an unlikely one, not only because of the age difference but also because of their contrasting backgrounds. Rachel came from a wealthy family who had sent her to exclusive schools and the Sorbonne to be educated. Thomas was a first generation American with only a high school education. However, both Thomas and Rachel shared a zest for life and love of the theater. Rachel's friends described her thus: "She… is like champagne bubbles…she effervesces, sparkles, and bubbles in her conversation."[12] Similarly, Thomas was said to have a "complete and gusty enjoyment of life and likes practically everything and everyone."[13]

Thomas's enjoyment of "everything and everyone" is best illustrated by his active social life in Hollywood. He became a member of John Barrymore's "entourage of drinkers and raconteurs," which also included W.C. Fields, Errol Flynn, Roland Young, and Anthony Quinn. [14] According to the *New York Times,* Thomas's idea of a perfect evening was to spend it in "an alehouse...in the company of enlightened and

THOMAS MITCHELL, SIXTH FROM LEFT, IN *STAGECOACH* (1939). COURTESY OF JERRY MURBACH.

convivial friends, haranguing on all possible topics." [15] Thomas's meetings with this group of friends resembled 16th century actor, poet, and playwright Ben Jonson's clan, which met at the fabled Mermaid Tavern in London. Members of Jonson's group included great writers and thinkers such as Frances Bacon, John Donne, and William Shakespeare. Thomas claimed his ambition was to make a "huge phonograph album recreating Ben Jonson's 'Mermaid Tavern', using well-known actors in principal roles." [16] According to Thomas, Ben Jonson was the perfect model of a man who "captured to the fullest the beauty of life and the enjoyment of living." [17]

Thomas's enjoyment for living showed in his vivid performances throughout the 1930s. His success continued in films like *Theodora Goes Wild* (1936), in which he was at home portraying a newspaperman, and the Leo McCarey drama *Make Way for Tomorrow* (1937), which tells of the perils of old age. He hit his stride in 1939 as did the rest of the film industry. The year is known as the best in Hollywood's history, producing such classics as *The Wizard of Oz, Gone With the Wind, Mr. Smith Goes to Washington, Stagecoach*, and *Goodbye Mr. Chips*. Thomas appeared in three of these films, playing an introspective alcoholic in each one.

In *Gone With the Wind*, Thomas plays Gerald O'Hara, Scarlett's willful Irish father who, in a moment of rebellion against the Yankees, jumps a fence with his horse and breaks his neck. Gerald O'Hara may have been comfortable with horses, but Thomas was fearful of them. Only did he sit on a horse after director Victor Fleming "bullied him into it." [18] Nevertheless, Thomas gave a noteworthy performance and spoke one of the most famous lines from the film:

> GERALD O'HARA: *It will come to you, this love of the land. There's no gettin' away from it if you're Irish...Land is the only thing in the world worth workin' for, worth fightin' for, worth dyin' for because it's the only thing that lasts.* [19]

Although Thomas's part as the drunken reporter "Dizzy" in *Mr. Smith Goes to Washington* was less emotionally demanding than the part of Gerald O'Hara, his scenes with Jean Arthur exhibit a subtle tenderness. This tenderness is most apparent in the scene when he declares he would become sober if she would agree to marry him.

Thomas's most demanding role of 1939 was as the whisky-slugging, philosophical Doc Boone in *Stagecoach*. In one soliloquy, he declares to Marshal Curly Wilcox:

> DOC BOONE: *I'm not only a philosopher, sir, I'm a fatalist. Somewhere, sometime, there may be the right bullet or the wrong bottle waiting for Josiah Boone. Why worry when or where?* [20]

For his portrayal of Doc Boone, Thomas took home the Oscar for Best Supporting Actor.

Although Thomas had hit the peak of his film career in 1939, his personal life was less stellar. The May-December romance between Thomas and Rachel Hartzell ended in divorce in 1939. But, in true Hollywood style, Thomas remarried his first wife, Anne, in 1941. He purchased a 3,000-acre farm in Carlton, Oregon with plans to move there with Anne at the end of the year. However, as the *Los Angeles Times* read: "His

[Thomas's] friends in Hollywood say they did not believe he intends interrupting his screen career." [21]

Indeed, Thomas showed no signs of leaving Hollywood as he continued to appear in a steady flow of films, including *The Immortal Sergeant* (1943) and *The Fighting Sullivans* (1944). Although he did claim to be writing a play with plans to direct it in New York, he explained to the *New York Times* that, "A lot of people say I've deserted my art because I left Broadway. Hell, I'm no artist. I've got a trade just like any other mechanic and I follow my trade where the work is...acting is my work, you can call it 'art' if you want to. I call it work." [22]

The bulk of Thomas's work was in Hollywood, but he did return to Broadway in 1941 to perform in *Crazy with Heat* and in 1947 to appear in *An Inspector Calls*. However, his best work of the 1940s is evident in his films, most notably the 1946 Capra holiday classic, *It's a Wonderful Life*. He exhibited his underrated comedic abilities in his portrayal of the forgetful, drunken Uncle Billy. His most humorous scene takes place after his nephew's wedding party when he declares to George Bailey: "I feel so good I could spit in Potter's eye! I think I will." [23] He then proceeds to stagger down the street, singing "My Wild Irish Rose" until he collides with a row of tin garbage cans. The other noteworthy performance of his later career was in a less comic role as a judge in the western classic *High Noon* (1952). Following this film, he devoted most of his time to television and theater.

Thomas's most substantial role in theater came in 1949 when he replaced Albert Dekker in the Arthur Miller classic *Death of a Salesman*. For his performance, he received the best notices of his career. *The Pittsburgh Post Gazette* wrote: "Mr. Mitchell gives substance to 'Death of a Salesman' as a play and stature to himself as an actor...it is a performance to move boulders." [24]

Never one to possess pretensions, Thomas unhesitatingly turned to the small screen after his one-and-a-half-year run in *Death of a Salesman*. He appeared in a variety of weekly specials including *Studio One* and *The O. Henry Playhouse*. In 1953, he won an Emmy as television's Best Actor.

The same year, the tireless actor returned to Broadway to appear in his first musical show. Titled *Hazel Flagg*, the play was a musical version of the Carole Lombard screwball classic *Nothing Sacred* (1937). Thomas took on the role of the drunken country doctor that Charles Winninger had played in the film. He won a Tony Award for his performance, thus becoming the first actor to win the Triple Crown of awards: an Oscar, Emmy, and Tony. [25]

Following *Hazel Flagg*, Thomas went into semi-retirement. He did appear on two television series, *Glencannon* and *Mayor of the Town*, as well as a final film in 1961, *Pocketful of Miracles*, which paired him for the fourth time with Frank Capra.

Thomas remained active until the end of his life in 1962 when he died at his home at the age of seventy. He left his entire estate of $150,000 to his widow, Anne, and his daughter. [26]

At the time of Thomas's death, he was known to three generation of audiences, beginning with theatergoers of the 1910s and 1920s, continuing with filmgoers of the 1930s and 1940s, and ending with television viewers of the 1950s and early 1960s. Thomas communicated a unique ebullience on screen no matter how troubled his characters were. His resilient characterizations, most notably in Capra's films, resonated with audiences, particularly those of the 1930s and 1940s. He represented the average working man's struggle to survive and find meaning in the lean Depression and war years. Despite his considerable intellectualism in philosophy and writing, Thomas never revealed on screen that he had begun as a Shakespearean actor. Instead, his stocky build, ruffled hair, twinkling eyes, and Irish brogue made him among the most accessible, familiar, and lovable character actors of the screen. Undoubtedly when honing his skills as an actor, Thomas followed hero Ben Jonson's philosophy:

> *"Good men are the stars, the planets of the ages wherein they live, and illustrate the times."* [27]

FILMOGRAPHY

Year	Film	Role
1961	*Pocketful of Miracles*	Judge Henry G. Blake
1961	*By Love Possessed*	Noah Tuttle
1960	*Too Young to Love*	Judge Bentley
1958	*Handle with Care*	Mayor Dick Williston
1956	*While the City Sleeps*	John Day Griffith (Sentinel *managing editor*)
1954	*Destry*	Reginald T. 'Rags' Barnaby
1954	*Secret of the Incas*	Ed Morgan
1952	*High Noon*	Mayor Jonas Henderson
1951	*Journey Into Light*	Gandy
1949	*The Big Wheel*	Arthur 'Red' Stanley
1949	*Alias Nick Beal*	Joseph Foster
1948	*Silver River*	John Plato Beck

1947	*The Romance of Rosy Ridge*	Gill MacBean
1947	*High Barbaree*	Capt. Thad Vail
1946	*It's a Wonderful Life*	Uncle Billy Bailey
1946	*The Dark Mirror*	Lt. Stevenson
1946	*Three Wise Fools*	Terence Alaysius O'Davern
1945	*Adventure*	Mudgin
1945	*Within These Walls*	Warden Michael Howland
1945	*Captain Eddie*	Ike Howard
1944	*The Keys of the Kingdom*	Willie Tulloch
1944	*Dark Waters*	Mr. Sydney
1944	*Wilson*	Joseph Tumulty
1944	*Buffalo Bill*	Ned Buntline
1944	*The Fighting Sullivans*	Mr. Thomas F. Sullivan
1943	*Flesh and Fantasy*	Septimus Podgers *(Episode 2)*
1943	*Bataan*	Cpl. Jake Feingold
1943	*The Outlaw*	Pat Garrett
1943	*Immortal Sergeant*	Sgt. Kelly
1942	*The Black Swan*	Tom 'Tommie' Blue
1942	*Tales of Manhattan*	John Halloway
1942	*This Above All*	Monty
1942	*Moontide*	Tiny
1942	*Song of the Islands*	Dennis O'Brien
1942	*Joan of Paris*	Father Antoine
1941	*The Devil and Daniel Webster*	Daniel Webster in some long shots *(uncredited)*
1941	*Out of the Fog*	Jonah Goodwin
1941	*Flight from Destiny*	Prof. Henry Todhunter
1940	*The Long Voyage Home*	Driscoll
1940	*Angels Over Broadway*	Gene Gibbons
1940	*Our Town*	Dr. Gibbs
1940	*Three Cheers for the Irish*	Peter Casey
1940	*Swiss Family Robinson*	William Robinson
1939	*The Hunchback of Notre Dame*	Chopin
1939	*Gone with the Wind*	Gerald O'Hara
1939	*Mr. Smith Goes to Washington*	Diz Moore
1939	*Only Angels Have Wings*	Kid Dabb
1939	*Stagecoach*	Doc Boone
1938	*Trade Winds*	Commissioner Blackton
1938	*Love, Honor and Behave*	Dan Painter
1937	*The Hurricane*	Dr. Kersaint

THE PATRICIAN VIXEN
AGNES MOOREHEAD

AGNES MOOREHEAD CIRCA 1944. COURTESY OF JERRY MURBACH.

Agnes Moorehead, sometimes referred to as the woman of 1,000 faces, [1] conquered every entertainment medium from theater to radio to film to television. With equal ease, the regal redhead could portray a slovenly aunt in *Johnny Belinda* (1948), a catty socialite in *Since You Went Away* (1944), a histrionic member of fallen gentility in *The Magnificent Ambersons* (1942), or a flamboyant witch on the television series *Bewitched* (1964-1972). No matter what role she filled, she strove to be "sincere but detached." [2] This aloofness enabled her to retain the aura of mystery she felt was crucial to Hollywood stardom. A portion of her distance was due to her patrician demeanor and the fact that she was among Hollywood's most educated actresses, holding Master's and Doctorate degrees. She may have been best known for playing tart-tongued shrews, but in reality she was like a beneficent queen ruling over her people with a guiding and generous hand. Her friend, Mary Roebling, keenly summarized Agnes when she stated: "Agnes Moorehead is the model of the civilized human being. She served others, made the world a better place in which to live without sacrificing her own center, her own individuality." [3]

Agnes Moorehead was born in December 6, 1900 in Clinton, Massachusetts, not far from the blue-blooded cities of Cambridge and Boston. Her staunch Presbyterianism was instilled in her early in life by her father, who was a minister of the faith. Her love for the performing arts was helped along by her mother, a former mezzo soprano opera singer. Her father did not discourage her interest in performing either; he arranged her first performance when he taught her to recite "The Lord's Prayer" at his church. At three years old, she was already a gifted public speaker. The majority of Agnes's acting occurred in daily life. She created characters to fit every mood; if she was particularly melancholy one day, she was "Cynthia," not Agnes. [4] Her imagination extended outside her own characterizations to ones of those about her. While strolling the streets with her father, she would mimic passersby, a game in which her father willingly entered with her. Mr. Moorehead not only encouraged Agnes's imagination, he also taught her graciousness towards other people. "I think I learned of the happiness of being with people from my father. He was so warm and outgoing," [5] Agnes recalled.

Agnes continued to progress in her ambitions as she joined the St. Louis Municipal Opera Company in her teens. However, upon her high school graduation her father ordered that she acquire a formal education upon which she could fall if her acting endeavors failed. Agnes attended Muskingham College in Ohio and graduated in 1923. She went on to teach English at a public school in Wisconsin before attaining a Master's

Degree in Public Speaking and English. She went on to earn a doctorate in literature from Bradley University in Illinois. "I believe the more you know about what goes on around you, the better prepared you would be for any parts that might come along,"[6] Agnes explained when asked about the value of her education. After attaining her degree, Agnes received her father's blessing to travel to New York, where she was enrolled in the Academy of Dramatic Arts. Agnes graduated with honors in 1929.

Despite Agnes's promise, her venture into Broadway was short-lived and she never progressed to significant parts. She was not earning enough to fill her needs; consequently, she took other modes of employment to supplement her income including working as a library assistant, waitress, and teacher.[7] During one particularly lean period, she went four days without food. Agnes did not begin earning steady income until she turned to the Depression era's most popular entertainment form: radio. Through her work on the airwaves, she met fellow actor and radio personality Jack G. Lee and married him in 1930.

Agnes quickly eclipsed her husband in the radio business as she became the medium's most popular star. Often, she performed in several programs in one day. She lent her voice to every type of program there was, from children's hours like *The Gumps* to mystery dramas like *Suspense* to comedy hours, in which she would be the female foil to masters, including Bob Hope and Fred Allen. She displayed her wit and singing talents as the "Lonelyhearts" columnist on Phil Baker's radio journal where she "dispensed a great deal of useless advice and features a song now and then."[8] The versatility Agnes would later exhibit on screen began in the breadth of radio work in which she was involved. "Radio was a wonderful boon to an actor," she said. "You could use your imagination and your voice to create all sorts of characterizations."[9]

Radio work reunited Agnes with Orson Welles, a young man whom she had first met at age five. This fortuitous meeting would be the connection that led to Agnes becoming a luminary in her field. Welles featured Agnes in the broadcast that shook the entire nation, "War of the Worlds." So pleased was he with her work that, in 1937, he invited her to join his theatrical group, the Mercury Theater. Less than three years later, when RKO invited Welles to work in Hollywood, he took Agnes and fellow group member Joseph Cotten with him.

In Hollywood, Welles produced and directed his own films, most of which were sophisticated fare done in experimental styles. The first, *Citizen Kane* (1941), gave Agnes her first on screen role. Her part as Kane's poverty-stricken, sober mother was a small but pivotal one; she alone represented the childhood to which Kane yearned to return when he uttered "Rosebud" on his deathbed. One year after *Citizen Kane*, Agnes appeared in a second Welles film in a more substantial part that fully displayed her abilities. *The Magnificent Ambersons* (1942) centers on a wealthy southern family that over the passage of time, falls from grace into genteel poverty. Agnes plays Fanny, an emotional spinster aunt who is most affected at having to relinquish her patrician life. Like Fanny, Agnes went through life, rich or poor, with a royal countenance and the expectation of being treated like a lady. On the sets of her films, she carried a Bible with her and instilled reverence and morality in all those about her. "Whenever she was on the set, there was such respect," actor Cesar Romero recalled. "She seemed to demand it by her very presence more than anything else. The 'grips' would stop swearing when she appeared." [10] However like Fanny Agnes was, she was not a method actress and thus was not about to fall into poverty. Her incessant work and drive left little possibility of an empty bank account. "Everything she had she earned herself," Cesar Romero explained. "I felt sometimes she had an almost obsessive fear that she would not ever have enough to live on." [11]

Agnes's fears continued despite the considerable praise she received for her work as Fanny. She garnered her first Oscar nomination and won the New York Film Critics award for Best Supporting Actress. The following year, Agnes returned to radio in what would be her most famous broadcast. In *Sorry Wrong Number*, Agnes acts as a selfish, bed-ridden woman whose phone line is crossed with a murderer. As she listens, terrified, to the murderer plotting his crime, she learns she is the intended victim of the plot. The show held the record for the most repeated performances in the history of radio. When the program was later adapted for the screen, Barbara Stanwyck filled Agnes's role.

Though she was a leading lady in radio, she continued to act in supporting roles in film. Most often she portrayed catty and pretentious society vixens, most notably in the patriotic melodrama *Since You Went Away* (1944). As socialite Emily Hawkins, Agnes provides the primary source of conflict in a film otherwise populated by pleasant characters. When eighteen-year-old Jane (Jennifer Jones) explains she is foregoing college in favor of training as a nurse's aide, Emily (Agnes) is unashamedly rude in her response:

A nurse's aide? Oh! What a revolting idea for an unmarried girl of your age. Well, our whole code of living seems to be completely ignored these days. [12]

Agnes filled such roles so convincingly that she seldom was offered sympathetic parts. "I've never wanted to be a personality," Agnes said in some dismay. "I've always tried to be completely different in my characterizations." [13] Agnes did indeed give a different characterization in her next film, *Mrs. Parkington* (1944). She offers a moving performance as the likeable, if world-wise and at times pessimistic baroness. She received a

AGNES MOOREHEAD IN *SUMMER HOLIDAY* (1948). COURTESY OF JERRY MURBACH.

second Oscar nomination, but again lost. The glamorous part of the baroness led to more diverse roles, one of which gave Agnes the rare opportunity
to be the love interest of the leading man. In the classic Humphrey Bogart
noir film *Dark Passage* (1947), Agnes is the archetypal "other woman" to
Lauren Bacall. "It's gratifying," Agnes declared, "to play something besides
dowdy old shrews or imbecilic harridans…I wear an elegant wardrobe
and speak fairly intelligently." [14] Following *Dark Passage*, Agnes turned
to a role on the opposite end of the spectrum when it came to glamour.
As the hard-edged Aunt Aggie in *Johnny Belinda* (1948), Agnes wears
ragged clothing and no make-up. Whatever Aunt Aggie lacked in looks
she made up for in character; she remains a strong female presence to
her vulnerable and motherless, deaf-mute niece (Jane Wyman) before
and after the girl's father is killed. Wyman won the Best Actress Oscar
for the film, but Agnes only received a nomination for her performance.

   Glowing with success and earning $6,000 a week from her M-G-M
contract, Agnes and her husband purchased a 320-acre farm near
Cambridge, Ohio. There, Agnes became what she called "a gentleman
farmer," growing alfalfa, wheat, oats, corn and raising cattle, hogs, and
chickens. [15] Though Agnes behaved like a member of nobility, she was
actually close to the earth and its creatures in many respects. She was
known to return from farmer's markets with pounds of produce in the
trunk which she would freeze and later use to hand-make her own meals.
Though she ate meat, her fondness for all animals made her often consider vegetarianism. Apart from her beloved pet dogs and self-professed
adoration for pigs, she also showed a fondness for deer and always left
a salt block out on her front yard. Agnes's farm was a place of solace to
which she could retreat for much needed peace and privacy. Her lack of
candor about her personal life was well known throughout Hollywood,
but Agnes preferred to remain enigmatic. "There must be glamour and
mystery where stars are concerned," [16] she stated.

   As much as Agnes's lifestyle fostered her wish for "good solid family
life," [17] her marriage with Jack Lee was less than solid. In 1950, Lee
filed for divorce, claiming that Agnes barred him from her room due
to his snoring and "berated him because of his dress, speech, posture,
and manner of eating." [18] His inadequacy was further perpetrated when
Agnes ordered her servants to answer the phone with "Miss Moorehead's
residence." The divorce was granted with Lee paying Agnes a laughable
one dollar per year in alimony. [19]

   Agnes was more than able to support herself as she found success in the
theater to rival that of her work on screen. In 1951, she began touring with

Charles Laughton's company in *Don Juan in Hell*. The play, composed of four actors reciting the works of George Bernard Shaw, played to capacity houses for twenty weeks of every year from its opening in 1951 to its closing in 1955. At the suggestion of Laughton, Agnes staged her own one-woman show before and after *Don Juan in Hell*, which she called *The Fabulous Redhead*. Each night's performance was unique as Agnes never gave the same readings twice. She read from such varied works as the Bible, the works of James Thurber, Ring Lardner, Marcel Proust, and even the telephone directory! The *Herald Tribune* hailed her as the heir to Ethel Barrymore. [20] Agnes preferred the stage to any other medium. Like her father, she was an excellent public speaker with a message to communicate. "She was always trying to improve people in the theater and improve on the theater," Joseph Cotten explained. "It was like a mission in life for her — she did it evangelically and even with apostolic zeal." [21]

In Hollywood, Agnes won praise for her performance in a film that she felt was an improving one: *Magnificent Obsession* (1954). In the film, she plays a noble nurse to the blind Jane Wyman. The film's message of faith and love as a healing power was one in which Agnes believed wholeheartedly. It took a great deal of fighting for Agnes to win the role of a "good" woman, [22] but her persistence paid off as she received her fourth Oscar nomination for her role.

The year prior to *Magnificent Obsession*, Agnes married actor Robert Gist. But, the union ended five years later. Due to her high moral sense, religious devotion, and need for privacy, marriage was difficult for Agnes. "Women operate on a different plane," she once said. "Our feelings are emotional, not physical...why always bring up sex?" [23] Her lack of interest in conventional romance led to rumors that she was bisexual, but the allegations were never substantiated.

Despite her failed marriages and need to retain her privacy from columnists, Agnes was the most popular party hostess among the Hollywood elite. Journalist Dorothy Manners commented: "It has always struck me as an anomaly that Agnes Moorehead, one of the most intellectual ladies of her profession...is also one of the most indefatigable partygoers in town." [24] Agnes's annual Christmas party was an event of interest nationwide, with newspapers covering it on both coasts. The soirees were held at her Mediterranean style mansion, Villa Agnese. The home boasted a marble fireplace, a veranda, and a pool decorated with a ceramic tile mosaic of the Madonna. Her bedroom and clothing were almost completely lavender, a color she would have copyrighted as her own if she could. Her own favorite shade of lavender she called "Moorehead

Mauve." [25] Her love for the color was such that many dubbed her "The Lavender Lady." [26] It is appropriate she chose a variation of purple, the color of royalty, as her favorite.

When not acting as hostess, Agnes spent her free time in her massive library. She played Scrabble, taught herself French, and discussed religion and philosophy with friends. "Something higher than the usual gossip," [27] she said. Outside of her home, she was active with many charities including the Illinois Cancer Society and organizations fostering Jewish welfare.

Agnes's career still progressed though she was much occupied with her social and intellectual pursuits. She received her fifth and final Oscar nomination for her portrayal of the cynical and suspicious housekeeper in the Bette Davis thriller *Hush, Hush Sweet Charlotte* (1964). However, her name was known in every household not as a result of her film work but due to her role on the television series *Bewitched*. As Endora, Elizabeth Montgomery's flamboyant and critical mother who also happens to be a witch, she became a cultural icon. Endora was more acid-tongued than even the bluntest harridans she played on screen. Her main source of pleasure was to throw barbs at her mortal son-in-law, as shown in this typical exchange between them:

DARRIN STEPHENS: *You know, Endora, sometimes you can be almost human.*

ENDORA: *This is no time to be insulting.* [28]

As fun as the Endora character was to portray, Agnes was quick to remind her fans of her distinguished career pre-*Bewitched*. She was not eager to be solely identified as a witch. Television she found tedious and "tiring...the most difficult of all entertainment mediums." [29] As much as Agnes sometimes regretted being entwined with Endora, she believed in *Bewitched* due to its upholding of family values and fostering of imagination. "Nothing is as dull as constant reality," [30] Agnes stated. "The way it [the show] brings order out of chaos. Everybody likes that." [31]

Agnes's fame on television made younger audiences and performers seek her out as a mentor. She began teaching budding actors in the 1960s and 1970s, educating them in Shakespeare, technique, and movement. She felt it her duty to redirect young people away from the sordidness of modern entertainment. "It doesn't take talent to say dirty words and take off your clothes...sensuousness of that type — that isn't art...it's leading to the breakdown of morality," Agnes lamented after the premiere of the controversial Broadway musical *Hair*.

Agnes remained active into the 1970s despite the fact that she had been diagnosed with cancer. In 1956, Agnes had done location filming in St. George, Utah, for the John Wayne epic about Genghis Khan, *The Conqueror*. The site was not far from a nuclear test area in Yucca Flat, Nevada. Director Dick Powell had died of cancer in 1963 and several other cast and crew members on the film had been stricken too. "I should never have taken that part,"[32] Agnes stated in 1974.

While battling her cancer, Agnes continued to make television appearances as well as join a Broadway revival of *Gigi*. She was forced to leave the production when she became too ill. It was typical of her impeccable manners that, even while she was in pain in the hospital, she found time to write thank you notes to every person who had sent her bouquets and gifts. "Her absolute conviction in God...enabled her to endure suffering with rare grace,"[33] her friend Mary Roebling said. Agnes's suffering ended in April 1974.

Agnes Moorehead possessed the rare ability to become a beloved cultural icon despite the fact she played mostly haughty and unlikeable women on screen. Perhaps she became so beloved because, through her caustic behavior, audiences could see the wit and kindness of the woman behind the insults she read in her script. "She was severe with herself but ever forgiving of others,"[34] her biographer, Warren Sherk, explained. A remote and private woman to the public, she was known by close friends to be a gracious and charitable lady with an eye for beauty. The words of her most famous character, Endora, aptly describe the enigmatic nature of Agnes Moorehead, the star:

> ENDORA (about being a witch): *We are quicksilver, a fleeting shadow, a distant sound...our home has no boundaries beyond which we cannot pass. We live in music, in a flash of color...we live on the wind and in the sparkle of a star!*[35]

FILMOGRAPHY

1973	*Charlotte's Web*	The Goose *(voice)*
1972	*Dear Dead Delilah*	Delilah Charles
1971	*What's the Matter with Helen?*	Sister Alma
1966	*The Singing Nun*	Sister Cluny
1964	*Hush...Hush, Sweet Charlotte*	Velma Cruther

1963	*Who's Minding the Store?*	Mrs. Phoebe Tuttle
1962	*How the West Was Won*	Rebecca Prescott
1962	*Jessica*	Maria Lombardo
1961	*Bachelor in Paradise*	Judge Peterson
1961	*Twenty Plus Two*	Mrs. Eleanor Delaney
1960	*Pollyanna*	Mrs. Snow
1959	*The Bat*	Cornelia van Gorder
1959	*Night of the Quarter Moon*	Cornelia Nelson
1958	*Tempest*	Vassilissa Mironova
1957	*The Story of Mankind*	Queen Elizabeth I
1957	*Raintree County*	Ellen Shawnessy
1957	*Jeanne Eagels*	Nellie Neilson
1957	*The True Story of Jesse James*	Mrs. Samuel
1956	*The Opposite Sex*	Countess
1956	*Pardners*	Mrs. Matilda Kingsley
1956	*The Revolt of Mamie Stover*	Bertha Parchman
1956	*The Swan*	Queen Maria Dominika
1956	*Meet Me in Las Vegas*	Miss Hattie
1956	*The Conqueror*	Hunlun
1955	*The Left Hand of God*	Beryl Sigman
1955	*All That Heaven Allows*	Sara Warren
1955	*Untamed*	Aggie *(Kildare's governess)*
1954	*Magnificent Obsession*	Nancy Ashford
1953	*Those Redheads from Seattle*	Mrs. Edmonds
1953	*Main Street to Broadway*	Mildred Waterbury
1953	*Scandal at Scourie*	Sister Josephine
1953	*The Story of Three Loves*	Aunt Lydia
		(segment "The Jealous Lover"*)*
1952	*The Blazing Forest*	Jessie Crain
1951	*The Blue Veil*	Mrs. Palfrey
1951	*Show Boat*	Parthy Hawks
1951	*Adventures of Captain Fabian*	Aunt Jezebel
1951	*Fourteen Hours*	Christine Hill Cosick
1950	*Caged*	Ruth Benton
1950	*Captain Blackjack*	Mrs. Emily Birk
1949	*Without Honor*	Katherine Williams
1949	*The Great Sinner*	Emma Getzel
1949	*The Stratton Story*	Ma Stratton
1948	*Johnny Belinda*	Aggie MacDonald
1948	*Station West*	Mrs. Mary Caslon

1948	*The Woman in White*	Countess Fosco
1948	*Summer Holiday*	Cousin Lily
1947	*The Lost Moment*	Juliana Borderau
1947	*Dark Passage*	Madge Rapf
1945	*Her Highness and the Bellboy*	Countess Zoe
1945	*Our Vines Have Tender Grapes*	Bruna Jacobson
1945	*Keep Your Powder Dry*	Lieut. Colonel Spottiswoode
1944	*Tomorrow, the World!*	Aunt Jessie Frame
1944	*Mrs. Parkington*	Baroness Aspasia Conti
1944	*The Seventh Cross*	Mme. Marelli
1944	*Dragon Seed*	Third Cousin's Wife
1944	*Since You Went Away*	Mrs. Emily Hawkins
1943	*Jane Eyre*	Mrs. Reed
1943	*Government Girl*	Adele–Mrs. Delancey Wright
1943	*The Youngest Profession*	Miss Featherstone
1943	*Journey Into Fear*	Mrs. Mathews
1942	*The Big Street*	Violette Shumberg
1942	*The Magnificent Ambersons*	Fanny
1941	*Citizen Kane*	Mary Kane

THE WIZARD OF COMEDY
FRANK MORGAN

FRANK MORGAN CIRCA 1942. AUTHOR'S COLLECTION.

He was an endearing milquetoast, "perpetually stammering his way through life"[1] with a timid smile nearly hidden beneath a white mustache. He was known as Hollywood's first gentleman, for his polite, mild manners and graciousness he showed both on and off screen. His name was Frank Morgan, but few modern film viewers would identify him this way. Rather, they would recall him as the loveable, humbug Wizard in the classic musical and staple of American culture, *The Wizard of Oz* (1939). But Frank's work reached far beyond the Wizard. Indeed, even in *Oz* he proved his versatility by playing no less than five roles, ranging from a phony seer to a weepy palace guard. Frank confessed to dying his hair gray far before it lost its color for the express purpose of playing character roles such as these. With his kind, bemused face and trademark fluttery stammer, Frank was perfectly suited for colorful supporting roles. However, by the late 1930s he had become so popular with audiences that it was not uncommon for him to land his own starring vehicle. Screenwriters called him a dream actor, for he could take any material and make it look good, whether he was the star or not. Mickey Rooney, who co-starred with Frank on numerous occasions, ideally described the master comedian with these words: "He was born to be an actor. He has done everything else in his lifetime but he was…bound to wind up entertaining people. He was bound to wow 'em."[2]

Frank was born as Francis Wupperman in New York City on June 1, 1890. He was the youngest in a brood of six boys and five girls. His family had made their name and fortune through the distribution of Angostura-Wupperman bitters, used in drinks and cocktails.[3] Frank was expected to follow the family business but from an early age, but he demonstrated more talent in positions that required showmanship. In his youth he worked at everything from selling toothbrushes to bronco busting. The family's healthy income allowed Frank to attend Cornell University, where he joined a fraternity and took part in campus dramatic productions. His brother Ralph helped to steer Frank toward the theater. Ralph had graduated from Cornell with a law degree, but abandoned it to become an actor after performing in a varsity show. Another brother, Carlos, also showed talent in acting as well as playwriting. To the chagrin of his parents, Frank quit school to follow his brothers' paths. Because his mother was a member of the WCTU and considered acting a bit on the immoral side, Frank changed his surname to Morgan to avoid disgracing the family.[4] Mr. Wupperman muttered, "It must be Goethe" as an explanation for his sons' dramatic preferences, for Goethe was a distant relation of the Wuppermans and the "only person in their ancestry who has the faintest connection to the stage."[5]

Frank made his stage debut in 1914 in a vaudeville skit entitled "The Last of the Quakers."[6] It was penned by Edgar Allen Woolf, who would incidentally have much to do with the writing of *The Wizard of Oz* twenty-five years later. The year 1914 also marked Frank's marriage to Alma Muller. They would remain wed until Frank's death. They had one son, George, in 1916. Even as a new father and husband, Frank found time to work his way up in show business through stock companies until he landed a role in his first full-length play, *A Woman Killed with Kindness*. However, due to mounting debts and too little pay, Frank turned to a different, and decidedly more lucrative, medium: film. In 1916, he went to Vitagraph Studios looking for a part and someone mistook him for actor Earl Williams. "That led to my first movie job," Frank said.[7] The film was *The Suspect*, shortly followed by a picture starring John Barrymore entitled *Raffles*.

After only a year, Frank confessed he was "sick of pictures"[8] and returned to the stage. He did not make the wrong choice; beginning in 1922, he appeared in little else but shows that were smashing successes. The first was *Seventh Heaven* (1922-1924) and next was *Firebrand* (1924-1925). The latter production had him portraying a duke. He proved apt at playing members of the upper class; some of his best roles in plays and future films would be as assorted royals or wealthy businessmen. A case in point is when he portrayed Henry Spoffard, target for gold diggers in *Gentlemen Prefer Blondes* (1926-1927), and the childish Royal Highness Cyril in Florenz Ziegfeld's musical production *Rosalie* (1928). Frank's roles were invariably supporting, comical ones but this is precisely how the actor wanted it. "I don't like gay, romantic heroes," he stated. "In fact, I was never so delighted as when I put on weight and no one could cast me for that type of part...I don't like to dance around, and I never could get excited about being romantic...Why they always had to be so energetic and full of youthful zest is beyond me."[9] Frank would later recall the day he grayed his hair was the day he became a character actor, and he recalled it with pride.

The same year the stock market crashed was the year Frank's star soared. In 1929, he landed the role of a timid, benign jeweler duped by a baron's dishonest dealings in the comedic play *Topaze*. The role sealed the type he would portray for the rest of his career: a mild man who never failed to be a bit puzzled by events surrounding him. The play ran for a year and its popularity led to its swift revival in late 1930. Frank found the opportunity to show his versatility the following year in *The Band Wagon*. In the musical revue, he showed not only his comedic skill but his singing one as well. Frank was thrilled at the chance and quipped, "Hitherto, my singing was confined to the privacy of my bath and I sang in public only when properly or improperly stimulated by illegal stimulants." [10] Apparently he sang well enough to please audiences; the show ran for over a year. Off stage, Frank's personality was untouched by his considerable success. Upon being invited by a small repertory company to reprise his role in

FRANK MORGAN WITH MARY FORBES AND JEAN HARLOW IN *BOMBSHELL* **(1933).** COURTESY OF JERRY MURBACH.

Firebrand, he studied "like mad" [11] for a week, shirking all engagements so as not to let the little company down. He was equally selfless in his social life. According to his friends, Frank had the ability to make everyone he met or mentioned in conversation sound "intensely interesting." [12]

Following *The Band Wagon's* success, Hollywood again beckoned to Frank. Now that talkies had replaced silent films, the medium held more opportunities for an actor who relied on his befuddled stutter for much of his comedy. Though his first role had him strangely cast as a villainous bank robber in the Helen Kane vehicle *Dangerous Nan McGrew* (1930), he soon settled into roles as puzzled but good-hearted middle-aged men. Among the most notable of his early roles were as an aging trouper in *Broadway to Hollywood* (1933) and as Florenz Ziegfeld's rival producer, Jack Billings, in *The Great Ziegfeld* (1935). He won an Academy Award nomination for his performance as a cuckolded duke in *The Affairs of Cellini* (1934). He was again a royal in *Naughty Marietta* (1935) and the film rendition of *Rosalie* (1937). His performance in *Rosalie* is Frank at his comedic best. As the king of the fictional country of Romanza, he is more interested in demonstrating his talent at ventriloquism with his dummy, Nappy (short for Napoleon), than attending to his royal duties. The comedy of his ineptitude is heightened in scenes he shares with his dominating onscreen wife, Edna May Oliver, who has no patience for him or Nappy.

In 1939, Frank found the opportunity for a role that would even better showcase his talents: the Wizard of Oz. After W.C. Fields dropped out of the cast, Frank seized the chance to take the part and asked the film's doubtful producers to allow him to do "an ad lib test." He erased any doubts as to his suitability for the role immediately. Frank's trademark air of confusion made him perfect for the character described by author L. Frank Baum as " a little old man, with a bald head and wrinkled face, who seemed to be as much surprised as they [Dorothy and her friends] were." [13] A colleague recalled Frank's performance as "marvelous" and "funny as Buster Keaton." [14] Frank lent his comedy not only to the Wizard, but to the roles of the dishonest fortune-teller, Professor Marvel, a crotchety gatekeeper of the Emerald City, a volatile guard for the Wizard, and the cabby for the horse of a different color. Of the array of characters he plays, he is at his best as the Wizard and Professor Marvel. The professor's feigned exalted status is humorously transparent when, talking to his horse, he declares, "There's a storm blowing up, a whopper! Just speaking the vernacular of the peasantry..." His exalted status is equally transparent, and equally humorous, when he is awarding Dorothy and her friends their wishes. Attempting to be dignified, he tries to give the name of men who spend all day using their hearts. "They're called phila-phila...good deed doers!" he declares. Frank plays the title role of the film, and he is deserving of it. His sympathetic portrayal of a character who is a "very good man" despite all his facades and faults truly embodies what the writers meant in the movie's preface when they describe the timeless, kindly philosophy at the heart of the film.

On the set of *Oz*, Frank was as full of surprises as the Wizard himself. Margaret Hamilton, who portrayed Miss Gulch/Wicked Witch in the film, recalls her discovery of his alcoholism. Frank carried a briefcase containing a mini-bar to the set each day; his drink of choice was champagne. However, the suitcase stayed in his dressing room and his drinking habit never affected his ability to deliver a performance. Hamilton called him

a "very, very professional player…but he did like his drink." [15] He liked it
to the extent that he functioned less well without it. When he attempted
to go on the wagon while he was rooming with director Victor Fleming,
he grew irritable and short-tempered. Fleming remarked, "Get back on
your liquor so we can live together." [16] While working on the film *By Your
Leave* (1934), Hamilton took a more sensitive view of Frank's addiction
to alcohol. She remembered him confiding in her about "how rotten" he
felt because the studio did not allow drinks on the set. Hamilton managed
to secretly get him one and recalled how "tickled" she was that such an
important star would be so candid with her. After obtaining him a drink,
Frank showed his appreciation by inviting her into his dressing room "for
a little snifter." [17] "He was a very loveable, very sweet, very considerate, one
of the nicest people I ever knew," Hamilton concluded. [18]

Frank's pleasant personality made him many friends. He was considered a member of Hollywood's "Irish Mafia," which also included Frank
McHugh, James Cagney, and Pat O'Brien. Frank enjoyed a practical
joke, and his friends knew it. On his twenty-fifth wedding anniversary,
Frank's buddies put the anchor of his sail boat on his doorknob, render-
ing it impossible to open. "He knew how to enjoy it [his life]," Mickey
Rooney observed. "No matter how busy, he can always find time to enjoy
himself…he has a habit of drifting into any house in the neighborhood
whenever a party is in the making. He seems to sense a good time." [19]
Aside from socializing, Frank's favorite way to enjoy himself was through
hunting, yachting, and sailing. In 1947, he entered his boat in a yacht
race and, though he slept past the festivities, was flabbergasted to awake
to the news that his boat had won. He was awarded a Koa-wood model
of a Polynesian canoe, which he declared he would rather have than a
Hollywood Oscar. [20]

Frank proved to be as popular on radio as on film. He was regular
guest on the program *Good News of 1938,* hosted by Robert Taylor. Frank's
broadcasts were so popular with audiences that when he tried to go on
a vacation he had been planning for two years, the show's sponsors grew
frantic as to what they would do without him. Frank selflessly gave up
his trip to do the show. "At least I had the fun of shopping and packing
a lot of clothes," he laughed. [21]

Frank would give several Oscar worthy performances as he continued
to be one of the busiest supporting players of the 1930s and 1940s. In
The Shop Around the Corner (1940), Frank gives a well-rounded performance as Mr. Matucheck, owner of a leather goods store. At one
moment, he is hilarious as he asks his clerks their honest opinion of a

musical cigar box, only to fly into a rage when they criticize it. At the
next moment, he is chilling in a scene when he attempts suicide after
discovering his wife's infidelity. In *Tortilla Flat* (1942), Frank played an
entirely different brand of character: a Mexican migrant worker. His
character, described by one reviewer as "the tiredest old man" [22] he had
ever seen, earned Frank a second Academy Award nomination. The
following year, Frank was exceptional as the alcoholic manager of a
telegraph office in *The Human Comedy* (1943). A scene in which he
has lost consciousness from overdrinking, leaving delivery boy Mickey
Rooney to desperately try to rouse him as a telegraph message comes
through, is among the most effective in the film, though Frank does
not utter a word.

Frank graduated to starring roles in several smaller, but no less entertaining, films in the late 1930s and early 1940s. In *Paradise for Three* (1938)
he is a wealthy businessman pretending to be poor while vacationing in
Germany; in *Hullabaloo* (1940) he lampoons the bedlam that ensued after
Orson Welles's broadcast of "War of the Worlds"; and in *The Vanishing
Virginian* (1942) he is at his comedic best as a politician who is all bark
and no bite. Though Frank's leading roles were few, he saw his customary
supporting status as a chance for opportunity rather than handicap. He
argued that he avoided the trap in which the aging John Barrymore had
fallen: the failure of transitioning from leading man to character actor.
"That is a hard thing to do," Frank said. "It generally takes ten years of
idleness to make the jump." [23] Frank continued to be adaptable with every
change in motion pictures, from his silent beginnings to his heyday of
screwball comedies, to the ventures into Technicolor musicals he would
make in the later 1940s. "The actor goes on fitting himself into whatever
change may come about," Frank observed.

Frank received a part in the musical version of *Ah, Wilderness!* called
Summer Holiday (1948), a part which required him to sing. Unfortunately,
the movie was a flop. But this did not discourage M-G-M from casting
him as Buffalo Bill Cody in a decidedly more successful musical, *Annie
Get Your Gun* (1950). He was ideal for the white-haired, mustachioed
showman. However, viewers would never realize this, for, after shooting
only the opening scene of the film, Frank died in his sleep of a heart attack.
His death was unexpected and tragically premature. Though he led audiences to believe he was older, he was only sixty at his death.

Frank was once called Hollywood's best ambassador. The title was a
fitting one, for he was as much beloved on screen as he was off. Mickey
Rooney described his endearing character type as having "fluttering

eyebrows and shuffling jitters." [24] But, Rooney also observed that he could make people cry as well, even if they were "happy tears." [25] Despite his failing battle with alcoholism, it was his talent and good humor that were more often remembered. Ray Bolger hailed him a "divine man." [26] Margaret Hamilton would agree; she once confessed that she cried each time she watched the scene in which the Wizard takes gifts from his black bag to bestow upon the Tin Man, Scarecrow, and Cowardly Lion. "Frank Morgan was like that in real life," she said. "Very generous." [27]

FILMOGRAPHY

1950	*Key to the City*	Fire Chief Duggan
1949	*Any Number Can Play*	Jim Kurstyn
1949	*The Great Sinner*	Aristide Pitard
1949	*The Stratton Story*	Barney Wile
1948	*The Three Musketeers*	King Louis XIII
1948	*Summer Holiday*	Uncle Sid
1947	*Green Dolphin Street*	Dr. Edmond Ozanne
1946	*Lady Luck*	William Audrey
1946	*The Cockeyed Miracle*	Sam Griggs
1946	*Courage of Lassie*	Harry MacBain
1945	*Yolanda and the Thief*	Victor Budlow Trout
1944	*Casanova Brown*	Mr. Ferris
1944	*Kismet*	Narrator *(voice, uncredited)*
1944	*The White Cliffs of Dover*	Hiram Porter Dunn
1943	*A Stranger in Town*	John Josephus Grant
1943	*The Human Comedy*	Willie Grogan
1942	*White Cargo*	The Doctor
1942	*Tortilla Flat*	The Pirate
1942	*The Vanishing Virginian*	Robert Yancey
1941	*Honky Tonk*	Judge Cotton
1941	*Washington Melodrama*	Calvin Claymore
1941	*The Wild Man of Borneo*	J. Daniel 'Dan' Thompson
1940	*Keeping Company*	Harry C. Thomas
1940	*Hullabaloo*	Frankie' Merriweather
1940	*Boom Town*	Luther Aldrich
1940	*The Mortal Storm*	Professor Roth
1940	*The Ghost Comes Home*	Vernon 'Vern' Adams
1940	*Broadway Melody of 1940*	Bob Casey
1940	*The Shop Around the Corner*	Hugo Matuschek

1939	*Balalaika*	Ivan Danchenoff
1939	*Henry Goes Arizona*	Henry 'Hank' Conroy
1939	*The Wizard of Oz*	Professor Marvel / The Wizard of Oz / The Gatekeeper / Cabby-Driver / Guard in Emerald City
1939	*Broadway Serenade*	Cornelius Collier Jr.
1938	*Sweethearts*	Felix Lehman
1938	*The Crowd Roars*	Brian McCoy
1938	*Port of Seven Seas*	Panisse
1938	*Paradise for Three*	Rudolph Tobler, aka Edward Schultz
1937	*Rosalie*	King Fredrick Romanikov
1937	*Beg, Borrow or Steal*	Ingraham Steward
1937	*Saratoga*	Jesse Kiffmeyer
1937	*The Emperor's Candlesticks*	Colonel Baron Suroff
1937	*The Last of Mrs. Cheyney*	Lord Francis Kelton
1936	*Dimples*	Prof. Eustace Appleby
1936	*Piccadilly Jim*	James Crocker–Sr. / Count Olav Osric
1936	*Trouble for Two*	Col. Geraldine
1936	*Dancing Pirate*	Mayor Don Emilio Perena
1936	*The Great Ziegfeld*	Billings
1935	*The Perfect Gentleman*	Major Horatio Chatteris
1935	*I Live My Life*	G.P. Bentley
1935	*Escapade*	Karl
1935	*Lazybones*	Tom
1935	*Naughty Marietta*	Gov. Gaspar d'Annard
1935	*Enchanted April*	Mellersh Wilkins
1935	*The Good Fairy*	Konrad
1934	*The Mighty Barnum*	Joe *(uncredited)*
1934	*By Your Leave*	Henry Smith
1934	*There's Always Tomorrow*	Joseph White
1934	*A Lost Lady*	Daniel 'Dan' Forrester
1934	*The Affairs of Cellini*	Alessandro, Duke of Florence
1934	*Sisters Under the Skin*	John Hunter Yates
1934	*Success at Any Price*	Raymond Merritt
1934	*The Cat and the Fiddle*	Jules Daudet
1933	*Bombshell*	Pops Burns
1933	*Broadway to Hollywood*	Ted Hackett
1933	*Best of Enemies*	William Hartman
1933	*When Ladies Meet*	Rogers Woodruf
1933	*The Nuisance*	Dr. Buchanan Prescott
1933	*The Kiss Before the Mirror*	Paul Held

THE SLAPSTICK
SOPHISTICATE
JULES
MUNSHIN

JULES MUNSHIN IN *ON THE TOWN* (1949). AUTHOR'S COLLECTION.

A pompous French waiter. A goofy baseball player. A skirt-chasing sailor on twenty-four hour leave. Though these three characters seem to have nothing in common, they were all portrayed by one versatile comedian: Jules Munshin. He appeared in a mere ten films, half of which are completely forgotten; however, he cemented his place in Hollywood history as Ozzie, the clumsy and zany sailor in *On the Town* (1949). He was as colorful off screen as he was on. In New York and Hollywood he was a welcome addition to any party and counted among his friends such luminaries as Frank Sinatra and Helen Hayes. The *Daily Boston Globe* described him as "a rather tall, dark, young man with blue eyes and dark hair. What you remember about him most is the little curl up on top of his head, which stands up like a small flag and gives him a particularly engaging look of youth." [1] It was indeed this "engaging look of youth" that made every moment of Jules's screen time sparkle with his own eccentric brand of humor that blended slapstick with sophistication.

Jules Munshin was born on February 22, 1915 in New York City, the very location he would sing was a "wonderful town" in his most famous film. He was the oldest of the three Munshin children, but he later wrote that his brother and sister "allowed me through my trickery and their graciousness to become the youngest in the family." [2] Jules's innate sense of comedy was a trait common to the Munshin family. Jules explained that "my mother and father…bestowed upon me the greatest gift of all — a home that might have lacked a material thing or two but never lacked the magic of laughter." [3]

The warm atmosphere of the Munshin household nurtured Jules's many interests, the strongest of which was comedy. As a teenager, he gained notice by being the loudest singer in his class. "I sang so loud they couldn't stop me. Then and there an entertainer was born," [4] Jules declared in 1952. He performed in a number of school shows and continued to pursue a career in acting immediately after graduation. He joined a stock company for a gig in the Catskills before moving into vaudeville, where he became a singer for the George Olsen band. [5]

Jules's first Broadway appearance came in the midst of World War II in a show which Americans' patriotism and loyalty to its servicemen made a success. Jules, who served in the Army, performed in *The Army Play by Play* for a three-month run in 1943 and continued with a tour in another Army show, *About Face*. When the tour ended, Jules won his first substantial role in the musical revue *Call Me Mister*, which tells of the "plight of soldiers reduced to civilian life." [6] Jules performed in many roles in the revue, including a sergeant, a Marine, a floorwalker, Senator

Burble, and a senator's song singer. He won the Donaldson Acting Award for his efforts. The show ran ninety weeks from April 1946 to January 1948, long enough for him to be spotted by the best producer of musicals in Hollywood.

Arthur Freed of Metro-Goldwyn-Mayer invited Jules to appear in a small but memorable role as a scene-stealing French waiter in the Fred Astaire and Judy Garland film *Easter Parade* (1948). It would be the top-grossing film of the year. Like a Method actor, Jules studied real waiters to prepare for his role. "I visited a dozen restaurants and watched the head waiters at every one of them," Jules explained. "Such disdain for the common folk on their faces! Such scorn of tips. That's when I realized I'd never become important enough not to worry about what the waiter thought of me."[7] Jules's arrogant, sophisticated waiter caricature is a work of comedic genius. His disdain is all too apparent with every lift of his nose or narrowing of his eyes. The *piece de resistance* is his hammy, over-the-top explanation of Salad Francoise to his customers, Judy Garland and Peter Lawford. He begins to giddily pretend that he is spreading a host of food before him as he enumerates the ingredients:

> *Spice from India, herb from Africa, garlic, perfume for a gourmet.* (He dabs behind his ears as if using garlic for perfume). *I gentle rub the inside of the bowl...egg...from a chicken. Lemon...you must be ruthless!* (He mimes squeezing a lemon vigorously)...*onion... you slice it very thin. This gives the salad flavor, makes it bright, refreshing, and gay* (He wipes tears from his eyes as if he were truly sniffing onions).

At the end of the performance, he, with a theatrical flourish, pre-tends to be mixing the salad with the utterances: "Mix mix, toss toss, toss toss, mix mix!" He then holds an invisible fork to his lips, takes a bite, puts his hand over his heart and closes his eyes, murmuring, "Mmm!" Anticlimactically, Peter Lawford says, "I don't think so," at which point Jules points his nose in the air and turns on his heel.[8]

Jules's hilarious performance won him enough favor with Arthur Freed to be cast in the producer's next two films. The first was *Take Me Out to the Ballgame* (1948) alongside Gene Kelly and Frank Sinatra. He held his own beside the musical legends in the comedic song and dance number, "O'Brien to Ryan to Goldberg" (Jules portrayed Nat Goldberg). The trio of Kelly-Sinatra-Munshin worked harmoniously enough on the screen to be reunited for the film adaptation of the Broadway hit *On the Town.* Jules provided the film's primary conflict. While flirting with Ann Miller, he clumsily knocks down a reconstructed dinosaur skeleton at the Museum of Natural History, thus forcing the sailors to flee from the police everywhere from the top of the Empire State Building to Coney Island. Jules also performed a comic song and dance to the tune of "Prehistoric Man," as sung by Ann Miller after she declares Jules is the exact likeness of a *pithecanthropus erectis.* The film was an artistic and commercial success; however, rather than lead to bigger and better roles for Jules, it proved to be a peak he would be unable to top. He next received a role in a less prestigious Kathryn Grayson and Mario Lanza operetta, *That Midnight Kiss* (1949). Jules, as stage manager Mr. Pemberton, provided variety to the mild film with his spastic pantomime of a conductor leading an orchestra and his vigorous thrashing of a temperamental tenor's dressing room.

Jules did not remain in supporting roles for long. He returned to Broadway in 1950 for the principal role in *Bless You All,* a revue by Harold Rome and Arnold Auerbach, the same authors of his first hit, *Call Me Mister.* It was also at this point in his life that he married for the first time, though the exact date is undocumented. His first wife was actress Ann Anderson with whom he would have two sons, David and Stephen. Like Jules, Ann was "far funnier than she was musical." [9] It was as a comedian rather than a musical star that Jules truly wished to be recognized.

"The hardest job in the theater is to gain recognition as a young comic," Jules said in 1953. "It takes experience and years of work for a comedian to make people laugh. Once you get to the top, people will roar at the very things they received in bored silence when you were starting out. I don't want to direct plays or pictures — I don't want to be a producer. All I want to be is a good comedian." [10] Despite his lack of interest in producing or directing, Jules did possess ambitions, including doing a comic Don Juan, writing a play about the theater, and learning ballet (though he admitted he did not know what he would use it for).

Jules received his opportunity to "be a good comedian" in the Helen Hayes play *Mrs. McThing.* In the play, he portrayed Poison Eddie, a "hoodlum...ready to kill anybody...but scared of true authority like his mother." [11] During the run of the show in 1952 and 1953, Jules stated: "It's important to be happy in your work and right now I'm happy in *Mrs. McThing.*" [12] Jules's success in the show made him among the most sought-after guests and host of Broadway parties. He was often pressured by his friends to give parties, and he usually obliged. However, he found ways to prevent his constant entertaining from draining his finances. In an

invitation to M-G-M musical arranger Roger Edens and his wife, Jules
wrote: "It will be a great honor to have you both at the party, despite the
fact that I have been so grazed by you and the rest of the guests into giving
this soiree that I now have nightmares, cold sweats, traumas, and all sorts
of nervous ailments unbecoming to a handsome leading man..." He went
on to request that Edens and the other guests sign a paper verifying that
the party was a business dinner, thus making it deductible. [13]

It was at one of the many parties Jules attended that he met the novel-
ist Norman Mailer. Not long after their meeting, Mailer's book *The Deer
Park* was published. Jules was shocked to find that "the archvillain of the
book, a real creep, has the somewhat familiar name of Munshin." [14] Jules
wrote the author a letter, asking why he had been portrayed as a bum, but,
with his usual good humor, he suggested that if the book were adapted to
the screen he be allowed to play his namesake. Mailer fired back, denying
that he had ever met Jules. "Why don't you take all the rights to all the
characters? Eight microphones on an empty stage...you play all eight
roles simultaneously," [15] the curmudgeonly author wrote. Though Jules had
his attorney prepare a lawsuit, he and Mailer reconciled after a lengthy
correspondence.

As full as Jules's life was in New York, his momentum slowed after the
close of *Mrs. McThing*. In the late 1950s, he and Ann Anderson divorced.
It is not doubtful the divorce was brought on by Jules's more casual view
of love, as evidenced in his words: "Real love is a deeper emotion to a man
than it is to a woman...this has something to do with a woman's being
monogamous and man's being polygamous." [16]

With little to keep him in New York, Jules returned to Hollywood. In
1954, he appeared alongside Audrey Hepburn in a French-produced film,
Monte Carlo Baby. The *New York Times* found little to praise in the film
as one reviewer scoffed: "Jules Munshin apes and grimaces offensively
throughout and it is not surprising that the whole vulgar mess collapses
in a shrill cacophony." [17] His next film, *Ten Thousand Bedrooms* (1957),
in which Jules portrayed Dean Martin's servant, Arthur, was marginally
more successfully, but it was ultimately a forgettable film. Better fortune
came in 1958 when he was invited to return to the Arthur Freed fold in
the musical adaptation of *Ninotchka* (1939), renamed *Silk Stockings* and
starring Fred Astaire. Jules portrays Bibinski, a Russian commissar, who
had "not smiled in thirty years." [18]

Unlike Bibinski, Jules lightened the mood of the set with his practical
joking, including writing a song he performed impromptu for the director, Rouben Mamoulian. "When you work for sweet Mamoulian, it's like

working for Napoleon," [19] was one line he delivered. Jules's jokes were largely lost on Fred Astaire, whom Jules said he ruffled "by coming in everyday with a tricky new dance step." [20] Astaire demanded that Jules's dressing room be moved to a more distant location to prevent him from arriving early and upstaging him. "I find it very tiring to jump around like a nut, especially after that long trek from the dressing room, which is located on the Arizona border of California," [21] Jules lamented.

His unsatisfactory experience in Hollywood encouraged him to look into other means of income, most notably writing. Always an avid letter writer, Jules penned a unique book on the subject titled *Dear Anybody*. His love of his subject is evident through his words: "Most of us are mailbox watchers…the trip to the mailbox is the chief thrill of getting letters." [22] *The Milwaukee Sentinel* described it as a "slightly fey volume" that "is a glib exposition of Munshin's faith in the pen…it is an amusing little book, notable for the actor-comedian's obvious intoxication with his chosen subject." [23]

Writing was not a steady job to be certain, and Jules did not have any serious intentions of abandoning his art of comedy. However, *Silk Stockings* was Jules's last picture of artistic substance. His screen time after the picture was primarily on television. He appeared on a variety of weekly television series including *Kraft Theater, Dick Powell Theater,* and *That Girl* in the late 1960s. He most often garnered positive receptions, as in his portrayal of Ichabod Crane in a 1958 television adaptation of *The Legend of Sleepy Hollow*. One critic noted that "Jules Munshin saved it from going under with a bright and spiritual and elegant performance… he swiped the show." [24] During this period, Jules met and married his second wife, dancer Bonnie Lynn Pohlmann. They would remain married from 1962 until Jules's death.

Jules remained in Hollywood for the bulk of 1960s before returning to Broadway. He only appeared in three more films. The first was a forgettable Tony Curtis comedy told through the viewpoint of a poodle, *Wild and Wonderful* (1964), followed by a piece of Disney fluff starring Maurice Chevalier, *Monkeys, Go Home* (1967). His final film, *Mastermind* (1976), was a bizarre science fiction story starring Zero Mostel in which Jules plays an Israeli agent. The offbeat film was not released until 1976, six years after Jules's death.

Jules's career was much brighter in New York . He returned to Broadway in 1960 in *The Good Soup* and next performed in two 1961 musicals, *Show Girl* and *The Gay Life*. He also appeared in shows off-Broadway including *Oliver!, Oklahoma,* and Paddy Chayefsky's *The Latent*

Heterosexual. In 1967, he played Victor Velasco in the Neil Simon hit *Barefoot in the Park.* His final play was a revival of the 1920s play *The Front Page,* in which he portrayed a Chicago mayor.

During the run of his final play, Jules fell ill and withdrew from it. He went into a less strenuous production at an experimental theater, American Place, to perform in a one-character play titled *Duet for Solo*

JULES MUNSHIN WITH MARLO THOMAS IN THAT GIRL (1965). AUTHOR'S COLLECTION.

Voice. The run of his show was cut short when he was again taken ill and forced into bed rest. On February 19th, only days after he left the show, he suffered a fatal heart attack. He died at the age of fifty-four, three days before his fifty-fifth birthday.[25]

In *Dear Anybody,* when Jules encouraged everyone to send letters, he stated: "Remember — just getting something from you will make someone happy."[26] Throughout his brief Hollywood career and lengthy Broadway one, Jules made countless people happy. He gave audiences quirky characters, that, though often absurd, carried a certain elegance thanks to Jules's sophisticated intonations and impeccable comic timing. His "particularly engaging look of youth" brings back to audiences the ability to laugh as candidly and spontaneously as children.

FILMOGRAPHY

1976 *Mastermind*..Israeli Agent #1

1967 *Monkeys, Go Home!*.. Monsieur Piastillio

1964 *Wild and Wonderful*.............................. Rousseleau, TV Director

1957 *Silk Stockings*.. Bibinski, Commisar

1957 *Ten Thousand Bedrooms*...Arthur

1953 *We Go to Monte Carlo*..Antoine

1949 *On the Town*.. Ozzie

1949 *That Midnight Kiss*..................................... Michael Pemberton

1949 *Take Me Out to the Ball Game*................................Nat Goldberg

1948 *Easter Parade*..Headwaiter François

MISS FROZEN FACE
VIRGINIA O'BRIEN

VIRGINIA O'BRIEN, CIRCA 1944. COURTESY OF JERRY MURBACH.

"Now fellas, Virginia O'Brien, the girl with only one expression."[1]

So Mickey Rooney spoke in *Thousands Cheer* (1944) when he introduced a tall and lithe brunette with wide eyes and elegantly long features. When the brunette launched into "In a Little Spanish Town," her shoulders moved back and forth, her voice lifted and dropped in rhythm with the song — but her face remained immobile. The more frozen her features remained, the more thunderous the audience's applause became. This was Virginia O'Brien's trademark that earned her nicknames, including Miss Ice Glacier, Miss Red Hot Frozen Face, and Miss Deadpan.[2] Virginia often appeared as herself in films, performing a specialty number to liven up whatever picture in which she was assigned. However, she more often appeared in a scene-stealing supporting role that made her, as biographer Bill Takacs wrote "an audience favorite by the sheer force of her personality, polished vocals, and comic quips."[3] Virginia was type-cast as the rejected, wise-cracking, and lovelorn sidekick of her films' leading ladies. However, she managed to stand out in each of her films even while sharing screen time with such musical and comedy legends as Judy Garland, Ray Bolger, Lucille Ball, and Red Skelton. Her filmography may be short, but Virginia O'Brien's one-of-a-kind talent distinguished her as one of the most memorable character performers from 1940s musicals.

Virginia Lee O'Brien was born on April 18, 1919 to a respected and illustrious family. Her middle name was given in honor of ancestor Robert E. Lee, and her first name was Lee's home state. Her Irish father was employed as the captain of detectives of the Los Angeles Police Department and he was later promoted to the position of the city's deputy district attorney.[4] Being born in Los Angeles gave Virginia added interest in pursuing a career as a performer. Also in her favor was the fact that her uncle was Lloyd Bacon, the director of the quintessential backstage musical *42nd Street* (1933). Virginia made only one isolated venture into filmdom at the age of two-and-a-half when she had a walk-on role in a Mack Sennett short.[5]

Virginia's formal training for show business did not take shape until she was in high school. As an adolescent, she took singing lessons and studied tap dancing for five years. Her idols were tap dance queen Eleanor Powell and singer/actress Ethel Merman. "I love show business," Virginia stated in 1975. "I guess I'm a ham. But in the beginning I didn't think I would ever be a performer. The deadpan singing was an accident."[6] Indeed, Virginia aspired to model herself after Ethel Merman, but the accident of which she spoke made this unlikely.

The accident occurred on the night of Virginia's stage debut in a 1939 musical revue, *Meet the People*, at Los Angeles's Assistance League

Playhouse. Though Virginia was hired as a straight vocalist, she became the comedic sensation of the show.

"When the spotlight hit me, I froze...my knees actually knocked together like castanets. My arms were paralyzed at my sides, my eyes were wide with fright...the best I could do was move my shoulders. So I did. Everything else was rigid except my mouth," Virginia recalled in a 1975 interview. "The audience wasn't sure what it was seeing. They were very quiet at first. Then people began to laugh. They roared. But I kept singing." [7]

After her number, Virginia ran into the wings and wept, thoroughly humiliated. Little did she know that among those roaring in the audience was studio mogul Louis B. Mayer, who was anything but displeased with her performance. "I was awful, but I was the hit of the show," Virginia chuckled. [8] Mayer invited her for a screen test and subsequently signed her to a seven-year contract. Virginia found the fact of her winning a contract surprising, given her appearance for the screen test. "I wore this yellow dress that made me look taller than the Empire State Building!" [9] she declared. Despite her five years of tap dancing and competent ability in the medium, she was only considered for vocal assignments to begin with. Virginia explained: "If you study your dancing like I did, you'll end up just like I did...a deadpan singer." [10]

Before Virginia made her first film appearance, she won a role in her first and only Broadway show, a musical revue titled *Keep Off the Grass*. Though the main attraction of the show was headliner Jimmy Durante, *New York Times* critic Brooks Atkinson singled Virginia out for special praise. He explained her as "a deadpan singer who convulses the audience by removing the ecstasy from high pressure music." [11]

Virginia returned to Hollywood the same year of her Broadway debut to make a brief appearance in the unmemorable Frank Morgan vehicle *Hullabaloo* (1940). She portrayed a smart aleck manicurist, but her primary function in the film was to sing "Jeanie with the Light Brown Hair." The following year, 1941, saw Virginia's roles improve as she was assigned to higher caliber films. She was cast in supporting roles in two musicals based upon Broadway shows, *Lady Be Good* (1941) and *Panama Hattie* (1942). In both she was paired with Red Skelton, who would ultimately be her most oft-repeated co-star. In *Lady Be Good*, Virginia was hilarious as Red's skinny girlfriend, Lull, who was not content unless she was eating. In *Panama Hattie*, Virginia portrayed a cigarette girl who is the sidekick to leading lady, Ann Sothern. Her character was presented as strictly comic relief as she was shown pursuing the middle-aged character actor Alan Mowbray. Virginia did stand out above Ann Sothern when she performed a number Sothern considered in bad taste: "Did I Get Stinkin' at the Savoy." [12]

Although Virginia played unlucky girls in love on screen, she was fortunate off screen. In 1942, she married actor John Feggo, known professionally as Kirk Alyn. He was anything but awkward or unromantic like Virginia's screen romancers, Red Skelton and Alan Mowbray; Alyn gained fame as being the first Superman in film.

At the outbreak of World War II, Kirk Alyn joined the Coast Guard and his Hollywood career all but ended. WWII led to an uptick in the production of cheerful musicals, many of which were formatted to mimic the revue style of USO shows. While her husband's career ended in part because of the war, Virginia's soared in the wake of the musical's popularity. She appeared as herself in the June Allyson film *Two Girls and a Sailor* (1944) and the patriotic *Thousands Cheer* (1944). She was again paired with Red Skelton in *Ship Ahoy* (1942), which also starred her idol, Eleanor Powell. Among her best roles was as Ginny the cigarette girl, who yearns after Red Skelton in *DuBarry Was a Lady* (1943). The film boasted a Cole Porter score and the talents of Lucille Ball and Gene Kelly. Virginia portrays, as usual, a lovesick and wisecracking second fiddle to the leading lady. In one scene, she forlornly watches as Red Skelton ogles Lucille Ball.

GINNY: *You never look at me like that.*

LOUIS BLORE (RED): *You never look like that.* [13]

When seen beside the glamorous Lucille Ball, it is puzzling why Virginia was not considered equally alluring. She is never more seductive than when she performs "Salome Was the Queen of Them All" near the film's beginning.

Virginia was again cast beside Lucille Ball in 1944's *Meet the People*, a film adaptation of the show that marked Virginia's stage debut. The film was updated with new tunes, one of which was "Say We're Sweethearts Again," a disturbingly comic song delivered by Virginia. With an unperturbed, blasé expression, Virginia sings:

"I never knew that our romance had ended until you poisoned my food…I never knew you and I had finished until that bottle hit my head… put down that hatchet and say we're sweethearts again." [14]

Though Virginia successfully delivered the song as a humorous specialty number, it could not have been easy for her deliver a piece about a violent partner when Kirk Alyn had gotten in the habit of striking her. Despite her marital difficulties, she remained Mrs. Kirk Alyn, perhaps because she desired to keep the family intact for the sake of her first daughter Theresa, who was born the following year, 1945.

Virginia was an expert multi-tasker as she took on the roles of mother and movie star in 1946, the year which would prove to be the apex of her career. She received roles in three all-star, Technicolor musicals. The first, *Ziegfeld Follies*, gave her a small specialty number in which she was mounted on a carousel horse, bedecked in an elaborate feather headdress, singing the parody "Bring on The Wonderful Men." She is at her comedic best as she deadpans:

> *I'm afraid I've a terrible yen for those beautiful M-E-N...I know the men are few, but what's a gal to do? I'll get a man before I'm through...hey you in the third row!* (At which point she drops the deadpan and, smiling, winks at the audience) *Bring on those wonderful men!* [15]

Her next picture, *Till the Clouds Roll By* (1946), the musical biopic of composer Jerome Kern, saw Virginia performing "Life Upon the Wicked Stage" from *Show Boat*. Widely considered to be her best performance in film, it is also a rare opportunity to see her singing without her Frozen Face trademark.

To cap off the stellar year, Virginia received the role she would later claim to be her favorite: Alma, the hearty and fearless waitress who, along with a dozen other young women, set out to civilize the Wild West with the Harvey House restaurant chain. Though Virginia appears to be at the peak of her attractiveness, she, as usual delivers self-deprecating lines in *The Harvey Girls* (1946):

> *I sent my picture in to one of the lonely hearts clubs and they sent it back, saying 'We're not that lonely!'* [16]

In the picture, Virginia performs two excellent musical numbers. The first, "It's a Great Big World" also included the talents of Judy Garland and Cyd Charisse. The second, "The Wild, Wild West," is arguably the best scene in the film. In it, Ray Bolger plays a blacksmith deadly afraid of horses. The scene's comic aspect would have been heightened all the more had viewers been aware that in actuality, Virginia was the one who suffered from equinophonia. Yet, she appears unperturbed when she walks in and shoes a horse for Bolger, all the while singing the lament, "*I was hopin' to be ropin' somethin' wild in the wild wild wild west...I reads about them desperado guys...the only one who's desperate is me!*"[17]

Given the high quality of Virginia's scenes in the film, it is puzzling to viewers why her character disappears halfway through the film with-

VIRGINIA O'BRIEN WITH JUDY GARLAND AND CYD CHARISSE IN *THE HARVEY GIRLS* **(1946). COURTESY OF JERRY MURBACH.**

out any explanation. The reason behind her abrupt departure was that she was pregnant with another daughter and the camera was unable to conceal it any longer. With Alyn, Virginia's family grew to include two daughters and a son.

Despite Virginia's growing family, she returned to work in 1947 to appear alongside Red Skelton in a non-musical, *Merton of the Movies*. Virginia later claimed it was the "worst picture ever made."[18] *Variety* disagreed and glowingly wrote: "Virginia O'Brien proves herself a capable leading lady without recourse to deadpan vocalizing. The erstwhile canary doesn't have a number to chirp throughout and sells herself strictly on talent merits in the romantic lead opposite Skelton. The manner in which she delivers should further her career."[19]

Unfortunately, *Variety's* prophesy was never actualized. Though she was offered the plum role of Annie Oakley in *Annie Get Your Gun* (1950), Virginia's equinophobia nullified the offer. Her M-G-M contract was not renewed.

Virginia disappeared from the public eye until 1955 when papers reported that "deadpan singer Virginia O'Brien is all smiles after a trip to court...she termed her divorce yesterday from Kirk Alyn the happy end of a 'very sad situation'."[20] Waving alimony payments, Virginia returned to the movies for a brief role in the Donald O'Connor comedy *Francis in the Navy* (1955).

Virginia's primary source of income was earned in nightclubs or on television. She appeared on various variety shows including those hosted by Ed Sullivan, Steve Allen, and Merv Griffin. Between jobs, she found the time to fall in love and marry electronics engineer Vern Evans. Though the marriage produced one child, it would end in divorce eight years later in 1966. She eventually found happiness in 1968 with her third husband, Harry B. White, a retired contractor, aviator, and inventor. Together, they acquired property in Los Angeles and Nevada, one of which included a gold mine.[21]

Virginia's newfound contentment extended into her professional life when she found a niche in nightclubs. "I stayed scared for years," she stated. "Not anymore. I discovered I could sing well. But I never had a chance to prove it in those M-G-M musicals. In fact, they wouldn't even let me smile."[22] Though she made one last appearance in film as a reporter in Disney's 1975 feature *Gus*, she found greater success on the stage. In 1984, she portrayed the cantankerous Parthy Ann in Long Beach's Civic Light Opera's production of *Show Boat*. Throughout the 1980s, she performed in her own one-woman show which led to the release of her own album, "A Salute to the Great M-G-M Musicals."[23] "I sing a lot and dance a little. I never do the same show twice. But I can't drop the deadpan numbers. People yell for them,"[24] she explained. Her most requested number was "Say We're Sweethearts Again."

Virginia made a surprise appearance at a 1980 USC seminar in honor of director Charles Walters with whom Virginia had worked with on *Dubarry Was a Lady* (1943). During a question and answer session with Walters and Lucille Ball, an audience member asked, "Whatever happened to Virginia O'Brien?" from somewhere in the back of the theater. Virginia, in her inimitable voice, called: "She's back here in the cheap seats!"[25] The delighted audience broke into applause, proving Virginia was certainly not forgotten.

In her old age, Virginia rejoiced in being grandmother to her seven grandchildren. She remained in semi-retirement until her death at the age of eighty-one in 2001.

Lucille Ball once told Virginia, "You were always best at what you did. You were always right on the money." [26] Virginia O'Brien was not only best at what she did — she was the *only* one who did what she did. Today, with the meticulous preservation of M-G-M's Technicolor musicals and release of remastered DVD editions, Virginia appears as bright and striking as she was in the 1940s. The moment the audience sees a tall, thin woman with wide eyes and flowing black hair and hears her voice — rich and deep with a lazy Western accent, tinged with irony — they know it is Virginia O'Brien.

FILMOGRAPHY

1976	*Gus*	Reporter
1955	*Francis in the Navy*	Nurse Kittredge
1947	*Merton of the Movies*	Phyllis Montague
1946	*The Show-Off*	Hortense
1946	*Till the Clouds Roll By*	Ellie May Shipley *(segment "Show Boat")* / Herself
1946	*The Harvey Girls*	Alma from Ohio
1946	*Ziegfeld Follies*	Performer
1945	*The Great Morgan*	Herself
1944	*Meet the People*	'Woodpecker' Peg
1944	*Thousands Cheer*	Herself
1944	*Two Girls and a Sailor*	Herself
1943	*Du Barry Was a Lady*	Ginny
1942	*Panama Hattie*	Flo Foster
1942	*Ship Ahoy*	Fran Evans
1941	*Lady Be Good*	Lull
1941	*Ringside Maisie*	Virginia O'Brien, Singer
1941	*The Big Store*	Kitty
1940	*Hullabaloo*	Virginia Ferris
1940	*Sky Murder*	Lucille LaVonne *(uncredited)*
1940	*Forty Little Mothers*	Granville Girl *(uncredited)*

"OH, REALLLY!"
EDNA MAY OLIVER

EDNA MAY OLIVER CIRCA 1938. AUTHOR'S COLLECTION.

"With a horse face like mine? What else can I do but play comedy?"[1]

So quipped Edna May Oliver, one of the most brilliant character comediennes of 1930s cinema. Her "horse face" proved to be her greatest asset in each role she played. It was ideal for the dour spinsters, busybodies, and aunts she invariably portrayed. But what set Edna apart from other character actresses specializing in these types of roles (namely Margaret Hamilton and Agnes Moorehead) was her unique grand dame manner that made her simultaneously cantankerous and loveable. Her brand of comedy became so recognized and beloved by filmgoers that her distinctive face, tall, bottom-heavy build, and "low, claxonish voice" were fondly caricatured in Warner Bros. cartoons of her day. Edna's signature utterance in animation and in live action was a consternated "Oh, *reallly!*" accompanied by a loud sniff of her nose.[2] Outspoken and unconventional in her films, Edna May Oliver was an independent-minded individualist off screen who rivaled her screen characters in eccentricity and quirkiness.

She was born Edna May Nutter on November 9, 1883 in Malden, Massachusetts. Though she would oft be mistaken for a Briton in later life, Edna's lineage was solidly New England. She could even trace John Quincy Adams as one of her ancestors.[3] As a girl, Edna's father hoped his daughter would follow a career in singing. Her father's dream appealed to Edna and thus she was groomed for the opera with the goal of studying in Italy when she was of age. But her aspirations were put on hold after her father died when Edna was fourteen years old.[4] She left school and took jobs as a milliner and dressmaker to help support her family. However, she continued to school herself after work in performing arts, dance, speech, and piano.[5] Her independent studies served her well when her uncle secured her a job singing in a light opera company. She traveled to Boston and sang at the Oliver Street Humanitarian Church and later she toured New England in open air opera shows.[6] Overuse of her voice and exposure to bad weather damaged her vocal chords, permanently blunting any real hope Edna had of being a legitimate opera singer. Edna took a job as pianist with a ladies' touring orchestra but missed the glamour of being in the spotlight on stage.[7] She began to consider acting as an attractive alternative to music. She had taken part in amateur theatrical productions as "a tiny girl in pigtails." She and her brother had erected a backyard tent and staged shows for the neighborhood children, for which Edna shrewdly charged "as high as six pins for choice seats." In her productions, the young Edna chose her characters from Dickens's *Child's History of London*.[8]

With only her amateur childhood experience behind her, Edna took small acting jobs with stock companies around New England. Her debut came in 1911 in a Boston company's production of *Miss Wiggs of the Cabbage Patch*. Edna continued to tour with stock groups until 1916 when she set her sights on Broadway and moved to New York. It was a hard-scrabble life for the lanky, plain young woman. Even when she did land her first Broadway role in *The Master*, she received little monetary reward; she had to pay for her costumes and, according to Edna, was left with "about two cents a week."[9]

In 1917, Edna's luck changed. She was fortuitously cast in what would become her archetypal spinster aunt role in Jerome Kern's smash hit musical comedy *Oh Boy!* The show garnered her positive notices and a higher salary. For the next decade, Edna would not see a year in which she was not essaying a role on Broadway. She played solid supporting parts in Victor Herbert operettas such as *The Rose of China* and *The Golden Girl*, both comedies, and in a drama, *Icebound*, produced in 1923. When the play won a Pulitzer Prize, Hollywood talent scouts took notice of everyone involved in it. Edna appeared in a silent screen version of the play, but she was not ready to abandon the stage for the camera. Upon returning from a trip to France in 1927, the actress declared that "there was no truth in the report that she thought of returning to the movies anytime soon."[10] Edna's decision was wise; she had just received the best notices of her career for her performance in the comedy *Cradle Snatchers* and was now cast as Parthy, Captain Andy's no-nonsense wife in Florenz Ziegfeld's monumental production of *Show Boat*.

During the run of *Show Boat*, Edna surprised everyone by marrying Newark stock broker David Pratt, a man five years her junior. Their wedding dinner was served at New York's Hotel Warwick. Among the guests were Edna's *Show Boat* colleagues Florenz Ziegfeld and Helen Morgan, and other theater luminaries such as George Jessel and Norma Terris.[11] Not a few eyebrows must have been raised when Edna explained that she and the groom planned to maintain separate residences. One wonders if Katharine Hepburn's famous remark, "Sometimes I wonder if men and women really suit each other. Perhaps they should live next door, and just visit now and then"[12] was inspired by the unconventional Edna.

In 1931, Edna could no longer ignore the lure of Hollywood. She accepted a role as Tracy Wyatt in the Academy Award-winning film adaptation of Edna Ferber's novel *Cimarron* (1931). She briefly returned to New York to reprise her role of Parthy in a revival of *Show Boat*, but her future now lay in Hollywood. Not even her marriage held her back. In

1931 Edna gave a statement to the press that her husband "said that marriage represented bonds and fetters and that he was going to be free." [13] Edna further testified that though she married Pratt in January of 1928, he had left her on March 1st of that same year. "He said he didn't desire to be married any longer," she said. "Later he wrote me urging me to get a divorce." [14] Edna was officially divorced in 1931 and never remarried.

Her career was not hurt by her marital difficulties. In 1932 she became what critics proclaimed "a star in her right" in the "homely comedy and witty satire" film entitled *Ladies of the Jury*. [15] Edna portrayed an overzealous juror determined to prove a showgirl's innocence. Her success in this mystery/comedy led to her being cast as a teacher turned amateur sleuth, Miss Hildegard Withers in *The Penguin Pool Murder* (1932), which would prove to be the first in a series of Withers films. Her "sagacious" and "fussy" character was the perfect foil to co-star James Gleason, who portrayed a "routine minded" police inspector. Audiences so enjoyed the light-hearted who-dunnits that one critic bemoaned to RKO Pictures, "One Gleason-Oliver picture a year seems awfully stingy. Couldn't we have two or three?" [16]

As successful as Edna was in the mystery genre, she was even more so in film adaptations of literary classics. One biographer asserted that Edna was "born to play the classics of American and British literature." Indeed, her "droll warmth" added "soul, wit, and depth" [17] to the otherwise unglamorous spinsters and gossips she played. It is as the spinster aunt, Betsy Trotwood, in M-G-M's 1935 star-studded adaptation of *David Copperfield* that Edna permanently established her archetypal crotchety grand dame persona. Edna is the first person viewers see in the film, rushing to her niece, Clara's, home unperturbed through a windstorm. She raps on the window and invites herself inside, then unapologetically begins to plan her soon-to-be-born great niece/nephew's life. "What will you call your girl?" she asks. "Perhaps it will be a boy," Clara says. "Don't contradict!" Betsy argues. "I have a pre-sentiment that it will be a girl. And I shall be her godmother. She shall be christened Betsy Trotwood Copperfield. She must be well brought up, I shall see to that. Far better than my impractical nephew could have done." [18] Other amusing moments in the film are when Aunt Betsy runs from her house in a frenzy each time she sees visitors approaching. More often than not they are riding donkeys (of which she has an untold horror), and she loses no time shooing them and the animals away, hospitality be damned! Betsy saves her graciousness only for her rather mad friend Mr. Dick. It is only his bizarre advice she takes seriously. Upon the film's release, critics remarked that only Charlie

Chaplin or W.C. Fields could not have a scene stolen from them...unless they were acting alongside Edna May Oliver. [19]

It was in another superb 1935 Dickensian adaptation that Edna most shone: *A Tale of Two Cities*. She lent her talent as Miss Pross, the outspoken nurse to the film's heroine, Lucie Manette. One particularly humorous scene is one in which she crossly tells balding, craggy faced Mr. Jarvis

MADGE EVANS, EDNA MAY OLIVER, AND FRANK LAWTON IN *DAVID COPPERFIELD* (1935). COURTESY OF JERRY MURBACH.

Lorry after he says he would not let Lucie's husband handle a child of his, "As to that, you haven't got one...and from the looks of you, you're not likely to have one." [20] As Miss Pross, Edna proved to be not only a topnotch comedienne but a swashbuckler who was "worthy of the toughest male scrappers in the Westerns." What earned this laudation is a scene in which she fights the villainous Madame Dufarge to the death with the war cry, "You might, from your appearance, be the wife of Lucifer, yet you shall not get the better of me. I'm an Englishwoman! I'm your match!" [21]

Edna would star in three more films adapted from British classics. She was the Red Queen in *Alice in Wonderland* (1933), Juliet's nurse in *Romeo and Juliet* (1936), and the judgmental Lady Catherine de Bourgh in *Pride and Prejudice* (1940). She also immortalized American literature as Aunt March in the definitive adaptation of *Little Women* (1933). When not bringing characters to life from the pages of literature, she starred in a screen version of the Ziegfeld show *Rosalie* (1937) as Frank Morgan's exasperated but domineering wife and as a wealthy widow who helps settlers in the days of the Revolutionary War in John Ford's epic *Drums Along the Mohawk* (1939). She received an Academy Award nomination for the latter film, but lost to Hattie McDaniel in *Gone With the Wind* (1939).

By the late 1930s Edna was one of the most, if not the most, celebrated character actresses in filmdom. However, in her private life Edna was shy and shunned Hollywood parties, instead "preferring the pleasures of her garden, playing the piano, singing, or reading."[22] Edna had never lost her early love of classical music and it served as a constant companion in her solitude. She had a phonograph system installed in her home with remote control buttons. Any room in which she stood, all she had to do was press one of the buttons and a symphony would flood the air.[23] She later drily commented to one reporter that she loved Tchaikovsky, Brahms, and Wagner so much that she was indecisive as to whether to be a symphony conductor or continue her career as an actress.[24] When not enjoying her own company, Edna surrounded herself with old friends. She was nothing like Betsy Trotwood in this aspect; indeed, she once took three childhood friends in "moderate circumstances" on a trip to Honolulu.[25] Though Edna never appeared lonely, she revealed some regret over her spinsterhood in a candid interview. "Oh yes, I'm grateful in a way for this face, now that I've gotten used to it. I know it's brought me this success. I know it's given me the chance to make and save enough money so I won't spend the end of my days in an old ladies' home somewhere. But all the same I'm a woman, and what woman doesn't want to be beautiful?"[26]

Edna was just as candid about her feelings regarding never having had any children. The actress responded with refreshing honesty that, while fond of them, "I guess the Lord was wise when he didn't give me children. He knows I would have spoiled them to death one minute and clomped them over the head the next, for I am very nervous."[27]

Edna combated her "nervousness" with not only music and friends, but also astrology. Just as Betsy Trotwood would only take advice from the mad Mr. Dick, Edna would never make a decision without consulting her horoscope. She once related how astrology helped her overcome a brush with death she experienced while swimming in the Mediterranean:

"I said to myself, 'Don't be afraid, Oliver. You know your horoscope says water is your friend. You can't drown.' And so, with that calming thought, I fought my way through the seaweed."[28]

Edna continued to fight through nerve-wracking experiences into the 1940s. Despite bouts with intestinal illness, the actress added much needed color to a 1941 comedy entitled *Lydia*. In it, she portrayed Merle Oberon's hypochondriac grandmother who spouts about her doctor, "He has the brain of a worm...looks like one, too...The *nerve* of him, telling me my liver is perfect!" [29] In a twist of tragic irony, the film would be her last as her own illness became so severe that she was forced to cancel radio and screen engagements. She spent time in the hospital and was twice released before again being admitted in October of 1942. Edna's death took place on what would have been her fifty-ninth birthday.

"She died without ever being aware of the gravity of her condition," a lifelong friend commented after Edna passed away. "She just peacefully went to sleep." [30]

Though her career was all too brief, Edna stands as one of the most well-remembered character actresses in American cinema. Her tart tongue and haughty indignation were so unusual for a woman of her era that audiences could not help but laugh both in surprise and amusement at her quips. She made insult into an art, thus paving the way for later acid-tongued actors like Monty Woolley. Initially appearing to be supercilious and antisocial on and off screen, Edna countered her sharper side with an unexpected warmth and selflessness that endeared her to audiences and friends. It is a line spoken by Betsy Trotwood that could have been the motto by which Edna lived her life: "Never be mean in anything. Never be false. Never be cruel. Avoid these three vices, and I can always be hopeful of you." [31]

FILMOGRAPHY

Year	Film	Role
1941	*Lydia*	Sarah MacMillan
1940	*Pride and Prejudice*	Lady Catherine de Bourgh
1939	*Drums Along the Mohawk*	Mrs. McKlennar
1939	*Nurse Edith Cavell*	Countess de Mavon
1939	*Second Fiddle*	Aunt Phoebe
1939	*The Story of Vernon and Irene Castle*	Maggie Sutton
1938	*Little Miss Broadway*	Sarah Wendling, owner, Hotel Variety
1938	*Paradise for Three*	Mrs. Julia Kunkel, Tobler's Housekeeper
1937	*Rosalie*	Queen of Romanza
1937	*My Dear Miss Aldrich*	Mrs. Lou Atherton

1937	*Parnell*	Aunt Ben Wood
1936	*Romeo and Juliet*	Nurse to Juliet
1935	*A Tale of Two Cities*	Miss Pross
1935	*No More Ladies*	Mrs. Fanny 'Grandma' Townsend
1935	*Murder on a Honeymoon*	Hildegarde Withers
1935	*David Copperfield*	Aunt Betsey
1934	*We're Rich Again*	Maude Stanley
1934	*Murder on the Blackboard*	Hildegarde Withers
1934	*The Last Gentleman*	Augusta Pritchard, Cabot's sister
1934	*The Poor Rich*	Harriet Spottiswood
1933	*Alice in Wonderland*	Red Queen
1933	*Little Women*	Aunt March
1933	*Only Yesterday*	Leona *(as Edna Mae Oliver)*
1933	*Meet the Baron*	Dean Primrose
1933	*Ann Vickers*	Malvina Wormser
1933	*It's Great to Be Alive*	Dr. Prodwell
1933	*The Great Jasper*	Madame Talma
1932	*Penguin Pool Murder*	Miss Hildegarde Martha Withers
1932	*The Conquerors*	Matilda Blake
1932	*Hold 'Em Jail*	Violet
1932	*Ladies of the Jury*	Mrs. Livingston Baldwin Crane
1931	*Fanny Foley Herself*	Fanny Foley
1931	*Newly Rich*	Bessie Tate
1931	*Cracked Nuts*	Aunt Minnie Van Varden
1931	*Laugh and Get Rich*	Mrs. Sarah Cranston Austin
1931	*Cimarron*	Mrs. Tracy Wyatt
1930	*Half Shot at Sunrise*	Mrs. Marshall
1929	*The Saturday Night Kid*	Miss Streeter
1926	*Let's Get Married*	J.W. Smith
1926	*The American Venus*	Mrs. Niles
1925	*Lovers in Quarantine*	Amelia Pincent
1925	*The Lucky Devil*	Mrs. McDee
1925	*The Lady Who Lied*	
1924	*Manhattan*	Mrs. Trapes
1924	*Icebound*	Hannah
1924	*Restless Wives*	Benson's Secretary
1923	*Three O'Clock in the Morning*	Hetty
1923	*Wife in Name Only*	Mrs. Dornham

MR. SUAVE
CLAUDE RAINS

CLAUDE RAINS CIRCA 1940. COURTESY OF JERRY MURBACH.

He stood only 5'6" in height. Some would call him stocky. Yet he was a more powerful and imposing presence on the silver screen than the archetypal tall, dark, and handsome leading man. Perhaps it was his "whispery baritone"[1] voice, or perhaps it was his unique ability to act as much with his eyes as with his body. Whether it was his appearance or traits that were more effective, they culminated in an actor who could be both suave and sinister, one who was so multidimensional those who saw him on film could "hate and admire him in the same glance."[2] His name was Claude Rains. Nominated for four Academy Awards in his over thirty-year screen career, he remains in a class apart: a supporting actor with A-list stardom. Claude Rains's remarkable versatility and seeming inability to give a bad performance have made him, in the apt words of one reporter, as much "a cinematic institution as the modicum itself."[3]

Claude should not have been an actor; all odds were against him. Born in London on November 10, 1889, his mother gave him a French name that when translated had the unfortunate definition of "lame" or "limpy."[4] He eventually adopted the more conventional name of William and made "Claude" less conspicuous as a middle name. As if his name were not enough to diminish the boy's confidence, his sporadically employed father, Frederick, physically abused him and his mother was psychologically unstable and institutionalized during his young adulthood. Claude's schooling was no smoother than his home life. He was the target of much taunting because of his Cockney dialect and inability to pronounce his r's. His peers called him "Willie Wains." Claude later described his early years: "I was a wretched little boy, you know, with no education, and for the most part, still am."[5]

Claude's unhappiness led him to, more often than not, play hooky. He found escape in the choir at the Church of Immaculate Conception in Mayfair. His decision was based on his admiration for the attractive uniforms choir members wore. The boy's choir position led him to be cast in a play called *Sweet Nell of Old Drury* for ten shillings. From then on, Claude carried a large part of the burden for the family finances. Claude worked as everything from a call boy to a stage prompter to an assistant stage manager. However, his pay was not enough to cover streetcar fare and meals. In 1901, he was caught stealing money from a leading man's coat pockets to use for food and was fired. But it was not long before his choirmaster got the boy a job at His Majesty's Theater, which was run by the well-established actor Herbert Tree. His association with Tree was a fortuitous one; indeed, it would mold him into the graceful, suave actor he would later become. Tree's public relations man, Walter Crichton, saw promise in Claude and took the boy under his tutelage. He gave Claude volumes of Thackery and Stevenson to read aloud to improve his speech impediment. Claude further learned proper posture and bearing. Soon he was a well-spoken young man and "Willie Wains" became a distant memory. [6]

Claude remained with Tree's company and went on extensive tours until 1910. At that time, Tree refused Claude a raise and the prideful young actor switched to the Theater Royal Company. It was in this company that he met the woman who would become his first wife, Isobel Jeans. Claude still worked as a stage manager but had also graduated to acting roles. He won praise essaying the role of a fifty-year-old man in the Shavian production *You Never Can Tell*. [7] He appeared to be a happily married and reasonably successful actor until World War I erupted. Claude joined the London Scottish Regiment, largely because he liked the kilts they wore as uniforms. [8] During his service, Claude was gassed and hit by shrapnel at Vimy Ridge, the damages of which blinded him in his right eye and paralyzed his vocal chords. The latter damage was what gave Claude his "husky timbre" that would later become his trademark in motion pictures. [9]

Claude remained in the Army and rose to the rank of camp captain before returning home. His homecoming was not a happy one; he found Isobel was having an affair with another actor. Despite attempts at reconciliation, they divorced in 1918 after Isobel miscarried her lover's child. [10] Claude avoided brooding by throwing himself back into theater work. He found it difficult to attain good roles because of his height, a fact which would later lead him to confess, "All the years I was in the theater I used to pray at night that I would wake up with three inches added to my height." [11] He did find success in a production of *Julius Caesar* at St. James's Theater. During the play's run, he met Marie Hemingway and made her his second wife. The marriage became a debacle of such proportion that it nearly ruined Claude's career on the stage. After refusing Marie on their first night together because she was intoxicated, she tried to throw herself from their hotel window. Claude regretted the impetuous marriage and hopelessly stated, "I can't stand another failure. I hate failure." [12] He turned to his friend Noël Coward for help. Coward hired a girl to stay in a room with Claude overnight, thus providing grounds for divorce. The plan backfired and reporters villainized Claude with headlines screaming intolerable cruelty on his part. "No decent theater would hire me," Claude said after the divorce. [13]

With no theater work presenting itself, he made what would be his only silent film *Build Thy House* (1920). [14] He found more reliable work at the Royal Academy of Dramatic Arts as a teacher. He was ahead of his time, using Stanislavsky's approach of building up characters and grounding them in psychological motivation that would manifest itself as the "Method" in the 1950s. [15] Among his students were Charles Laughton, Lawrence Olivier, and John Gielgud. Gielgud described his teacher thus: "He had a twinkling eye and a very good sense of humor. He didn't take himself too seriously, which I think is frightfully important for an actor." [16]

Claude always came to work dressed in immaculate double-breasted dark suits, large buttoned ties, and fine linen cuffs. His dapper dress added to his "twinkling eye," "good sense of humor," and ability to communicate with the subtle twitch of his brow gained him much admiration from his female students. One such student, Beatrix Thompson, performed with him in Shaw's *Getting Married.* They took the play's name seriously and wed, but the union was not, like Claude's previous marriages, fated to be a long one. Beatrix grew disillusioned that her husband's life was not the exciting one befitting an actor, and so they remained married in name only while separately pursuing their careers. Still hampered by his small stature, Claude continued to battle for good roles.

With no leading roles offered, Claude took predominantly supporting ones as various sinister characters. He played cocaine smugglers and drug addicts to much acclaim. But his small successes were not enough to keep him in England. When Beatrix landed the lead in *The Constant Nymph* on Broadway, Claude followed her to New York and took a supporting role as a butler. Ironically, though his part was small, it led to a breakthrough in his career while Beatrix's failed. He joined the Theater Guild and would ultimately appear in over twenty Broadway productions. During his time in the theater, Claude's colleagues found him at once egocentric and introverted. One company member described him as brazenly questioning every line to the stage manager, but at the same time he was "very quiet, to himself, reticent." [17] Claude's own description of his feelings reveal not a cocky actor or a retiring introvert, but rather a highly strung man full of an inflexible, high expectation of himself. "The fear doesn't diminish," he admitted about performing on the stage. "The longer I do it, the worse the fear. Always there's the same misery as you strive for perfection." [18]

Claude's anxiety could not have been helped by his marital difficulties. While performing in *Marco Millions*, he and Beatrix were living apart. Claude met eighteen-year-old Frances Proper and a relationship bloomed between them that ultimately led to Claude divorcing Beatrix. Though Claude and his new wife had a considerable number of years between them, their marriage was destined to be the longest lived and fairly happy.

In 1932, Claude landed a role in a bizarre melodrama that would change the course of his career. It was *The Man Who Reclaimed His Head*. Claude, as a disfigured writer, gained unprecedented levels of acclaim for his performance. Even Hollywood began to take notice. Now that the movies talked, his unique, slightly raspy voice and British accent in a man of such small stature presented intriguing possibilities. However, Claude was the last one to see them. After watching a screen test he made for an upcoming film, *The Invisible Man*, perfectionist Claude recalled: "When I saw the test, I was horrified. I stank. I knew immediately that I hadn't the slightest chance of a film career."[19] Director James Whale did not share his view. Though studio executives advised against casting the short stage actor, Whale declared, "I don't care what he looks like; that's the voice I want."[20]

Claude was signed for the role. Ironically, he need not have worried about his physical appearance in it. He is only seen for approximately ten seconds at the end of the movie. For the majority of the film, his dis-embodied character was masked by heavy, claustrophobic bandages. He proved to be aloof on the set, as he had been in the theater. But he was wholly engrossed and enthusiastic about his role, no matter how reserved he seemed to his co-stars. One cannot help but both fear and laugh with him when he nonchalantly utters such chilling words as, "We'll begin with a reign of terror, a few murders here and there, numbers of great men, numbers of little men, to show we make no distinction."[21]

It was Claude's ability to so convincingly be maniacal, dynamic, sinister, and comical all at once that would type him as a villain in a good portion of his films, namely *The Mystery of Edwin Drood* (1934), *The Clairvoyant* (1935), and *The Phantom of the Opera* (1943). Claude did not complain about being typed as various madmen in these pictures. He once said, undoubtedly with his tongue in his cheek, "Often we secretly like to do the very things we discipline ourselves against…in the movies, I can be as mean, as wicked as I want to — and all without hurting anybody. Look at that lovely girl I've just shot!"[22] Though he had gained considerable success in film, Claude could not shed his constant self-doubt. He and Frances bought a forty-acre farm in Pennsylvania, a place where Claude claimed he could become a gentleman farmer if Hollywood failed him.[23]

For the remainder of the 1930s, Claude was kept busy with an amalgam of both benign and devious historical, literary, and contemporary charac-ters. He seamlessly adjusted his nuances and his voice from a murmur to a growl for each separate role. The year 1939 marked the beginning of a decade that would be the peak of his screen career. His string of successes began when he was cast in *Mr. Smith Goes to Washington* as Senator Paine, a man who attempts suicide from guilt over his corruption. His performance earned him the first of his four Academy Award nominations. In the 1930s, he also proved his versatility by appearing as loveable music professor Dr. Lemp, the father in *Four Daughters* (1938). Claude reprised his role as Dr. Lemp in the sequels *Four Wives* (1939) and *Four Mothers* (1941). Upset at how minuscule his now prestigious name had appeared on the *Four Daughters* poster, Claude declared it a breach of contract. The studio knew the treasure they had in Claude and honored his request; his salary also leapt to a staggering $7,600 a week for the next four years. Claude grew richer not only in his career but in his home life. Frances had given birth to what would be his only child, a daughter named Jennifer.

Jennifer would later recall her father as at his best when he was at his Pennsylvania farm. He had increased his property to 600 acres and, according to Jennifer, it was the pride of his life. "He just couldn't wait to get back to it after he had completed a film," she said. [24] Claude did not relish the Hollywood life, calling it "bare and cold to look at." [25] Jennifer remained remarkably unaffected by her father's fame and allegedly told her classmates that he was simply a farmer. Jennifer further recalls Claude as a sympathetic father, especially when she developed a stammer. He helped her overcome it by teaching her to sing everything she said. The Rains' dinners were amusing affairs, with Beatrix, Claude, and Jennifer singing such innocuous words as "Please pass the biscuits."

Though he disliked Hollywood, Claude had earned a great deal of prestige in the town. Thus, his name alone brought added class to melodramas like *Kings Row* (1942) and *Now Voyager* (1942). In the former, he provides a haunting performance as a doctor who murders his daughter and then commits suicide. More substantial was his role as the kindly, wise Dr. Jaquith with a dry sense of humor in *Now Voyager*. Bette Davis grew so fond of her co-star during filming that she claimed her character and Dr. Jaquith should have gotten together at the end of the film rather than her and Paul Henreid. Davis and Claude would appear together twice more, first in *Mr. Skeffington* (1944) and then in *Deception* (1946). Claude would earn another Academy Award nomination for his role as a Jewish banker in the former film.

Aside from *The Invisible Man* (1933), it is Claude's role in *Casablanca* (1942) for which he is best remembered. He portrays Captain Louis Renault, a slippery man who professes that Rick (Humphrey Bogart) is the only man in Casablanca with fewer scruples than himself. As Renault, Claude uses the dry humor of the Invisible Man and Dr. Jaquith, Edwin

Drood's darkness, and Dr. Lemp's charm. He never displays his many sides better than in the following exchange when he enters Rick's Café, declaring he is there to close it down:

> RENAULT: *I'm shocked,* shocked *to find that gambling is going on in here!*

> (A croupier hands him a pile of money)

> CROUPIER: *Your winnings, sir.*

> RENAULT (sotto voce): *Oh, thank you very much.* (aloud): *Everybody out at once!* [26]

His performance in no small part made *Casablanca* an instant classic. It earned him another Academy Award nomination. His growing standing in the industry also gave Claude one of his few leading roles in the ultimately unsuccessful, over-budget adaptation of Shaw's *Caesar and Cleopatra* (1945).

In the film that would earn him his final Academy nomination, Alfred Hitchcock's *Notorious* (1946), his performance as a Nazi plotting to kill his wife was thoroughly effective despite the height discrepancy between him and the film's stars, Ingrid Bergman and Cary Grant. Critics agreed, lauding his performance with these words: "It is difficult not to find Rains' baggy-eyed, shrewd-faced villainy more interesting and therefore more sympathetic than the virtue of Cary Grant." [27]

Notorious would mark the end of Claude's career peak. Warner Bros. did not renew his contract, leaving the actor with ample time to spend at his beloved farm. But Claude could not enjoy it. He began drinking more heavily and made such self-disparaging remarks as, "I have no other talent other than acting. I can't write, direct. I certainly can't produce." [28] Because of the farm's proximity to New York, Claude took what roles he could get in television and the theater. He appeared on four episodes of *Alfred Hitchcock Presents* and a stage production called *Darkness of Man*. After a seventeen-year absence from the stage, Claude was paralyzed with fright and drank heavily to assuage his anxiety. On his first performance, his alcohol consumption was not evident, but his voice was hoarse from overuse in rehearsals and thus inaudible. However, by the time the play reached Broadway, Claude had overcome the worst of his anxiety by muttering under his breath before the performance, "To hell with them out there! To hell with everybody!" [29] He won a Tony Award for his work.

Though Claude found some success in his career, his marriage was failing. A friend of Claude's blamed his and Frances's eventual divorce on Claude's need to be the center of attention and his leaning toward "chauvinism in a quiet way." [30] The dissolution of his marriage led Claude to go on a drunken binge that ended in a car accident and an odd affair with a local farmer's wife. Things got worse when, in 1959, he impetu-

CLAUDE RAINS AND CONRAD VEIDT IN *CASABLANCA* (1942). COURTESY OF JERRY MURBACH.

ously married Agi Jambor, a pianist from Bryn Mawr. The marriage ended within a year. Claude was allegedly disgusted by the porn Agi brought in the house to stimulate him. Agi condemned him as an overly moral man and skinflint who, in the entire year of their marriage, had only given her $9.50 for groceries. [31]

It is fitting that during this period in the actor's life he was working on an autobiography with a title that reflected how he must have felt in life: *Lost and Found*. In 1960, Claude was "found" by a widowed housewife named Rosemary Clark Schrode. The marriage was described by many, including Claude's daughter, as the happiest of his life. He and Rosemary moved to New Hampshire and Claude kept busy fixing up their new home. He also kept active in film, making two stellar appearances in *Lawrence of Arabia* (1962) and *The Greatest Story Ever Told* (1965). His last appearance was on stage at the Westport County Playhouse. He forgot his lines during the performance and went into a sort of self-exile. His loneliness was not helped by Rosemary's untimely death from cancer. Her passing so affected him that he kept her last letter to him pinned on his bedside pillow.

Claude followed Rosemary in 1967 when he collapsed in his garden and died of internal hemorrhage. Only eleven people attended his funeral. [32] It was a gray, lifeless event unbefitting of a man who brought such sophisticated humor, charisma, and chills to the stage and screen for sixty years.

For a man whose entire life was shadowed by feelings of inadequacy and self-doubt, Claude Rains rose to become a top-notch supporting player who always left audiences wanting more. The type of man he played on screen was as unpredictable as the man he could be in life; he was at once charming and disdainful, vain and self-loathing; he was a loving father and a volatile alcoholic. Perhaps Louella Parsons described his intriguing, dueling qualities best: "He's one of those birds who gets under your skin, and it's difficult to explain because he's not an impressive looking man, nor is his voice particularly easy to take. Maybe it's because he's a good actor." [33]

FILMOGRAPHY

Year	Film	Role
1965	*The Greatest Story Ever Told*	King Herod
1963	*Twilight of Honor*	Art Harper
1962	*Lawrence of Arabia*	Mr. Dryden
1961	*Il pianeta degli uomini spenti*	Prof. Benson
1960	*The Lost World*	Prof. George Edward Challenger
1959	*This Earth Is Mine*	Philippe Rambeau
1956	*Lisbon*	Aristides Mavros
1952	*The Paris Express*	Kees Popinga
1951	*Sealed Cargo*	Capt. Skalder
1950	*Where Danger Lives*	Mr. Lannington
1950	*The White Tower*	Paul DeLambre
1949	*Song of Surrender*	Elisha Hunt
1949	*Rope of Sand*	Arthur Martingale
1949	*One Woman's Story*	Howard Justin
1947	*The Unsuspected*	Victor Grandison
1946	*Deception*	Alexander Hollenius
1946	*Angel on My Shoulder*	Nick

1946	*Notorious*	Alexander Sebastian
1945	*Caesar and Cleopatra*	Julius Caesar
1945	*This Love of Ours*	Joseph Targel
1945	*Strange Holiday*	John Stevenson
1944	*Mr. Skeffington*	Job Skeffington
1944	*Passage to Marseille*	Capt. Freycinet
1943	*Phantom of the Opera*	Erique Claudin
1943	*Forever and a Day*	Ambrose Pomfret
1942	*Casablanca*	Captain Louis Renault
1942	*Now, Voyager*	Dr. Jaquith
1942	*Moontide*	Nutsy
1942	*Kings Row*	Dr. Alexander Tower
1941	*The Wolf Man*	Sir John Talbot
1941	*Here Comes Mr. Jordan*	Mr. Jordan
1941	*Four Mothers*	Adam Lemp
1940	*Lady with Red Hair*	David Belasco
1940	*The Sea Hawk*	Don José Alvarez de Cordoba
1940	*Saturday's Children*	Mr. Henry Halevy
1939	*Four Wives*	Adam Lemp
1939	*Mr. Smith Goes to Washington*	Sen. Joseph Harrison Paine
1939	*Daughters Courageous*	Jim Masters
1939	*Sons of Liberty (short)*	Haym Salomon
1939	*Juarez*	Emperor Louis Napoleon III
1939	*They Made Me a Criminal*	Det. Monty Phelan
1938	*Four Daughters*	Adam Lemp
1938	*The Adventures of Robin Hood*	Prince John
1938	*Gold Is Where You Find It*	Col. Christopher 'Chris' Ferris
1938	*White Banners*	Paul Ward
1937	*They Won't Forget*	District Attorney Andrew J. 'Andy' Griffin
1937	*The Prince and the Pauper*	Earl of Hertford
1937	*Stolen Holiday*	Stefan Orloff
1936	*Anthony Adverse*	Marquis Don Luis
1936	*Hearts Divided*	Emperor Napoleon Bonaparte
1935	*The Last Outpost*	John Stevenson
1935	*The Clairvoyant*	Maximus
1935	*Mystery of Edwin Drood*	John Jasper
1934	*The Man Who Reclaimed His Head*	Paul Verin
1934	*Crime Without Passion*	Lee Gentry
1933	*The Invisible Man*	The Invisible Man
1920	*Build Thy House*	Clarkis

SPREADING
COMMON SENSE
THELMA
RITTER

THELMA RITTER CIRCA 1950. AUTHOR'S COLLECTION.

She was tactless. She was not one to give sympathy. Her voice, with its flat Brooklyn accent, more often than not tossed out insults thinly disguised as wisecracks. Her bleak expression, shuffling walk and ill-fitting, inexpensive wardrobe spoke of a maid or a working-class housewife. Such a drab description does not immediately bring to mind a woman who would be considered one of the cinema's most beloved character actresses. However, such a description can be attached to the six-time Oscar nominee, Thelma Ritter. Beneath her unflinching and salty exterior was a funny and motherly woman with more common sense to share than *Reader's Digest*. Most often she portrayed maids and mothers, but sometimes she strayed into roles as unglamorous as a panhandler and as glamorous as a millionairess. Thelma was known as one of Hollywood's most dependable actresses due to her lack of vanity and uncomplaining demeanor. "I don't care what I do," she once said. "I just want to be in show business." [1]

Thelma Ritter was born on February 14, 1902 in Brooklyn, New York. She was the only child of a church soloist and his wife. Even as a girl, she possessed her trademark common sense in her life outlook, as she explained in a 1959 interview: "An only child has a great luxury — the luxury of being lonely. People today don't appreciate the advantages of being lonely individually. They seek loneliness en masse." [2] Thelma did not brood in her loneliness; rather, she found ways to engage with others through performing. At age eight, she was doing monologues in clubs and churches, which she later declared were "terrible." [3] She found further success in grammar school plays and was overall, in her words, an "obnoxious child actress." [4] She was so well-received in her childhood ventures that she felt confident enough to leave school at age sixteen to pursue her career. She applied to the Academy of Dramatic Arts in New York, but the judges told her to finish school first. Thelma obeyed. But, immediately after graduation, she went to work to earn her tuition for the Academy. She took whatever job she could find. Her first, as a "girl office boy" [5] at Chase National Bank, she kept only long enough to save for one year's tuition. Once she was enrolled at the Academy, she worked "jobbing in stock," which meant she was "the maid or the friend of the family; but whatever you are, you keep on the outer fringe of any stage group." [6]

By 1926, Thelma was working steadily in stock companies up and down the East Coast. She made two brief forays onto Broadway in 1926's *The Shelf* and 1931's *In Times Square*. However, for the next fourteen years, she worked primarily in stock, going from one show to another for forty-eight weeks out of every year. Thelma admitted that "the plays were pretty bad. They didn't require much talent."[7] Her standing as a predominantly stock actress made her looked down upon by Broadway actors. "The fact that we did one play a week made us hacks, and because we did things fast,"[8] Thelma explained. However, she was unfazed by this prejudice. She preferred stock actors' company to Broadway stars, who she considered too slow. Hack or not, Thelma later recalled her days in touring companies, when she "lived and breathed"[9] the theater, as great fun. In her stock company days, she was described quite differently from the way she would later appear on screen: a "shy, sweet girl...who could win a beauty prize."[10] Her beauty attracted the attention of fellow stock actor Joe Moran. Thelma and Joe fell in love and caught what time they could together between engagements, rehearsing each other in their lines for their respective shows.

By 1927 Joe's and Thelma's steady salaries enabled them to marry. However, their security crashed with the stock market in 1929. Joe earned spare cash through radio slogan contests, but, most of the time, Thelma remembered "we never had a teaspoonful of gravy."[11] After weeks of hunger and unemployment, Thelma admitted she was "tired and disgusted with the life. I threatened to take a nine to five job."[12] Before Thelma could abandon her career, Joe decided he would "concentrate on the bread and beans"[13] and found work in an advertising firm. Twenty-three years later, he would be vice president of the firm. While Joe worked, Thelma found employment in unspectacular Broadway shows before venturing into radio. By the end of the 1930s, she and Joe were earning enough to consider children. They had their first child, Tony, in 1937, and their second, Monica, in 1940.

Though Thelma was what reporter Howard Thompson called "an unassuming cheerful, simply dressed...typical housewife," she became a virtual overnight star after an uncredited cameo as a harried Christmas shopper in the holiday classic *Miracle on 34th Street* (1947). Twentieth Century-Fox head Darryl Zanuck was so impressed with her reading of the one-line part that he ordered the screenwriters to expand her role. Subsequently, he signed her to a three-picture-a-year contract.[14] When the film was released, Thelma began a pattern she would follow throughout her career. Rather than attend private screenings, she went to regular theaters and sat in the audience with ordinary people. She recalled that when she first viewed *Miracle on 34th Street*, the woman beside her leaned in close when Thelma came on screen and whispered, "My God, look at the face on that one!" More humorous feedback came when she went to see her next film, *A Letter to Three Wives* (1949), and her children bounced up and down in their seats crying "There's Mama!" when only the back end of Thelma was visible as she leaned over a stove. [15]

A Letter to Three Wives (1949) gave Thelma her first substantial part as Sadie Dugan, a slovenly and work-weary friend of fellow character actress, Connie Gilchrist. Thelma's stoic resignation is comical as she seems not to notice the way the foundation of Gilchrist's home shakes each time a train rattles by on the overpass visible outside the window. Joseph Mankiewicz, the film's director, wrote the part especially for Thelma. The following year, he wrote a significantly more important role for her in the sophisticated satire *All About Eve* (1950). In the film, Thelma is Margo Channing's (Bette Davis) wardrobe assistant. Thelma is perhaps the single most relatable character in the film, which is populated with society wits and stars whose highbrow in-jokes and barbs are often beyond the comprehension of average, working-class Americans. As Birdie, Thelma humanizes every scene in which she appears with her everyday wisdom and wry humor. In one exchange, Birdie's unflinching honesty is cause for a fit of temperament from Margo:

MARGO CHANNING: *Birdie, you don't like Eve, do you?*

BIRDIE: *You looking for an answer or an argument?*

MARGO CHANNING: *An answer.*

BIRDIE: *No.*

MARGO CHANNING: *Why not?*

BIRDIE: *Now you want an argument.* [16]

Thelma received her first Academy Award nomination for her performance. Though she did not win the statuette, the nomination made her a much sought-after actress by Hollywood's top producers and writers. Prominent screenwriter Charles Brackett tailored his script for the domestic comedy *The Mating Season* (1951) to be appropriate for Thelma. As Ellen McNulty, Thelma plays a woman who loses her hamburger stand and must move in with her son and his wife. Complications and comedy ensue when Ellen arrives and her daughter-in-law mistakes her for a maid. Ellen does not correct the mistake and plays the role of house maid as she endears herself to her unsuspecting daughter-in-law. "When people like Mankiewicz and Brackett start writing roles especially for you, that's something new and exciting," [17] Thelma declared in 1951. Though Thelma's role was equal to leading lady Gene Tierney's part in the film, Thelma received only a Supporting Actress nomination for her performance.

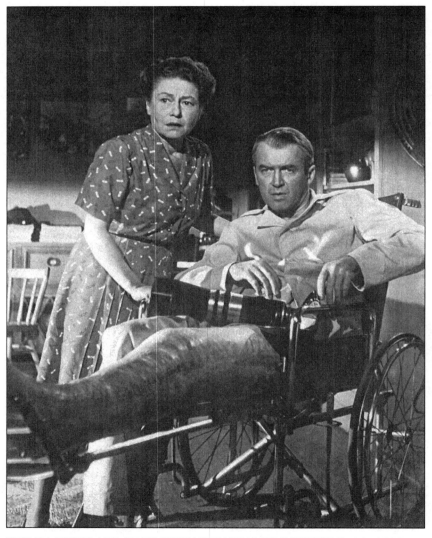

THELMA RITTER AND JAMES STEWART IN *REAR WINDOW* (1954). COURTESY OF JERRY MURBACH.

Thelma again lost the Oscar, but she was nevertheless treated like an award winner at each personal appearance. "I always traveled by bus and sometimes by day coach. Now they give me a drawing room. I like it," [18] Thelma stated after a train trip to Boston to promote her new film. Once she arrived at her hotel, she was given the best suite and received bouquets from the management. The drawback to her newfound fame was being unable to spend time with her husband and children, all of whom lived in Baltimore where Joe's firm was based. Yet, her new life was superior to the hand-to-mouth existence she had previously known. They at least enjoyed more than a teaspoonful of gravy for dinner. Thelma was in no danger of starving as her career continued on an upward trend. She received her third Academy Award nomination for her portrayal of Susan Hayward's dedicated nurse in *With a Song in My Heart* (1952). The following year, she was nominated a fourth consecutive time for her portrayal of a necktie peddler with underworld ties in the gritty crime drama *Pickup on South Street* (1953). After her fourth loss, she quipped: "I'm the William Jennings Bryan of the acting profession. Always nominated — never elected." [19]

Though her defeats were disheartening, Thelma was as resilient as her screen characters. She uncomplainingly accepted more supporting roles. "If the picture isn't good, the public doesn't blame anyone in the supporting roles," [20] she smilingly said. She did not believe that star status was an accurate measure of an actor's talent. She had her own ideas: "Many fine actors aren't stars and some very big film stars aren't actors... there should be one star stars, two star stars, three star stars...just like the military." [21] Thelma was a three star star in her best role of the mid-1950s, which went unrecognized by the Oscars. As Stella, James Stewart's no-nonsense nurse in the Alfred Hitchcock classic *Rear Window* (1954), Thelma played a woman not unlike herself: happily married and eager to share her common wisdom with discontented individuals. When she catches her invalid patient, James Stewart, watching his neighbor through binoculars, she philosophizes:

STELLA: *We've become a race of Peeping Toms. What people ought to do is get outside their own house and look in for a change. Yes sir. How's that for a bit of homespun philosophy?*

JEFF: *Readers Digest, April 1939.*

STELLA: *Well, I only quote from the best.* [22]

As accepting as Thelma was towards the types of roles she was given, she sometimes wished to leave Hollywood behind. With the exception of *The Farmer Takes a Wife* (1953), in which she was "the richest woman on the Eerie Canal," Thelma rarely wore pearls or heels in her films. She admitted to the *Boston Globe* that she was tired of playing maids.

However, it was the lack of glamour in her roles that gave her a starring role on Broadway. Her portrayal of the streetwise panhandler, Moe, in *Pickup on South Street* (1953) made her first choice to support the cast of a musical version of *Anna Christie*, re-named *New Girl in Town*. Despite the fact she had never performed in a musical and had not been on Broadway in eighteen years, Thelma gave a stellar performance as Marthy, "an amiably disreputable and elderly delinquent of the waterfront." [23] The highlight of the show was Thelma's rendition of the bawdy song "Flings," which even Evangelical spokesman Billy Graham called "great fun." [24] Though Thelma had been trying to steer away from maid's roles, Marthy was decidedly less glamorous than a maid. Her costume consisted of an oversized cardigan and floppy boots that amounted to a "look of raffish abandon." [25] Nevertheless, the role made Thelma an unlikely matinee idol. "The way those girls [in the audience] buy the part, they all must want to wear old sweaters and let their hair down. It bewilders me," [26] Thelma declared. After years of fruitless nominations, Thelma finally won an award for her performance as Marthy. Though she won the 1958 Tony Award, she had to share the spotlight with her co-star Gwen Verdon, with whom she tied.

Thelma returned to Hollywood with a wealth of prestige. However, her role as Marthy only increased her being typed in the same category of parts. In one particular role for *How the West Was Won* (1963), director Henry Hathaway had her costumes cut down from men's clothes. "I won't say I don't like pretty clothes, but I do find that usually my best parts are the ones out on left field," [27] Thelma stated. Thelma received the rare opportunity to wear pretty clothes in *For Love or Money* (1963), which boasted costumes by the famous Jean Louis. Yet, it was still the working-class character parts that won Thelma acclaim. She was back at the top of Hollywood's supporting players as early as 1959. She received her fifth Academy Award nomination for her role as Alma, Doris Day's boozy maid in *Pillow Talk* (1959). In 1962, she was nominated for the sixth and last time for her portrayal of Burt Lancaster's mother in *The Birdman of Alcatraz* (1962). Her dramatic talent was also showcased in her role as Marilyn Monroe's landlady in *The Misfits* (1961) while her comedic gifts were well-used in *Move Over, Darling* (1963), in which she portrayed James Garner's mother.

After working at a rapid pace in a string of successful films, Thelma finally admitted in 1963: "I am exhausted...I'm going home to cook." [28] Thelma may have been taking a vacation from show business, but her children were just beginning. Monica co-starred in the James Stewart comedy *Take Her, She's Mine* (1963) and Tony announced he wished to pursue the stage after he co-starred with Thelma in 1956's *The Proud and the Profane.* "Who knows? Maybe we're starting a new theatrical dynasty," Thelma grinned. "...they've been around actors long enough to know what it's all about. They've got no dust in their eyes." [29]

Thelma still kept up to date in the acting community despite her absence from the screen. She was aware most of her colleagues went regularly to psychoanalysts, but she did not wish to fill her newfound leisure time in a doctor's office. "My husband says if I did, I'd have the psychiatrist going to a psychiatrist," [30] she remarked. She studied Method acting at her son's suggestion but decided that her acting was based on instinct. "I don't have a method. It's like a recipe, I guess, like the French or the Italian school of cooking," [31] she explained. Thelma made use of her recipe after her brief vacation. She appeared frequently on the small screen in programs including *Alfred Hitchcock Presents* and *The General Electric Theater* and returned to the big screen in less prestigious films such as *Boeing Boeing* (1965) and the Mary Tyler Moore comedy *What's So Bad About Feeling Good?* (1968). The latter film would prove to be her last. The year following its release, Thelma suffered a fatal heart attack nine days before her sixty-seventh birthday.

Thelma Ritter cemented her place in cinema history over the course of her twenty-year, thirty-film career. By elevating average comedies and dramas with her wisecracks and old-fashioned American common sense, she saved "many a picture from floundering away inside." [32] More significant is her work in above average films. In each of her scenes, she dominated Hollywood's top actors, including Bette Davis, Grace Kelly, and Burt Lancaster. Her unapologetic, middle-class housewife persona was refreshing in an era when films most often showed wives and mothers as being bland and unrealistically made-up in heels and pearls. Though Thelma was not a ham when it came to her appearance, she was not ashamed to be called a ham. "I never resent it because ham is good," she said. "There are many fine actors who never make the grade because they have no ham in them and so they lack that essential flavor for the audience." [33]

Thelma, without a doubt, possessed that essential flavor.

FILMOGRAPHY

1968	*What's So Bad About Feeling Good?*	Mrs. Schwartz
1967	*The Incident*	Bertha Beckerman
1965	*Boeing (707)*	Bertha
1963	*Move Over, Darling*	Grace Arden
1963	*A New Kind of Love*	Leena
1963	*For Love or Money*	Chloe Brasher
1962	*How the West Was Won*	Agatha Clegg
1962	*Birdman of Alcatraz*	Elizabeth Stroud
1961	*The Second Time Around*	Aggie Gates
1961	*The Misfits*	Isabelle Steers
1959	*Pillow Talk*	Alma
1959	*A Hole in the Head*	Sophie Manetta
1956	*The Proud and Profane*	Kate Connors
1955	*Lucy Gallant*	Molly Basserman
1955	*Daddy Long Legs*	Alicia Pritchard
1954	*Rear Window*	Stella
1953	*The Farmer Takes a Wife*	Lucy Cashdollar
1953	*Pickup on South Street*	Moe Williams
1953	*Titanic*	Maude Young
1952	*With a Song in My Heart*	Clancy
1951	*The Model and the Marriage Broker*	Mae Swasey
1951	*As Young as You Feel*	Della Hodges
1951	*The Mating Season*	Ellen McNulty
1950	*All About Eve*	Birdie
1950	*I'll Get By*	Miss Murphy
1950	*Perfect Strangers*	Lena Fassler
1949	*Father Was a Fullback*	Geraldine
1949	*City Across the River*	Mrs. Katie Cusack
1949	*A Letter to Three Wives*	Sadie Dugan *(uncredited)*
1948	*Call Northside 777*	Receptionist *(uncredited)*
1947	*Miracle on 34th Street*	Peter's Mother *(uncredited)*

JOLLY JOWLS
S.Z. SAKALL

S.Z. SAKALL CIRCA 1945. AUTHOR'S COLLECTION.

He looked like a chubby teddy bear with his quivering jowls and jiggling stomach. But he was a bear entirely benign in nature. With his quaint European accent and trademark cry of exasperation, "Sheesh!" (uttered while slapping his hands on either plump cheek), he could not be anything but endearing, fussbudget though he was. His formal name was S.Z. Sakall, but he was more fondly known to filmgoers as "Cuddles." Though not a musical man, he played in more sunny, Technicolor musicals than any musical star ever did between the years of 1939 and 1955. [1] He made his way into Americans' hearts as "an endless succession of excitable theatrical impresarios, loveable European uncles, and befuddled shop-keepers." [2] Other actors had mastered these types before, namely Edward Everett Horton and Frank Morgan, but S.Z. made the character his own through his conspicuously fleshy appearance and funny accent. In the time when much of Europe was under Hitler's shadow, S.Z. represented the Europe Americans wanted to save. Off screen, S.Z. Sakall was even more reflective of the optimism he brought to America onscreen in wartime and after.

S.Z. Sakall's good disposition was not gained by chance. He was born as Eugene Gero Sakall on February 2, 1883 in Budapest to parents who were optimism personified. His father was a poor sculptor and stone cutter who specialized in tombstones. His work did not prove lucra-tive enough to support his wife and four children, forcing the family to live in an old tenement house across from a cemetery. Yet the Sakalls were a happy brood; Mr. Sakall managed to make light of the most depressing environments. "This is the best place to sell tombstones in," he once joked. "The customers are right on our doorstep." [3] But tragedy struck when Mrs. Sakall died in childbirth. Her sister, Emma, came to help the family and ended up marrying Mr. Sakall. S.Z.'s description of his aunt could have been a description of himself: "There was only one Aunt Emma in the world. She always brought excitement, glamour, and laughter into our lives." [4] She was also close friends with Sigmund Freud and his wife, and S.Z. recalled some of his earliest memories as those when the distinguished psychoanalyst brought him and his siblings toys at Christmastime.

The Sakalls did not enjoy their time together for long, for Mr. Sakall died of pneumonia shortly after his remarriage. However, Aunt Emma did not let the tragedy color their lives. "We knew how hard it was to make ends meet," S.Z. wrote in his memoirs. "But Aunt Emma tackled the most fantastic enterprises with such self assurance, good humor, and shrewdness that we considered the problem of earning our daily bread the funniest thing in the world."[5] Among the fantastic enterprises that kept food on the table was a chicken farm, selling hand-rolled cigarettes, and bottling Cognac from a barrel a rich uncle in France had sent the family.

Surrounded by a family that knew the importance of laughter, S.Z. grew up a natural comedian. He was the sensation of his grammar school promotion ceremony when he recited an eccentric poem entitled "The Naughty Little Bladder." As he reached adolescence, S.Z. honed his comedic skills by writing short stories and skits for vaudeville. "Before I left high school, something miraculous happened to me," S.Z. recalled. "A well-known Budapest comic accepted one of my pieces…it was a funny song…I collected five crowns."[6] He took to signing his sketches "E.G.," for the theater was still looked upon as not quite respectable[7] at this time. Respectable or not, his efforts allowed the family to live more comfortably. But S.Z.'s attempts at anonymity soon became impossible. "While he was directing one of his own plays, he started reading the comedian's lines to show how he wanted the part played," a *New York Times* reporter would later write. "His demonstration was so good that he found himself on the stage instead of behind it."[8] S.Z. was only seventeen years old. He changed his name to Szoeko Szakall which, when translated, means "blonde beard." It was a nickname his colleagues gave him after he cultivated a goatee in order to appear older.[9]

S.Z.'s reputation as one of Budapest's leading comedians grew fast. His success allowed him to marry and live what he described as "a settled, decent middle-class life."[10] He did not remain settled for long; his wife, Giza, died after two years of their marriage. S.Z. admitted he had known she was an invalid when he married her, but this made her loss no less devastating. More upheaval came when the Great War broke out. S.Z. tried to enlist but was (unbelievable as it may seem) rejected for being too thin. After putting on some pounds, he was accepted.

As successful as he was as a comedian, he was equally unsuccessful as a soldier. When on firing squad duty, S.Z. recalled sobbing and admitting his inability to do it. "I'm a comedian…a professional funny man…I'll lose my humor forever,"[11] he declared. A priest personally excused him from duty with words S.Z. would carry with him throughout his career: "Go on making people laugh you — you sad comedian!"[12] Perhaps one of the first conscientious objectors, S.Z. professed his hatred of fighting from an early age: "What possible reason could we [enemy soldiers] have for anger, personal animosity? We had never met before!"[13] He spent most of the war in convalescence after he was severely wounded by a

Russian bayonet. The war's end did not bring immediate solace to S.Z.; he returned home to find his Aunt Emma had died. With no family to return to, S.Z. threw himself into his work.

S.Z. picked up where he left off as Hungary's leading comedian. While performing at the Royal Orpheum Theater, he met and married Bozsi Kudos, the secretary of the music hall. It was Bozsi who helped to move S.Z.'s career to the next level when she suggested he start his own touring production company. He did just that and worked in "practically every country in Europe." [14] Though he knew little of languages besides Hungarian, he was hailed as a favorite comedian in any country he toured. It was during a tour of Germany that S.Z. got his first taste of filmmaking. A Viennese producer asked him to appear in a German motion picture and S.Z. accepted, though he had to learn his lines by rote without a clue as to what he was saying. The producer assured him that, "ignorance of the language would only heighten my [S.Z.'s] success. A comedian was really funny if he did not know something and made constant mistakes." [15] S.Z. proved to be "really funny" making mistakes in an impressive 106 German movies. He found he loved the film medium and the people who made it possible. Among the friends he made behind the scenes were Michael Curtiz and Joe Pasternak. The actor's creation of S.Z. Sakall Films, Ltd. permanently converted him to a screen rather than stage actor. S.Z. found his greatest acclaim in *Her Majesty Love* (1929), which was later remade in America with W.C. Fields in S.Z.'s role. "We were very happy," S.Z. wrote of his family and company during this golden period in his career. "The Hungarian colony in Berlin was a tight, close knit one." [16]

Nazi occupation in Berlin too soon broke up the close-knit community S.Z. loved. He decided to leave the city immediately after Adolf Hitler himself made clear his disapproval of the comedian's work. "Aren't you ashamed to make such stupid, senseless pictures?" [17] he asked after seeing S.Z.'s adaptation of Gogol's *The Inspector General* (1933). S.Z. and his wife fled to Vienna, to Holland, and finally to London to escape Hitler's reign. However, it was Joe Pasternak who offered the Sakalls the safest and most permanent means of escape: a role for S.Z. in Deanna Durbin's next picture, *It's a Date* (1939). S.Z. accepted the offer and came to what he called the "most blessed country," America. When he and Boszi became U.S. citizens in 1946, they kept their citizenship papers proudly displayed on their mantle [18]. S.Z.'s love for America was due in no small part to the fact that all three of his sisters perished in Nazi concentration camps. Their deaths and the destruction the Nazis brought to his homeland filled him with the type of violent anger of which he had been incapable as a soldier in World War I. "I hate the evil murderers with all my heart and without regulations. I shall hate them as long as I live, and if there is any life beyond death, I shall hate them in the other world, too," he wrote. [19]

S.Z.'s new country embraced him as much as he embraced his new

S.Z. SAKALL IN *THANK YOUR LUCKY STARS* (1943). COURTESY OF JERRY MURBACH.

country. He still learned his lines by rote and thus strengthened his characteristic fluster and perplexity on screen. Audiences loved it. Following *It's a Date,* he appeared in a succession of more lightweight films, one of which was *Spring Parade* (1940). "I loved my part," [20] S.Z. said of his role as a baker in the picture. What he did not love so much was the trademark this film imprinted upon him, one he "did not find funny at all." In a scene when he sits behind the counter of his bakery, he suddenly glances up in surprise when a customer enters. "Mr. Koster, the director, burst out laughing...," S.Z. recalled. "If I jerked my head suddenly my jowls started to shake, and this was funny." [21] From then on, in each of his movies his jowls had to "quiver and shake in a bigger and better way. It was the same with the other gestures...They liked the way I buried my dejected head in my hands…they ordered me to slap my cheeks with both hands." [22] S.Z. further wrote to the readers of his memoirs that he liked these antics "as little as you do." [23]

Contrary to his belief, audiences *did* like S.Z.'s gestures. He "quivered and shook" plenty as Olivia DeHavilland's music teacher in *My Love Come Back* (1940), as Charles Coburn's butler in *The Devil and Miss Jones* (1941), as one of seven professors Barbara Stanwyck teaches slang in *Ball of Fire* (1941), and as a slightly lecherous backer for songwriter George M. Cohan's shows in *Yankee Doodle Dandy* (1942). It was the same year he appeared in *Yankee Doodle Dandy* that he initially rejected the role that would cement his reputation in Hollywood. The role was as Carl, the waiter at Rick's Café in *Casablanca* (1942). No doubt he was glad he reconsidered and accepted the part, for not only was it directed by his friend, Michael Curtiz, but the film also gave S.Z. lines of script that helped exorcize some of his resentment toward the Nazis. In one scene, he is instructed to give a Nazi officer "a good table close to the ladies." Carl flippantly replies, "I have already given him the best, knowing he is German and would take it anyway." [24] After gaining exposure in Grade A films, S.Z.'s wife observed that: "People began to recognize him on the streets…they smile at him…strange ladies walk up to him and chuck him under the chin…what more does a 'ham' need?" [25]

It was little surprise his fans behaved so familiarly toward him; he was so loveable on screen it was hard to dissociate the actor from the man in real life. Perhaps his most endearing roles were as Barbara Stanwyck's Uncle Felix in *Christmas in Connecticut* (1945) and as Judy Garland's boss in a music shop in *In the Good Old Summertime* (1949). In the former, S.Z. portrays what seemed to be his favorite character, a baker. He is priceless when he assures Stanwyck that everything is "hunky dunky" when she professes her ignorance of cooking. "I show you how to flip flop the flop flips," [26] he says in his broken English while showing her how to make pancakes. Another scene that uses S.Z.'s "Mittle European" understanding of English to good advantage is when, at his restaurant, Felix (S.Z.) asks one of his waiters what "catastrophe" means:

WAITER: *It's from the Greek. It means 'a misfortune, a cataclysm, or a serious calamity.'*

FELIX: *Is it good?*

WAITER: *No, bad.* [27]

Christmas in Connecticut has become a staple of the holiday season since its release, due partly to S.Z.'s charming performance. He is less charming and more flustered in a film produced by Joe Pasternak, *In the Good Old Summertime* . He portrays Mr. Oberkugen, the manager of a music shop. Perhaps the most humorous scenes in the film are those in which Mr. Oberkugen plays his Stradivarius, closing his eyes in bliss as if he is producing heavenly sounds, while everyone around him must wear earplugs to blunt his deplorable playing. At one point in the film, his nephew (played by Buster Keaton) drops and falls on what Mr. Oberkugen thinks is his violin. He lets out a shriek, calls Keaton a *dumkoff*, and must be calmed with smelling salts. The scene would be tragic if S.Z.'s flummoxed hysterics were not so hilarious to watch.

S.Z. continued to appear in comedies and musicals that, though often predictable, were elevated by his distinctive performances. Among his most notable later films were those in which he appeared with Doris Day: *Romance on the High Seas* (1948), *My Dream Is Yours* (1949), *Tea for Two* (1950) and *Lullaby of Broadway* (1951).

By the mid 1950s, S.Z.'s popularity with film audiences had reached such proportions that he had three fan clubs devoted to him. S.Z. proudly called the members of these clubs "my cheeldren." [28] In fact, some of them were children who so believed S.Z. was the avuncular kind man on screen that they felt comfortable with making him their confidante. One little girl in Holland penned him a letter reading: "Dear Uncle Sakall, Why aren't you my daddy? My daddy is so thin and is always in bad spirits." [29] Perhaps S.Z. had such a following because his fans could sense that he was not dissimilar to the man he portrayed on screen. "He has remained the same good-hearted, friendly and warm man of his European days when he and his wife could be seen talking and playing cards in various cafes of Vienna and Budapest," [30] one columnist observed. He even brought a homey atmosphere to his workplace. He was given the privilege of driving his car on the studio lot because his wife accompanied him to work each day and could not carry the knitting, boxes of treats, and thermos of goulash she brought with her. The studio was happy to accommodate him. "I made many friends," S.Z. wrote of his colleagues in the United States. "They called me Yanni [short for his birth name, Eugene] Sakall and treated me as if I had been born among them." [31]

As much as S.Z. loved and was beloved by Hollywood, he was eager to do more independent work that would allow him to write his own roles. His merry disposition seldom led him to reveal his dissatisfaction with his film parts, though he confessed to the *New York Times* that he was tired of the oftentimes ridiculous lines he was given. "I can mix up these languages much better than he," [32] S.Z. said in reference to a screenwriter. In 1951, S.Z. was released from his Warner Bros. contract and had ample opportunity to pursue projects more tailored to his preferred brand of comedy. He made the news when he penned his own screenplay entitled *Cook's Tour*. The film would follow the humorous misadventures of a chef traveling across the continent by train. [33] Alexander Korda purchased the film and it appeared S.Z. was on the brink of resurrecting S.Z. Sakall Films, Ltd. "Always I wanted to act, I am too modest to say so, so in my script I put in a character which is me," [34] S.Z. stated. It is a great loss to cinema that the genuine "Yanny" was never seen in *Cook's Tour*. S.Z. died in February 1955 of heart disease before the film was made. He was sixty-seven years old.

S.Z. Sakall may not have lived in America for long, but in the sixteen years he was on U.S. soil, he managed to leave an indelible mark on its cinema. He may have seemed to be Americans' unrealistic stereotype of a jolly, if befuddled, immigrant, but in more ways than one, he *was* that stereotype. As S.Z. had described his beloved Aunt Emma, he helped to bring "glamour, laughter, and excitement" to the films of Hollywood's golden age. To the end of his life, his heart and mind were still in making films that, by his own description, would "tell funny stories and make people laugh with gusto." [35] S.Z. came to Hollywood during a dark time in America's history and, generations later, he is still making people laugh with gusto through each new dark time that comes. It is his genuine optimism that brings such warmth to his onscreen portrayals and makes audiences believe that there could be a world as colorful and sunny as a Technicolor musical. "I believe with fanatical faith," S.Z. wrote, "that within a short time we'll walk on the sunny side again." [36]

FILMOGRAPHY

1954	*The Student Prince*	Joseph Ruder	*(as S. Z. "Cuddles" Sakall)*
1953	*Small Town Girl*	Papa Eric Schlemmer	
1951	*It's a Big Country*	Stefan Szabo	
1951	*Painting the Clouds with Sunshine*	Uncle Felix	
1951	*Lullaby of Broadway*	Adolph Hubbell	
1951	*Sugarfoot*	Don Miguel Wormser	*(as S. Z. Sakall)*
1950	*Tea for Two*	J. Maxwell Bloomhaus	
1950	*The Daughter of Rosie O'Grady*	Miklos 'Mike' Teretzky	*(as Cuddles Sakall)*

1950	*Montana* .... Papa Otto Schultz *(as S.Z. 'Cuddles' Sakall)*
1949	*Oh, You Beautiful Doll* ....Fred Fisher
	AKA Alfred Breitenbach
1949	*In the Good Old Summertime* ....Otto Oberkugen
	(as S.Z. 'Cuddles' Sakall)
1949	*Look for the Silver Lining* .... Shendorf
1949	*My Dream Is Yours* ....Felix Hofer
1948	*Whiplash* ....Sam
1948	*Embraceable You* .... Sammy
1948	*Romance on the High Seas* .... Uncle Lazlo Lazlo
1948	*April Showers* .... Mr. Curley
1947	*Cynthia* .... Prof. Rosenkrantz
1946	*The Time, the Place and the Girl* ....Ladislaus Cassel
	(as S.Z. 'Cuddles' Sakall)
1946	*Never Say Goodbye* .... Luigi Restaurateur
	(as S.Z. 'Cuddles' Sakall)
1946	*Two Guys from Milwaukee*................................... Count Oswald
1946	*Cinderella Jones* .... Gabriel Popik
1945	*San Antonio* ....Sacha Bozic *(as S.Z. "Cuddles" Sakall)*
1945	*The Dolly Sisters* .... Uncle Latsie Dolly
1945	*Christmas in Connecticut* .... Felix Bassenak
1945	*Wonder Man* .... Schmidt
1944	*Hollywood Canteen*.................................. S. Z. 'Cuddles' Sakall
1944	*Shine on Harvest Moon* ....Poppa Carl
1943	*Thank Your Lucky Stars*................... Dr. Schlenna *(as S.K. Sakall)*
1943	*Wintertime*..................................Hjalmar Ostgaard
1942	*Casablanca* .... Carl *(as S.K. Sakall)*
1942	*Seven Sweethearts*...........................Mr. Van Maaster, the Father
1942	*Yankee Doodle Dandy* .... Schwab
1942	*Broadway*.. Nick
1941	*Ball of Fire* ....Prof. Magenbruch
1941	*That Night in Rio* ....Arthur Penna
1941	*The Devil and Miss Jones* .... George–Merrick's Butler
1941	*The Man Who Lost Himself*..Paul
1940	*Spring Parade*..............................Laci Teschek–the Baker
1940	*My Love Came Back*......................................Geza Peyer
1940	*Florian* ....Max
1940	*It's a Date*..Karl Ober
1937	*The Lilac Domino* ....Sandor
1937	*Bubi* .... Moller *(as Szöke Szakall)*

1936 *Fräulein Lilli*............................ Prokurist Seidl *(as Szöke Szakall)*

1936 *Barátságos arcot kérek* .... Blazsek Mátyás fényképész
(as Szöke Szakáll)

1935 *Affairs of Maupassant*.................... Dr. Walitzky *(as Szöke Szakall)*

1935 *Viereinhalb Musketiere* .... Sattler, drummer *(as Szöke Szakall)*

1935 *Bretter, die die Welt bedeuten*..........Franz Novak *(as Szöke Szakall)*

1935 *Affairs of Maupassant* .... *(as Szöke Szakall)*

1934 *Ende schlecht, alles gut* ...... Anton Polgar, Stationery Shop Owner
(as Szöke Szakall)

1934 *Room for the Aged*.............Polgár papírkereskedō *(as Szöke Szakáll)*

1934 *Wenn du jung bist, gehört dir die Welt*....... Beppo *(as Szöke Szakall)*

1934 *Everything for the Woman*................................. *(as Szöke Szakáll)*

1933 *Az ellopott szerda*..............Schmidz,fotóriporter *(as Szöke Szakáll)*

1933 *Frühlingsstimmen*...............Krüger, Schuldiener *(as Szöke Szakall)*

1933 *Skandal in Budapest* .... Stangl *(as Szöke Szakáll)*

1933 *Abenteuer am Lido*............................ Michael *(as Szöke Szakall)*

1933 *Pardon, tévedtem*........................Strangel úr, Murray menedzsere
(as Szöke Szakáll)

1933 *Großfürstin Alexandra*............... Dimitri, Chefkoch im Hause der
Großfürstin *(as Szöke Szakall)*

1933 *Muß man sich gleich scheiden lassen*.. Professor Friedrich Hornung

1933 *Es war einmal ein Musikus*................ Häberlein *(as Szöke Szakall)*

1933 *A Woman Like You*.............................. Theobald Roehn, Fabrikant
(as Szöke Szakall)

1933 *The Emperor's Waltz* .... Leitner–Fabrikant aus Budapest
(as Szöke Szakall)

1933 *The Town Stands on Its Head*...........................Der Bürgermeister

1933 *Tokajerglut*............. Schmidt, Pressephotograph *(as Szöke Szakall)*

1932 *Glück über Nacht* ....Haase

1932 *Mein Name ist Lampe (short)* .... *(as Szöke Szakall)*

1932 *Gräfin Mariza* ....Lampe

1932 *I Do Not Want to Know Who You Are*.............................. Ottokar
(as Szöke Szakall)

1932 *Ein harmloser Fall (short)*..............Herr Werner *(as Szöke Szakall)*

1932 *Right to Happiness* ....Bernhard

1932 *Mädchen zum Heiraten* .... Alois Novak

1932 *Ahoi–Ahoi! (short)* .... Herr Lampe *(as Szöke Sakall)*

1932   Besserer Herr gesucht zwecks…*(short)*

1932 *Streichquartett (short)*..

1931 *The Unknown Guest* ....Leopold Kuhlmann *(as Szöke Szakall)*

1931 *The Soaring Maiden* .... Onkel Lampe *(as Szöke Szakall)*

1931 *The Woman They Talk About....* Salewski Moretti *(as Szöke Szakall)*

1931 *Meine Cousine aus Warschau*......................Burel, Luciennes Gatte

1931 *The Squeeker* .... Bill "Billy" Anerley *(as Szöke Szakall)*

1931 *Der Stumme von Portici* .... Ehemann *(as Szöke Szakall)*

1931 *Ich heirate meinen Mann* ....Adolphe *(as Szöke Szakall)*

1931 *Walzerparadies* .... Schwartz, Theateragent *(as Szöke Szakáll)*

1931   Ihr Junge *(as Szöke Szakall)*

1931 *Die Faschingsfee* .... Matthias, Diener *(as Szöke Szakáll)*

1931 *Kopfüber ins Glück*....................Baron Monteuil *(as Szöke Szakall)*

1931 *Her Majesty Love*........... Bela Török/Lias Vater *(as Szöke Szakall)*

1930 *The Jumping Jack* .... Eickmeyer–Parfümfabrikant
                  (as Szöke Szakall)

1930 *Susanne macht Ordnung*................. Dr. Fuchs, juristischer Berater
                  (as Szöke Sakall)

1930 *Rendez-Vous*.. Crepin *(as Szöke Szakall)*

1930 *Twice Wedding* ....Grafenbergs Schwager

1930 *Zwei Herzen im Dreiviertel-Takt* .... Der Theaterdirektor
                  (as Szöke Szakall)

1929 *Why Cry at Parting?* ...... Gottgetreu, Kassierer von Harder & Co.

1929 *The Jolly Peasant*............................. Dorfpolizist *(as Szöke Szakall)*

1929 *Großstadtschmetterling* .... Paul Bennet, Maler

1928 *Whirl of Youth* .... Sam, ein Artist *(as Szöke Szakall)*

1928 *Mary Lou*....................................Der Jongleur *(as Szöke Szakall)*

1927 *Familientag im Hause Prellstein* ....Sami Bambus
                  (as Szöke Szakall)

1927 *Der Himmel auf Erden*... Geschäftsführer

1927 *Make Up*..................................Theaterdirektor *(as Szöke Szakall)*

1926 *Wenn das Herz der Jugend spricht* ...... Dr. Hecht *(as Szöke Szakall)*

1917 *A dollárnéni* ....

1916 *Az újszülött apa* .... *(as Szöke Szakáll)*

FATHER CONFESSOR
LEWIS STONE

LEWIS STONE CIRCA 1933. AUTHOR'S COLLECTION.

"Twenty years ago, I came to Metro as a star. I will go out as a character actor."[1]

Lewis Stone offered this prescient remark in 1943 and it could not have been more accurate. As an original member of M-G-M's constellation of stars when the studio opened in 1924, his distinguished looks and prematurely gray hair made him the perfect leading man in drawing room dramas. He was cast alongside Greta Garbo no less than seven times. However, it was character roles to which he was relegated as he grew older that, though considerably smaller, made him a star. To old and modern film audiences alike, Lewis and his role as Mickey Rooney's shrewd, kindly father in the long-running *Andy Hardy* series (1937-1946) are forever entwined. Lewis may have appeared in 200 films in his long career, but it is because of his role as Judge Hardy in only fourteen of them that his name will never fall into obscurity. As typed as Lewis became in Hollywood, off screen he managed to live a life more action-packed than any blockbuster film could hope to be. One reporter summed up the tireless actor's escapades thus: "He has gone hungry in stock companies, survived Krag slugs, fever and rotten beef with Teddy Roosevelt in Cuba; skippered his own yacht to Alaska, investigated the snake-dancing Hopi Indians for the War Department, and served as a major in World War I."[2] With such a wealth of life experience, it is little wonder that Lewis Stone was so convincing as the endlessly knowledgeable and wise Judge Hardy.

Lewis was born on November 15, 1879 in Worcester, Massachusetts. His father, Bertrand, made his living as a partner at a shoe and boot making factory. Bertrand's family had the theater in their blood; they were responsible for founding a theatrical troupe called the Bostonians as well as establishing the Old Boston Opera Company.[3] Though young Lewis loved the theater, he claimed, "I never had any great desire to act."[4] At ten years old, Lewis and his family moved to Manhattan, where he would have ample exposure to the theater. It was not acting, but writing, for the theater in which Lewis expressed interest. He succeeded in writing a vaudeville comedy sketch and selling it to an agent. However, the agent had one condition: that Lewis act in the sketch himself. The Spanish-American war broke out before Lewis had a chance to make his stage debut; instead, the burgeoning actor enlisted with the New York Volunteers. He went to Cuba and was present at the battle of San Juan Hill. Later, after he rose to the rank of lieutenant, he was stationed beside Walter Reed when Reed discovered the cure for yellow fever.[5]

After his eventful service in the Army, Lewis returned to New York with the all-encompassing problem of employment on his mind. "I had heard that a lot of men were needed for jobs at the Boston Navy Yard and I went up there to see about it," he later recounted. He investigated what jobs were available, but was fortuitously distracted by a story he read in a magazine he picked up on his way back from job searching. He perceived the story to have "dramatic possibilities" and adapted it into a play. With the help of an uncle with connections in the theater, Lewis was directed to an agent who was impressed enough with the young man's talents to hire him as a replacement for an actor who had fallen ill in the Detroit Stock Company. [6] He traveled with the company to Canada, planning to stay with them for only two weeks "as a lark" in a show called *Side-Tracked*. [7] However, the play ran a year and he stayed with it for the entire time. Any notion that he was an actor just "as a lark" had long vanished.

Lewis had to wait until 1906 until he was truly recognized for his craft. His break came in the Laurette Taylor production *The Bird of Paradise*. It established him as a romantic lead; indeed, one reporter later said he was "the Clark Gable of his day." [8] His romantic appeal was not limited to the stage. The same year he made his first true success on Broadway, he married Margaret Langham, a member of his stock company. Lewis enjoyed more luck when he was invited to be a guest star at the Morosco theater circuit in Los Angeles. While there, Thomas Ince convinced the actor to appear in *Honor's Altar* (1915), the film that would ultimately mark Lewis's entrance into movies. He made enough of an impression in it to be cast in two more films. But Lewis again put his career on hold to serve his country. In 1916, he was sent on a mission by Theodore Roosevelt to film the Hopi Indian's tribal dances and customs. A reporter commented on Lewis's impressive ability to gain the indigenous people's trust, an ability he would later communicate so aptly as the stolid Judge Hardy: "Their [the Hopi] first distrust soon turned to friendship and respect for the quiet, reserved white man who could shoot, ride, and even speak their language." [9]

Lewis continued on his call to duty when America entered World War I. He again enlisted and served in the cavalry, using his exceptional skills as a horseman to help win the war. [10] After the Armistice, his career picked up right where it left off. He appeared in *Scaramouche* (1923) and *Helen of Troy* (1927) before becoming one of the first stars to join the newly formed Metro Studio. Lewis was perfect for portraying "tycoons and drawing room parts" in his early films. [11] He starred alongside the era's most glamorous women, namely Jean Harlow and Greta Garbo. In *Red-Headed Woman* (1932) he was the father of the wealthy man gold digger Harlow sets her sights upon; in *The Girl from Missouri* (1934) his role was reversed and he was the wealthy man subject to Harlow's attention. In Harlow's *Suzy* (1936), he portrays an affluent baron, and finally, in Harlow's *China Seas* (1935) he steps out of the tycoon mold and essays the role of an officer presumed to be a coward. With Garbo, he appeared as her dull older husband in *Wild Orchids* (1929), her doctor in *A Woman of Affairs* (1929), and her lover in *Romance* (1930). He appeared

LEWIS STONE WITH GRETA GARBO IN *A WOMAN OF AFFAIRS* (1928).
COURTESY OF JERRY MURBACH.

with her three more times: in *Inspiration* (1931), *Mata Hari* (1931), and *Queen Christina* (1933). But it was in Garbo's *Grand Hotel* (1932) that he became firmly established as arguably the best supporting actor in M-G-M's stable of stars. As war-scarred Dr. Ottenschlag, Lewis gives a chillingly realistic portrayal of the bitter aimlessness so many veterans of the Great War faced. It is the doctor who utters the now iconic line from the film: "Grand Hotel...always the same. People come, people go. Nothing happens." [12]

Lewis was considerably less grave off screen. He later fondly recalled his early days at M-G-M. He watched Will Rogers "rope his goats on the back lot" and conjectured "what new make-up magic Lon Chaney was concocting behind his mysteriously locked door."

"On summer evenings we'd sit on the porch, chairs tilted back, and serenade the girls with barbershop harmony," Lewis further reminisced. "Lionel Barrymore, Lew Cody, John Gilbert, and myself. No old shoes were thrown in spite of what we did to 'Sweet Adeline' and 'Good Old Summertime.'" [13]

The actor's contentment in his career did not extend to his personal life. After his first wife died in 1910, Lewis married another actress, Florence Oakley. The marriage was an unhappy one, ending in a messy divorce in 1929. Lewis again married in 1930 to a young woman named Hazel Scott. Lewis was fifty and the bride was twenty, but the marriage would endure until Lewis's death over twenty years later. [14] He had two daughters, Barbara and Virginia.

Lewis continued to appear in films in rapid succession. He proved his versatility in roles that took him out of the "drawing room" or "tycoon" mold. He appeared as the crusty Captain Smollet in *Treasure Island* (1934) and then made a rare appearance in a horror film, *The Man Who Cried Wolf* (1937). Lewis maintained that his favorite roles were with Garbo in *A Woman of Affairs* (1929), with Ruth Chatterton in *Madame X* (1929), and with Helen Hayes in *The Sin of Madelon Claudet* (1931). [15] However, it was in a small, low budget picture absent of any gods or goddesses of the screen that would change Lewis's career forever. The picture was *You're Only Young Once* (1937), a sequel to the homespun *A Family Affair*, released the previous year. The film, depicting the life and misadventures of Judge Hardy and his family in the small town of Carvel, was like a modern day rendition of Tom Sawyer that appealed to both young and old. Lewis replaced Lionel Barrymore in the role of the judge and would do it more than its justice for the next decade.

Lewis's portrayal of Judge Hardy, an even-tempered, calm, and intelligent man never short of glib advice, was the perfect contrast to Mickey Rooney's oftentimes over-the-top, rambunctious portrayal of his son, Andy. Lewis was the kind of man everyone would want as their father confessor. He never raised his voice, even when he had to bring Andy down to earth to prevent him from being (in the words of the judge) "Too big for his britches." Instead of argumentatively confronting Andy when he suspected the boy of hiding something, he would pry the information out of Andy in such a roundabout manner that he fooled the boy into confiding the truth to him. A case in point is in *Life Begins for Andy Hardy* (1941). Andy has made a disaster of his first attempt to leave home for the big city but continues to maintain the façade of a big shot in front of his friends and family. The judge and Andy have the following exchange:

JUDGE: *Looks like you have life by the tail.*

ANDY: *Well, I've had a couple of experiences but I'm all right now.*

JUDGE: *Nothing to warrant talking about, eh?*

ANDY: *Nah. Nothing to talk about.* [16]

Of course, the moment Andy says he has nothing to talk about, he inadvertently goes on to tell his father all about his debacle of a start in the big city.

Lewis's stolid portrayal of Judge Hardy earned him fans all around the world. The actor once claimed that after eight years as a judge he probably knew more about motion picture law than anyone else alive. [17] It was not uncommon for Lewis to receive requests for legal advice in place of fan mail. "It's my movie fans who ask my advice," he said ruefully. "No one else does. My married daughters have never asked me for advice, neither have my grandchildren!" [18]

As beloved as Lewis became in the role that made him a household name, he had mixed feelings about it. It was the inextricable association with Judge Hardy that forced Lewis to give up certain pursuits unseemly for a man of the law; namely "beating out boogie woogie on the orchestra drums in local bistros." [19] But what most bothered Lewis about the permanent association was his claim that it virtually took him out of pictures. "There have been other things I could have done but now I'm so identified as the Judge that I don't get a chance at anything else," he stated. [20]

However, off screen Lewis got ample opportunity to do something else. When America entered World War II, as a member of the California State Guard, Lewis took it upon himself to form an Evacuation Regiment as a unit within the guard. The regiment came to include over 100 station wagons, most of them owned by local businessmen. While carrying out his duties in the State Guard, it seemed that Lewis might never have been an actor. Once when in uniform a lawyer in the regiment asked him about his career and Lewis refused to speak about it. Instead, he asked the man: "What are you now in that uniform? A lawyer or a soldier?"

"A soldier," the man replied.

"So am I. I'm not acting now," Lewis said. [21]

Aside from the more sobering duties for which the war called, Lewis was versatile in his recreational activities. An expert horseman, he was a member of the Sheriff's Posse in southern California, a group that made regular jaunts on horseback in traditional Western style. He also belonged to the Vistadores, an organization that made a horseback pilgrimage to ranches in Santa Barbara each year. Contrary to his early roles as sophisticates and later as a suburban judge, Lewis was a man who felt most himself when close to the earth. For a period in the late 1940s, Lewis had settled into the life of a "gentleman farmer" in the San Fernando Valley.[22] At this time he professed to have no ambitions aside from tending to his land and to "go on giving the repressed, at ease performances that have won him the respect of audiences and actors alike."[23] Perhaps the best expression of Lewis's down-to-earth, simple way of life was reflected in his philosophy about his longevity. "I made up my mind at the age of sixty-five that I would do one thing religiously — keep breathing. That's about all I can say — I've kept breathing."[24]

After the Andy Hardy series wrapped up in 1946, Lewis had more time to pursue his recreational activities as his roles were slower in coming. Among the most notable of his later portrayals were as Angela Lansbury's irate, politically minded father who commits suicide in Frank Capra's *State of the Union* (1948), and as a similarly suicidal man in the Clark Gable vehicle *Any Number Can Play* (1949). In the latter film, he plays a drunken gambler, more than proving that he was still apt at playing someone besides Judge Hardy. In the late 1950s, he appeared in such swashbuckling films as *Scaramouche* (1952) and *The Prisoner of Zenda* (1952). Incidentally, he was in the silent production of both these films as well. Because film roles were scarcer as he grew older, Lewis was not averse to the new medium of television. "I'm watching it because it's a new phase of our business that I might have to know about someday," he commented.[25]

As he aged into his seventies, Lewis remained remarkably sharp and curious about the modern age around him. Indeed, he was so keen that he never seemed part of an antiquated personage of an era long past and forgotten. When asked if he ever considered retirement, he raised his eyebrows and quipped, "What? And miss all this?"[26]

Lewis kept breathing and did not miss a thing until he was seventy-three years old. On September 13, 1953 his wife stated that some disreputable boys invaded the Stones' backyard and threw their garden furniture in the pool. Lewis was watching television when he heard the prowlers and went out to investigate, though Hazel pleaded with him not to exert himself so. But the veteran was not about to turn his back on a battle, even it meant death.

Lewis collapsed on the sidewalk and died of a heart attack after chasing the delinquents from his home. [27]

Lewis's death was like the passing of a king who has ruled a country for so long that inhabitants cannot recall a time when he was not on the throne. His was a rule that was welcome. He endeared himself to young and old alike. He once admitted that young people did not have the same opportunities in the theater as they did when he was starting his career, and thus he made it a point to be beneficent to movie beginners. He was a hero to all generations and served as a role model not only on screen but on the battlefield and at home. As Judge Hardy, he truly made the film series worthy of the honorary Oscar bestowed upon it in 1943 for representing the American way of life. Actor Henry Silva recalled in 1959 the influence Lewis had on him as a child in the slums of Harlem: "Judge Hardy became like a father to me and…a lot of the guys…When they balked at doing something, their fathers told them, 'Do it or I'll break your neck.'…Lewis Stone would say, "Now let's sit down and talk this over.' That made a big impression on us." [28] With his reassuring, calm intelligence and wise screen presence, he has continued to make an impression. Filmgoers can heartily agree with a statement he made in 1952 that if he had it to do all over again, he would live his life exactly the same way. [29]

FILMOGRAPHY

1953	*All the Brothers Were Valiant*	Captain Holt
1952	*The Prisoner of Zenda*	The Cardinal
1952	*Scaramouche*	Georges de Valmorin
1952	*Talk About a Stranger*	William J. Wardlaw
1952	*Just This Once*	Judge Samuel Coulter
1951	*It's a Big Country*	Church sexton
1951	*The Unknown Man*	Judge James V. Hulbrook
1951	*Bannerline*	Josh
1951	*Angels in the Outfield*	Arnold P. Hapgood
1951	*Night Into Morning*	Dr. Horace Snyder
1951	*Grounds for Marriage*	Dr. Carleton Radwin Young
1950	*Stars in My Crown*	Dr. Daniel Kalbert Harris, Sr.
1950	*Key to the City*	Judge Silas Standish
1949	*Any Number Can Play*	Ben Gavery Snelerr
1949	*The Sun Comes Up*	Arthur Norton
1948	*State of the Union*	Sam Thorndyke
1946	*Love Laughs at Andy Hardy*	Judge Hardy

1946	*Three Wise Fools*	Judge James Trumbell
1946	*The Hoodlum Saint*	Father Nolan
1944	*Andy Hardy's Blonde Trouble*	Judge James K. 'Jim' Hardy
1942	*Andy Hardy's Double Life*	Judge James K. Hardy
1942	*The Courtship of Andy Hardy*	Judge James K. Hardy
1942	*The Bugle Sounds*	Colonel Jack Lawton
1941	*Life Begins for Andy Hardy*	Judge James K. 'Jim' Hardy
1941	*Andy Hardy's Private Secretary*	Judge James K. Hardy
1940	*Sporting Blood*	Davis Lockwood
1940	*Andy Hardy Meets Debutante*	Judge James K. 'Jim' Hardy
1940	*Andy Hardy's Dilemma: A Lesson in Mathematics...and Other Things (short)*	Judge Hardy
1939	*Judge Hardy and Son*	Judge James K. Hardy
1939	*Joe and Ethel Turp Call on the President*	The President
1939	*Andy Hardy Gets Spring Fever*	Judge James K. 'Jim' Hardy
1939	*The Hardys Ride High*	Judge James K. Hardy
1939	*The Ice Follies of 1939*	Douglas 'Doug' Tolliver Jr.
1939	*Loews Christmas Greeting (The Hardy Family, short)*	Judge James K. Hardy
1938	*Out West with the Hardys*	Judge James 'Jim' K. Hardy
1938	*The Chaser*	Dr. Delford Q. Prescott
1938	*Love Finds Andy Hardy*	Judge James K. Hardy
1938	*Yellow Jack*	Maj. Walter Reed
1938	*Stolen Heaven*	Joseph Langauer
1938	*Judge Hardy's Children*	Judge James K. Hardy
1937	*The Bad Man of Brimstone*	Mr. Jackson Douglas
1937	*You're Only Young Once*	Judge James K. Hardy
1937	*The Man Who Cried Wolf*	Lawrence Fontaine
1937	*The Thirteenth Chair*	Inspector Marney
1937	*Outcast*	Anthony Abbott *(lawyer)*
1936	*Don't Turn 'em Loose*	John Webster
1936	*Sworn Enemy*	Doctor Simon 'Doc' Gattle
1936	*Suzy*	Baron
1936	*Small Town Girl*	Doctor Dakin
1936	*The Unguarded Hour*	Gen. Lawrence
1936	*Three Godfathers*	James 'Doc' Underwood
1936	*Tough Guy*	Davis *(scenes deleted)*
1935	*Shipmates Forever*	Adm. Richard Melville
1935	*China Seas*	Davids
1935	*Woman Wanted*	District Attorney Martin

1935	*Public Hero #1*.. Warden Alcott
1935	*West Point of the Air*...Gen. Carter
1935	*Vanessa: Her Love Story*... Adam Paris
1935	*David Copperfield* .... Mr. Wickfield
1934	*Treasure Island*.. Captain Smollett
1934	*The Girl from Missouri* .... Frank Cousins
1934	*The Mystery of Mr. X*... Supt. Connor
1934	*You Can't Buy Everything* ....John Burton
1933	*Queen Christina*... Oxenstierna
1933	*Bureau of Missing Persons*...........................Police Captain Webb
	(as Lewis S. Stone)
1933	*Looking Forward*..Gabriel Service Sr.
1933	*The White Sister*...............................Prince Guido Chiaromonte
1933	*Men Must Fight*...Edward 'Ned' Seward
1932	*The Son-Daughter* .... Dr. Dong Tong
1932	*The Mask of Fu Manchu* .... Commissioner Sir Nayland Smith
1932	*Divorce in the Family* .... John Parker
1932	*Unashamed*..Henry Trask
1932	*Red-Headed Woman*...........................William 'Will' Legendre Sr.
1932	*New Morals for Old*..Mr. Thomas
1932	*Letty Lynton* .... District Attorney Haney
1932	*Night Court*.......................................Judge William 'Will' Osgood
1932	*Grand Hotel* ....Doctor Otternschlag
1932	*The Wet Parade* ....Col. Roger Chilcote
1931	*Mata Hari* .... Andriani
1931	*Strictly Dishonorable*..Judge Dempsey
1931	*The Sin of Madelon Claudet* ....Carlo Boretti
1931	*The Phantom of Paris*... Costaud
1931	*The Bargain*... Maitland White
1931	*Always Goodbye*..John Graham
1931	*My Past*.. Mr. John Thornley
1931	*The Secret Six*...Richard 'Newt' Newton
1931	*Father's Son* .... William Emory
1931	*Inspiration* ....Raymond Delval
1930	*Passion Flower* ....Antonio 'Tony' Morado
1930	*The Office Wife*......................................Lawrence 'Larry' Fellowes,
	also spelled Fellows
1930	*Romance*... Cornelius 'Corny' Van Tuyl
1930	*The Big House*.. Warden
1930	*Strictly Unconventional*........................ Clive Champion-Cheney

1929	*Their Own Desire*	Henry 'Hal' Marlett
1929	*Madame X*	Louis Floriot
1929	*Wonder of Women*	Stephen Trombolt
1929	*The Trial of Mary Dugan*	Edward West
1929	*Wild Orchids*	John Sterling
1928	*A Woman of Affairs*	Dr. Hugh Trevelyan
1928	*Freedom of the Press*	Daniel Steele
1928	*The Patriot*	Count Pahlen
1928	*The Foreign Legion*	Col. Destinn
1927	*The Private Life of Helen of Troy*	Menelaus
1927	*The Prince of Headwaiters*	Pierre
1927	*Lonesome Ladies*	John Fosdick
1927	*The Notorious Lady*	Patrick Marlowe/John Carew
1927	*An Affair of the Follies*	Hammersley
1926	*The Blonde Saint*	Sebastian Maure
1926	*Midnight Lovers*	Maj. William Ridgewell, RFC
1926	*Don Juan's Three Nights*	Johann Aradi
1926	*Old Loves and New*	Gervas Carew
1926	*The Girl from Montmartre*	Jerome Hautrive
1926	*Too Much Money*	Robert Broadley
1925	*What Fools Men*	Joseph Greer
1925	*Fine Clothes*	Earl of Denham
1925	*The Lady Who Lied*	Horace Pierpont
1925	*The Talker*	Harry Lennox *(as Lewis S. Stone)*
1925	*Confessions of a Queen*	The King
1925	*The Lost World*	Sir John Roxton *(as Mr. Lewis Stone)*
1925	*Cheaper to Marry*	Jim Knight *(as Lewis S. Stone)*
1924	*Inez from Hollywood*	Stewart Cuyler *(as Lewis S. Stone)*
1924	*Husbands and Lovers*	James Livingston *(as Lewis S. Stone)*
1924	*Cytherea*	Lee Randon
1924	*Why Men Leave Home*	John Emerson
1924	*The Stranger*	Keith Darrant
1923	*Scaramouche*	The Marquis de la Tour d'Azyr
1923	*You Can't Fool Your Wife*	Garth McBride
1923	*The World's Applause*	John Elliott
1923	*The Dangerous Age*	John Emerson
1922	*Trifling Women*	The Marquis Ferroni
1922	*The Prisoner of Zenda*	Rudolf Rassendyll / King Rudolf
1922	*A Fool There Was*	John Schuyler
1922	*The Rosary*	Father Brian Kelly *(as Lewis S. Stone)*

1921   The White Mouse *(short)*..

1921   *Pilgrims of the Night* .... Philip Champion/Lord Ellingham
(as Lewis S. Stone)

1921   *The Child Thou Gavest Me*................................. Edward Berkeley

1921   *Don't Neglect Your Wife*..................................... Langdon Masters

1921   *The Golden Snare*..Sergeant Philip Raine

1921   The Northern Trail *(short)*

1921   *Beau Revel*.................... Lawrence 'Beau' Revel *(as Lewis S. Stone)*

1921   *The Concert*........................ Augustus Martinot *(as Lewis S. Stone)*

1920   *Held by the Enemy*... Capt. Gordon Haine

1920   *Nomads of the North*.................Cpl. O'Connor *(as Lewis S. Stone)*

1920   *Milestones* ....John Rhead

1920   *The River's End* ....Derwent Conniston/John Keith

1919   *Man's Desire*................................ Tom Denton *(as Lewis S. Stone)*

1918   *The Man of Bronze* .... John Adams *(as Lewis S. Stone)*

1918   *Inside the Lines*.. Captain Cavendish

1916   *According to the Code* .... Basil Beckenridge *(as Lewis S. Stone)*

1916   *The Havoc*... Richard Craig

1916   *Honor's Altar*...........................Warren Woods *(as Lewis S. Stone)*

1915   *The Man Who Found Out (short)*........ Undetermined Minor Role
(uncredited)

1914   The Bargain ....

A REAL ANGEL
HENRY TRAVERS

HENRY TRAVERS IN *THE INVISIBLE MAN* (1933). AUTHOR'S COLLECTION.

He has been said to resemble a leprechaun with his sweet, pudding face, curling, whiskery eyebrows, and wispy voice.[1] There never seemed to have been a time when he did not have gray hair and wrinkles that gave him a loveable, grandfatherly look. Yet, even with gray hair and wrinkles, he managed to seem more youthful than his glossy-haired, smooth-faced costars. Appearing in over fifty motion pictures, his is a face audiences immediately recognize. But if asked his name, filmgoers would likely call him Clarence Oddbody instead of his real name: Henry Travers. It is inarguable that Henry is known today by virtue of his performance as Clarence Oddbody, James Stewart's bumbling guardian angel in the holiday classic *It's a Wonderful Life* (1946). His endearing, if clumsy, persona as Clarence was precisely the type of character Henry had made his own more than a decade before *It's a Wonderful Life* was released. One can see Clarence in each father, grandfather, judge, doctor, or other avuncular gentlemen he essayed in his long list of film credits. On screen and off, Henry Travers's was a kindly and reassuring presence, but one not absent of the impish humor that provoked James Stewart to call him a trifle "off his nut."[2]

Henry Travers's life story is nearly as elusive as an angel's. Sources disagree on whether he was born in Ireland or in the English locations of Berwick and Prudhoe. However, all sources agree he is of Irish extraction and was born as Travers John Geagerty on March 5, 1874.[3] His father, Daniel, was an Irish doctor in County Cork. Around 1876, Daniel and his family settled in Tweedmouth at Berwick-upon-Tweed. Berwick was a quaint, small English town probably not unlike the Bedford Falls of Henry's most famous film. Henry's home was located on a corner over a railway bridge. Allan Foster, film expert, called it not substantial, "just an average looking house."[4] Henry seemed like just an average boy as he grew up and was educated at Berwick Grammar School. The *New York Times* later reported that the actor's "early years were carefully directed by his parents in the fondly delusive notion that he was to be an architect."[5] However, at sixteen years old Henry "discouraged this idea"[6] and instead joined the Tweedside Minstrels.[7]

For the next six years, the young actor enjoyed performing in local amateur shows around Britain and the Canadian provinces. His first big break as an actor came in Montreal when a stock manager scouting England for leading men discovered Henry. The manager hired him not for leading parts but for character roles. The fact that Henry's being hired resulted in "the discharge of the man already engaged for the work"[8] is a testament to what talent young Henry must have honed in his years traveling England and the provinces. In 1901, Henry briefly came to America to appear on Broadway in a melodrama entitled *The Price of Peace*.[9] It only lasted sixty performances, after which time Henry returned to England. In 1905 he joined the James Wallace Quintet and became as ubiquitous on the British stage as he would later become in American films. Although still comparatively young, Henry was already playing "befuddled old men."[10]

At age forty-five, Henry returned to America to appear in *The Pipes of Pan* (1917). It was much more successful than his first foray onto Broadway and ran nearly a year.[11] Now having established himself in New York, Henry decided lay down roots in America. In 1919, he joined the Theater Guild, an organization of which he remained a member until his retirement from the stage.[12] From 1917 to the early 1930s, there was not a year that passed in which Henry was not appearing in one or more Broadway productions. And yet, he remained fairly unknown, leading the *New York Times* to report in 1923 that the "task of discovering him should be very easy for the professional discoverer, for...he has been around these many years."[13] He proved to be as versatile in his roles as he was prolific. Though he was usually relegated to the supporting part of an elder gentleman, these gentlemen could be of any ethnicity or class in comedies, dramas, and tragedies. In *The Betrothal*, described as a fantastical "fairy play,"[14] he portrayed Daddy Tyl. The next year found him in as a bookie in the drama *Jenny Clegg* and as a burglar in the comedy *Heartbreak House*. In 1922, he played Clown Jackson in Richard Bennett's allegorical tale *He Who Gets Slapped*. Between 1925 and 1927, he played a Roman, an Italian, and a Russian in *Caesar and Cleopatra*, *Arms and the Man*, and *The Brothers Karamazov*, respectively.[15]

In 1926, he won the lead role of Professor Higgins in *Pygmalion* and gained further prominence by appearing alongside the acclaimed Alfred Lunt in a satire on Marco Polo's Asian travels, *Marco Millions*. He continued into another Asian based play as Wang Lun's father in *The Good Earth*.[16] But it was in a subsequent Alfred Lunt production, *Reunion in Vienna* (1931), that Henry permanently endeared himself to audiences. It was in his role as the German Herr Krugg that he forever established himself as a winning, bemused old man. The *New York Times* summarized that he was highly effective "doddering around amusingly as a gossiping father-in-law."[17] So popular did Henry and the play prove to be that a film version of it was produced just two years later, with Henry reprising his role as Herr Krugg. One reviewer lauded Henry as "the curious, loveable old fellow who lives for his enjoyment and the excitement in other lives — is incomparable and the true highlight of the picture." [18] His performance was so well received that M-G-M signed him for a contract. [19]

But Henry was not ready to give up the stage for the screen yet. In 1936, he was never more in his element than as the whimsical, if a bit kooky, Grandfather Vanderhof in the hit play *You Can't Take It with You.* The role of a young-old man who attends commencement speeches for

HENRY TRAVERS AND GREER GARSON IN *MRS. MINIVER* (1942). COURTESY OF JERRY MURBACH.

the fun of it, collects stamps, and slides down his stair banisters with his grandchildren was Henry's ideal swan song to Broadway. The play ran for two years. When it was recreated by director Frank Capra on screen, Lionel Barrymore was cast in Henry's role.

Though Henry had not won the role of Grandfather Vanderhof in Capra's film, this did not deter him from pursuing his film career. He played only mild variations of the same type of loveable, if flighty town gossip/father/doctor/professors over the next decade. Stand-out performances were as Claude Rains's flustered doctor in *The Invisible Man* (1933), Bette Davis's father in *The Sisters* (1938), Joan Leslie's sly, knowing grandpa in *High Sierra* (1941), and as an impish professor in *Ball of Fire* (1941).

It was in 1942 that Henry was cast in what he would later call his favorite role: that of Mr. Ballard, a meek fellow who works at a railway station by day but breeds beautiful roses in his spare time. The film, *Mrs. Miniver*, was arguably the best of the patriotic, home-front pictures to come out of World War II. Never was Henry more endearing as when he modestly tells Greer Garson's Mrs. Miniver, "What goes to make a rose ma'am is breeding, and budding…and horse manure, if you'll pardon the expression."[20] He earned an Academy Award nomination for Best Supporting Actor of 1942, but lost to Van Heflin in *Johnny Eager* (1942).

Henry may have lost the Academy Award, but he turned in no less stellar performances in his following films. In 1943 he proved his top-rate comedic skills in what Alfred Hitchcock would later call the favorite of all the films he made: *Shadow of a Doubt*. Henry was cast as Mr. Newton, who was (predictably) a rather befuddled father figure, but this role had an intriguing variation: Mr. Newton's way of relaxing is to read gory mystery stories and follow murders in the news. Among the best darkly humorous scenes in the film are those in which Mr. Newton and his friend Herb argue the pros and cons of methods in which to murder each other. At one point Mr. Newton blithely dismisses Herb's idea of poisoning him with a mushroom. Waving his hands and shaking his head he corrects his friend's faulty logic with, "I had a better idea, thought of it while I was shaving… a bathtub, pull your legs out from under you, hold you down. It's been done, but it's still good."[21] The following year Henry turned in a meatier performance in *Dragonseed* (1944) as an impoverished Chinese farmer. Shockingly against type, Henry "delivers a terse monologue describing how he regained his self respect by beating his shrewish wife."[22]

It was 1946 that would ultimately be Henry's zenith in film. After playing a small part as a gossipy storekeeper in the feel-good family classic *The Yearling*, the year would see him star in two more films that are now considered staple holiday classics. The first, *The Bell's of St. Mary's*, cast Henry against type as Mr. Bogardus, a Scrooge-like businessman constructing a building next door to St. Mary's Parish that nuns hope he will donate to the church as a new school. Many critics argued that Henry should have been nominated for a second Academy Award for his performance. He was convincing at the beginning of the film as a villain, cursing schoolchildren and slamming windows shut so angrily he shatters them. However, he was equally convincing as hero at the end as he experiences a Dickensian change in heart and is all eagerness to donate his building to St. Mary's Church and commit other good deeds, like helping a puppy across the street and an elderly woman into a bus. But

Henry's true gift is his ability to avoid becoming a maudlin caricature; at the close of the film, he nonchalantly whispers to a friend, "A gift to the church — it's deductible."[23]

His next film, *It's a Wonderful Life* (1946), found him filling a completely different role. Rather than be Scrooge, he played angel to Scrooge-like James Stewart. His performance as Stewart's wingless guardian angel with "the IQ of a rabbit," Clarence Oddbody, is essential Henry Travers. He is simultaneously charming, bumbling, and thought-provoking in his portrayal. Audiences cannot help but laugh watching him order "flaming rum punch" from a bartender who only serves "hard liquor for men who want to get drunk quickly" or when he slips on an out-dated night shirt and casually declares, "I passed away in it." Though James Stewart bitterly mumbles that Clarence is "just about the kind of angel I'd get," the witless angel is not as dumb as he seems. He provides much to ponder through his words, full of truth with their disarming simplicity, "Strange, isn't it? Each man's life touches so many other lives. When he isn't around, he leaves an awful hole, doesn't he?" Henry is the symbol of the kindly philosophy behind *It's a Wonderful Life;* indeed, it is his character that coined the now iconic phrase "No man is a failure who has friends."[24]

Behind the scenes, James Stewart had the opportunity to observe Henry's well-honed acting technique. Declaring what a joy it was to work with him, the actor further recalled in an interview: "Henry! Of course, he was just exactly right...there couldn't have been anybody better than Henry Travers for Clarence...His timing and his looks and the way he played it straight. You could see he was absolutely guarding himself against anything that would be a comic strip type of thing. Because he was an angel." Stewart went on to describe how well Henry performed without rehearsal. In the scene following Stewart and Henry's dive from the bridge, director Frank Capra began filming with no previous practice. Stewart was all anxiety, but Henry was as unaffected as his angelic character. "I was just fascinated by that man," Stewart declared. "His timing, and always putting the humor where it belonged. Looking up every once in awhile when I talked and then when I said I wished I'd never been born...the way he did it. The take wasn't fake, but it, you know, it just sort of amazed."[25]

It's a Wonderful Life would prove to be Henry's last great film. He retired from pictures in 1949 at the age of seventy-five. His final performance was in a movie that was all fluff, *The Girl from Jones Beach* starring Ronald Reagan. But Henry was singled out for praise in his portrayal as a judge and "managed to steal several scenes of the show."[26]

The sincerity and realism Henry brought to each of his roles until the end of his career was in no small part due to the fact that he was the same man off screen. Little is known about his two marriages, first to Amy Forest Rhodes, who died in 1954, and then to a nurse named Ann G. Murphy. He did not have any biological children; thus, most insight into Henry's warm character comes from the step-grandchildren from his second wife. Granddaughter Peggy Hess claimed, "Grandpa was exactly as he was in the movies. Always even-tempered. I never heard him raise his voice at anyone. He was the type of person who thought about what he would say before he said it, so when he said something, people listened."

Peggy further described how Henry had a suite built onto his and his wife's pink stucco Hollywood home specifically for his grandchildren to stay in when they visited. When Peggy and her siblings awoke in the morning, they would always find Henry enjoying a cup of coffee in the house's beautiful sunroom. In the evenings, they would invariably find him in his office where "he read and drank whiskey on the rocks," Peggy recalled. "He and my father got along well and liked the same things. They would spend their time outside under the palm trees in the garden… sometimes they would tell us kids stories." The stories never dealt with Henry's screen career; according to Peggy, he spoke very little of his films. She did not even know he worked with Humphrey Bogart until she saw *High Sierra* (1941) late at night on television when she was a teenager. However, he did not stop socializing with old friends from filmdom. Gary Cooper was one of the closest of the Travers' family friends. Cooper and Henry attended the same Catholic church and the actor even helped Henry select a book on the saints for Peggy's confirmation. [27]

Henry spent most of his time in retirement at the little pink stucco house. He grew increasingly frail and most often had to walk with the aid of a cane. Though he always seemed such a "young" old man, age finally caught up with him when, in 1965, he died of arteriosclerosis. Henry died in tragic obscurity; no major or minor newspapers printed an obituary for him.

It is only in recent years that Henry's name has become better known. He did not live to see the phenomenal popularity *It's a Wonderful Life* gained after its television premiere in 1979, a popularity that made his face, if not his name, recognizable to generations of film viewers. Miles Gregory, theater and cinema director in Henry's hometown of Berwick, stated, "He's the kind of chap people would have actually seen many times without possibly realizing it was indeed Henry Travers…It's easy to overlook actors who have had a very successful career and who have been in employment throughout their careers — the sum of their contribution is far greater than the individual parts they play."[28] In 2010, Henry's hometown opened The Travers Studio, a structure that seats 120 people and was built to "recognize his links with the theatrical community…in Berwick."[29]

The individual parts Henry played may have been almost indistinguishable from one another, but, added together their sum is a grandfather every child would wish to have, a man with a mischievous smile and curious, innocent nature that makes him all the more loveable because he is like a child himself. "The gentle, friendly squeaky-voiced person you see on film is exactly who Henry Travers was," his granddaughter attested. "He was very unpretentious. He was casual, friendly, and a real angel."[30]

FILMOGRAPHY

1949	*The Girl from Jones Beach*	Judge Bullfinch
1949	*The Accused*	Blakely–Romley's Assistant *(uncredited)*
1948	*Beyond Glory*	Pop Dewing
1947	*The Flame*	Dr. Mitchell
1946	*It's a Wonderful Life*	Clarence
1946	*The Yearling*	Mr. Boyles
1946	*Gallant Journey*	Thomas Logan
1945	*The Bells of St. Mary's*	Horace P. Bogardus
1945	*The Naughty Nineties*	Capt. Sam Jackson
1945	*Thrill of a Romance*	Hobart Glenn
1944	*The Very Thought of You*	Pop Wheeler
1944	*Dragon Seed*	Third Cousin
1944	*None Shall Escape*	Father Warecki
1943	*Madame Curie*	Eugene Curie
1943	*The Moon Is Down*	Mayor Orden
1943	*Shadow of a Doubt*	Joseph Newton
1942	*Random Harvest*	Dr. Sims
1942	*Pierre of the Plains*	Percival Wellsby
1942	*Mrs. Miniver*	Mr. Ballard
1941	*Ball of Fire*	Prof. Jerome
1941	*I'll Wait for You*	Mr. Miller
1941	*The Bad Man*	Mr. Jasper Hardy
1941	*A Girl, a Guy, and a Gob*	Abel Martin
1941	*High Sierra*	Pa
1940	*Wyoming*	Sheriff

1940	*Anne of Windy Poplars*	Matey
1940	*Edison, the Man*	Ben Els
1940	*Primrose Path*	Gramp
1939	*Remember?*	Judge Milliken
1939	*The Rains Came*	Rev. Homer Smiley
1939	*Stanley and Livingstone*	John Kingsley
1939	*On Borrowed Time*	Dr. Evans
1939	*Dark Victory*	Dr. Parsons
1939	*Dodge City*	Dr. Irving
1939	*You Can't Get Away with Murder*	Pop, Sing Sing Librarian
1938	*The Sisters*	Ned Elliott
1936	*Too Many Parents*	Wilkins
1935	*Seven Keys to Baldpate*	Adalbert 'Lem' Peters / The Hermit
1935	*Pursuit*	Thomas 'Tom' Reynolds
1935	*Escapade*	Concierge
1935	*Four Hours to Kill!*	Mac Mason
1935	*Captain Hurricane*	Captain Ben
1935	*After Office Hours*	Cap
1935	*Maybe It's Love*	Mr. Woodrow Halevy
1934	*Ready for Love*	Judge Pickett
1934	*The Party's Over*	Theodore
1934	*Born to Be Bad*	Fuzzy
1934	*Death Takes a Holiday*	Baron Cesarea
1933	*The Invisible Man*	Dr. Cranley
1933	*My Weakness*	Ellery Gregory
1933	*Another Language*	Pop Hallam
1933	*Reunion in Vienna*	Father Krug

SHE'S GOT SPUNK

NANCY WALKER

NANCY WALKER CIRCA 1965. AUTHOR'S COLLECTION.

She's been described as having the "grace of a cement mixer" and the "ferocity of a spiteful steam valve." [1]

She's been described as "having a kind of angelic spirit hovering over her, making her beautiful…" [2]

Whether she's a cement mixer or an angelic spirit, there was one thing everyone who knew her agreed upon: she was a comic genius. Today, audiences recognize her as Rhoda Morgenstern's mother or as Rosie the waitress, responsible for coining the phrase: "Bounty, it's the quicker picker upper." Not many would expect that in her youth, Nancy Walker was proclaimed to be the "best slapstick comedienne of her generation," [3] destined to be the next Fanny Brice or Beatrice Lily of Broadway.

Though she gained fame through portraying the stereotypical Jewish mother, Nancy Walker was born what she called "black Irish." Her given name was Anna Myrtle Swoyer, born to vaudevillians Myrtle and Dewy Barto on May 10, 1922. Her father was a comedic acrobat and her mother was a singer. As she grew up, Nancy would learn to blend her father's talent at humor with her mother's talent at singing. She made her acting debut at the age of ten months when she crawled on stage during her parents' act. [4]

Nancy officially became a stock company actress when she was three and went on to tour Europe throughout her childhood with her parents' "Barto and Mann Vaudeville Team." Nancy was mostly raised backstage by her father, for her mother died early in Nancy's life, after she gave birth to a second daughter, Betty Lou. Like her father, Nancy was very short, only 4'11" and thus found it difficult to be cast in anything but comedy. Her unconventional looks, once described as resembling a "toy bull," and her voice, which has been described "like sandpaper" [5] only made casting more problematic. As a teenager, Nancy turned to a medium where physical appearance need not apply: radio. She was featured on a serial *The Lady Next Door*. [6] However, Nancy dreamed of doing more glamorous work and set a goal of becoming a torch singer. Though her voice was rather abrasive, when she sang it was surprisingly rich and lovely. Her later rendition of "Long Ago and Faraway" is more than enough proof of her abilities.

In 1941, Nancy sought to make her big break by auditioning on Broadway for director/ producers George Abbott and Richard Rodgers, who were currently casting their new show, *Best Foot Forward*. Hugh Martin, the songwriter for *Foot*, remembered his first impression of the young actress: "What a bonanza her discovery was because this young lady possessed genuine comic genius…She had been rejected by every director in town, but she was so persistent that she was finally allowed to audition for Abbott and Rodgers...Nancy sang a torch song and sang it perfectly straight. Some quirk in her unique personality shone through the mediocre material, and that great old eagle...Mr. Abbott...had to stuff a handkerchief in his mouth to keep from laughing and hurting the poor kid's feelings..." [7]

No matter how she wished it were so, Nancy did not have the makings of a sultry torch singer — unless she was depicting one in satire. It was her deadpan delivery that "seemed never to try for a laugh" [8] that led Abbott and Rodgers to see a future for her as sort of female Buster Keaton. They came up with the idea of writing an entire new character into the play designed for Nancy: a plain, awkward girl with a gift for wisecracks who is attending the school prom as a blind date. After securing her role, Nancy adopted the stage name Nancy Walker.

Besides her cute, attractive co-stars June Allyson and Victoria Schools, Nancy certainly must have felt "plain and awkward." Like Nancy, Hugh Martin was also a newcomer to Broadway and remembers bonding with her during the show. He saw a soft, vulnerable side to her that was in sharp contrast to her sarcasm and, as Martin recalls, "her wild profanity," which she used to cover up her insecurities.

"Nancy and I were a couple of babes in the woods. She was a total stranger to the world of romantic relationships...We were both shy, clumsy, insecure, inarticulate. In spite of our naiveté, we had a great time together," [9] Martin wrote. The songwriter later learned that Nancy had a schoolgirl crush on him and whenever he entered a room, she reverently never uttered a four letter word. Their friendship boosted both of their egos enough to give them the confidence necessary for spectacular Broadway debuts.

Martin showcased Nancy in two musical numbers in the play: "Just a Little Joint with a Jukebox" and "The Three B's." The latter was sung by the three female leads, but Nancy's hip, jazzy lines dominated the rest: "I love the boogie 'coz it tickles my spine...It's got a kick like mountain liquor, and it's as slick and hard to take as Veronica Lake!" [10]

Along with her scene stealing lines in the musical numbers, the show's script also gave her ample chance to utilize her deadpan delivery. Take, for instance, this exchange between her and June Allyson:

JUNE: *It looks like we have a lot in common.*

NANCY: *If it's common, we've got it.* [11]

George Abbott's instinct for her talent proved to be correct, for her talent at jazz and her flair for comedy made her, in Martin's words, "walk off with the show" on opening night. [12]

Finally Nancy's unconventional looks and personality began to work in her favor. After *Foot*, she landed another excellent role as the lady cab driver, Hildy, in *On the Town*. The role was later popularized by Betty Garrett in

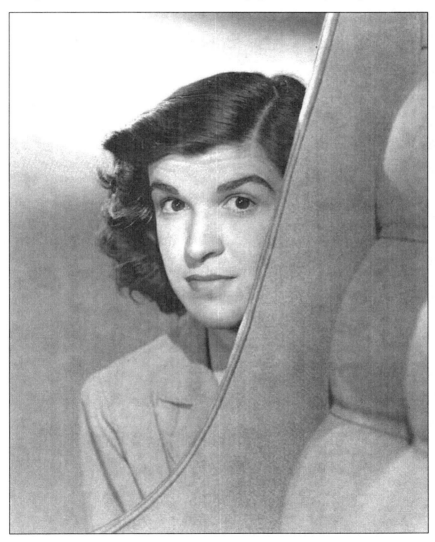

NANCY WALKER CIRCA 1942. AUTHOR'S COLLECTION.

the Gene Kelly film adaptation of the play. As in *Foot,* Nancy played the girl no one really wants, but who continues to be persistent in the face of all rejection. Nancy packed as much humor as she could into the show's lyrics, which were rather risqué and filled with double entrendres absent from the later film version. One song stood out in particular, entitled "I Can Cook": "I'm a man's ideal of a perfect meal...I'm a pot of joy for a hungry boy." [13]

Nancy received rave reviews and attracted the attention of Hollywood in 1943 for the film version of *Best Foot Forward.* The same year, she had a small part in the Mickey Rooney-Judy Garland picture *Girl Crazy.* She was again the kooky girl no one wants. Her self-image could not have been boosted by this exchange between her and Judy in the film:

JUDY: *You're gonna get fat if you don't stop eating all those bananas.*

NANCY: *When you look like me from the neck up, the neck down's no problem.* [14]

Nancy appeared in only one more film before returning to the stage. The film was *Broadway Rhythm* (1944) starring George Murphy and Gloria DeHaven. In her one musical number, Nancy, dressed as a woman welder just off a swing shift, sings the sassy "Milkman Keep Those Bottles Quiet." It was the highlight of an otherwise predictable film.

By 1948 Nancy was back on Broadway and was reunited with Hugh Martin in his new show *Look Ma, I'm Dancin'!, New York Times* critic Brooks Atkinson lauded her "robustious comic ability" as making her the funniest woman since "Fanny Brice crossed her eyes and looked grotesquely comic in songs and revue sketches." [15] Another hit followed in 1949 in *Along Fifth Avenue.* Nancy again had the audience in stitches acting as a plain girl singing "Chat D'Amour" to the object of her desire. [16]

Though Nancy's professional life was booming, her personal one was filled with anything but comedy. In 1948, she married actor Gar Moore but was divorced from him less than a year later. Nancy had never had an easy time with romance, and the failed marriage only reinforced her sagging self-image. She entered therapy and would remain in and out of it throughout her entire life, battling feelings of insecurity, depression, and hostility. She later confessed to *TV Guide:* "I'm filled with rages. I'm the most irate woman I've ever known. Most of the time, I'm quiet. You never knew I could kill. Oh yes. I explode." [17]

Her frustrations began to extend to her singing. In 1949, she sought help from vocal coach and composer David Craig. "I couldn't stand David when I first met him," Nancy admitted to *People* magazine. "I told her she wasn't really committed to her career," Craig continued. "And she got so furious that it got us together — the old negative approach." [18]

Like a plot from a classic romantic comedy, the sparring couple fell in love and married in 1951. In 1952, they had their only child, a daughter named Miranda. Craig wrote two shows for Nancy. One of them, *Phoenix '56*, earned her a Tony nomination, an honor she would again receive in 1960 for her performance with Phil Silvers in *Do Re Mi*. Her popularity in musicals led her to release an album called *I Hate Men*. The record featured a hilarious selection of songs themed with exasperation for the opposite sex such as "I'm Going to Wash That Man Right Out of My Hair." Perhaps Nancy was still working through her insecurities, but her marriage with Craig was proving to be a happy one. "I rely on David more than either of us realizes," Nancy stated. "I fight him about it, because that's my ego. But the result has always worked." [19] She and David enjoyed being curmudgeons together and unapologetically dozed off or walked out of shows or parties that were excruciatingly dull to them. Nancy often found the company of her two cats, named Fanny Brice and Willie Howard, preferable to the glitz of Hollywood life. She described herself as a "big lady for commitments to my family." She enjoyed staying at home with her cats and sewing clothes for her daughter until her fingers were cramped. [20] Her daughter fondly remembered Nancy's devotion as "a fierce, wonderful love that no one will ever give me again." [21]

It was Nancy's wish to have a more settled life with her family that led her to turn her attention to television, a medium which was reliable and offered a healthy salary. "I saw the handwriting on the wall for New York," Nancy said. "Both professionally and as a place to live.'

Nancy made brief appearances on television in 1960, but by the latter half of the decade, she and her family had permanently relocated to Hollywood. They moved into a beautiful hilltop mansion with a pool in Studio City. "I've gotten to an age where I like to be comfortable. I spent decades in scroungy dressing rooms. Now I work in nice studios with nice people," [22] Nancy stated. She soon found her niche on TV. She appeared on many popular shows, including *Family Affair* and *The Carol Burnett Show*. She was most acclaimed for her portrayal of a "prototypically possessive Jewish mother, evoking a lifetime of smother love in a single arched eyebrow" in *Rhoda*. She was not lacking in her customary sass as Mrs. Morgenstern, either, as evidenced in an example of one of the many outrageous comic moments she created on the show. While being examine by a doctor, she enquires why he and not a woman is conducting the check-up.

DR. HENRY GERBER: *Why? Why do you think?*

IDA MORGENSTERN: *Because I think you get your kicks from seeing a woman my age naked.*

DR. HENRY GERBER: *Mrs. Morgenstern, I examine naked people all day long. I've been doing it for over 20 years.*

IDA MORGENSTERN: *Aw, come on doctor, you mean to say if uh, you don't see an extraordinary body, you don't let that stethoscope linger a little?* [23]

Nancy's appearances on *Rhoda* succeeded in giving the series a much-needed boost in ratings. Buoyed by her success as Mrs. Morgenstern, Nancy attempted to create a showcase for herself in *The Nancy Walker Show* in 1976, but it only lasted one season before being canceled. However, this failure did not dampen her ability to bring laughs in other recurring roles, such as on Rock Hudson's *McMillan and Wife*. Her portrayal of a "sardonic housekeeper, whose disdainful shrugs and shriveling glares make her a foil to cutey smooty Susan St. James." [24] Next, Nancy's character of Rosie the waitress on Bounty paper towel commercials from 1970-1990 made her face recognizable to fifty million people, more than all the people she performed to during her thirty years in the theater. She earned a total of seven Emmy nominations, the last of which was for a single appearance she made on *Golden Girls*.

In 1986, Nancy's seemingly indomitable energy was tested when she was diagnosed with lung cancer. Her health slowly deteriorated until 1992. Her last wish was to have a fortieth anniversary party with her husband and eerily, her flagging health rose just in time for the occasion. She turned to Craig and said, "Now I can go in peace. This was the last dream of my life come true." [25]

In 1992, Nancy Walker died at age sixty-nine. She was cremated and scattered at sea. To the end, she never lost her spunk and brassy sense of humor. Her co-star Valerie Harper stated, "I love the fact that she went out like she came in, with grease paint on." [26]

However, until the end Nancy used her "greasepaint" as the comic mask she had worn since her beginnings on Broadway. Harold Gould of *Rhoda* saw the mask fall, as Hugh Martin did in 1941. Gould recalled, "I saw her privately give way to tears of frustration when she felt her performance wasn't going right." [27]

Plagued by depression and insecurity her entire life, Nancy Walker managed to create a persona brimming with "sass and grit." She left an indelible print on Broadway and television and continues to bring laughter to modern audiences, whether in her appearances on the small screen or the big screen. "You can't teach someone to be Bert Lahr," her husband stated. "Or Nancy Walker." [28]

FILMOGRAPHY

1976	*Murder by Death*	Yetta—Maid
1976	*Won Ton Ton: The Dog Who Saved Hollywood*	Mrs. Fromberg
1973	*40 Carats*	Mrs. Margolin
1973	*The World's Greatest Athlete*	Mrs. Petersen
1972	*Stand Up and Be Counted*	Agnes
1954	*Lucky Me*	Flo Neely
1944	*Broadway Rhythm*	Trixie Simpson
1943	*Girl Crazy*	Polly Williams
1943	*Best Foot Forward*	Nancy, Blind Date

THE MENACING,
THE PATHETIC, THE GRATEFUL
H.B. WARNER

H.B. WARNER CIRCA 1930. AUTHOR'S COLLECTION.

"I am supposed to be associated with that awful word, dignity. That is what Cecil B. DeMille did for me, as I'm not at all dignified or saintly really." [1]

Anyone who has seen H.B. Warner's over one hundred film performances would be inclined to disagree with his above statement. Though he began his career on stage playing thugs, detectives, and crooks, it is his performances as Jesus in *The King of Kings* (1927) and his small but pivotal roles in Frank Capra's socially conscious films of the 1930s and 1940s that have made him associated with virtue and morality. With his slight, almost fragile build, pensive eyes, and soft, whispery voice, one could hardly imagine him playing anyone but a wise, impeccably natured gentleman. It is the quiet dignity of which he seems unaware that makes him seem so (though he would be the first to protest against it) saintly yet mysterious. One critic aptly described H.B. Warner's effect in film: "No matter how much one tries to gage the acting of Mr. Warner, one soon forgets the actor and remembers only the glorified role which he plays. This seems to be the highest type of acting, and consequently, Mr. Warner is most satisfactory." [2]

He started life as Henry Byron Warner on October 26, 1875. "I was born calm — and in England," [3] he later said. He was also born more or less in the theater; his father, Charles, and his grandfather, James, were both well-established actors of the British stage. H.B. did his share of acting as early as the tender age of seven. He made his stage debut at that age quite by accident. "My father was playing in Hanley, Staffordshire, England at the Theater Royal," H.B. recalled. "...A hurry call was sent to my nurse, who brought me to the theater...With her holding my hand, I walked on stage with a group of extras as part of a big fire scene." [4] Though his father was active in drama as H.B. continued to grow, he wished for his son to study medicine. H.B. studied little of medicine or drama when he entered college; he was more interested in sports such as rugby and crew. But as a graduate student at University College, he could not help but try his hand at theater again. His niche as moralistic, holy men started early; in his first college production, he portrayed the Rev. Mr. Eden in a play entitled *Never Too Late to Mend.* [5] Sportsman, actor, or doctor — H.B. was adept at all three callings but nevertheless confessed: "When I came out of University College...I hadn't the remotest idea what I wanted to do." [6]

H.B. must have had an idea what he did *not* want to do, for he quit his medical studies and instead traveled to Italy and France to study acting. Accepting that his son would follow the family tradition, Charles Warner took H.B. into his stock company and helped him hone his craft. When not working with his father, H.B. ventured into film, making his debut as the Duke of Monmouth in *English Nell,* a British short produced in 1900.[7] He made his official stage debut in *Drink,* a play that would have a record-breaking run but did not necessarily lead to meatier roles for H.B. "I had been playing juvenile roles in England and it looked as if I would go on playing them until I was 200 years old," he stated. "I wasn't satisfied. Perhaps I should have been, for I was doing what was called mighty well for a young man, but I was ambitious…I longed for a change."[8] He was granted his wish for change in 1906 when an American stage producer asked him on a Monday to come to the States by Thursday to become a leading man to Miss Eleanor Robson in *Merely Mary Ann*[9]. H.B. recalled that he was "carried off his feet" by the offer, as was his father. Never having made it to America himself, Charles told H.B., "Boy, if you ever get a chance to go to America, take it. I know you'll succeed and if you do you'll never come back."[10]

When H.B. first arrived in America, he plunged into his work to assuage the feelings of loneliness that overtook him there. He enjoyed a string of successful shows that were mostly light romantic comedies until 1910, when he starred in the show that would be the pinnacle of his career thus far: *Alias Jimmy Valentine.* The show was a heavy drama dealing with the plight of inmates imprisoned for life. H.B. played a prisoner himself; juvenile roles were a thing of the past. H.B.'s gripping performance made him the toast of Broadway. He would never return to England.

"I'm playing in America and my interests are American,"[11] the patriotic H.B. declared. He married an American girl, Mary Hamlin, in 1912 and together they bought an idyllic summer home near Boston. At his door, H.B. had a golf course and the ocean only steps away. H.B. claimed he would not change his seaside cottage for a mansion in England. "I love my old home, but I love America, too," he said. "Give me the open country, a chance to swim, a tennis racquet, and a set of golf clubs and my vacation is complete."[12] Aside from renewing his love of athletics, H.B. found a new love in animals. He was eager to share his enthusiasm for them to reporters. He told one columnist for the *Boston Globe:* "I love all kinds of animals and I like to have them around…I'm so strong for animals that I'm planning for a pigeon loft."[13] His love of animals also manifested when he was at work. At the theater, he went out of his way to make a large gray tabby cat feel welcome. "I'm sort of like this cat," he told an interviewer. "She makes friends with everybody. At nights and on matinee days she sits at the stage entrance until all the company has

arrived, and then she visits around the dressing room. I wouldn't hurt that
cat's feelings for anything." [14]

H.B.'s love of America and its creatures, human or animal, was never
more evident than when he (like a character from the pages of a Frank
Capra screenplay) took on the justice system himself. In 1910, he not only
proposed to donate the proceeds of a performance of *Alias Jimmy Valentine*
to better the conditions of "lifers" in prison, but also set about proving the
innocence of two black men accused of murder. He succeeded, and even
President Taft agreed that the prisoners had been "grievously wronged". [15]
One of the freed prisoners became H.B.'s valet and accompanied him
faithfully to his seaside cottage each year. H.B., though he described
himself as the opposite of a saint, seemed not unlike a St. Francis of Assisi
to animals or a Moses freeing the slaves of Egypt.

H.B.'s streak of good fortune came to an abrupt halt in the spring of
1913 when his wife was killed in an automobile accident not moments
away from their idyllic home. H.B. was in the car as well but miraculously
escaped the accident with no more than bruises. It would be six years
before H.B. felt ready to marry again. His second wife was Rita Stanwood.
They had two children together, Joan and Buddy. H.B.'s dressing room
table would never be without framed photographs of the girl and boy. [16]

After his first wife's death, H.B.'s work was increasingly in film. He
appeared in another short, *Harp of Tara,* in 1914 and the same year
reprised his role in *The Ghost Breaker,* which he had performed on stage
the previous year. The film was directed by Cecil B. DeMille, the man
who would ultimately prove the most influential in H.B.'s career. It was
DeMille who came to H.B. thirteen years later with a proposal for the film
King of Kings, which was to deal with the life of Christ. "I listened intently
and saw myself in the role of Judas," [17] H.B said, for he had become so
accustomed to playing unsavory characters on stage. He could hardly
believe it when DeMille told him it was Christ he wanted H.B. to play.

As effective as his later roles in film would be, *King of Kings* is considered to be the zenith of H.B.'s career. His performance was enhanced by
the silent screen, for it allowed viewers to imagine how Jesus would sound.
Also, without words, the ever-present, pensive look in H.B.'s eyes had
increased profundity. Though H.B.'s casting had initially spread doubt in
Hollywood, he was lauded by critics, including this review from the *Boston
Daily Globe:* "After seeing Mr. Warner it is hard to imagine anyone playing the part with more sympathy and good taste. Each person to whom
religion means a great deal has a different ideal of Jesus, but Mr. Warner
seems to have assembled all the ideals and struck a happy average... *The*

King of Kings is Hollywood's answer to the accusation that modern films are without exception cheap in treatment and commercial in their aims."[18]

The film may not have been commercial in its aims, but H.B. insisted that he held sheer entertainment above the most profound and thought-provoking of movies or plays. "Our mission is to amuse and not to inform or uplift,"[19] he stated. He himself preferred amateur theatrics, much to the chagrin of some of his high-brow contemporaries. As much as H.B. wanted to be a simple entertainer as his father and grandfather had been, after *King of Kings,* audiences could not dissociate H.B. from message pictures. H.B. once ruefully said that DeMille had put him on the cross, and he had been martyred ever since in one film after the other.

H.B. did indeed play his fair share of martyred men in his following pictures. Most notable was his performance as a war veteran father who sacrifices everything for his child in *Sorrell and Son* (1928). When talking pictures arrived, H.B. became one of the most ubiquitous supporting players on screen. His unobtrusive appearance and silken voice made him ideal to play men of all ethnicities: Americans, Britons, and Asians. He appeared as Gabelle, a French tutor in *A Tale of Two Cities* (1935), as Chen Tsu in *The Adventures of Marco Polo* (1938), and as a maharajah in *The Rains Came* (1939). However, no matter what his color or creed in film, his roles were almost invariably men of the highest moral standing. Look at his credits and there will usually be a "Col.," "Dr.," "Judge," or "Rev." attached to his character's name.

In 1936, H.B. appeared in his first Frank Capra film, *Mr. Deeds Goes to Town.* He would appear in five more Capra works. His roles in this sextet of films gave him a range of character he had not enjoyed since *King of Kings.* In *Mr. Deeds* he portrays a judge, in *Mr. Smith Goes to Washington* (1939) he portrays a shady senator, in *You Can't Take It with You* (1938) he is a businessman, and in *Lost Horizon* (1937) he is a holy man. His role in *Lost Horizon* is one audiences would most expect from him. As a guide to a group of stranded refugees in a plane crash who stumble upon Shangri-La, he offers such sage observations as:

> *Age is a limit we impose upon ourselves. You know, each time you Westerners celebrate your birthday, you build another fence around your minds.* [20]

H.B. received an Academy Award nomination for his performance in the film. His next role as Mr. Ramsey in *You Can't Take It with You* lasts only one minute, but the monologue he gives in that moment intensely conveys the message of the entire film. Shouting without raising his voice at the antagonist of the film, he expresses regret over what had been his lifelong mission of gaining money at the expense of family and friendship:

> RAMSEY: *I never gained one moment's happiness out of it. I warn you Anthony...in spite of your victories you can't shut out every decent impulse and survive. You're top heavy with power right now, Anthony, and you're going to crack under it; you're bound to crack under it! You know what's going to happen Mr. Anthony P. Kirby, you'll scream for help and suddenly find yourself alone in the world... that's what happened to me and it'll happen to you, that's what happens to all men like us Anthony. It's coming to us.* [21]

At the end of his speech he collapses and moments later is found dead in the washroom. The mix of fragility, anger, and remorse he poured into every word in his performance leads one to ponder why he was not nominated by the Academy for this film too.

Though Capra's films gave H.B. recognition, the salary of a supporting actor could not cover his living expenses. Once one of the highest paid actors in film, in 1943, H.B. declared bankruptcy. It did not help that he had divorced his wife in 1933, which had resulted in a hefty property settlement. H.B. returned to the stage in 1945 in *A Doll's House* and declared that he was "exceedingly glad" to be back in the theater, working in sequence instead of on small blocks of unrelated film. It was not surprising that the man who had professed to "love everybody" valued people's approval of his work, something that was more intangible in film than in live theater. "There's something fine about having an audience reaction, too," he said. [22] As much validation as he felt from his audiences, he still confessed he was glad that his son did not wish to carry on the often hardscrabble and unreliable family tradition of acting. Instead, his boy chose to join the Tank Corp in Patton's army. [23]

In 1946, H.B. appeared in his last Capra film, *It's a Wonderful Life.* As the drunken druggist Mr. Gower, he was cast decidedly against type but gives perhaps his best performance in a talking picture. He worked tirelessly at the role. Bobbie Anderson, who plays James Stewart as a child in the film, remembers H.B. as a "Method" actor. H.B. began drinking at the beginning of each shooting day in order to be realistically inebriated on film. In the famous scene when H.B. slaps Anderson when the boy tries to tell him he has mistakenly put poison in some medicine capsules, Anderson recalled, "He actually bloodied my ear...My face was red and

I was in tears." But he quickly added, "H.B. was perfect. He reached the crescendo. At the end, when it was all over, he was very loveable. He grabbed me and hugged me and he meant it." [24]

Mr. Gower would prove to be H.B.'s last great role. He appeared in a succession of forgettable pictures in the 1950s, with the exception of a cameo in the classic *Sunset Blvd.* (1950) as one of aged star Norma

ANNA Q. NILSSON, GLORIA SWANSON, BUSTER KEATON, WILLIAM HOLDEN, ERICH VON STROHEIM, AND H.B. WARNER IN *SUNSET BLVD.* (1950).
COURTESY OF JERRY MURBACH.

Desmond's friends the film's sarcastic narrator describes as "a Waxwork." The role was a self-deprecatory one, and reflective of H.B.'s obscure status by the end of his career. His final role was as Amminadab in Cecil B. DeMille's *The Ten Commandments* (1958), an appropriate swan song for the man who epitomized Christ to generations of filmgoers. H.B. died on December 21, 1958 at the age of eighty-three.

Though one of the most prolific supporting players in filmdom, it is a sad truth that H.B. Warner is an actor time has largely forgotten. His roles often amounted to less than two minutes on screen, yet they managed to be more profound and well-drawn than many leading actors' performances. H.B. admitted to be the furthest thing from a saint there could be off screen, yet his every action warred with this notion. He was a kind patron to humans and animals alike and once confided that he could never criticize even the least talented of amateurs because, "I would rather boost than knock." [25] Perhaps H.B. was described best when he was said to be a man who "wore his manners well." Indeed, his manners continue to wear well with each new viewing of his film roles, whether they are, in one writer's words, "the menacing, the pathetic" or "the grateful." [26]

FILMOGRAPHY

Year	Title	Role
1956	*The Ten Commandments*	Amminadab
1951	*Journey Into Light*	Wiz, the Wino
1951	*Here Comes the Groom*	Uncle Elihu
1951	*Savage Drums*	Maou
1951	*The First Legion*	Fr. Jose Sierra
1950	Sunset Blvd.	Himself
1949	*The Judge Steps Out*	Chief Justice Hayes
1949	*Hellfire*	Brother Joseph
1949	*El Paso*	Judge Fletcher
1948	*The Prince of Thieves*	Gilbert Head
1947	*High Wall*	Mr. Slocum
1947	*Driftwood*	Rev. J. 'Grandpappy' Hollingsworth
1946	*It's a Wonderful Life*	Mr. Gower
1946	*Gentleman Joe Palooka*	Sen. McCarden
1946	*Strange Impersonation*	Dr. Mansfield, plastic surgeon
1945	*Captain Tugboat Annie*	Judge Abbott
1944	*Rogues Gallery*	Professor Reynolds
1944	*Faces in the Fog*	Defense Attorney Rankins
1944	*Enemy of Women*	Col. Eberhart Brandt
1944	*Prices Unlimited (short)*	Uncle Sam *(uncredited)*
1944	*Action in Arabia*	Abdul El Rashid
1943	*Women in Bondage*	Pastor Renz
1943	*Hitler's Children*	The Bishop
1942	*The Boss of Big Town*	Jeffrey Moore
1942	*A Yank in Libya*	Herbert Forbes
1942	*Crossroads*	Prosecuting Attorney
1941	*The Corsican Brothers*	Dr. Enrico Paoli
1941	*The Devil and Daniel Webster*	Justice John Hathorne
1941	*South of Tahiti*	High Chief
1941	*Ellery Queen and the Perfect Crime*	Ray Jardin
1941	*City of Missing Girls*	Captain McVeigh

1941	*Topper Returns*	Mr. Henry Carrington
1940	*New Moon*	Father Michel
1940	*The Man from Dakota*	Undetermined Supporting Role *(scenes deleted)*
1939	*Mr. Smith Goes to Washington*	Senate Majority Leader–Agnew
1939	*The Rains Came*	Maharajah
1939	*Nurse Edith Cavell*	Hugh Gibson
1939	*Bulldog Drummond's Bride*	Colonel Nielson
1939	*The Gracie Allen Murder Case*	Richard Lawrence
1939	*Bulldog Drummond's Secret Police*	Col. Nielson
1939	*Let Freedom Ring*	Ned Rutledge
1939	*Arrest Bulldog Drummond*	Colonel Nielsen
1938	*Bulldog Drummond in Africa*	Col. J.A. Nielsen
1938	*You Can't Take It with You*	Ramsey
1938	*Army Girl*	Col. Armstrong
1938	*The Toy Wife*	Victor Brigard
1938	*Kidnapped*	Angus Rankeiller
1938	*The Adventures of Marco Polo*	Chen Tsu
1938	*The Girl of the Golden West*	Father Sienna
1937	*Victoria the Great*	Lord Melbourne
1937	*Torpedoed*	British Consul Brent
1937	*Lost Horizon*	Chang
1936	*Along Came Love*	Dr. Martin
1936	*Blackmailer*	Michael Rankin
1936	*Mr. Deeds Goes to Town*	Judge May
1936	*Moonlight Murder*	Godfrey Chiltern
1936	*The Garden Murder Case*	Major Fenwicke-Ralston
1936	*Rose of the Rancho*	Don Pasqual Castro
1935	*A Tale of Two Cities*	Gabelle
1935	*Born to Gamble*	Carter Mathews
1934	*Night Alarm*	Henry B. Smith
1934	*Behold My Wife*	Hubert Carter
1934	*In Old Santa Fe*	Charlie Miller–her father
1934	*Grand Canary*	Dr. Ismay
1934	*Viva Villa!*	Man *(scenes deleted)*
1933	*Sorrell and Son*	Captain Stephen Sorrell
1933	*Christopher Bean*	Maxwell Davenport
1933	*Jennie Gerhardt*	William Gerhardt
1933	*Supernatural*	Dr. Carl Houston
1933	*Justice Takes a Holiday*	John Logan

1932	*The Son-Daughter*	Sin Kai
1932	*The Phantom of Crestwood*	Priam Andes
		(Harbor National Bank)
1932	*The Crusader*	Phillip Brandon
1932	*Tom Brown of Culver*	Dr. Brown
1932	*Unholy Love*	Dr. Daniel Gregory
1932	*Cross Examination*	Gerald Waring, Defense Attorney
1932	*A Woman Commands*	Col. Stradimirovitsch
1932	*The Menace*	Inspector Tracy
1932	*Charlie Chan's Chance*	Inspector Fife
1931	*Expensive Women*	Melville Raymond
1931	*Five Star Final*	Michael Townsend
1931	*The Reckless Hour*	Walter Nichols
1931	*A Woman of Experience*	Major Hugh Schmidt
1930	*Princess and the Plumber*	Prince Conrad of Daritzia
1930	*Liliom*	Chief Magistrate
1930	*On Your Back*	Raymond Pryor
1930	*Wild Company*	Henry Grayson
1930	*The Second Floor Mystery*	Inspector Bray
1930	*The Furies*	Oliver Bedlow
1930	*The Green Goddess*	Major Crespin
1929	*Wedding Rings*	Lewis Dike
1929	*Tiger Rose*	Dr. Cusick
1929	*The Show of Shows*	The Victim, Guillotine sequence
1929	*The Argyle Case*	Hurley
1929	*The Gamblers*	James Darwin
1929	*The Trial of Mary Dugan*	District Attorney Galway
1929	*The Divine Lady*	Sir William Hamilton
1929	*Stark Mad*	Prof. Dangerfield
1929	*The Doctor's Secret*	Richard Garson
1928	*Conquest*	James Farnham
1928	*The Naughty Duchess*	Duke de St. Maclou
1928	*Romance of a Rogue*	Bruce Lowry
1928	*Man-Made Women*	Jules Moret
1927	*French Dressing*	Phillip Grey
1927	*Sorrell and Son*	Stephen Sorrell
1927	*The King of Kings*	Jesus, the Christ
1926	*/ Silence*	Jim Warren
1926	*Whispering Smith*	'Whispering Smith'
1924	*Is Love Everything?*	Jordan Southwick

1923	*Zaza*	Bernard Dufresne
1921	*When We Were 21*	Richard Carewe
1920	*Dice of Destiny*	Jimmy Doyle
1920	*Felix O'Day*	Felix O'Day
1920	*One Hour Before Dawn*	George Clayton
1920	*Uncharted Channels*	Timothy Webb Jr
1920	*The White Dove*	Sylvester Lanyon
1919	*Haunting Shadows*	John Glenarm
1919	*A Fugitive from Matrimony*	Stephen Van Courtlandt
1919	*The Gray Wolf's Ghost*	Doctor West/Harry West
1919	*For a Woman's Honor*	Captain Clyde Mannering
1919	*The Pagan God*	Bruce Winthrop
1919	*The Man Who Turned White*	Captain Rand/aka Ali Zaman
1917	*Danger Trail*	John Howland
1917	*God's Man*	Arnold L'Hommedieu
1917	*The Seventh Sin*	Feodor / The Grand Duke
1917	*Wrath*	Feodor / The Grand Duke
1917	*The Seven Deadly Sins*	Feodor / The Grand Duke, Wrath & Seventh Sin
1916	*The Vagabond Prince*	Prince Tonio
1916	*Shell 43*	William Berner
1916	*The Market of Vain Desire*	John Armstrong (as Henry B. Warner)
1916	*The Beggar of Cawnpore*	Dr. Robert Lowndes
1916	*The Raiders*	Scott Wells (as Henry B. Warner)
1914	*The Ghost Breaker*	Warren Jarvis
1914	*The Lost Paradise*	Reuben Warren
1914		Harp of Tara (short)
1900	*English Nell (short)*	Duke of Monmouth

QUEEN OF
THE WHEELCHAIRS
MARY WICKES

MARY WICKES CIRCA 1960. AUTHOR'S COLLECTION.

"She has been called the last of the great character actresses, and that was right. When Mary came on, you knew you were in for a lot of laughs."[1]

So spoke Madelyn Davis in 1995 after the passing of her friend Mary Wickes. Mary was indeed among the best character actresses who enlivened so many films of the 1940s through the 1960s (and into the 1990s, in Mary's case). Mary Wickes occupied a niche somewhere between Thelma Ritter and Marjorie Main, most often playing nurses and housekeepers. She was not as irascible as Main and was a touch more sentimental than Ritter; however, like these two women, Mary's sharp wit and dry sense of humor elevated every film in which she appeared. Following her most famous role as the long-suffering Nurse Preen in *The Man Who Came to Dinner* (1942), Mary Wickes became typed to such an extent that she dubbed herself "The Queen of the Wheelchairs."[2] Despite her type-casting, Mary was much more than a Queen of Wheelchairs. She was a talented comedienne who could hold her own against the best-known female comedy star of the 1950s, Lucille Ball. However, her lanky 5'10" build, weak chin, and prominent nose relegated Mary to character parts without the glamour of the red-headed Lucy. But, Mary was content with her place in Hollywood. As she said: "They may not ask for my autograph, as long as they sign my paycheck."[3]

Born on June 13, 1910 as Mary Isabella Wickenhauser in St. Louis, Missouri, Mary was brought up in a well-to-do family in the southern tradition. Her father, a banker, and her mother even arranged a debutante party for her when she came of age. The Wickenhausers also were patrons of the theater throughout Mary's childhood. Mary later reminisced about her first taste of the stage at the age of seven: "I remember crying when a play was funny because I was so happy."[4] However, it did not occur to the young Mary to pursue show business. She explained: "I never thought I'd be an actress. They seemed like a whole 'nother race to me as I watched them growing up."[5]

At eighteen, Mary entered Washington University in St. Louis as a Political Science major. The school had no drama department aside from a course on one-act plays. Mary chose this class to fill her elective requirement. To her amazement, her professor suggested Mary try out for the St. Louis Little Theater. Mary heeded the advice and won a role in the theater's production of *The Solid South*. Like the cliché plot of a 1930s backstage film, Mary was spotted in the little play by Broadway director F. Cole Strickland. He invited her to join his summer stock company at the Berkshire Playhouse in Stockbridge, Massachusetts. However, before Mary could accept, her protective father demanded that he "audition"[6] the director to be sure his character was above reproach. Strickland must have passed Mr. Wickenhauser's test, for Mary appeared in summer stock productions each year for the remainder of her college career. "I was actually paid to have a good time," Mary declared. [7]

Mary graduated with a degree in Political Science, but she had little use for it. She packed up for New York to pursue acting. In 1934, she won a walk-on part in *The Farmer Takes a Wife*, a show in which Henry Fonda was the leading man. Mary went on to gain steady employment in several plays, the most notable of which was *Stage Door*. The play, co-written by George S. Kaufman, was to be the first of many Kaufman shows in which Mary appeared. Mary's parts were exclusively secondary roles that often called for a woman older than her. In a 1979 interview, Mary explained that she had to lie about her age to play character parts and that "later on when I tried to straighten it out, they looked at me like — sure, sure, everyone wants to be younger than they really are. I had to present my birth certificate." [8]

Aside from *Stage Door*, the bulk of Mary's early work was in shows that received less than laudatory reviews. Her luck changed in 1939 when she played the harassed Nurse Preen in the George S. Kaufman and Moss Hart comedy *The Man Who Came to Dinner*. Although Mary had had a few dramatic parts in summer stock productions, she claimed that "both [drama and comedy] require a feeling for timing, but I found once you get comic timing down the other comes easy." [9]

Unlike most of Mary's roles in which she portrayed an outspoken character, Nurse Preen called for her to be cowering and easily daunted. Nurse Preen speaks her mind only once at the end of the show when she has lost patience after one too many insults from her acid-tongued patient, Sheridan Whiteside (played by the hilarious Monty Woolley). Her monologue is among the most memorable in the play and in her career:

NURSE PREEN: *After one month with you, Mr. Whiteside, I'm going to work in a munitions factory. From now on, anything I can do to help exterminate the human race will fill me with the greatest of pleasure. If Florence Nightingale had ever nursed you, she'd of married Jack the Ripper instead of founding the Red Cross. Good day!* [10]

So pleased was Kaufman with Mary's performance that he kept her in the role of Nurse Preen for the play's two-year run and subsequent tours. Kaufman was later quoted as saying Mary was his "favorite comedienne." [11]

Rather than keep Mary on the stage, her hit on Broadway whisked her off to Hollywood. In 1942, Warner Bros. engaged her to recreate her role alongside Monty Woolley in the film adaptation of *The Man Who Came to Dinner*, which co-starred Bette Davis. Mary had little difficulty finding subsequent parts in films, although the bulk of them were forgettable B films, including the Abbott and Costello spoof on the detective genre, *Who*

MARY WICKES, FRANK SINATRA, MICHELE MORGAN, AND JACK HALEY IN *HIGHER AND HIGHER* **(1943).** AUTHOR'S COLLECTION.

Done It? (1942) and the Andrews Sisters vehicle *Private Buckaroo* (1942). The only picture of substance in which she appeared during this period was another Bette Davis film, *Now, Voyager* (1942). In it, she was again cast as a nurse — though in this film she was far more outspoken than the submissive Nurse Preen. The *St. Petersburg Times* noted in 1943: "Mary Wickes is one actress who looks into the mirror each morning and hopes bags are forming under her eyes...this gangling, six foot...actress...is finding the movies pay off quite handsomely on homeliness as well as beauty." [12]

Despite Mary's success in Hollywood, she had no immediate plans for staying there permanently. In 1945, she returned to Broadway, and for the next three years appeared in exclusively Kaufman shows: *Hollywood Pinafore, Town House,* and *Park Avenue.*

Mary returned to Hollywood in 1948 to perform in a role written especially for her (again as a nurse) in *The Decision of Christopher Blakeley*. It would be decades before she would return to the stage, so in demand did she become in the movies. Mary was resigned to her type of part, though she did retain a wistful fondness for the stage. "In film, I'm always someone's housekeeper, but in the theater I tend to get dressed up more, if you know what I mean,"[13] she said in a 1990 interview.

Mary appeared as a reporter in another Bette Davis film, *June Bride* (1948) but was back to playing a caretaker role in three delightful Doris Day films: *On Moonlight Bay* (1951), *By the Light of the Silvery Moon* (1951), and *I'll See You in My Dreams* (1951). Her most prestigious picture since *Now, Voyager* came in 1954 when she portrayed the innkeeper's wife in the Irving Berlin holiday classic *White Christmas*. Playing her signature type as a blunt woman always ready with a witty comeback, Mary stole every scene in which she appeared with her snappy one-liners:

GEN. THOMAS WAVERLY: *I got along just fine without you in the Army.*

EMMA (Mary): *Yeah, it only took 15,000 men to take my place.*[14]

Mary's employment was steady in films, but she accepted the fact that television was eclipsing movies in popularity. Because there would always be a need for supporting character actors, she was more easily able to adapt to changing times than leading ladies and gentlemen. In television, she continued to pursue her forte of playing servants, teachers, and other working-girl types. Most people hold the name Mary Poppins as synonymous with Julie Andrews, but it was actually Mary who first portrayed the flying babysitter on a 1949 CBS special. She was ubiquitous on a variety of television series, guest starring alongside comedy legends including Jack Benny, Red Skelton, and Bob Hope and playing regular roles on *Make Room for Daddy* and *Dennis the Menace*. In 1961, she won an Emmy nomination for Best Supporting Actress for her performance on *The Gertrude Berg Show*.

Among Mary's most memorable small screen appearances was as Lucille Ball's ballet teacher in *I Love Lucy*. The chemistry between Mary and Lucy worked so well on screen due to the fact that the two women were close friends off screen. Mary was a frequent visitor to the Arnaz home on Sundays after church.

"For my brother and me," Lucy recalled, "Mary was just like one of the family. If any of us were sick or even in bed with a cold, Mary would show up at the back door with a kettle of chicken soup. She could be loud and boisterous and as demanding as any of the characters she played, but she was also very loving and giving. What a lady!"[15]

More of Mary's friends besides Lucy were accustomed to her hospitality. She often hosted small buffets at her apartment which consisted of baked ham, chicken salad, and baked beans with her famous pumpkin, apple, or peach pies for dessert.[16]

The "loving and giving" personality Mary possessed would lead one to believe she had the potential of being an ideal mother and wife. Although she was not known to have had many romances, she is said to have been the longtime companion of playwright Abby Conrad. The nature of their relationship remains unclear, but, in any case, they never wed.[17] Mary later admitted regret at never having had a family, but she was overall content, stating: "It [her life] just didn't work out that way. But I'm a cheerful, happy woman and I love my work."[18]

Indeed, the bulk of Mary's life was absorbed with her work. She returned to the big screen for a cameo in *The Music Man* (1962) and donned a nun's habit in *The Trouble with Angels* (1966) alongside Rosalind Russell. She even acted as the live-action stand-in for Cruella De Vil in Disney's animated feature *101 Dalmatians* (1961). However, the majority of her work revolved around television with more appearances throughout the 1970s and 1980s in shows like *M*A*S*H*, *Here's Lucy*, and as a regular character on *Doc*. In each of these series, she played — unsurprisingly — a nurse. Mary also appeared in a variety of plays including *Arsenic and Old Lace*. It was not until 1979 that she returned to Broadway for the first time since 1948 to appear in a revival of *Oklahoma!*

"Theater is my background," she stated. "But I love television and movies too. If it's a good script, they're just as much fun. But I guess if I had my druthers I'd take the stage."[19]

Mary may have preferred the stage, but at sixty-nine, she was ready to settle down and "quit living out of a suitcase."[20] Returning to Los Angeles, she settled into her home in a modern apartment building. Her place was filled with her great-great grandmother's wedding furniture from 1834, including a mahogany loveseat and ornate candelabras. She had no pets due to the building's rules, but she made do, stating: "It's cruel for a performer to keep an animal alone all day."[21] She would not venture into the swimming pool, preferring to sit in the sun dressed in her wardrobe of "dresses and suits" (she was not fond of wearing pants). She kept the schedule of a farmer with food to match. Waking a seven-thirty she fixed "a truck driver's breakfast of fruit, cereal, eggs, and toast." Mary arrived for work at nine-thirty, never without a home-packed salad for lunch. In the evening, she would dine out on Mexican, French, Chinese, or Italian cuisine and retire by eight o'clock. [22] Her lifestyle certainly did not mimic that of most actresses', but rather mimicked that of an ordinary working girl. This translated on screen and made audiences able to relate to Mary and identify with her as if she were their aunt or mother.

Aside from work at CBS-TV, Mary's interests branched outside of acting into volunteer work and education. She was a regular volunteer at the UCLA Hospital where she would visit the rooms of friendless patients. When she was not volunteering, she kept busy working on a master's thesis at UCLA. St. Louis University, her alma mater, had given her an honorary Doctor of Arts degree in 1968, which had sparked her interest in returning to school. She relished completing research for her thesis on the St. Louis Municipal Opera (in which she had appeared in fourteen productions). [23] In a 1979 interview, she declared: "I'm a campus bum and I think I could live in a research library. I just love the smell of them." [24]

Prolific on and off screen until the end of her life, Mary experienced a resurgence of popularity in the 1990s. She played a straight-talking rectory housekeeper from 1989-1991 on television's *Father Dowling Mysteries* and again donned a habit in the Whoopi Goldberg comedy *Sister Act* (1992) and its 1993 sequel. "It's amazing," she said. "When you are in the habit you get quieter as far as your gestures are concerned. You find yourself quite relaxed and reposed, which is new for us." [25]

Mary's final film appearance proved that her talents had not diminished over the years. As the curmudgeonly Aunt March in the 1994 adaptation of *Little Women*, she is darkly funny and hateful at the same time. Her final job in Hollywood was as the voice for a gargoyle in the posthumously released Disney film *The Hunchback of Notre Dame* (1996).

Mary's non-stop work ended in 1995 when she was hospitalized with multiple ailments including kidney failure, breast cancer, and gastrointestinal bleeding. She passed away on October 24, 1995. Her will left two million dollars to set up a memorial fund in honor of her parents called the Isabella and Frank Wickenhauser Memorial Fund for TV, Film, and Theater Arts. [26]

Mary's funeral was so well attended there was standing room only. Lucille Ball spoke at the service and rallied those in attendance to rise for one last ovation. Although Mary was not in the same realm as Valentino or Monroe, she had gained a following all her own. "Women like me," Mary once said. "They think I'm wholesome or something." [27]

Audiences spanning from the 1940s to the 1990s know Mary Wickes. Some may remember her as Nurse Preen, baby boomers may remember her as Miss Cathcart on *Dennis the Menace* while younger moviegoers will remember her as Sister Mary Lazarus in *Sister Act*. She is the caretaker audiences all wish they had — one who keeps them in line and calms their extraneous worries with a no-nonsense retort. She managed to be comforting despite her blunt demeanor because her manner always contained an undercurrent of mirth and warmth that made any comment, no matter how honest, a statement born from caring rather than one meant only as a judgmental barb.

"I love playing comedy with a heart," Mary stated. "Comedy which touches the audience." [28]

FILMOGRAPHY

1996	*The Hunchback of Notre Dame*	Laverne *(voice)*
1994	*Little Women*	Aunt March
1993	*Sister Act 2: Back in the Habit*	Sister Mary Lazarus
1992	*Sister Act*	Sister Mary Lazarus
1990	*Postcards from the Edge*	Grandma
1980	*Touched by Love*	Margaret
1972	*Snowball Express*	Miss Wigginton
1972	*Napoleon and Samantha*	Clerk
1972	*Open Window (short)*	Mrs. Sappleton
1968	*Where Angels Go Trouble Follows!*	Sister Clarissa
1967	*The Spirit Is Willing*	Gloria Tritt
1966	*The Trouble with Angels*	Sister Clarissa
1965	*How to Murder Your Wife*	Harold's Secretary
1964	*Dear Heart*	Miss Fox
1964	*Fate Is the Hunter*	Mrs. Llewlyn
1962	*The Music Man*	Mrs. Squires
1961	*The Sins of Rachel Cade*	Marie Grieux
1961	*One Hundred and One Dalmatians (voice)*	
1960	*Cimarron*	Mrs. Neal Hefner
1959	*It Happened to Jane*	Matilda Runyon
1958	*The Proud Rebel*	Mrs. Ainsley *(uncredited)*
1957	*Don't Go Near the Water*	Janie
1956	*Dance with Me, Henry*	Miss Mayberry
1955	*Good Morning, Miss Dove*	Miss Lorraine Ellwood
1954	*Destry*	Bessie Mae Curtis

1954	*White Christmas*	Emma Allen
1954	*Ma and Pa Kettle at Home*	Miss Wetter
1953	*The Actress*	Emma Glavey
1953	*Half a Hero*	Mrs. Watts
1953	*By the Light of the Silvery Moon*	Stella
1952	*Bloodhounds of Broadway*	Lady at Laundry *(uncredited)*
1952	*The Story of Will Rogers*	Mrs. Foster, Landlady
1952	*Young Man with Ideas*	Mrs. Jasper Gilpin
1951	*I'll See You in My Dreams*	Anna
1951	*On Moonlight Bay*	Stella
1950	*The Petty Girl*	Prof. Whitman
1949	*Anna Lucasta*	Stella
1948	*The Decision of Christopher Blake*	Clara
1948	*June Bride*	Rosemary McNally
1943	*Higher and Higher*	Sandy Brooks
1943	*Happy Land*	Emmy *(uncredited)*
1943	*My Kingdom for a Cook*	Agnes Willoughby *(uncredited)*
1943	*Rhythm of the Islands*	Susie Dugan
1943	*How's About It*	Tracy
1942	*Who Done It?*	Juliet Collins
1942	*Keeping Fit (short)*	Ann–Andy's wife
1942	*Now, Voyager*	Dora Pickford
1942	*The Mayor of 44th Street*	Mamie
1942	*Private Buckaroo*	Bonnie-Belle Schlopkiss
1942	*Blondie's Blessed Event*	Sarah Miller
1942	*The Man Who Came to Dinner*	Miss Preen
1939	*Seeing Red (short)*	Mrs. Smith *(uncredited)*
1938	*Too Much Johnson (short)*	Mrs. Battison
1935	*Watch the Birdie (short)*	*Bottom right at 1:18 into scene (uncredited, unconfirmed)*

AMERICA'S TEXAN COUSIN
CHILL WILLS

CHILL WILLS CIRCA 1945. COURTESY OF JERRY MURBACH.

"I don't care how big or how small a role is. All I want is something to make people say 'that dad-blamed guy was pretty good'." [1]

If this was veteran actor Chill Wills's ambition, he fulfilled it in no uncertain terms during his forty-year career on the screen. He appeared in over 130 films from the late 1930s to the late 1970s, and, though by his own admission he had "laid plenty of bombs," [2] he gave his best to each and every role, whether it was in a top-rate production or a forgettable B picture. A tall and unrefined Westerner with a "mouth like a carpet bag [and] a meandering nose," [3] Chill was primarily distinguished by his low and croaky Texas drawl and friendly manner. He was often considered a "poor man's Will Rogers," [4] due to their similar folksy screen personae. Like Rogers, Chill ingratiated himself to strangers and friends alike, even going so far as to meet everyone with the same greeting: "Hello Cousin." Despite his similarities to Rogers, Chill's affinity with Texas, which was not so much a state to him as an identity, set him in a category of his own. He proudly stated in 1971, "I'm a professional Texan and proud of it." [5]

Chill Wills was born as Theodore Childress Wills on July 18, 1902 in Seagonville, Texas. However, he was never called Theodore and would later tell amusing tales of how he came by the unconventional name of Chill. "I was seventh in the family an' I reckon they run out o' common ones [names]. They named me Chill Theodore. Imagine me usin' a silly name like Theodore. No siree! I dropped it quickly," [6] Chill later explained. Aside from Chill's explanation, another reason once given for the origin of his name was the fact that that July 18th was the hottest day ever recorded in Seagonville's history. Before he could walk or talk, his name already predestined him to be adept at comedy.

Chill's father, who worked as a druggist, and Chill's mother were nurturing parents to their sizable brood. "My mother was a wonderful cook — she did all those big, rich Sunday dinners that were so delicious you never knew when to stop eating," [7] Chill once reminisced. Chill inherited his passion for cooking from his mother and would later concoct meals that outdid the richest dinners his mother had made. However, as a child and young adult, Chill's main ambition was to perform. His interest in this pursuit began at age eleven after his father gave him a guitar for his birthday. Before too long, he was a member of a quartet that sang for the Dallas First Baptist Church.

Chill's career accelerated with such speed that by age fourteen he was traveling through Texas and Oklahoma in tent shows. "I know how easy I've got it today after years of rigorous training in tents shows…I'd do nine different plays in a single week with completely different characterizations

in each,"[8] Chill explained in 1956. The different characterizations ranged
from whiskered old men to villains to cowboys. However, it was his musical ability that allowed him to graduate from tent shows to vaudeville. "I
was in on its last gasp," he wryly stated. "I played everywhere from the
opery house in Hogtown (Desdemona) to the Cocoanut Grove in Los
Angeles."[9] It was in one of his vaudeville skits that Chill coined what
would become his signature greeting: "Hello Cousin." He kept it as part
of his repertoire because, as he explained, "It sort of pleased people —
made them feel friendly right off."[10] Aside from vaudeville, Chill also
participated in stock company productions in which he performed in
every sort of role except female impersonations. By 1928, the young actor's
steady income gave him enough security to wed a dancer named Betty
Chapelle. They would remain married until his death. According to one
1977 reporter, Chill "was courtly with the ladies and warm with children...
[he had] old-fashioned virtues."[11]

By the 1930s, Chill was leader of his own harmony group, the Avalon
Boys. The group eventually disbanded after making several uncredited
singing appearances in Hollywood films beginning in 1934. After a
gig in *Anything Goes* (1936), Chill was offered a contract. He turned
it down when the studio stipulated that he would be sent to a studio
school to learn how to act, which he perceived as an insult to his innate
abilities. Chill continued to perform in clubs and hotels for two years
until he accepted a second contract offer during a gig at the Trocadero.
Given that he was a Texan, he was placed in Western roles by default.
The director of his first film, *Lawless Valley* (1938), accused him of exag-
gerating his accent for unneeded comic effect. He insisted it was his
natural voice, and, for the rest of his career, it was his drawl that made
him instantly recognizable. Chill went on to appear in several Westerns.
The best one was *The Westerner* (1940), in which he portrayed Gary
Cooper's friend.

The first role that brought Chill significant recognition was as
Harmony, a whiskered cook who travels with oil prospectors Clark Gable
and Spencer Tracy in the all-star movie *Boom Town* (1940). His role
was no great stretch from his true identity given that Harmony was a
talented cook. Chill later boasted, "I cook any man's food. I can cook
Jewish, Japanese, or Chinese food."[12] His particular specialties were crepes
suzette, blintzes, preserves, shish kabob, and chili. Chill's success in *Boom
Town* was not only because he felt comfortable with the character, but
also because of the cooperation of his costar, Clark Gable. When the
director objected to Chill putting in a few of his "corny ad libs," Gable

"stepped out of character and said 'Leave them in; we're probably going to need them'." [13] Chill's naturalistic style onscreen was fostered by men such as Gable and Tracy who, like Chill, did not believe in "suffocating or burying yourself in the script." [14] Chill received excellent reviews for his performance as Harmony. The *New York Times* raved: "When a comparatively unknown actor stands out in a picture here he is in competition

DARRYL HICKMAN, CHILL WILLS, JEANNE CRAIN, AND CORNEL WILDE IN *LEAVE HER TO HEAVEN* **(1945).** AUTHOR'S COLLECTION.

with Gable, Lamarr, [Frank] Morgan…and Marion Martin…it requires no stretch of the imagination to conclude that he has something in the way of ability." [15]

For the remainder of the 1940s and through the 1950s, Chill would become an ever-present face in both A pictures and B pictures. One of his most memorable, if brief roles, was as Mr. Neely, the ice man in 1944's *Meet Me in St. Louis.* His rapport with children is evident as he humors young Margaret O'Brien's belief that her doll is dying of "four fatal diseases." He stepped out of type in *See Here, Private Hargrove* (1944) as a sarcastic sergeant who torments the new recruits. In 1945's Technicolor noir film, *Leave Her to Heaven,* Chill's vaudeville training worked in his favor when he sang folksy ballads as Thorne, the groundskeeper of a secluded mountain cabin. He was at his comedic best in *The Harvey Girls* (1946) as Judy Garland's fiancé, whom she knows only through written correspondence. When Garland arrives in the uncivilized Wild West town of Flagstaff, Chill's explanation as to why he would make a less than ideal husband is among his most memorable monologues:

> *Miss Bradley, it's only fittin' you know somethin' more about me. For instance, I chew tobbacah and I drink. I'm a terrible drinker and I gamble. Gamblin's my downfall!......so please ma'am, please say no!* [16]

Chill's other standout moments in the film come when he unwittingly antagonizes the testy Marjorie Main, a comedienne with whom he shared a remarkable chemistry on screen. Chill's roles became varied to such an extent that he could no longer be called a formulaic character in unremarkable westerns. In 1950, the *Times Daily* aptly described his evolution: "From his bearded character in *Boom Town*, Chill was dubbed as the Walter Brennan type. Following a mug role in *Belle Star* he became 'another Wallace Beery,' and after acting as a bashful youngster in *The Harvey Girls* he was classified with silent star Charles Ray." However, Chill remarked that the "greatest comparison" he ever had was when he was told: "Chill, you don't remind me of anybody but Chill Wills." [17] Chill's likeable persona on and off screen made him a popular entertainer in Army and children's hospitals during World War II. Hedda Hopper wrote that she had "added Chill Wills' name to those for whom I ask God's blessing" [18] due to his contributions to America's morale during the war.

Though Chill had become a star in his own right during his M-G-M contract days, he did not choose to continue there, preferring instead to freelance and "not be tied to a deal that wouldn't give him a choice of roles." [19] Chill's decision to freelance was not due to an urge to find bigger roles that would give him more fame. It was the complete opposite; he requested he receive no credit for providing voices in both *Stella* (1950) and *Francis the Talking Mule* (1950). His request baffled Hollywood. Despite his desire to be uncredited, he gained more fame than ever before as Francis the Mule. The film, starring Donald O'Connor, proved popular, and spawned an entire series of Francis films. Theaters, feeling it was unfair that Chill receive no credit, ran an addendum to the Francis trailers that read: "The voice of Francis you just heard was your friend and ours, Chill Wills." [20]

Chill's status as "friend" to all was well known by Hollywood executives and public relations departments. They used this to its best advantage by enlisting him to "plug causes for filmdom," all of which he willingly performed. He stood on street corners, shaking hands and engaging people in "homespun, folksy" conversation. [21] At each personal appearance, he distributed batches of autographed photographs signed, "Howdy Cousin." His position as the "unofficial ambassador of goodwill" [22] made him a top candidate to portray Will Rogers in the actor's biopic. Though Chill and Rogers had been good friends, Chill turned down the role and it was appropriately filled by Rogers' own son.

Chill's popularity continued into the 1950s as he appeared in what he would later say was his favorite film, *Giant* (1956). The multigenerational story of a Texas family was, according to Chill, "going to be bigger than *Gone With the Wind.*" [23] As the easy going and philosophical Uncle Bawley, Chill provided a steadying presence onscreen, though it was not completely devoid of his usual penchant for comedy. When his nephew, played by Rock Hudson, remarks: "Just remember, one of these days, that bourbon's gonna kill you," Uncle Bawley wryly retorts: "Okay, it'll be me or it. One of us has gotta go." [24]

It was another Texan epic that gave Chill his next most substantial role. *The Alamo* (1960), starring John Wayne, had Chill portraying the "Bee Keeper," Davey Crockett's companion. The role won him his first Oscar nomination; however, the honor ultimately developed into a fiasco due to a publicity stunt concocted by Chill's agent, W.S. Wojciechowicz. The agent placed an advertisement in multiple Hollywood trade papers that read: "We of *The Alamo* cast are praying harder — than the real Texans prayed for their lives in The Alamo — for Chill Wills to win the Oscar." In addition, there were letters signed in Chill's name prompting his "cousins" at the Academy of Motion Picture Arts and Science to vote for him. [25] John Wayne openly condemned such campaigning and denied any of the cast had condoned it. The stunt did not please the Academy either and ultimately led to a new rule being made that outlawed any campaigning by stars to win an Oscar. Needless to say, Chill did not win the Academy Award for Best Supporting Actor, losing it to Peter Ustinov for his role in *Spartacus.*

After the Oscar unpleasantness, Chill redirected his energy towards television but did not abandon the big screen altogether. He starred in one season of the CBS show *Frontier Circus* (1961-61) and later appeared as a rancher in ABC's series *The Rounders* (1966). He continued to make appearances on the big screen including an unlikely role as a monsignor in Otto Preminger's *The Cardinal* (1963). In 1967, Chill stepped away from show business for a time and considered running as governor of Texas despite the fact he no longer was considered a Texas resident. He denied he had made any certain decision but smilingly told reporters, "I'm an actor now. But then that didn't stop [George] Murphy or Reagan did it?"[26] Though he was conservative, he gave a nod to the liberal point of view when it came to women's lib. "What I say about women, is, let 'em,"[27] he said.

Though Chill's film career was not as prolific as it had been in the 1940s, his wealth did not appear to be affected. His elaborate automobile was more of a character than he was. The $23,000 convertible Pontiac contained sixteen chromium-plated six shooters and ten derringers, steer horns on the grill, and a silver saddle in the area between the two front seats. In addition, it boasted a $4,000 stereo sound system and a horn than whinnied like a horse. Chill stipulated in his will that the car would go to the Cowboy Hall of Fame in Oklahoma City upon his death.[28] Chill's lack of poverty was also apparent in the gold jewelry he wore at parties, often hosted at his ranch in San Antonio or his second home in the San Fernando Valley. Chill's income was supplemented by his entry into the business world. He owned a chain of restaurants as well as his own chili manufacturing business. He sent gallons of his homemade chili to troops in Vietnam, claiming that it was health food. "I make mine so that it doesn't have a bit of grease in it. Doctors have said chili is especially good for people with heart trouble,"[29] he declared.

Hollywood did not forget Chill despite his less frequent presence on screen. In 1970, he received a star on the Walk of Fame directly in front of Grauman's Chinese Theater. In temporary lettering below his name was his motto: "Hello Cousin." Chill arrived to his star's unveiling in his cowboy car, resplendent in boots with spurs and a ten gallon hat. Kneeling down with tears in his eyes, he "dropped to his knees and kissed the cold ornament." He told reporters, "Anything in show business I feel good about."[30] Though he felt "good about" show business, he experienced personal tragedy in 1971 when his wife of over forty years died. He remarried two years later to Novadeen Googe and would remain her husband until his death five years later.

Though he was content in his personal and professional life, Chill found appropriate films harder to find as he grew older. "I generally enjoy working...I'm a great one for family pictures, but the script I've been asked to do next has the filthiest language in it I've ever seen. I just don't think I need that one. Now, I'm not a prude, mind you. However, there's a limit to what a man ought to do for money," [31] he explained in 1977. True to his word, Chill never accepted a role in a film that he would be ashamed to show to his two children, three grandchildren, or wife.

Shortly after Chill made his final film appearance as a janitor in 1978's *Stubby Pringle's Christmas,* he succumbed to cancer at the age of seventy-six. Though a veteran of over a hundred films, his fame at the time of his death and today is primarily attributed to his association with Francis the Talking Mule. His inimitable drawl was a major part of his character, but it was his physical appearance that completed his identity. His 6'2 frame, affable grin, and rough-around-the-edges manner coupled with western garb define the quintessential American cowboy. Yet, Chill's lack of pretense or star power make him like a "cousin" rather than a cardboard cutout disembodied on the screen. In the 1970s, he, according to one reporter, "refused to admit there was a recession in the movies, said his greatest reward always has been in the warmth expressed by audiences." [32] Chill returned the love of his audiences by giving them warm and endearing performances for four decades. Though not as well known as Will Rogers, his own words bear a remarkable resemblance to the philosophy of the man to whom he was often compared: "I never saw people I couldn't get along with." [33]

FILMOGRAPHY

1977	*Poco…Little Dog Lost*	Big Burt
1977	*Mr. Billion*	Col. Clayton T. Winkle
1973	*Pat Garrett & Billy the Kid*	Lemuel
1973	*Guns of a Stranger*	Tom Duncan
1971	*The Steagle*	Tall-Guy McCoy
1970	*The Liberation of L. B. Jones*	Mr. Ike
1969	*Big Daddy*	
1966	*Fireball 500*	Big Jaw
1965	*The Rounders*	Jim Ed Love *(owner, Love Ranch)*
1963	*The Cardinal*	Monsignor Whittle
1963	*The Wheeler Dealers*	Jay Ray Spinelby
1963	*McLintock!*	Drago
1962	*Young Guns of Texas*	Preacher Sam Shelby
1961	*The Little Shepherd of Kingdom Come*	Major Buford
1961	*The Deadly Companions*	Turk
1961	*Gold of the Seven Saints*	Doc Wilson Gates, MD
1960	*Where the Boys Are*	Police Captain

1960	*The Alamo* ....Beekeeper
1959	*The Sad Horse*...Capt Connors
1958	*From Hell to Texas* .... Amos Bradley
1957	*Gun Glory*.. Preacher
1957	*Gun for a Coward* .... Loving
1956	*Giant*...Uncle Bawley
1956	*Santiago*............................Captain 'Sidewheel' Jones
1956	*Kentucky Rifle* .... Tobias Taylor
1955	*Francis in the Navy*. Francis the Talking Mule *(voice) (uncredited)*
1955	*Timberjack* ....Steve Riika
1954	*Hell's Outpost* .... Kevin Russel
1954	*Ricochet Romance* .... Tom Williams
1954	*Francis Joins the WACS*..... Gen. Benjamin Kaye *(voice, uncredited)*
	Francis the Talking Mule *(voice, uncredited)*
1953	*Tumbleweed* .... Sheriff Murchoree
1953	*The Man from the Alamo* ....John Gage
1953	*City That Never Sleeps*...................Sgt. Joe, the 'Voice of Chicago'
1953	*Francis Covers the Big Town* ...... Francis the Talking Mule *(voice)*
1953	*Small Town Girl* .... 'Happy', Jailer *(uncredited)*
1952	*Ride the Man Down*..................................... Ike Adams
1952	*Francis Goes to West Point*...................... Francis the Talking Mule
	(voice, uncredited)
1952	*Bronco Buster* .... Dan Bream
1951	*Screen Snapshots: Hollywood Goes Western (short)* ....
	Rodeo Performer
1951	*The Sea Hornet* .... Swede
1951	*Cattle Drive*...Dallas
1951	*Francis Goes to the Races*....................... Francis the Talking Mule
	(voice, uncredited)
1951	*Oh! Susanna*.................................... Sergeant Barhydt
1950	*Rio Grande*...................Dr. Wilkins *(regimental surgeon)*
1950	*High Lonesome* .... Boatwhistle, Ranch Cook
1950	*Stella*..Chief Clark *(uncredited)*
1950	*Rock Island Trail* .... Hogger McCoy
1950	*Francis* .... Francis the Talking Mule *(voice, uncredited)*
1950	*The Sundowners*.. Sam Beers
1950	*The Grass Is Always Greener (short)* ....Windy
1949	*Red Canyon*... Brackton
1949	*Tulsa*.. Pinky Jimpson *(Narrator)*
1948	*Loaded Pistols*.. Sheriff Cramer

1948	*Family Honeymoon*	Fred
1948	*That Wonderful Urge*	Homer Beggs, Justice of the Peace, Monroe Township
1948	*The Saxon Charm*	Captain Chatham
1948	*Northwest Stampede*	'Mileaway' James
1948	*The Sainted Sisters*	Will Twitchell
1947	*Heartaches*	Boggie Mann/Vic *(voice)*
1947	*High Barbaree*	Lars *(uncredited)*
1946	*The Yearling*	Buck Forrester
1946	*Gallant Bess*	Chief Petty Officer
1946	*The Harvey Girls*	H.H. Hartsey
1945	*Leave Her to Heaven*	Leick Thome
1945	*What Next, Corporal Hargrove?*	Sgt. Cramp
1944	*I'll Be Seeing You*	Swanson
1944	*Sunday Dinner for a Soldier*	Mr. York
1944	*Meet Me in St. Louis*	Mr. Neely
1944	*Trailin' West (short)*	Old Man Coffey
1944	*Barbary Coast Gent*	Sheriff Hightower
1944	*The Immortal Blacksmith (short)*	Tom Davenport
1944	*Rationing*	Bus driver
1944	*See Here, Private Hargrove*	First Sgt. Cramp
1943	*Best Foot Forward*	Chester Short
1943	*A Stranger in Town*	Charles Craig
1942	*Stand by for Action*	Chief Boatswain's Mate Jenks
1942	*Apache Trail*	'Pike' Skelton
1942	*The Omaha Trail*	Henry Hawkins
1942	*Her Cardboard Lover*	Judge
1942	*Tarzan's New York Adventure*	Manchester Montford
1942	*Mister Gardenia Jones (documentary short)*	Hotel Employee
1942	*The Bugle Sounds*	Sergeant Larry Dillon
1941	*Honky Tonk*	The Sniper
1941	*Belle Starr*	Blue Duck
1941	*Billy the Kid*	Tom Patterson
1941	*The Bad Man*	'Red' Giddings
1941	*Western Union*	Homer Kettle
1940	*Tugboat Annie Sails Again*	Shiftless
1940	*Sky Murder*	Sheriff Beckwith
1940	*The Westerner*	Southeast
1940	*Wyoming*	Lafe *(uncredited)*
1940	*Boom Town*	Harmony Jones

THE OLD TROUPER
CHARLES WINNINGER

CHARLES WINNINGER CIRCA 1935. AUTHOR'S COLLECTION.

He was a performer from what was once called "that happy yesterday of entertainment...vaudeville." [1] He may have oversold his songs and overhammed his comedy, but one would not wish him to be any different. His short, chubby frame and twinkling eyes bring to mind a mischievous leprechaun full of vim and vigor at any age. This was no coincidence. The great entertainer in question, Charles Winninger, had an innate joviality that endeared him to generations of theater and filmgoers. His presence on screen is unique in that he often played only slight variations of himself: loveable old codgers always ready to perform and show young whippersnappers a thing or two about entertainment. Having won fame under such scions of Broadway as Florenz Ziegfeld and George M. Cohan, Charles knew quality showmanship. Yet, he never grew jaded at vaudeville's passing and the loss of his own glorious place in that arena. Rather, into old age he "spun tales of the theater with the enthusiasm of any stage struck youngster." [2] Charles's enthusiasm is palpable in his films; it shows new generations why vaudeville was such a favorite pastime of their grandparents and makes them question why it ever went out of fashion.

Charles Winninger was born in the proverbial trunk as Karl Winninger on May 26, 1884. His Austrian father had immigrated to Wisconsin with his wife before Charles was born. Though a respected violinist and bandmaster in his country, Mr. Winninger did not know which career to seek in America. Charles alleged that if it had not been for his father's stubbornness when seeking a new career, the family would never have entered show business. "Father would ask every tradesman if his business was good and the answer was always in the affirmative," Charles recalled. "One day he approached a traveling preacher and he also said opportunities were good in all trades. That burned father. 'What kind of business isn't good to go into?' he asked. 'Show business' he was told, so father went right out, bought a costume, and started immediately in show business." [3] The business that had been so warned against became a lucrative family affair. Mr. and Mrs. Winninger, Charles, and his five siblings all contributed to what became the Winninger Family Concert Company, and later grew into a medicine show called Winninger Family Novelties [4]. However, the company had its beginning as a nomadic tent show. Charles's childhood "under the big top" provided rich experience that the actor could still recall with amazing clarity and nostalgia decades later: "It's like nothing else in the world. The smell of kerosene...the clomping of work horses...the shouts of roustabouts, the call to chow... and opening nights! These are memorable impressions of my boyhood." [5]

Charles started out as a "boy soprano"[6] in the show at the age of six. By age eight, he had left school to devote himself entirely to entertaining people. He began to double on the trapeze, fancying himself to be like his earliest hero, Harry Houdini. Incidentally, Mr. Winninger had discovered Houdini during a tour in Appleton, Wisconsin.[7]

Mr. Winninger could also be credited with discovering Charles himself. It was he who gave Charles his first chance to perform, initially in acrobatic stunts and then in serious acting roles. After the company's leading man left, Charles was told to replace him. "I had to learn and perform six different plays in a week," Charles explained. "Luckily, I've always had a photographic memory. Learning a part has never been a problem for me."[8] By 1907, Charles had proved himself proficient enough an actor to strike out on his own and head for vaudeville. Before he found himself behind the footlights of Broadway, he was employed as an actor on a Mississippi show boat.[9] After finding such work made him too seasick to perform, he was forced to seek alternate means of earning money. At one time, he earned fifty dollars after winning a bet that he could not swim a mile across a treacherous current that threatened to suck him under every minute[10]. He found less dangerous employment in entertainment not dissimilar to that which he had known as boy. He described it as "everything from medicine shows to opera. At medicine shows, we'd also sell blood purifier. And we carried along a nurse to pull teeth."[11]

In 1912, Charles finally landed his first role on Broadway and left the more colorful existence of a traveling performer. The show was entitled *The Wall Street Girl*. It was during the play's run that he met Blanche Ring, an already well-known actress thirteen years his senior. He acted as stage manager for her and the two fell in love. They quietly married at the Westminster Hotel in New York. The press described the couple as "happy as two turtledoves."[12] They would perform in some shows together, but the couple found themselves separated quite often as Charles tried his luck in film. From 1915 to 1916, Charles appeared in some comedic shorts, but silent film did not allow his brand of comedy to fully translate to audiences. He returned to the stage and not a moment too soon; in 1916, George M. Cohan cast him in his yearly *Cohan Revue*. It was Charles's big break. He returned to Cohan's show in 1918 and was then tapped by the two other major players in the Broadway syndicate: the Shuberts and Florenz Ziegfeld. He was in the Shubert's *Passing Show of 1919*, followed in quick succession by the *Ziegfeld Follies of 1920*. He was hilarious in a skit with comedienne Ray Dooley in which she played an infant becoming drunk on milk punch. Charles strolled through a park "drinking and flirting while Dooley carried on." [13] It would not be the last time Charles would get big laughs from being tipsy.

Charles's continued to enjoy stage successes throughout the 1920s. In 1921 he appeared with Blanche Ring in *The Broadway Whirl;* in 1925 he was in *No, No Nanette,* followed in 1927 by the amusingly titled *Yes,*

CHARLES WINNINGER, FAR RIGHT, WITH EMMA DUNN, SIDNEY FOX, AND BETTE DAVIS IN *THE BAD SISTER* (1931). AUTHOR'S COLLECTION.

Yes Yvette. It was on the heels of *Yvette* that Charles landed the role that would define him for the rest of his career: Cap'n Andy in Ziegfeld's groundbreaking musical adaptation of Edna Ferber's *Show Boat.* Except for the fact that he was prone to seasickness, the role could have been Charles himself. Andy was jolly with mischievous, salty humor. No doubt Charles used his experience working on a show boat to his advantage in the play. *Show Boat* was Ziegfeld's, and Charles's, greatest success. It ran uninterrupted for two years and was revived in 1932, during which it enjoyed a six-month run even at the height of the Great Depression. Charles was happy to go on playing Cap'n Andy indefinitely; he once told Ziegfeld that he would play the part for nothing rather than see it done by another actor. [14]

Flush with the success of *Show Boat,* Charles now had the means to indulge in leisurely pursuits. The *Daily Boston Globe* heralded him as "the best all round actor-athlete"[15] there was. He was an exceptional golfer, baseball player, and one of the top shots in the American Trap Shooters Association. He also "played tennis like a youngster" and occasionally "boxed on rainy days."[16] Charles used his considerable athletic talents in his acting as well. In 1935, he showed his agility by performing his role in a play entitled *Revenge with Music* despite the fact that he had a broken leg and heavy cast. In true "show must go on" fashion, he simply used a cane on stage.[17] The play would prove to be his last Broadway appearance for over a decade. Hollywood had taken sharper notice of the silver-haired "song and dance man"[18] and decided he would be a welcome presence in talking pictures. He appeared in dominantly comedy films, among them *Soup to Nuts* (1930) with the Three Stooges and *God's Gift to Women* (1931) with fellow stage veteran Frank Fay. Though comedy was his forte, Charles lent his unique "warm-hearted presence"[19] to dramatic pictures as well. He was notable in Bette Davis' *The Bad Sister* (1931) and Helen Hayes's *The Sin of Madelon Claudet* (1931). Charles was often the archetypal father who is all bark and no bite in these pictures. However, he would later joke that he should have a "Dr." before his name and an "M.D." after it, for he more often portrayed a physician, notably in *Flying High* (1932) with Bert Lahr.[20]

It was not until 1936 that Charles found the fame in film he had won on stage. Again, it was *Show Boat* that brought him this success. He reprised his role as Cap'n Andy along with a stellar cast, including Irene Dunne, Allan Jones, and Hattie McDaniel. It would be the greatest performance of his career. Silent films had not accommodated his humor; his comedy relied on words and not pantomimic gags. Now, audiences enjoyed hearing such mischievous exchanges as the following, after Cap'n Andy bids goodnight to his wife:

CHORUS GIRL: *Pops, who was that?*

CAP'N ANDY HAWKS: *That was Parthenia, my wife.*

CHORUS GIRL: *Oh, my mistake!*

CAP'N ANDY HAWKS: *No...mine!*[21]

Charles provided more laughs with quips that were humorous because of the manner in which they took the audience by surprise. One would not expect the good-natured Cap'n to reveal such a fact as he does in the following exchange with his "mistake":

PARTHY: *Andy Hawks, are you going to stand there and let your only child marry a murderer?*

CAP'N ANDY HAWKS: *Oh don't be so narrow minded, Mrs. Hawks, I killed a man myself once.* [22]

As much as Charles had embraced film and film had embraced him, the old trouper still held fast to the belief that movies could never replace legitimate theater. "You simply can't get that sense of contact with your audience in the movies," he asserted. "And the movies are going to have to have real actors more and more, actors who can have that sense of feeling for an audience whether it is there or not...That is why youngsters who are being heard of in the movies today are those who have come up as real actors and actresses before they went into the movies." [23] Charles proved his ability to reach an audience just as effectively through film over the course of the next decade. He maintained the high standards of the theater in now classic films such as *Nothing Sacred* (1937) and *Destry Rides Again* (1939). In the former he delighted audiences as a quack doctor looking to make a profit from publicizing a patient's brave (but feigned) fight against death. The enthusiasm he brings to the part dispels any doubt that he was once part of a medicine show selling snake oil to gullible customers. In *Destry Rides Again,* he brings the same enthusiasm to his role as a drunk who is elevated to the position of sheriff for the sole purpose that he will not try to bring law and order to his rough and tumble town.

Charles made more good use of his talent for playing inebriates as Judy Garland's grandfather in *Little Nellie Kelly* (1941). He is believable as an easily flustered Irishman who favors whiskey over work, which he claims to be "the curse of civilization."

It is in two other Garland films that audiences are given the most personal glimpse into what Charles was like off screen. In *Babes in Arms* (1939) and *Ziegfeld Girl* (1941) he portrayed a veteran actor looking to resurrect his act. As Mickey Rooney's father in *Babes in Arms,* he gives Rooney and Garland stiff competition when he brashly performs his own acts. He makes the audiences believe his every word when he declares:

That's an idea, a road show! With a lot of old timers!...They say vaudeville is dead? Not with a lot of old troupers like us it isn't![24]

In *Ziegfeld Girl* he manages to poke fun at some of the less appealing
acts in vaudeville, most evident in a scene when he tries to teach Garland
to sell a song with overbroad gestures and an almost shouting voice that
would likely scare the audience away rather than hook them in. More
effective is when he performs an act with real-life vaudevillian and fellow
Ziegfeld alum, Al Shean. Shean and Charles, as Mr. Gallagher, seem to
enjoy themselves as much as the audience as they sing such mischievous
banter as:

MR. GALLAGHER: *Oh Mr. Shean, of Mr. Shean, when she sunk
I dove down like a submarine, dragged her out upon the shore and
now she's mine forevermore...*

MR. SHEAN: *The lady, Mr. Gallagher?*

MR. GALLAGHER: *No, the rowboat Mr. Shean.* [25]

Charles offered audiences more nostalgic views into vaudeville in pictures such as *Goodbye Broadway* (1938), *Broadway Rhythm* (1944), and
Give My Regards to Broadway (1948). For the latter film, two vaudevillians
were hired to teach the actors stunts for their skits. When Charles found
that the two men were unemployed after the close of the picture, he had
an agent seek them out so he could hire them for part of the entertainment during the centennial celebration of his home state, Wisconsin.
He was full of sentiment and nostalgia himself during the celebration,
a festivity for which he had broken two film commitments to attend.
"Why, the biggest thrill of my life was when I went up to Ashton [his
hometown] the other day. I was walking down the street and saw a girl
whom I hadn't seen in more than fifty years. I yelled, 'Hey Maggie' and
she was running to me with tears in her eyes," Charles related. "...No sir,
I wouldn't have missed this...for all the picture deals they could throw
at me in Hollywood."[26]

As much as Charles treasured times past, he was not one to shun
modernity. He unhesitatingly tried his luck in television when it gained
popularity in the early 1950s. "I'm not ready to turn in the tools of my
profession yet," the aging actor said. He proved it by remaining ubiquitous in film, radio, theater, and television until the end of the decade. He
returned to Broadway in *Music in the Air* in 1951, performed in three

films back to back in 1953 alone, and made a memorable guest appearance as Fred Mertz's old vaudeville colleague on *I Love Lucy*. He also occasionally played variations of Cap'n Andy on the radio. Because he was so engrossed in his work, his marriage had suffered. Blanche Ring and Charles divorced in 1951, after which Charles remarried actress/writer Gertrude Walker. He had met Walker during the revival of *Show Boat* twenty years before and remained married to her until his death.

By 1960, Charles may have still been unwilling to turn in the tools his trade, but he was beginning to feel his age. He played Santa Claus in *The Miracle of White Reindeer* (1960) and later that year appeared in what would be his final film, *Raymie*. He did not have the opportunity to enjoy his retirement; in 1964, he broke his hip and the injury kept him in pain for five years. [27] In 1969, he passed away in his Palm Springs home at the age of eighty-four. It is doubtful Charles would have wanted his death to be a time of mourning. His long life had been well-lived, brimming with enough adventure and color to fill three lifetimes. Of all the veterans of *Show Boat,* Charles had by far the most prolific career in all mediums of entertainment. He was awarded a star on the Hollywood Walk of Fame for his work in radio, where his favorite role of Cap'n Andy reached a wider audience than even the stage play or film renditions.

Whether he was playing a drunk, a doctor, or his most oft-repeated role of an old trouper, Charles never failed to be likeable and warm. One of his final roles in film had been as Santa Claus, and never was an actor more appropriate for the part. With his silver gray hair and round, short stature, he looked like a benevolent, if impish, Saint Nicholas. It is this likeability that makes him approachable to audiences of any age and what made him the ideal man to bridge the gap between theater days of yore and the modern age of films and television. In *Ziegfeld Girl* (1941) he confidently tells a stagehand on his opening night at the *Ziegfeld Follies* that it was the first time since the annual show began that the people would get their money's worth. A humble statement by no means, but all too true. Indeed, it is just as true as one critic's remark that Charles "proves that it takes a great old-timer to bring back old times." [28]

FILMOGRAPHY

1960	*The Miracle of the White Reindeer*	Santa Claus
1960	*Raymie*	R.J. Parsons
1955	*Las Vegas Shakedown*	Ernest Raff
1953	*Champ for a Day*	Pa Karlsen

1953	*The Sun Shines Bright*..................... Judge William Pittman Priest
1953	*A Perilous Journey*............................ Captain Eph Allan
1952	*Torpedo Alley*...................................... Oliver J. Peabody
1950	*Father Is a Bachelor* ....Professor Mordecai Ford
1948	*Give My Regards to Broadway* .... Albert Norwick
1948	*The Inside Story* ....Uncle Ed
1947	*Something in the Wind* .... Uncle Chester Read
1947	*Living in a Big Way* ....D. Rutherford Morgan
1946	*Lover Come Back*...............................William 'Pa' Williams, Sr.
1945	*She Wouldn't Say Yes* .... Doctor Lane
1945	*State Fair* .... Abel Frake
1944	*Belle of the Yukon*................................... Pop Candless
1944	*Sunday Dinner for a Soldier*..........Dudley 'Granfeathers' Osborne
1944	*Broadway Rhythm*................................. Sam Demming
1943	*Flesh and Fantasy*.....................................King Lamarr *(Episode 3)*
1943	*A Lady Takes a Chance* ....Waco
1943	*Hers to Hold* ....Judson Craig
1943	*Coney Island*.................................... Finnigan
1942	*Friendly Enemies*.................................. Karl Pfeiffer
1942	*Mister Gardenia Jones (documentary short)* ....John Jones
1941	*My Life with Caroline*.................................Mr. Bliss
1941	*The Getaway*.................................... Doctor Josiah Glass
1941	*Ziegfeld Girl* .... 'Pop' Gallagher
1941	*Pot o' Gold*.....................................Charles 'C.J.' Haskell
1940	*Little Nellie Kelly* ....Michael 'Mike' Noonan
1940	*My Love Came Back*................................. Julius Malette
1940	*Beyond Christmas*.................................Michael O'Brien
1940	*If I Had My Way*...Joe Johnson
1939	*Barricade*...Samuel J. Cady
1939	*Destry Rides Again*...................................Washington Dimsdale
1939	*Babes in Arms*...Joe Moran
1939	*Three Smart Girls Grow Up*.......................................Judson Craig
1938	*Hard to Get* .... Benjamin Richards
1938	*Goodbye Broadway* .... Pat Malloy
1937	*You're a Sweetheart* .... Cherokee Charlie
1937	*Every Day's a Holiday*............. Van Reighle Van Pelter Van Doon
1937	*Nothing Sacred*................................... Dr. Enoch Downer
1937	*You Can't Have Everything* .... Sam Gordon
1937	*The Go Getter* .... Captain 'Cappy' Ricks
1937	*Woman Chases Man* .... B.J. Nolan

1937	*Café Metropole*	Joseph Ridgeway
1936	*Three Smart Girls*	Judson Craig
1936	*White Fang*	Doc McFane
1936	*Show Boat*	Cap'n Andy Hawks
1934	*Social Register*	Jonesie
1931	*Husband's Holiday*	Mr. Reid
1931	*Flying High*	Dr. Brown
1931	*The Sin of Madelon Claudet*	M. Novella–Photographer
1931	*Children of Dreams*	Dr. Joe Thompson
1931	*Night Nurse*	Dr. Arthur Bell
1931	*How I Play Golf by Bobby Jones, No. 2: Chip Shots (short)*	Golfer *(uncredited)*
1931	*God's Gift to Women*	Mr. John Churchill
1931	*Gun Smoke*	Tack Gillup
1931	*The Bad Sister*	Mr. Madison
1931	*Fighting Caravans*	Marshall
1930	*Soup to Nuts*	Otto Schmidt
1926	*Summer Bachelors*	Preston Smith
1926	*The Canadian*	Pop Tyson
1924	*Pied Piper Malone*	Louie *(the barber)*
1916	*A September Mourning (short)*	Artist
1915	*The Doomed Groom (short)*	The Groom
1915	Lizzie's Shattered Dreams *(short)*	

BOLD AND BRASSY
SHELLEY WINTERS

SHELLEY WINTERS IN *JOHNNY STOOL PIDGEON* (1949).
COURTESY OF JERRY MURBACH.

She was garish, audacious, and straight-talking. She was a quintessential Hollywood star, always good for a line in the juiciest of gossip columns. At the same time, she shunned Hollywood's glitz in favor of Broadway and the Actors Studio. Though she began her career with the nickname the Blonde Bombshell, she proved herself to be a serious actress in roles varying from simpering women to self-indulgent, nagging mothers to bold prostitutes. The actress who embodies the above personae is Shirley Schrift, better known as Shelley Winters. She once stated that "I've never really thought of myself as a leading woman type and I usually try to avoid parts where I'm supposed to be glamorous." [1] Shelley had her share of leading parts, but it is for outspoken supporting characters "created from her own inbred audacity and frankness…just this side of cheesy" [2] that she is best remembered. Whether she was the pathetic and abandoned Alice Tripp in *A Place in the Sun* (1951) or the abusive and bigoted prostitute mother in *A Patch of Blue* (1964), she gave each role her trademark of exaggerated but sincere emoting and an uncompromising determination to attain what she was after.

Shelley Winters (Shirley Schrift) was born August 18, 1920 in St. Louis, Missouri. She was born in a tenement to Jewish parents who struggled to afford shoes and coats for her and her sister. Among Shelley's earliest memories of her youth in St. Louis foreshadowed her future as a star. While playing a fairy in a neighborhood parade, the mayor approached her and declared "Baby, you're a natural!" The already outspoken young Shirley replied, "I know." [3] Shelley was less outgoing after her family relocated to Brooklyn. She became a loner in school and struggled to make passing marks in all subjects. Rather than play with her classmates, Shelley preferred playing hooky and sneaking into movie houses at every opportunity. "I developed a whole fantasy world during my childhood; reality was too unbearable. But it used to play hell with my real life. Even later in my life I often refused to see things as they really were, and would fantasize about something nicer," [4] Shelley explained in her 1980 memoir.

Shelley's idealism led her to develop a leaning toward liberal politics with a special interest in Socialism and the Soviet Union. After she quit high school, she was a card-carrying union member, not infrequently marching in strikes. As a worker herself, variously employed as a department store model and Woolworth's clerk, she was very much an advocate for workers' rights. During this period, her father's business caught fire and he was jailed with the accusation that he set the fire himself to collect insurance money. Her father's misfortune plus her hardscrabble existence thus far made Shelley banish her liberal ideology for the time being. "I decided since I wasn't personally able to do anything about the shits of the world, from now on I was going to take care of number one,"[5] she stated.

Taking care of number one meant focusing her energies and earnings on beginning a career in show business rather than marching in strikes. Her first optimistic foray into the business was auditioning for George Cukor during his nationwide search for the perfect Scarlett O'Hara. The director advised the inexperienced young girl to acquire training before she tried Hollywood. Heeding his advice, Shelley apprenticed in summer stock and performed in renditions of older hits including *Meet the People, Of Thee I Sing,* and the operetta *Rosalinda.* It was during the run of the operetta that she rechristened herself Shelley Winter, using her mother's maiden name of Winter and taking her first name from her favorite poet, Percy Shelley. Shelley's performance in *Rosalinda* attracted the attention of Columbia Studio's head, Harry Cohn. With her sister Blanche and her parents, Shelley relocated West with the promise of a screen test.

From the chest up, Shelley was remade by Columbia's make-up department. Her hair line was fixed with electrolysis, her teeth were capped, her bosom was stuffed, her hair was lightened, and her speech was altered to ferret out her Brooklyn accent. Shelley would later look back on her early experiences in Hollywood without a hint of nostalgia: "They made my hair pink and tried to make us all look like Rita Hayworth. For two years, I was running in and out of bit harem parts in veils. The pictures were awful and I certainly didn't know what the hell acting was about."[6] Shelley knew little more about marriage than she did about acting, yet, soon after she arrived in Hollywood, she met and wedded Captain Mack Paul Mayer. The union was never a greatly committed one due to Mayer's frequent time overseas and Shelley's busy schedule at the studio. She appeared in several uncredited or bit parts in films including *Cover Girl* (1944), *Living in a Big Way* (1947), and *Red River* (1948).

As she struggled to gain recognition, she made a simultaneous breakthrough in film and on stage. George Cukor asked her to portray Pat Kroll, the doomed waitress murdered by Ronald Colman in *A Double Life* (1948). Cukor taught her to be sincere and earthy rather than behave like the brainless blonde the studio was building her up to be. Hedda Hopper described her as "the new combination of Jean Harlow and Jean Arthur."[7] Shelley added much needed color to the dark and depressing film, but it was Ronald Colman who took home the Oscar for it. At the time she was cast as Pat, she was also handed the role of Ado Annie in *Oklahoma!* on Broadway. She left for the East after *A Double Life* wrapped up.

As successful as she had become in Hollywood, Shelley vowed not to return to California. In New York, she explained that she was "treated with respect as a serious actress…it's a different feeling being an actor in New York than being one in Hollywood. There's camaraderie among New York actors."[8] Like Shelley had brought color to *A Double Life*, she brought freshness to *Oklahoma!*, which had become stilted after its long run. She met fellow actor Marlon Brando during the time he was starring in *A Streetcar Named Desire*. The two thespians engaged in an affair that developed into a lifelong friendship. Brando encouraged Shelley to attend lectures at the Actors Studio where she became an ardent student of the Method.

Shelley's decision to banish Hollywood ended after she realized how much she missed her family. Universal Studios offered her a contract, and she accepted. Upon her return to California in 1948, she obtained an amicable divorce from her husband. She no longer had any wifely façade to feign; consequently, she thrust all her energy into her career. She was cast in second lead roles in films, most often as vulgar women who meet unfortunate ends, including *The Great Gatsby* (1949) and *Cry of the City* (1948). Because she had learned to respect her talent at the Actors Studio, Shelley resented her sexpot/bombshell image all the more. She rebelled by cutting her hair off in 1948, giving the explanation: "It was either that or kill myself."[9] The short haircut became her trademark and increased rather than decreased her popularity. She became a frequent name in tabloids, which relished reprinting her brazen statements such as: "It was so cold I almost got married" or "A girl can't be sexy all on her own. She's got to aim at somebody."[10]

Though Shelley proclaimed to be happy during this period, she later said that her inner self was chanting "wrong, wrong, WRONG."[11] Her struggle between "the Myth and the Mensch" led her to attend studies at esteemed actor Charles Laughton's house with others, including Robert Ryan, Paulette Goddard, and Charles Chaplin. Gossip columnists did not acknowledge her intellect and chose instead to focus on her serial dating patterns. It was true that she was seldom seen on the arm of the same man, but her feelings for her escorts were more serious than reporters led the public to believe. She had regular affairs with William Holden and had a serious romance with married actor Burt Lancaster.

Shelley's tutelage under Laughton led her to strive for quality in her pictures, even if it meant taking an unglamorous role. She campaigned for the part of Alice Tripp in George Stevens's masterful production *A Place in the Sun* (1951). Wearing her sister's old blouse and an ill-fitting skirt and with no make-up on her face, she auditioned for the astonished Stevens, who did not initially recognize her. Shelley gave her best performance thus far as Alice, the factory girl impregnated and abandoned by the boss's nephew, George Eastman. Shelley's whiny performance garners simultaneous resentment and sympathy from the audience. In her final scene alone with Eastman in a rowboat, she releases an effusion of unreciprocated enthusiasm for the marriage between her and her baby's father. All throughout her speech she is oblivious to the fact that Eastman is planning to murder her. Eastman is shown sweating and fidgeting miserably as he listens to her speak:

> ALICE TRIPP: *I'd like to live in a little house. Just big enough for the two of us...only there's gonna be more than two of us, isn't there?... I'll tell you what I wish. I wish you still loved me...you'll see...after a while you'll settle down and be contented with what ya got instead of working yourself up over what you can't have. After all, it's the little things in life that count. Sure, maybe we'll have to scrimp and save, but we'll have each other!* [12]

Shelley's use of Method acting in the film led to an intense psychological reaction that, compounded with her heartbreak at ending her affair with Burt Lancaster, resulted in a nervous breakdown. As she recovered at Cedars of Lebanon Hospital, she was cheered to hear she was being nominated for Best Actress for *A Place in the Sun*. Despite the prestige of the nomination, she was again thrust into dumb blonde roles, first in *Behave Yourself!* (1951) opposite Farley Granger. She and Granger were sent on an international publicity tour through Europe and Israel after the film's completion.

While in Rome, Shelley began her lifelong passion for all things Italian. She adored the fashion and the food, but mostly she was interested in the Italian actor Vittorio Gassman. He and Shelley married quickly and returned to Hollywood together. Their relationship was primarily based on physical attraction, for he spoke little English and his ideas concerning women were Old World in the least appealing sense. It was not until Gassman returned to Italy for a new film that his possessive nature began to emerge. While he was away, Shelley gave birth to their daughter, Vittoria. Marlon Brando drove her to hospital and stayed at her bedside in place of her husband. Vittorio's subsequent insistence that she move to Italy coupled with Shelley's knowledge that he was carrying on an affair with a teenage girl with whom he was co-starring led to a violent argument.

The fight left Shelley with a severely damaged eye. Shelley made ideal tabloid fodder once again during production of *Mambo,* an Italian-made film starring both Shelley and Gassman. When her husband brought his teenage girlfriend on the set, she heaved a mirror at him and left the girl with nail marks on her face. "Sure it happened,"[13] Shelley proudly told reporters as she sat at the bar of the Hotel De La Ville in Rome.

SHELLEY WINTERS AND MONTGOMERY CLIFT IN *A PLACE IN THE SUN* (1951).
COURTESY OF JERRY MURBACH.

Onscreen, Shelley was decidedly more submissive to men than she was in her private life. Her former teacher, Charles Laughton, cast her in the classic thriller *The Night of the Hunter* (1955), co-starring Robert Mitchum. Shelley portrays a gullible and spineless widow blind to the cruelty of her new husband, phony preacher Mitchum, towards her two children. After he slaps her across the face, she cries with a dazed smile: *I feel clean now. My whole body's just a-quiverin' with cleanness.*[14]

Following this laudable performance, Shelley once again returned to New York to establish herself as a serious actress. In *A Hatful of Rain,* Shelley played a "drab, faithless young wife of a narcotics addict."[15] Co-starring as her husband was young actor Anthony Franciosa, with whom Shelley fell in love. Critics were amazed at her performance and finally admitted she could act. Her role in the play was much like her former character, Alice Tripp. She was "a human being in low heels without make-up who didn't have a sex quality." [16] As commendable as her reviews for the show were, concurrent to the play's run was the release of a B picture she had grudgingly done, *I Died A Thousand Times* (1955). Reviewers said she was "piteously without skill" [17] in the picture. Shelley stated that though she "always fought for quality, for every good [film], I had to do a lousy Technicolor Western." [18]

Shelley returned to Hollywood in triumph with Franciosa at her side. She and the actor were married in 1957, but, like the union with Gassman, their dueling careers did not make for harmony. Shelley's career ascended as Franciosa's stagnated. In another George Stevens film, *The Diary of Anne Frank* (1959), she was cast as Mrs. Van Daan, her best role since Alice Tripp. Her portrayal of a nagging and tough yet loving wife and mother was the beginning of her transition away from her type casting as a sexy leading woman. Shelley won an Oscar for her performance, which she later donated to the Anne Frank Museum. "I'll never forget the night I brought the Oscar home," Shelley said. "Tony took one look at it and I knew my marriage was over." [19] They divorced in 1960.

As the new decade opened, Shelley fell into the category of character actress. "You gotta play mothers. If you don't, you won't get a long career in Hollywood," [20] she explained. She was cast as a "host of revoltingly bad mamas, blowsy matrons, and trashy madams," [21] according to her biographer Gary Brumburgh. And this was what she desired. She, according to journalist Vincent Canby, "fought tenaciously for the character parts she now cherishes." [22] Among the first revoltingly bad mothers she played was Charlotte Haze in Stanley Kubrick's *Lolita* (1962). Shelley is at her nagging and whining best as the less than protective mother jealous of her new husband's infatuation for her thirteen-year-old daughter. Her next most atrocious role was as Elizabeth Hartman's abusive, prostitute mother in the ground-breaking film showing love between a black man and a blind white girl, *A Patch of Blue* (1965). Shelley's role was as a woman the complete opposite of herself, particularly when it came to her views on race relations. "Can you imagine me using words like 'nigger' and 'wop'? I've always found something to like in the characters I've played but not this time. I really hate this woman…she blinds her daughter…and beats her…how's that for a role?" [23] Shelley declared.

In actuality, Shelley was a liberal Democrat known for her defense of civil rights and her support of candidates like John and Robert Kennedy. Despite her dislike for her character, Shelley gave a riveting performance that earned her a second Academy Award. Shelley's convincing work as a prostitute led her to win the part of America's best-known madam, Polly Adler, in *A House Is Not a Home* (1964) — a decidedly more sympathetic role to which she tried to give "a degree of dignity."[24] However, after the assassination of Robert Kennedy, Shelley turned toward gentler roles. She was among the first Hollywood actors to pledge not to make any more gratuitous films and helped organize the Committee for a Federal Gun Control Law.[25]

In the late 1960s, Shelley transitioned into making romantic comedies, including *Alfie* (1966) and *Buena Sera, Mrs. Campbell* (1968); however, she earned most accolades as "the harping Jewish wife/mother...with loud, flashy, unsubtle roles," most notably in *The Poseidon Adventure* (1972) and *Next Stop, Greenwich Village* (1976). In *The Poseidon Adventure*, Shelley put on over twenty pounds to portray a sarcastic, out-of-shape ex-swimmer. She won a Golden Globe for her performance and was nominated for another Oscar. Shelley noted that "In every film where I've either drowned or had to swim, such as in *Night of the Hunter* or *A Place in the Sun,* I have a great personal success."[26]

As successful as Shelley was in Hollywood, she returned to New York to "reclaim [her brain]."[27] She accomplished this by penning her own play, consisting of three one-act vignettes which "reflect the shifting position of the liberal since Hitler."[28] The show opened on Broadway and starred a young Robert DiNiro. She became increasingly unreliable on screen as her notorious temper flared on more than one occasion. In 1972, she walked off the set of *The Tonight Show* after dumping a bucket of ice water over guest Oliver Reed's head when she disagreed with his attitude towards women. A similar incident occurred during the filming of 1985's *Always,* during which she threw a tantrum backstage and was removed from the picture. She had better luck off screen, again due to her talent with the pen. Her 1980 five-hundred-paged autobiography made the top ten best sellers list. The expose style book had an equally candid sequel in 1989. "If there's a movie, I'd like Streisand to play me,"[29] Shelley joked.

Though Shelley was more successful with her offstage work in the latter half of her career, she still appeared in a steady flow of films and television specials. She had won an Emmy in 1964 for her performance on the *Bob Hope Chrysler Theater* and had proceeded to make frequent appearances on the small screen. In the early 1990s, she was best known for her recurring role as Roseanne Barr's sassy grandmother on *Roseanne.* Her final film appearance was in an unmemorable Italian picture, *La Bomba* (1999).

The new millennium saw Shelley's health failing, finally forcing her into a wheelchair. She had as her constant companion Gerry DeFord from 1987 to 2006. When she entered a nursing home with a failing heart, she ordered her goddaughter, who was an ordained minister, to join her and DeFord together in spiritual union. A few hours after the marriage, Shelley died. Though she had become a campy figure as her career waned, the dignity and excellence of her best work made her a legend in her own unique way. Shelley was an unsung Method actress, as dedicated to the technique as Brando or Clift.

At the end of Shelley's first autobiography, she stated: "Shelley Winter aka Shirley Schrift are now finally fused together."[30] It is the mix of Shelley Winters — brazen and gaudy Hollywood star — and Shirley Schrift — ambitious, socially conscious, and idealistic girl — that make Shelley so appealing on screen. Her onscreen gregarious women, working-class girls, and unsubstantial bombshells in costume westerns contain common elements of sensitivity, grit, and relatable human weaknesses. Shelley's offscreen persona alternated between a dignified Strasberg-trained actress and a schmaltzy blonde dame. Shelley once commented on this dichotomy with the quip:

"I get bursts of being a lady, but it doesn't last long."[31]

FILMOGRAPHY

1999	*La bomba*	Prof. Summers
1999	*Gideon*	Mrs. Willows
1996	*The Portrait of a Lady*	Mrs. Touchett
1995	*Raging Angels*	Grandma Ruth
1995	*Mrs. Munck*	Aunt Monica
1995	*Jury Duty*	Mom
1995	*Backfire!*	The Good Lieutenant
1995	*Heavy*	Dolly Modino
1994	*The Silence of the Hams*	Mrs. Motel *(The Mother)*
1993	*The Pickle*	Yetta
1991	*Stepping Out*	Mrs. Fraser
1990	*Touch of a Stranger*	
1989	*An Unremarkable Life*	Evelyn McEllany
1988	*Purple People Eater*	Rita
1986	*The Delta Force*	Edie Kaplan
1986	*Witchfire*	Lydia

1966	*The Three Sisters*	Natalya
1965	*A Patch of Blue*	Rose-Ann D'Arcey
1965	*The Greatest Story Ever Told*	Woman who is healed
1964	*A House Is Not a Home*	Polly Adler
1964	*Time of Indifference*	Lisa
1963	*Wives and Lovers*	Fran Cabrell
1963	*The Balcony*	Madame Irma
1962	*The Chapman Report*	Sarah Garnell
1962	*Lolita*	Charlotte Haze
1961	*The Young Savages*	Mary diPace
1960	*Let No Man Write My Epitaph*	Nellie Romano
1959	*Odds Against Tomorrow*	Lorry
1959	*The Diary of Anne Frank*	Mrs. Petronella Van Daan
1955	*I Died a Thousand Times*	Marie Garson
1955	*The Treasure of Pancho Villa*	Ruth Harris
1955	*The Big Knife*	Dixie Evans *(as Miss Shelley Winters)*
1955	*The Night of the Hunter*	Willa Harper
1955	*I Am a Camera*	Natalia Landauer
1954	*Cash on Delivery*	Myrtle La Mar
1954	*Mambo*	Toni Salerno
1954	*Playgirl*	Fran Davis
1954	*Executive Suite*	Eva Bardeman
1954	*Saskatchewan*	Grace Markey
1954	*Tennessee Champ*	Sarah Wurble
1952	*My Man and I*	Nancy
1952	*Untamed Frontier*	Jane Stevens
1952	*Phone Call from a Stranger*	Binky Gay
1951	*Meet Danny Wilson*	Joy Carroll
1951	*The Raging Tide*	Connie Thatcher
1951	*Behave Yourself!*	Kate Denny
1951	*A Place in the Sun*	Alice Tripp
1951	*He Ran All the Way*	Peggy Dobbs
1950	*Frenchie*	Frenchie Fontaine Dawson
1950	*South Sea Sinner*	Coral
1950	*Winchester '73*	Lola Manners
1949	*Johnny Stool Pigeon*	Terry Stewart
1949	*The Great Gatsby*	Myrtle Wilson
1949	*Take One False Step*	Catherine Sykes
1948	*Cry of the City*	Brenda Martingale
1948	*Larceny*	Tory

1948 *Red River*.............. Dance Hall Girl in Wagon Train *(uncredited)*

1947 *Killer McCoy*.................Waitress/Autograph Hound *(uncredited)*

1947 *A Double Life* .... Pat Kroll

1947 *The Gangster*.. Hazel *(uncredited)*

1947 *Living in a Big Way* .... Junior League Girl *(uncredited)*

1947 *New Orleans* .... Miss Holmbright *(uncredited)*

1946 *Abie's Irish Rose* .... Bridesmaid *(uncredited)*

1946 *Susie Steps Out* ....Female Singer *(uncredited)*

1946 *Two Smart People*..Princess *(uncredited)*

1946 *The Fighting Guardsman*................................Nanette *(uncredited)*

1945 *A Thousand and One Nights*....................Handmaiden *(uncredited)*

1945 *Escape in the Fog* .... Taxi Driver *(uncredited)*

1945 *Tonight and Every Night*................................Bubbles *(uncredited)*

1944 *Together Again* ....Young Woman *(uncredited)*

1944 *Dancing in Manhattan* .... Margie *(uncredited)*

1944 *She's a Soldier Too* ....'Silver' Rankin *(uncredited)*

1944 *Cover Girl*.. Chorus Girl *(unconfirmed)*

1944 *Knickerbocker Holiday*............. Ulda Tienhoven *(as Shelley Winter)*

1944 *Sailor's Holiday*........................... Gloria Flynn *(as Shelley Winter)*

1943 *What a Woman!*... Secretary *(uncredited)*

1943 *There's Something About a Soldier*.. Norma

THE LOVABLE GROUCH
MONTY WOOLLEY

MONTY WOOLLEY IN *LIFE BEGINS AT 8:30* (1942).

COURTESY OF JERRY MURBACH.

"Is there a man in the world who suffers as I do from the gross inadequacies of the human race?" [1]

So bemoans Sheridan Whiteside, the misanthropic celebrity author in the classic 1942 film *The Man Who Came to Dinner*. Such acerbic words were not just Sheridan Whiteside's trademark, but also that of the man who portrayed him: Monty Woolley. Today, Monty Woolley is recognized by audiences as a sort of malignant Santa Claus with a white beard and fierce blue eyes who throws out caustic yet witty remarks while clenching a cigarette holder between his teeth. Off screen, Monty insisted he was "mild-mannered and easy to get along with" and mourned that "being typed as a man with an acid tongue has just about ruined me." [2] Though he claimed his typecasting had ruined him, Monty Woolley would eventually use his screen character as a welcome shield for his true self which he kept largely concealed during his seventy-five years of life.

Monty had a wealth of personal experience to draw upon to make his sophisticated characters more genuine. He was born Edgar Montillion Woolley on August 17, 1888 in New York's elite Bristol Hotel. It was just one of the upper-crust establishments owned or managed by his father, William. William exposed his son to the highest echelons of society during the time he and his family lived in a home on the grounds of his Grand Union Hotel in Saratoga Springs. Among the luminaries Monty met were Lillian Russell, Diamond Jim Brady, and Victor Herbert. [3] The young man continued to soak in the culture of the upper-crust when he entered into Yale's class of 1907. He mingled with the "smart set," a group of boys reminiscent of characters that F. Scott Fitzgerald would later create who "owned pianos and studied wine lists" and dabbled in "dramatics and profligacy." [4] Charismatic and witty, Monty did not have any trouble attracting a group of friends. He was described by those who knew him best as the life of the party and by his senior year, the lavish, original costume balls he hosted became "the stuff of legend." [5] He was also closely involved with the university's dramatic association. More often than not, Monty played the starring role in the productions. He was so accustomed to being the star that initially, Monty did not take kindly to a sophomore named Cole Porter, whom he saw as a competitor. Monty accused Cole of being a "show off" when the young songwriter led everyone at a banquet in singing a tune he had written that became the school's anthem: "Bingo Eli Yale." [6] However, after becoming better acquainted, the two men became the closest of friends. They shared not only privileged upbringings and a love of theater and music, but they were also both closeted homosexuals. This, more than anything else, drew them together and allowed them to share confidences their other friends could not accept.

Cole and Monty proved to fuel each other's creative abilities. With Cole as lyricist and composer and Monty as flamboyant performer, they became the most lauded team of the Yale Dramatic Association. Monty was honing his skills as a dark-humored comedian and never displayed them better than in Cole's spoof on *Uncle Tom's Cabin* in which he played the villain who sings, "I take delight/ In looking for a fight/I have gotten/ a rep for being rotten/ I put poison in my mother's cream of wheat." [7] Cole later credited much of his early success to Monty. He stated that his friend was "one of my finest experiences at Yale" and that he had taught him "how to listen." [8]

By 1914, Monty had received his bachelor's degree from Yale and went on to graduate school at both Yale and Harvard. After graduating, Monty served as drama coach for Yale for three years. However, as a member of the National Guard, he enlisted as a lieutenant in the Army as soon as the United States entered World War I. He spent eight months in France. While on leave, he maintained the active social life he had left behind him at college. Cole had moved to Paris in 1917 and introduced his friend to such members of the intelligentsia as Elsa Maxwell, Elsie DeWolfe, and Archibald MacLeish. [9] His friendship with Cole strengthened during his much-needed vacations from battle and would continue to grow in the trying years ahead.

After the war, Monty found himself in a position to which he was unaccustomed: being unemployed and penniless. He went to New York to try his hand at directing but could only find sporadic work as a stage manager. In 1923, he was grateful to accept a job from his alma mater as lecturer on drama and director of undergraduate productions. During his years as professor at the university, Monty elevated the dramatic productions to new heights of sophistication and saw their popularity soar. Responsible for part of the show's popularity was also Cole Porter. Noting that his friend had grown despondent to the point that he was no longer writing songs, Monty asked him to write the score for Yale's Christmas show, *Out o' Luck*. Cole's friend H.C. Potter saw the genuine affection and concern Monty held for him. He later said, "I know that Monty had to use every bit of exuberant enthusiasm and persuasion...to nudge Cole out of...virtual retirement." [10] Monty's efforts paid off. The show was an enormous success and spurred Cole into years of prolific song-writing.

Monty's generosity and enthusiasm were reserved not only for his friends but also for his pupils. His loquacious and fun-loving personality endeared him to students (Thornton Wilder and Philip Barry included) and they would remain fiercely loyal to him when, in 1924, his job fell into jeopardy. After the school received a million-dollar grant to create the country's first official college drama department, a man named George Pierce Baker was appointed as head. Baker was a strong proponent of "experimental, proletarian shows" while Monty's forte was "witty, escapist sophistication." [11] The two men's differences proved to be insurmountable and in 1925, Monty's appointment was not renewed. Students staged furious protests and declared their beloved professor's termination as "a sinister plan of the Yale Corporation." [12]

Monty returned to New York. The boy who had grown up in such a rarefied atmosphere found himself again as penniless as he had been after the war. He was forced to appeal to his friends for money, a humiliating position for a man who exuded such confidence and dignity. However, in 1929, Cole Porter helped Monty just as his friend had helped him when giving him *Out o'Luck* to write. Cole was currently writing a Broadway production called *Fifty Million Frenchman* and decided Monty would be the perfect director. The show was unanimously loved by critics and audiences. Its success renewed Monty's confidence, and this new confidence manifested in an interesting way: he grew a beard. Monty claimed he grew it as a gesture of independence, for his mother had recently passed away and she had always told him how she hated the idea of him ever growing whiskers. Little did Monty know that this gesture would become his signature look.

Monty's rapid succession of stage hits included *Champagne Sec* and *The New Yorkers*. Even in the thick of the Depression, audiences lapped up the "escapist sophistication" that had led to his discharge from Yale University. His creativity and adeptness with language were at their apex, so much that it inspired the talents of those around him. In 1935 while on a world cruise with Cole Porter and his wife Linda, Monty sat watching a sunrise. Cole remarked, "It's delightful." Linda continued, "It's delicious." Monty concluded with what would become one of Cole's most popular lyrics, "It's de-lovely." [13]

Though Cole and Monty's combined talents seemed indomitable, the Depression finally affected them in 1936. Their most recent show, *Jubilee*, contained some of Cole's best efforts ("Begin the Beguine" and "Just One of Those Things"), but it lost a staggering amount at the box office and resulted in a severe monetary loss for Cole and Monty. His Broadway career had begun to falter, but looking to the opposite coast, Monty realized Hollywood was booming. Reluctantly he moved to California and hit what he called the low point of his career. He failed to land any directing or acting jobs and would have found himself penniless again if was not for an offer from Rodgers and Hart, who were currently producing a new Broadway show called *On Your Toes*. They wanted him to play the role of a flamboyant ballet impresario. Monty accepted and performed the role to such acclaim that film studios even began to take attention. Hollywood agents believed the pomposity and unapologetic brashness he brought to his roles could make for a unique character on screen; his distinctive beard certainly posed interesting possibilities, too.

Monty decided to give Hollywood a second chance but soon began to wonder why he had. Rather than utilizing his talents and distinct appearance, the studios he worked for made them a springboard for broad comedy. In his first film, *Live, Love, and Learn* (1937), Monty's beard was dunked in a pail of water. Similarly, in the Lana Turner vehicle *Dancing Co-Ed* (1939), he was dumped in a pool of water and spent "two days on a scene that had Robert Benchley and him rolling drunk in a wet gutter." [14] Monty finally received a few small roles in which he could display his talent for witty barbs, most notably as an exasperated producer in Judy Garland's *Everybody Sing* (1938). He utilized not wit but dignity as a doctor in *Young Dr. Kildare* (1938), a judge in Claudette Colbert's *Midnight* (1939) and jeweler in Freddie Bartholomew's *Lord Jeff* (1938).

Despite some token dignified roles, Monty maintained that he was "humiliated, disgusted, and desperate" [15] in the movies. He reached the point where he claimed that even approaching the studio filled him with the wish to meet with a car accident and die quietly and painlessly in a ditch. He began sleeping for twenty hours at a time, so depressed did he become.

Salvation again came in the form of a new Broadway show. Jolted awake in the middle of the night by the ring of his telephone, Monty picked up the receiver and found himself being offered a part in a Kaufman and Hart play entitled *The Man Who Came to Dinner*.

"That's a poor joke to play on a tired old man trying to get some sleep," [16] Monty told the playwrights. But Kaufman and Hart were playing him no joke. Monty was on the next train to New York, where he set about making the role Sheridan Whiteside his own. Whiteside is a caustic, out-spoken author who injures his hip while on tour and is forced to stay, wheelchair-bound, in his Midwestern hosts' home. He succeeds in turning the lives of all those around him upside down as he carries on his whirlwind, society lifestyle from his wheelchair. Kaufman and Hart feared their fellow Algonquin Round Table member, Alexander Woollcott, would take offense at the obvious parody of himself in Whiteside. However, on opening night critics proclaimed Whiteside as "more Woolley than Woollcott." [17] Monty flawlessly blended his dignity, humor, and sarcasm into his portrayal and created his own brand of character, a character so unique he can turn making insults into an art. Just a sampling of his outrageous jabs affirm that he could make the cruelest comment worthy of laughter:

> *"My great aunt Jennifer ate a whole box of candy every day of her life. She lived to be 102, and when she had been dead three days, she looked better than you do now."* [18]

> *"Will you take your clammy hand off my chair? You have the touch of a love-starved cobra."* [19]

Monty continued his success in Hollywood, where he brought his character of Sheridan Whiteside to the screen in the 1942 film adaptation of the play. The public took to him immediately, so much that he earned the affectionate nickname of "The Beard" among audiences.

More plum roles followed *The Man Who Came to Dinner.* Two of them, one in *The Pied Piper* (1942) and one in *Since You Went Away* (1944), earned Monty Academy Award nominations. Both films had him playing his now typical role of a curmudgeon whose bark is worse than his bite. He is at his acerbic best in *Since You Went Away* when he first enters Claudette Colbert's home, in which he hopes to rent a room during the housing shortage of World War II. As he enters, he declares:

> *My name is Smollett, William G., Colonel, United States Army, retired. Retired, I might add, by virtue of certain fatuous opinions held in the War Department which judge a man's usefulness neither by his experience nor his ability, but by the number of years since he was weaned.*

He goes on to wordily explain his experiences, ending on an ungracious, if ironic note:

> *Through a full, and somewhat protracted existence, I have learned to accept the natural tendency of all women to be garrulous.* [20]

In *Since You Went Away* and another notable role in *The Bishop's Wife* (1947), Monty succeeded in preventing the Christmas-themed films from sliding into overdone sentimentality. The 1940s closed with another substantial role in the glossy biopic of Cole Porter in which Monty played himself, *Night and Day* (1946).

Off screen, Monty found as welcome of a niche as he had found onscreen. In the early 1940s he met Cary Abbott, a man he was to carry on a deep and loving relationship with for the next five years. When

REGINALD GARDINER, BETTE DAVIS, AND MONTY WOOLLEY IN *THE MAN WHO CAME TO DINNER* (1942). COURTESY OF JERRY MURBACH.

Monty bought a home in Saratoga Springs, he and Cary moved into it together, though Cary did have to maintain the façade of being Monty's secretary. Monty loved being in his hometown, and his hometown loved it, too. In 1945, the townspeople elected him mayor by a write-in vote. Though Monty graciously turned down the appointment, he showed his appreciation by giving a special performance of *The Man Who Came to Dinner* for the community.

"My heart lies in Saratoga Springs," Monty said. "In Saratoga, I'm not Monty. I'm Edgar and that makes me happy indeed." [21]

Though he could not openly reveal his homosexuality even in his hometown, the warmth and friendship Saratoga Springs offered him allowed him to be the kind, generous man who went so unnoticed in the face of his overbearing archetype onscreen. Monty's happiness would prove to be all too short when in 1948, Cary Abbott died. Suddenly, "Edgar" all but disappeared and became the curmudgeonly man he portrayed in film. Monty became a virtual loner, most often dining alone at a gentleman's club owned by a man named Nathan Goldsmith. Goldsmith recalled that Monty began to drink a lot and would usually sit by himself at the bar reading Troybee's *A Study of History*. "I don't like to eat with other people," Monty said. "Most people like to have a drink and eat. I like to stretch the cocktails out leisurely." [22] Monty's loneliness only grew after his closest friend, Cole Porter, ended their relationship. Allegedly their falling out was over Cole's disapproval of an affair Monty had with his black manservant.

As much as Monty wanted solitude now, when he was dining, fans and waiters alike would be disappointed if they were not the recipients of Monty's famed barbs. He later said that he had formed such a reputation as a grouch that he had to insult people to make them leave him alone. One newspaper account told of a waiter leaving Monty's table, beaming, after Monty pelted him with insults about the quality of the food. As much as he seemed to become his misanthropic screen persona off camera, Monty mourned the loss of "Edgar," once regretfully stating, "I suppose I should feel fortunate that I am always able to say exactly what I think and not offend." [23]

As the 1950s continued, Monty appeared in several films, his final one being in *Kismet* (1955) in which he played Omar Khayyam. It was role so small that he declared, "I don't know why they need me." He began to feel increasingly out of place in a world that was becoming too fast paced. He loathed a live-television performance he gave of *The Man Who Came to Dinner*, deploring, "You simply can't condense a play like that into forty-five minutes. It's impossible." [24] He also loathed the plethora of acting schools that had cropped up in Hollywood, all of them promising a road to quick fame. "Why when I think of mine own kampf — why, damn it all, those arrant tricksters!" [25] he cried.

In 1963, Monty died of kidney and heart ailments at the age of seventy-five. On the night before his death, Cole Porter had refused to let him to stay the night at his home when a massive storm hit.

Though in his later years Monty became withdrawn, lonely, and depressed largely due to the frustration and loss he experienced as a closeted homosexual, the words that most readily came to those who knew him when asked to describe him were, "generous," "sweet," and "fun to be with." To generations of film and theater goers he has become a modern version of Heidi's grandfather: a man with a crusty exterior but a giving, soft heart. Without a doubt, his inimitable legacy to filmdom is, in the words Monty coined himself, "delightful and de-lovely."

FILMOGRAPHY

1955 *Kismet* ....Omar
1951 *As Young as You Feel* ....John R. Hodges
1948 *Miss Tatlock's Millions* ....Miles Tatlock
1947 *The Bishop's Wife* .... Professor Wutheridge
1946 *Night and Day* .... Himself
1945 *Molly and Me* ....John Graham
1944 *Irish Eyes Are Smiling* .... Edgar Brawley
1944 *Since You Went Away* .... Colonel William G. Smollett
1943 *Holy Matrimony* ....Priam Farrell
1942 *Life Begins at Eight-Thirty* ....Madden Thomas
1942 *The Pied Piper* ....John Sidney Howard
1942 *The Man Who Came to Dinner* ....Sheridan Whiteside
1939 *See Your Doctor (short)* .... Doctor *(uncredited)*
1939 *Dancing Co-Ed* ....Professor Lange
1939 *Honeymoon in Bali* ....Parker, Smitty's Publisher *(uncredited)*
1939 *Man About Town* .... Henri Dubois
1939 *Never Say Die* .... Dr. Schmidt
1939 *Midnight* ....The Judge
1938 *Zaza* .... Fouget
1938 *Artists and Models Abroad* .... Gantvoort
1938 *Young Dr. Kildare* .... Dr. Lane-Porteus
1938 *Vacation from Love* .... Wedding Guest in Car *(uncredited)*
1938 *Lord Jeff* ....Jeweler
1938 *Three Comrades* ....Dr. Jaffe
1938 *The Forgotten Step (short)* .... The Art Collector
1938 *The Girl of the Golden West* .... The Governor
1938 *Arsène Lupin Returns* .... Georges Bouchet
1938 *Everybody Sing* ....John 'Jack' Fleming
1937 *Nothing Sacred* ....Dr. Oswald Vunch *(uncredited)*
1937 *Live, Love and Learn* ....Mr. Bawltitude
1936 *Ladies in Love* .... Man in Box Seat *(uncredited, unconfirmed)*

THE REAL MR. TOPPER
ROLAND YOUNG

ROLAND YOUNG IN *TOPPER RETURNS* (1941).
COURTESY OF JERRY MURBACH.

In the escapist world of screwball comedies characterized by farcical situations, zany heiresses, and snappy repartee between the sexes, a meek, short-framed, balding man prone to mumbling would seem to have little place. But this man did have a place. His restrained comedy, once described as "faintly fatalistic and self-deprecatory," [1] provided perfect balance to the bedlam around him in screwball films. His relaxed, patrician air, immaculately tailored suits, and wispy mustache at first deceive film audiences as to his potential for humor. Look closer, and his subtle "covered laugh or sly, knowing wink" [2] will steal laughter from the most outlandish antics of his big name co-stars. This deceptively meek man's name is Roland Young. He is immortalized today as the title character in the ghostly 1937 madcap comedy of manners, *Topper*. However, off screen Mr. Young proved to be just as much an eccentric wit as the men he portrayed in his films.

Roland was born on November 11, 1887 in London, England. The son of a well-known architect, he was expected to follow the profession when he reached adulthood. But young Roland had other plans. Harboring a secret passion for the stage, the nearest he came to realizing his ambition as a youth was singing in the school choir. He was educated at Sherbourne, Albert the Great's alma mater. Roland's study room at Sherbourne was a 13th century monk's cell below ground level. The aspiring actor, discontent to remain in the confines of a cell, used the three pence he earned every Sunday in the choir to travel the world. He easily could have penned another *Innocents Abroad;* Roland visited everywhere from France, to Italy, to Switzerland, to Morocco, and to the Canary Islands. [3]

As much of the adventurer as he appeared to be, Roland could be as meek as his later screen persona. He "labored diligently in his father's office" for two years before expressing any of his acting ambition to his parents. [4] When he did hint at it, he received no encouragement from his father. It was when Roland was taken ill with a sore throat that the elder Mr. Young had the opportunity to make inquiries about his son's work. He gathered that though Roland was highly talented at the drafts and sketches required for architecture, the young man was not adept at the math. More than that, his heart was not in his work. Mr. Young demanded of his son, "What do you want to do?" Unable to audibly answer due to the sore throat, Roland's mother intervened with, "You know very well what he wants to do. He wants to be an actor." [5]

Roland's father finally consented and relieved his son from duties at the architectural office. Roland duly enrolled at the Academy of Dramatic Art. He stayed until 1911, when he landed a role in a drama entitled *Find the*

Woman. According to the *New York Times,* the "impression made by this play in London was not so great." Undaunted, Roland promptly went into another role, this time in a comedy called *Improper Peter.* It too did not make a great impression. It was now 1912, a year that would prove to be crucial for young Roland. His performances had impressed an influential woman known as Miss Horniman so much that she suggested him for a part in *Hindle Wakes,* a play being cast by successful American producer William Brady. Roland received the role and the play enjoyed a three-month run in Chicago, though it quickly folded on Broadway. Roland worked steadily until 1914 when Brady was again seeking British players for his next production. Roland haunted the lobby of the Savoy Hotel, where he made it his business to "accidentally" run into Brady. His waiting paid off, and Brady recommended he come to New York where they could plan a play together. Roland beat Brady to the States and waited in the producer's office every day for the hypothetical play Brady had promised. He was ignored until he resurrected his act of "accidentally" running into Brady, this time in the lobby of his New York hotel. Brady finally acknowledged him and gave the pesky Briton some names of other producers to bother.

Roland chose Emmanuel Reicher to bother, and he quickly was cast in a show called *Elysa.* Though it only played for one matinee before closing, Roland dove into another Reicher play. It had a comparatively long run of ten days. Undiscouraged, Roland joined the Washington Square Players for a season and found more success as a light comedian in their shows, most notably in *The Miracle of St. Anthony.* [6] Though he was most successful in comedy shows, he proved effective in such highbrow drama as Chekhov's *The Seagull* (1916), Ibsen's *A Doll's House* (1918), and the Clare Kummar play produced by Florenz Ziegfeld, *Rescuing Angel* (1918). [7] The latter play co-starred Billie Burke, an actress he would ultimately act alongside in seven films during the 1930s and 1940s.

As the 1910s drew to a close, Roland was comfortable in his life in New York and applied for American citizenship. It was as an American citizen that he served for a year fighting in World War I. Following his discharge, Roland lost no time in returning to the stage. He found most success in domestic comedies. Alexander Woollcott lauded his performance in the amusingly titled 1920 play *Scrambled Wives*: "The chief joy is Mr. Young," Woollcott wrote. "He is a delightfully droll comedian...the first thing you know some manager will present him in a role as good as he is. He seems to have all of the equipment that would fit him for a position equivalent to that of the Gerald du Maurier, who he so strikingly resembles in style, manner, and method." [8]

Roland enjoyed a string of hit shows in the early 1920s, including *Madame Pierre*, *The Devil's Disciple*, and *Rollo's Wild Oats*. It was in the latter play, written again by Clare Kummar, that he met the playwright's daughter Marjorie. They fell in love and were married in 1926. They wed on the vine-covered porch of the bride's summer cottage at Narragansett Bay. In a moment of comedy, a bridesmaid disrupted the ceremony when a grasshopper leapt down the front of her blouse. [9]

While Roland remained active on stage, like many other theater performers at the dawn of the Jazz Age, he tried his hand at acting in motion pictures. He had the plum role of the comically hesitant Dr. Watson to John Barrymore's Sherlock Holmes in a 1922 film of the same title. Based on his success as Dr. Watson, Roland was cast in an assortment of murder mysteries, including his first talkie directed by Lionel Barrymore entitled *Unholy Night* (1929). [10]

When not emoting in mysteries, Roland was cast in roles typifying him as an upper crust, often befuddled, aristocrat. His ability to appear both unperturbed and puzzled at the same time clicked with Depression-era audiences. More often than not, according to one critic, Roland's parts found him in "a dinner jacket" surveying "a drawing room with a dour or defeated expression, but with a glint of sarcasm in his eye." [11] He played such roles in Robert Montgomery's *Lovers Courageous* (1932) and Cary Grant's screen debut, *This Is the Night* (1932). The latter film cast him as a romantic lead, a role critics at first found hard to imagine but concluded was "delightful, ridiculous and charming." [12] He again ventured into a different type of role in *David Copperfield* (1936) as the villainous Uriah Heap. It was his performance as Heap that finally established him in Hollywood as a top-notch character performer.

Off screen as well as on, Roland gained a reputation as an intellectual wit and a bit of an eccentric. He rubbed elbows with writer Thorne Smith and tried writing himself. During the course of a play, Roland was supposed to "scribble royal edicts" and ended up penning so many that his friends convinced him to publish them. In 1930, he published a comical book of verse entitled *Not for Children*. One poem read: "The Billy goat's a handsome gent/ but has a most far reaching scent/ The nanny goat is quite a belle/ Let's hope she has no sense of smell." [13] Just as amusing as his poetry were his caricatures. The *New York Times* described them as "detached as a celluloid cuff" and further described the artist as "clever and merciless." [14] Roland showed his sardonic wit through the subtitles he gave his sketches. For instance, beneath Theodore Dreiser's picture was "From garbage cans to millionaires" and beneath theatrical/industrial designer Norman Bel Geddes' was "Megalo-Mania Trained and Tamed to Beauty." His favorite subject, however, were penguins simply because, like him, they "were different than anything on God's Earth." [15] His study at home was covered in sketches of the creatures. His love of animals also extended to cats. He owned a black feline delightfully named "Unex," short for "Unexpected." [16]

FREDDIE BARTHOLOMEW AND ROLAND YOUNG IN *DAVID COPPERFIELD* (1935). COURTESY OF JERRY MURBACH.

Roland's eccentricities made him much sought after by interviewers. However, interviewers found him reticent and distracted when answering questions. He prefaced nearly everything he said with "this can't be used of course" and when asked for an opinion, he answered either yes, no, or mumbled his reply to render it indecipherable. Interviewers did manage to glean the information that he disliked the factory-like system of filmmaking in Hollywood and that he was dissatisfied with his roles.

"Same thing you know," Roland murmured. "Sam the Sophisticate. Freddie the Faithful Friend. Nicky the Nut. Always one of the three. Funny, very funny. But tiresome. Same speeches. Same mannerisms. Um." He continued to explain how he preferred radio and stage work, and his face remained deadpan as he described his current role on Broadway. "A murderer. Very nice fellow really. Physician. Kills his wife. Buries her in the cellar...Nice part for me. Um." [17]

It was in Roland's next film role that he was able to blend both his macabre humor and dramatic abilities. He would rise above 'Sam the Sophisticate' or 'Nicky the Nut' and succeed in creating a character he would later admit he was most comfortable playing. The character was Cosmo Topper, a man invented by Roland's late friend Thorne Smith (Smith died in 1934). Some hold the theory that Smith created Cosmo Topper with Roland in mind. Based on Roland's Buster Keaton frown he could maintain in the bedlam of screwball comedy, Smith's description of Topper fits the actor perfectly: "An earthquake, an eruption or tidal wave would mildly move Cosmo Topper...Mr. Topper could not be troubled. His mental process ran safely, smoothly, and on the dot along well-signaled tracks; he resented trouble. At least he thought he did." [18] In a Topper-esque comment during a 1935 interview, Roland said that he disliked being bothered with the act of eating, much less at a dinner table, because it took time away time to "spend on truly entertaining things." [19] Topper and Roland were made for each other.

Topper is the story of a banker hen-pecked by his wife. His life is thrown into disarray when a fun-loving couple of ghosts (Cary Grant and Constance Bennett) try to do a good deed to get into heaven by reuniting him with his wife and teaching him how to have fun at the same time. Stand-out moments in the film include when Topper is intoxicated and slurs, "Oh no, we can't eat on an empty stomach" and proceeds to, in the words of one reviewer, "perform a licentious little dance with his respectably clad feet while his torso remains magnificently aloof in the depths of a lounge chair. It is an object lesson in controlled lunacy." [20] Also worthy of mention are Roland's scenes with onscreen wife Billie Burke. In a breakfast scene with Burke, priceless is Roland's long-suffering frown paired with his tongue-in-cheek humor when he responds to his wife's accusation that he is late. "Oh, better late than never," he says. "Only forty-four seconds anyhow." [21]

Roland earned the best reviews of his career for his performance in the film. His "talent for being harassed" as the "half-willing victim of the ghostly experiment" found "exquisite expression." [22] He earned an Academy Award nomination for Best Supporting Actor. Though he did not win the award, this did nothing to dampen the public's appetite for more Topper films. Two more followed. Based on his and Billie Burke's excellent screen chemistry, he appeared in four other films with her. Most notable among those not in the Topper series was 1938's *The Young in Heart* in which they play the mother and father in a family of lovable con artists. Roland's subtle, dignified befuddlement paired with Burke's not-so-subtle scatter-brained persona blend hilariously in the film. "I'm thunderstruck! Completely thunderstruck!" Roland declares at one point in the film. "Did I say thunderstruck?" he continues, to which Burke airily replies, "Yes, dear."[23] Several times throughout the film they sing an amusing little song together. Roland's mumbling monotone harmonizing with Burke's bird-like twitter could provoke laughs from even the sourest of audience members.

Roland's last great screen performance was as the bottom-pinching, constantly tipsy Uncle Willie in *The Philadelphia Story* (1940). Based on the fact that Roland was ignorant as to how to mix even a Manhattan, it is interesting to note how effective he was at being intoxicated on screen. "Aaw, this is one of those days that the pages of history teach us are better spent lying in bed," Uncle Willie moans after a night spent drinking[24]. Though Roland's talent for screwball comedy had reached its peak at the turn of the decade, the coming of World War II dampened the public's taste for such escapism and was replaced with an onslaught of gritty film noir or sentimental war dramas. Despite losing his niche in Hollywood, Roland did not lack for work. He resurrected *Topper* in a fifteen-episode radio serial in 1945 (sadly not with Burke as his wife)[25]. He retired from film in 1953 following the mediocre comedy, *That Man From Tangier*, in which he played the father of a wacky heiress. He acted as a suburban husband in another radio serial, *William and Mary*, in the 1950s. He also made regular appearances in *Lux Video Theatre, Studio One*, and *Chevrolet Theater*.[26] His final stage performance was in *Another Love Story*, which had had a healthy three-month run in 1944[27].

In his personal life, he found happiness with forty-year-old Dorothy Patience May DuCroz in 1948 after divorcing Marjorie Kummar in 1939. DuCroz survived her husband when, in 1953, Roland died in his sleep of natural causes.[28] He was sixty-five years old.

At the time of his death, Roland Young had appeared in over one hundred films and over thirty plays in England and America. Though at times he regretted being typed as the same dour, suave, but always humorous aristocrat, his unique character brought laughter and escape to Depression-era audiences when they needed it most. His performance as Mr. Topper continues to endear him to new generations of filmgoers. Both on and off screen, his wit and humor are as fresh today as they were seventy years ago.

"I am grateful," he once quipped. "that I belong to a generation that has produced such an exquisite example of architecture as Grauman's Chinese theater, the superb poetry of Edgar Allan Guest, and the measured prose and encyclopedic knowledge of the fan magazine."[29]

FILMOGRAPHY

1953	*That Man from Tangier*	George
1951	*St. Benny the Dip*	Matthew
1950	*Let's Dance*	Edmund Pohlwhistle
1949	*The Great Lover*	C.J. Dabney
1948	*You Gotta Stay Happy*	Ralph Tutwiler
1948	*Bond Street*	George Chester-Barrett
1945	*And Then There Were None*	Detective William Henry Blore
1944	*Standing Room Only*	Ira Cromwell
1943	*Forever and a Day*	Henry Barringer
1942	*Tales of Manhattan*	Edgar
1942	*They All Kissed the Bride*	Marsh
1942	*The Lady Has Plans*	Ronald Dean
1941	*Two-Faced Woman*	Oscar 'O. O.' Miller
1941	*The Flame of New Orleans*	Charles Giraud
1941	*Topper Returns*	Cosmo Topper
1940	*The Philadelphia Story*	Uncle Willie
1940	*No, No, Nanette*	Mr. 'Happy' Jimmy Smith
1940	*Dulcy*	Roger Forbes
1940	*Private Affairs*	Amos Bullerton
1940	*Irene*	Mr. Smith
1940	*Star Dust*	Thomas Brooke
1940	*He Married His Wife*	Bill Carter
1939	*The Night of Nights*	Barry Keith-Trimble
1939	*Here I Am a Stranger*	Professor Daniels
1939	*Yes, My Darling Daughter*	Titus 'Jay' Jaywood
1938	*Topper Takes a Trip*	Cosmo Topper
1938	*The Young in Heart*	Col. Anthony 'Sahib' Carleton
1938	*Sailing Along*	Anthony Gulliver
1937	*Ali Baba Goes to Town*	Sultan
1937	*Topper*	Cosmo Topper
1937	*King Solomon's Mines*	Cmdr. John Good
1937	*Call It a Day*	Frank Haines
1937	*Gypsy*	Alan Brooks

1936	*The Man Who Could Work Miracles*	George McWhirter Fotheringay
1936	*Give Me Your Heart*	Edward 'Tubbs' Barron
1936	*One Rainy Afternoon*	Maillot
1936	*The Unguarded Hour*	William 'Bunny' Jeffers
1935	*Ruggles of Red Gap*	Earl of Burnstead
1935	*David Copperfield*	Uriah Heep
1934	*Here Is My Heart*	Prince Nicholas/Nicki
1933	*His Double Life*	Priam Farrel
1933	*Blind Adventure*	Holmes the Burglar
1933	*Pleasure Cruise*	Andrew Poole
1933	*A Lady's Profession*	Lord Reginald Withers
1932	*They Just Had to Get Married*	Hillary Hume
1932	*Wedding Rehearsal*	Reggie Buckley Candysshe, Marquis of Buckminster
1932	*Street of Women*	Linkhorne 'Link' Gibson
1932	*This Is the Night*	Gerald Gray
1932	*One Hour with You*	Professor Olivier
1932	*A Woman Commands*	King Alexander
1932	*Lovers Courageous*	Jeffrey
1931	*The Guardsman*	Bernhardt the Critic
1931	*The Pagan Lady*	Dr. Heath
1931	*The Squaw Man*	Sir John 'Johnny' Applegate
1931	*Annabelle's Affairs*	Roland Wimbleton
1931	*The Prodigal*	Doc aka Somerset Greenman
1931	*All Women are Bad*	Herbert Drake
1930	*New Moon*	Count Igor Strogoff
1930	*Madam Satan*	Jimmy Wade
1930	*The Bishop Murder Case*	Sigurd 'Erik' Arnesson
1929	*Wise Girls*	Duke Merrill
1929	*The Unholy Night*	Lord 'Monte' Montague
1929	*Her Private Life*	Charteris
1928	*Walls Tell Tales (short)*	
1926	*Camille (short)*	Lord Kyne
1924	*Grit*	Houdini Hart
1922	*Sherlock Holmes*	Dr. Watson

SELECTED BIBLIOGRAPHY

Arden, Eve. *The Three Phases of Eve* (New York: St. Martin's Press, 1985).

Basinger, Jeanine. *The 'It's a Wonderful Life' Book* (New York, NY: Knopf, 1986).

Baum, L. Frank. *The Wonderful Wizard of Oz* (New York, NY: Scholastic, Inc., 1958).

Bickford, Charles. *Bulls, Balls, Bicycles, and Actors* (New York: Paul S. Eriksson, Inc., 1965).

Bogle, Donald. *Bright Boulevards Bold Dreams: The Story of Black Hollywood* (New York: One
    World Ballantine Books, 2006).

Bridges, Herb, and Terryl C. Boodman. *Gone With the Wind: The Definitive, Illustrated History,*

The Book, the Movie and the Legend (Lady Lake, FL: Fireside Books, 1989).

Bowers, Ronald and James Robert Parish. *The M-G-M Stock Company (*New York: Bonanza Books,
    1972).

Burke, Billie. *With a Feather on My Nose* (New York: Appleton Century Crofts, 1949).

Burke, Billie. *With Powder on My Nose* (New York, NY: Coward-McCann, 1959).

Cox, Stephen. *It's a Wonderful Life: A Memory Book.* (Nashville, TN: Cumberland House, 2003).

Deschner, Donald. *The Complete Films of Cary Grant (*New York: Citadel Press, 1983).

Fordin, Hugh. *M-G-M's Greatest Musicals* (New York, NY: Da Capo, 1996).

Golden, Eve. *Bride of Golden Image* (Albany, GA: BearManorBearManor Media, 2009).

Hadleigh, Boze. *Hollywood Lesbians* (New York: Barricade Books, 1994).

Harmetz, Aljean. *The Making of The Wizard of Oz* (New York: Tralfalgar Square, 1989).

Hayter-Menzies, Grant. *Mrs. Ziegfeld* (Jefferson, NC: MacFarland Press, 2009).

Higham, Charles. *Ziegfeld* (New York, NY: Regenery, 1972).

Jackson, Carlton. *Hattie: The Life of Hattie McDaniel* (London: Madison Books, 1990).

Kennedy, Matthew. *Joan Blondell: A Life Between Takes* (Jackson, MS: University Press of
    Mississippi, 2007).

Lanchester, Elsa. *Elsa Lanchester Herself* (New York: St. Martin's Press, 1983).

Marra, Kimberley Bell and Robert A. Schanke. *Passing Performances: Queer Readings of Leading Players in American Theater* (Ann Arbor, MI: University of Michigan Press, 1998).

Martin, Hugh. *Hugh Martin: The Boy Next Door* (Encinitas, CA: Trolley Press, 2010).

McBrien, William. *Cole Porter* (New York: Vintage Publishing, 2000).

Mitchell, Margaret. *Gone With the Wind* (New York: Warner Books, 1936).

Morley, Sheridan. *Gladys Cooper* (New York: McGraw-Hill Book Co., 1979).

Munshin, Jules. *Dear Anybody* (New York: Crown Publishers, 1957).

Piro, Rita. *Judy Garland: The Golden Years* (New York, NY: Great Feats Press, 2001).

Rogers, Ginger. *Ginger: My Story* (New York: HarperCollins, 1991).

Sakall, S. Z. *The Story of Cuddles: My Life Under the Emperor Francis Joseph, Adolf Hitler, and the Warner Bros.* (London: Cassell and Co. Ltd, 1954).

Sherk, Warren. *Agnes Moorehead: A Very Private Person* (Philadelphia, PA: Dorrance and Company, 1976).

Skall, David J. *An Actor's Voice* (Lexington, KY: University Press of Kentucky, 2009).

Smith, R.J. *The Great Black Way: L.A. in the 1940s and the Lost African-American Renaissance* (New York: Public Affairs, 2006).

Sobel, Bernard. *Broadway Heartbeat* (New York, NY: Hermitage House, 1953).

Stern, Keith. *Queers in History* (Dallas, Texas: BenBella Books, 2009).

Winters, Shelley. *Shelley: Also Known as Shirley* (New York: William Morrow and Co., 1980).

Young, Roland. *Not for Children* (New York: Garden City Publishing, 1945).

Ziegfeld, Richard and Paulette. *The Ziegfeld Touch* (New York: Harry N. Abrams, Inc. Publishers, 1993).

ENDNOTES

INTRODUCTION

1 Molly Haskell, "Oscars Films/Actresses: Where Have You Gone Fay Bainter and Joan Blondell?" *New York Times* (New York, NY) Mar. 4, 2001.

2 Aljean Harmetz, *The Making of The Wizard of Oz* (New York: Tralfalgar Square, 1989), p. 123, 177.

3 "Hattie McDaniel," *Internet Movie Database,* June 4, 2012, *http://www.imdb.com/name/ nm0567408/bio#trivia.*

4 "Constance Bennett," *Internet Movie Database,* Jun. 4, 2012, *http://www.imdb.com/name/ nm0000909/bio#trivia.*

5 Billie Burke, *With a Feather on My Nose* (New York: Appleton Century Crofts, 1949), p. 253.

EDDIE ROCHESTER ANDERSON

1 R.J. Smith, *The Great Black Way: L.A. in the 1940s and the Lost African-American Renaissance* (New York: Public Affairs, 2006), p. 16.

2 " 'Rochester of Jack Benny Show Dies of Heart Attack," *Ludington Daily News* (Ludington, MI), Mar. 1, 1977.

3 "Eddie (Rochester) Anderson, Featured on Jack Benny Shows," *Daily Boston Globe* (Boston, MA), Mar. 1, 1977.

4 Ibid.

5 Hal Humphrey, "Rochester Is Back," *The Victoria Advocate* (Victoria, TX), Nov. 10, 1968.

6 Donald Bogle, *Bright Boulevards Bold Dreams: The Story of Black Hollywood* (New York: One World Ballantine Books, 2006), p. 432.

7 R.J. Smith, *The Great Black Way: L.A. in the 1940s and the Lost African-American Renaissance* (New York: Public Affairs, 2006), p. 17.

8 Ibid, p. 18.

9 Ibid, p. 16.

10 Hal Humphrey, "Rochester Is Back," *The Victoria Advocate* (Victoria, TX), Nov. 10, 1968.

11 *Topper Returns,* DVD, Dir.: Roy Del Ruth, Perf.: Roland Young, Joan Blondell, and Carole Landis (1941; Los Angeles: Hal Roach Studios, 2002), Film.

12 "Entertainment Proposition," *Time* (New York, NY), Apr. 16, 1945.

13 "He Broke the Racial Bar," *St. Joseph News-Press* (St. Joseph, MO), Mar. 4, 1977.

14 R.J. Smith, *The Great Black Way: L.A. in the 1940s and the Lost African-American Renaissance* (New York: Public Affairs, 2006), p. 19.

15 Ibid, p 19.

16 "Negroes at War," *Life* (New York, NY), June 15, 1942, p. 89.

17 "Rochester's Hoss Ready," *Spokane Daily Chronicle* (Spokane, WA), Apr. 29, 1943.

18 "Eddie Rochester Anderson, 71, Dies," *Daytona Beach Morning* (Daytona Beach, FL), Mar. 1, 1977.

19 "The One Hundred Richest Negroes," *Ebony* (Chicago, IL), May 1962.

20 "Rochester Designs Own Speedster," *Popular Mechanics* (New York, NY), June 1951.

21 "Rochester Has Real Trouble: Son Arrested," *Ocala Star-Banner* (Ocala, Saskatchewan), Jul. 27, 1956.

22 "Eddie Rochester Anderson Comedian Actor, Hollywood Broadway Star 1905-1977," *Baltimore Afro-American* (Baltimore, MA), Jan. 1, 1985.

23 "Rochester, Jack Benny Reunited," *Washington Afro-American* (Washington D.C.), Nov. 12, 1968.

24 Donald Bogle, *Bright Boulevards Bold Dreams: The Story of Black Hollywood* (New York: One World Ballantine Books, 2006), p. 432.

25 "The Eddie Rochester Anderson Foundation," May 18, 2012, *http://www.teraf.org/*.

26 "Premiere Show," *The Jack Benny Program* (1950; Los Angeles: CBS), Television.

EVE ARDEN

1 Bob Thomas, "Eve Arden More Hep Than 'Miss Brooks,'" *The Miami News* (Miami, FL), June 23, 1954.

2 Lloyd Shearer, "All About Eve Arden," *Boston Globe* (Boston, MA), Oct. 28, 1962.

3 Ibid.

4 Liza Wilson, "Teacher's Pet," *The Milwaukee Sentinel* (Milwaukee, WI), Oct. 17, 1953.

5 Eve Arden, *The Three Phases of Eve* (New York: St. Martin's Press, 1985), p. 2.

6 Ibid, p. 11.

7 Ibid, p. 15.

8 Tony Fontana, "Eve Arden," *Internet Movie Database*, Apr. 23, 2012, *http://www.imdb.com/name/nm0000781/*.

9 "Eve Arden Is Long Past Typecasting as Miss Brooks," *The Milwaukee Journal* (Milwaukee, WI), Feb. 11, 1983.

10 Ibid.

11 Eve Arden, *The Three Phases of Eve* (New York: St. Martin's Press, 1985), p. 34.

12 Liza Wilson, "Teacher's Pet," *The Milwaukee Sentinel* (Milwaukee, WI), Oct. 17, 1953.

13 Lloyd Shearer, "All About Eve Arden," *Boston Globe* (Boston, MA), Oct. 28, 1962.

14 *Stage Door*, DVD, Dir.: Gregory La Cava, Perf.: Katharine Hepburn, Ginger Rogers, Andrea Leeds (1937; Hollywood: RKO, 2005), Film.

15 Percy Shain, "Eve Arden Is Back!," *Boston Globe* (Boston, MA), Jul. 23, 1967.

16 Eve Arden, *The Three Phases of Eve* (New York: St. Martin's Press, 1985), p. 45.

17 *Mildred Pierce,* DVD, Dir.: Michael Curtiz, Perf.: Joan Crawford, Ann Blyth, Jack Carson (1945; Hollywood: Warner Brothers, 2005), Film.

18 Ibid.

19 Virginia MacPherson, "Eve Arden's Wisecrack Roles Beginning to Pall," *St. Petersburg Times* (St. Petersburg, FL), Oct. 18, 1945.

20 Eve Arden, *The Three Phases of Eve* (New York: St. Martin's Press, 1985), p. 63.

21 Ibid, p. 66.

22 Lloyd Shearer, "All About Eve Arden," *Boston Globe* (Boston, MA), Oct. 28, 1962.

23 Tony Fontana, "Eve Arden," *Internet Movie Database,* Apr. 23, 2012, *http://www.imdb.com/ name/nm0000781/.*

24 Tony Fontana, "Eve Arden," *Internet Movie Database,* Apr. 23, 2012, *http://www.imdb.com/ name/nm0000781/.*

25 Percy Shain, "Eve Arden Is Back!," *Boston Globe* (Boston, MA), Jul. 23, 1967.

26 Eve Arden, *The Three Phases of Eve* (New York: St. Martin's Press, 1985), p. 140.

27 Aline Mosby, "Eve Arden Says World Needs More Grin and Less Grim," *The Deseret News* (Salt Lake City, UT), Dec. 31, 1950.

28 Ibid.

29 Lloyd Shearer, "All About Eve Arden," *Boston Globe* (Boston, MA), Oct. 28, 1962.

30 Percy Shain, "Eve Arden Is Back!," *Boston Globe* (Boston, MA), Jul. 23, 1967.

31 Eve Arden, *The Three Phases of Eve* (New York: St. Martin's Press, 1985), p. 218.

32 Ibid, p. 243.

33 Ibid, p. 280.

FAY BAINTER

1 " 'The Kissing Bandit' Is on for a Run." *New York Times* (New York, NY), May 10, 1918.

2 Fay Bainter, "Christmases I Have Known," *New York Times* (New York, NY), Dec. 21, 1918.

3 Ibid.

4 Ibid.

5 Rodney Lee, "Fay Bainter," *New York Times* (New York, NY), Oct. 2, 1916.

6 " 'The Willow Tree' A Thing of Beauty," *New York Times* (New York, NY), Mar. 7, 1917.

7 "'The Kissing Bandit' Is on for a Run." *New York Times* (New York, NY), May 10, 1918.

8 Fay Bainter, "Christmases I Have Known," *New York Times* (New York, NY), Dec. 21, 1918.

9 "Sympathize with Venable," *New York Times* (New York, NY), Aug. 27, 1920.

10 James Robert Parish and Ronald Bowers, *The M-G-M Stock Company* (New York: Bonanza Books, 1972), p. 47.

11 Ibid, p. 46.

12 *Jezebel,* DVD, Dir.: William Wyler, Perf.: Bette Davis, Henry Fonda, and Fay Bainter (1938; Hollywood: Warner Bros. 2000), Film.

13 Sheilah Graham, "Fay Bainter Wants to Be 'Bad Woman,'" The Hartford Courant (Hartford, CT), Jul. 1, 1938.

14 James Robert Parish and Ronald Bowers, The M-G-M Stock Company (New York: Bonanza Books, 1972), p. 48.

15 Molly Haskell, "Oscar Films/Actresses: Where Have You Gone Joan Blondell and Fay Bainter?" New York Times (New York, NY), Mar. 4, 2001.

16 "Fay Bainter Craves Crayfish," The Milwaukee Sentinel (Milwaukee, WI), Feb. 18, 1955.

17 Ibid.

18 Woman of the Year, DV, Dir.: George Stevens. Perf.: Spencer Tracy, Katharine Hepburn, and Fay Bainter (1942; Hollywood: M-G-M, 2000), Film.

19 Rick Cooney (nephew of Fay Bainter), interview by Sara Brideson, Sep. 8, 2011.

CHARLES BICKFORD

1 Charles Bickford, Bulls, Balls, Bicycles, and Actors (New York: Paul S. Eriksson, Inc., 1965), p. viii.

2 Ibid, p. 3.

3 Ibid, p. 4.

4 Ibid, p. 9.

5 Ibid, p. 19.

6 Ibid, p. 26.

7 "Charles Bickford," Internet Movie Database, Mar. 15, 2012, http://www.imdb.com/name/ nm0001948/.

8 Charles Bickford, Bulls, Balls, Bicycles, and Actors (New York: Paul S. Eriksson, Inc., 1965), p. 47.

9 Ibid, p. 54.

10 Ibid, p. 87.

11 Ibid, p. 91.

12 Ibid, p. 138.

13 Ibid, p. 143.

14 "Charles Bickford," Internet Movie Database, Mar. 15, 2012, http://www.imdb.com/name/ nm0001948/.

15 Charles Bickford, Bulls, Balls, Bicycles, and Actors (New York: Paul S. Eriksson, Inc., 1965), p. 154.

16 Ibid, p. 252.

17 Ibid, p. 253.

18 "Charles Bickford Likes to Choose His Own Roles," Daily Boston Globe (Boston, MA), Jan. 15, 1933.

19 Charles Bickford, Bulls, Balls, Bicycles, and Actors (New York: Paul S. Eriksson, Inc., 1965), p. 253.

20 Ibid, p. 268.

21 Ibid, p. 276.

22 Grace Turner, "He Likes His Meals Square," *The Milwaukee Journal* (Milwaukee, WI), May 15, 1938.

23 Ibid, p. 294.

24 Ibid, p. 307.

25 Charles Bickford, *Bulls, Balls, Bicycles, and Actors* (New York: Paul S. Eriksson, Inc., 1965), p. 308.

26 Bob Thomas, "Bickford Bids Stars Act Ages," *The Evening Independent* (St. Petersburg, FL), Feb. 28, 1949.

27 "Older Women Want to See Older Stars Make Love in the Movies," *The Daily Times* (Rochester, PA), Feb. 22, 1946.

28 Gene Handsaker, "Charles Bickford Refuses to Quit Work in Movies," *Reading Eagle* (Reading, PA), Aug. 4, 1966.

29 " 'Get Rid of the In-Between Pictures,' Says Bickford," *Daily Boston Globe* (Boston, MA), Jul. 22, 1956.

30 Gene Handsaker, "Charles Bickford Refuses to Quit Work in Movies," *Reading Eagle* (Reading, PA), Aug. 4, 1966.

31 Rick Du Brow, "Charles Bickford, Actor, One Man to Remember," *The Press-Courier* (Oxnard, CA), Nov. 10, 1967.

32 "Actor Bickford Asked There Be No Services," *The Lewiston Daily Sun* (Lewiston, MN), Nov. 11, 1967.

33 Charles Bickford, *Bulls, Balls, Bicycles, and Actors* (New York: Paul S. Eriksson, Inc., 1965), p. 3.

34 "Actor Bickford Asked There Be No Services," *The Lewiston Daily Sun* (Lewiston, MN), Nov. 11, 1967.

JOAN BLONDELL

1 "Dick Powell, Joan Blondell Reach End of the Road," *Miami News* (Miami, FL), Jan. 4, 1944.

2 Matthew Kennedy, *Joan Blondell: A Life Between Takes* (Jackson, MS: University Press of Mississippi, 2007), p. 5.

3 Ibid, p. 6.

4 Charles Higham, "Joanie's Still Bright, Brash and Blondell," *New York Times* (New York, NY), Aug. 20, 1972.

5 Matthew Kennedy, *Joan Blondell: A Life Between Takes* (Jackson, MS: University Press of Mississippi, 2007), p. 6.

6 Ibid, p. 20.

7 Ibid, p. 200.

8 *Gold Diggers of 1933,* DVD, Dir.: Busby Berkely, Perf.: Ruby Keeler, Dick Powell, and Joan Blondell (1933; Hollywood: Warner Brothers, 2006), Film.

9 Matthew Kennedy, *Joan Blondell: A Life Between Takes* (Jackson, MS: University Press of Mississippi, 2007), p. 47.

10 Ibid, p. 71.

11 *Dames,* DVD, Dir.: Busby Berkeley, Perf.: Dick Powell, Joan Blondell, and Ruby Keeler (1934; Hollywood: Warner Brothers, 2006), Film.

12   Matthew Kennedy, *Joan Blondell: A Life Between Takes* (Jackson, MS: University Press of Mississippi, 2007), p. 63.

13   Ibid, p. 126.

14   Ibid, p. 136.

15   Ibid, p. 144.

16   Ibid, p. 153.

17   Ibid, p. 157.

18   Ibid, p. 159.

19   *Desk Set*, Dir.: Walter Lang, Perf.: Spencer Tracy, Katharine Hepburn, and Joan Blondell (1957; Hollywood: 20th Century Fox, 2004), Film.

20   Matthew Kennedy, *Joan Blondell: A Life Between Takes* (Jackson, MS: University Press of Mississippi, 2007), p. 169.

21   Charles Higham, "Joanie's Still Bright, Brash and Blondell," *New York Times* (New York, NY), Aug. 20, 1972.

22   Ibid, p. 216.

23   Ibid, p. 231.

24   Ibid, p. 220.

ERIC BLORE

1   Mayme Ober Peak, "Need a Butler? Call Eric Blore," *Boston Globe* (Boston, MA), Apr. 17, 1939.

2   William McPeak, "Eric Blore," *Internet Movie Database*, Feb. 2, 2012, *http://www.imdb.com/name/nm0089314/*.

3   Mayme Ober Peak, "Need a Butler? Call Eric Blore," *Boston Globe* (Boston, MA), Apr. 17, 1939.

4   Ibid.

5   Ibid.

6   Ibid.

7   "Stage Life of Eric Blore," *Boston Globe* (Boston, MA), Apr. 1, 1928.

8   Mayme Ober Peak, "Need a Butler? Call Eric Blore," *Boston Globe* (Boston, MA), Apr. 17, 1939.

9   Ibid.

10   "The Merry Makers," *Wairarapa Daily* (Wairarapa, New Zealand), Aug. 13, 1908.

11   "Stage Life of Eric Blore," *Boston Globe* (Boston, MA), Apr. 1, 1928.

12   Ibid.

13   Ibid.

14   William McPeak, "Eric Blore," *Internet Movie Database*, Feb. 2, 2012, *http://www.imdb.com/name/nm0089314/*.

15   Mayme Ober Peak, "Need a Butler? Call Eric Blore," *Boston Globe* (Boston, MA), Apr. 17, 1939.

16   "Eric Blore," *Internet Broadway Database*, Feb. 5, 2012, *http://ibdb.com/person.php?id=32335*.

17 William McPeak, "Eric Blore," *Internet Movie Database,* Feb. 2, 2012, *http://www.imdb.com/name/nm0089314/.*

18 Ibid.

19 *Top Hat,* DVD, Dir.: Mark Sandrich, Perf.: Fred Astaire, Ginger Rogers, Edward Everett Horton (1935; Hollywood, RKO, 2005), Film.

20 Ginger Rogers, *Ginger: My Story* (New York: HarperCollins, 1991), p. 165.

21 *Shall We Dance,* DVD, Dir.: Mark Sandrich, Perf.: Fred Astaire, Ginger Rogers, Edward Everett Horton (1937; Hollywood, RKO, 2005) , Film.

22 Miriam Bell, "For Your Amusement," *The Miami News* (Miami, FL), Aug. 24, 1936.

23 Jimmie Fiddler, "Idol Chatter," *St. Petersburg Times* (St. Petersburg, FL), Apr. 5, 1939.

24 Mayme Ober Peak, "Need a Butler? Call Eric Blore," *Boston Globe* (Boston, MA), Apr. 17, 1939.

25 Ibid.

26 Ibid.

27 "Arthur Treacher, Eric Blore not bonafide butlers," *The Dispatch* (Lexington, NC), Nov. 22, 1974.

28 Ibid.

29 Molly Merrick, "Hollywood in Person," *The Milwaukee Journal* (Milwaukee, WI), Nov. 15, 1935.

30 Mayme Ober Peak, "Need a Butler? Call Eric Blore," *Boston Globe* (Boston, MA), Apr. 17, 1939.

31 "Eric Blore," *Internet Broadway Database,* Feb. 5, 2012, *http://ibdb.com/person.php?id=32335.*

32 "Marriage of Son Ended After 10 Days," *Los Angeles Times* (Los Angeles, CA), Apr. 2, 1954.

33 William McPeak, "Eric Blore," *Internet Movie Database,* Feb. 2, 2012, *http://www.imdb.com/name/nm0089314/.*

34 Miriam Bell, "For Your Amusement," *The Miami News* (Miami, FL), Aug. 24, 1936.

RAY BOLGER

1 "Ray Bolger, Last of Oz Foursome, Dies," *The Miami News* (Miami, FL), Jan. 16, 1987.

2 Paul F. Kneeland, "Ray Bolger Was a Timid Male Wallflower at Dorchester High Senior Prom," *Daily Boston Globe* (Boston, MA), Jul. 24, 1949.

3 "Where's Raymond? (1953)," *Internet Movie Database,* Apr. 3, 2012, *http://www.imdb.com/title/tt0045455/.*

4 Aljean Harmetz, *The Making of The Wizard of Oz* (New York: Tralfalgar Square, 1989), p. 114.

5 Paul F. Kneeland, "Ray Bolger Was a Timid Male Wallflower at Dorchester High Senior Prom," *Daily Boston Globe* (Boston, MA), Jul. 24, 1949.

6 Ibid.

7 Aljean Harmetz, *The Making of The Wizard of Oz* (New York: Tralfalgar Square, 1989), p. 114.

8 Harold Heffernan, "Ray Bolger Has Parental Advice," *The Pittsburgh Press* (Pittsburgh, PA), Jun. 28, 1961.

9   William Keefe, "Public Acclaim Makes Ray Bolger New Star in Spite of Program," *Evening Independent* (St. Petersburg, FL), Apr. 16, 1936.

10   Paul F. Kneeland, "Ray Bolger Was a Timid Male Wallflower at Dorchester High Senior Prom," *Daily Boston Globe* (Boston, MA), Jul. 24, 1949.

11   "Informal Interview with Ray Bolger," *Daily Boston Globe* (Boston, MA), Mar. 22, 1936.

12   Ibid.

13   "Ray Bolger," *Turner Classic Movies*, Apr. 2, 2012, *http://www.tcm.com/tcmdb/person/18584%7C127645/Ray-Bolger/*.

14   Paul F. Kneeland, "Ray Bolger Was a Timid Male Wallflower at Dorchester High Senior Prom," *Daily Boston Globe* (Boston, MA), Jul. 24, 1949.

15   "Informal Interview with Ray Bolger," *Daily Boston Globe* (Boston, MA), Mar. 22, 1936.

16   Ibid.

17   Paul F. Kneeland, "Ray Bolger Was a Timid Male Wallflower at Dorchester High Senior Prom," *Daily Boston Globe* (Boston, MA), Jul. 24, 1949.

18   L. Frank Baum, *The Wonderful Wizard of Oz* (New York, NY: Scholastic, Inc., 1958), p. 20

19   *The Wizard of Oz*, DVD, Dir.: Victor Fleming, Perf.: Judy Gar;and, Ray Bolger, and Frank Morgan (1939; Hollywood: M-G-M, 1999), Film.

20   "Ray Bolger Stars in 'The Entertainer,'" *News and Courier* (Charleston, SC), Mar. 6, 1976.

21   "Where's Raymond? (1953)," *Internet Movie Database*, Apr. 3, 2012, *http://www.imdb.com/title/tt0045455/*.

22   "Cambridge Nurse Lauds Ray Bolger as Morale Builder," *Daily Boston Globe* (Boston, MA), Sep. 13, 1943.

23   "Where's Raymond? (1953)," *Internet Movie Database*, Apr. 3, 2012, *http://www.imdb.com/title/tt0045455/*.

24   "Where's Charley?," *Internet Movie Database*, May 4, 2012, *http://www.imdb.com/title/tt0045325/*.

25   Henry Ward, "Ray Bolger Top star of Stanley Feature," *The Pittsburgh Press* (Pittsburgh, PA), Aug. 16, 1952.

26   Ibid.

27   "Ray Bolger Stars in 'The Entertainer,'" *News and Courier* (Charleston, SC), Mar. 6, 1976.

28   ??????????????

29   "Where's Raymond? (1953)," *Internet Movie Database*, Apr. 3, 2012, *http://www.imdb.com/title/tt0045455/*.

30   *Look for the Silver Lining*, DVD, Dir.: David Butler, Perf.: June Haver, Ray Bolger, and Gordan MacRae (1949; Hollywood: Warner Brothers, 2010), Film.

BEULAH BONDI

1   Richard K. Shull, "Beulah Bondi Returns in Series on Lincoln," *Youngstown Vindicator* (Youngstown, OH), Jan. 10, 1976.

2   Ibid.

3   Jon C. Hopwood, "Beulah Bondi," *Internet Movie Database*, Jan. 21, 2011, *http://www.imdb.com/name/nm0094135/*.

4   Phil Potempka, "The Beloved Mother" in *It's a Wonderful Life: A Memory Book,* by Stephan Cox. (Nashville, TN: Cumberland House, 2003), p. 63.

5   Ibid, p. 63.

6   Ibid, p. 63.

7   Ibid, p. 62.

8   "A Five-time mom to Jimmy Stewart, actress Beulah Bondi is a vital 87," *The Lewiston Journal* (Lewiston, MN), Mar. 15, 1980.

9   Jeanine Basinger, *The 'It's a Wonderful Life' Book* (New York, NY: Knopf, 1986), p. 82.

10 Ibid, p. 82.

11 "A Five-time mom to Jimmy Stewart, actress Beulah Bondi is a vital 87," *The Lewiston Journal* (Lewiston, MN), Mar. 15, 1980.

12 *Make Way for Tomorrow,* DVD, Dir.: Leo McCarey, Perf.: Victor Moore, Beulah Bondi, Fay Bainter (1937, Hollywood: Paramount Studio, 2010) Film.

13 Jon C. Hopwood, "Beulah Bondi," *Internet Movie Database,* Jan. 21, 2011, *http://www.imdb. com/name/nm0094135/.*

14 Phil Potempka, "The Beloved Mother" in *It's a Wonderful Life: a Memory Book,* by Stephan Cox. (Nashville, TN: Cumberland House, 2003), p. 67.

15 *It's a Wonderful Life,* DVD, Dir.: Frank Capra, Perf.: James Stewart, Donna Reed, Lionel Barrymore (1946, Hollywood: Republic Pictures, 2006), Film.

16 Richard K. Shull, "Beulah Bondi Returns in Series on Lincoln," *Youngstown Vindicator* (Youngstown, OH), Jan. 10, 1976.

17 Ibid.

18 Phil Potempka, "The Beloved Mother" in *It's a Wonderful Life: a Memory Book,* by Stephan Cox. (Nashville, TN: Cumberland House, 2003), p. 67.

19 Ibid, p. 67.

20 Ibid, p. 67.

21 "A Five-time mom to Jimmy Stewart, actress Beulah Bondi is a vital 87," *The Lewiston Journal* (Lewiston, MN), Mar. 15, 1980.

22 Jon C. Hopwood, "Beulah Bondi," *Internet Movie Database,* Jan. 21, 2011, *http://www.imdb. com/name/nm0094135/*

BILLIE BURKE

1   L. Frank Baum, *The Wonderful Wizard of Oz* (New York, NY: Scholastic, Inc., 1958), p. 150.

2   Billie Burke, *With a Feather on My Nose* (New York, NY: P. Davies, 1948), p. 47.

3   Grant Hayter-Menzies, *Mrs. Ziegfeld* (Jefferson, NC: MacFarland Press, 2009), p. 35.

4   Bernard Sobel, *Broadway Heartbeat* (New York, NY: Hermitage House, 1953), p. 113.

5   Billie Burke, "Temperament Is Essential," *New York Times* (New York, NY), Nov. 8, 1908.

6   Billie Burke, *With a Feather on My Nose,* (New York, NY: P. Davies, 1948), p. 120.

7   Bernard Sobel, *Broadway Heartbeat* (New York, NY: Hermitage House, 1953), p. 113.

8   Patricia Ziegfeld, *The Ziegfelds' Girl* (New York: Little Brown and Co., 1964).

9   Alexander Woollcott, "The Play," *New York Times* (New York, NY), Nov. 8, 1921.

10 Billie Burke, *With a Feather on My Nose* (New York, NY: P. Davies, 1948), p. 248.

11 Charles Higham, *Ziegfeld* (New York, NY: Regenery, 1972), p. 223.

12 Billie Burke, *With a Feather on My Nose,* (New York, NY: P. Davies, 1948), p. 250-51.

13 Billie Burke, *With Powder on My Nose* (New York, NY: Coward-McCann, 1959), p. 22.

14 *Dinner at Eight,* Video, Dir.: George Cukor, Perf.: Jean Harlow, John Barrymore, Billie Burke (1933; Hollywood: M-G-M, 1997), Film.

15 *Merrily We Live,* Video, Dir.: Norman Z. MacLeod, Perf.: Constance Bennett, Brian Aherne, and Billie Burke, (1938; Hollywood: M-G-M, 2011).

16 Grant Hayter-Menzies, *Mrs. Ziegfeld* (Jefferson, NC: MacFarland Press, 2009), p. 107.

17 Ibid, p. 204.

18 Ibid, p. 187.

19 Billie Burke, *With a Feather on My Nose* (New York, NY: P. Davies, 1948), p. 253.

20 Grant Hayter-Menzies, *Mrs. Ziegfeld* (Jefferson, NC: MacFarland Press, 2009), p. 203.

21 Ibid, p. 169.

SPRING BYINGTON

1 Charles Stumpf, "Spring Byington: Eternal Spring," Classic Images (Muscatine, IA), Jun. 2000.

2 Gary Brumburgh, "Spring Byington," Internet Movie Database, Nov. 30, 2011, *http://www. imdb.com/name/nm0001981/.*

3 Charles Mercer, "Spring Byington Offers Tips on Staying Young," Ocala Star-Banner (Ocala, FL), Oct. 20, 1958.

4 Charles Stumpf, "Spring Byington: Eternal Spring," Classic Images (Muscatine, IA), Jun. 2000.

5 Gary Brumburgh, "Spring Byington," Internet Movie Database, Nov. 30, 2011, *http://www. imdb.com/name/nm0001981/.*

6 Ibid.

7 "Spring Byington, Actress, Is Dead at 77," New York Times (New York, NY), Sep. 9, 1971.

8 Charles Stumpf, "Spring Byington: Eternal Spring," Classic Images (Muscatine, IA), Jun. 2000.

9 Gary Brumburgh, "Spring Byington," Internet Movie Database, Nov. 30, 2011, *http://www. imdb.com/name/nm0001981/.*

10 Charles Stumpf, "Spring Byington: Eternal Spring," Classic Images (Muscatine, IA), Jun. 2000.

11 "Be Your Age Has Moments of Gayety," New York Times (New York, NY), Feb. 5, 1929.

12 Charles Stumpf, "Spring Byington: Eternal Spring," Classic Images (Muscatine, IA), Jun. 2000.

13 You Can't Take It with You, DVD, Dir.: Frank Capra, Perf.: Lionel Barrymore, Jean Arthur, James Stewart (1938; Hollywood: Columbia, 2003), Film.

14 Charles Stumpf, "Spring Byington: Eternal Spring," Classic Images (Muscatine, IA), Jun. 2000.

15 "Picture Star Who Is Unmarried Proposes New Plan for Alimony," The Evening Independent (St. Petersburg, FL), Feb. 22, 1937.

16 Keith Stern, Queers in History (Dallas, Texas: BenBella Books, 2009), p. 83.

17 Boze Hadleigh, Hollywood Lesbians (New York: Barricade Books, 1994), p. 20.

18 Charles Stumpf, "Spring Byington: Eternal Spring," Classic Images (Muscatine, IA), Jun. 2000.

19 "The Grandfather Clock" in December Bride (1955; Hollywood, CA: Desilu Productions), Television.

20 "The Ecstatic December Bride," The Evening Independent (St. Petersburg, FL), Jun. 5, 1960.

21 Ibid.

22 Ibid.

23 Earl Wilson, "We Give Spring Byington Tips on Mother-in-Lawing," Pittsburgh Post Gazette (Pittsburgh, PA), Sept. 19, 1955.

24 Robert Peterson, "Spring Sparkles at 60-Plus," Sarasota Herald Tribune (Sarasota, FL), Dec. 27, 1958.

25 Ibid.

26 Gary Brumburgh, "Spring Byington," Internet Movie Database, Nov. 30, 2011, *http://www. imdb.com/name/nm0001981/.*

27 Charles Mercer, "Spring Byington Offers Tips on Staying Young," Ocala Star-Banner (Ocala, FL), Oct. 20, 1958.

28 Ibid.

29 Robert Peterson, "Spring Sparkles at 60-Plus," Sarasota Herald Tribune (Sarasota, FL), Dec. 27, 1958.

30 "The Ecstatic December Bride," The Evening Independent (St. Petersburg, FL), Jun. 5, 1960

CHARLES COBURN

1 Theodore Strauss, "A Man and His Monocle," *New York Times* (New York, NY), Jan. 18, 1942.

2 "Actor Charles Coburn Dies in New York," *The Evening Independent* (St. Petersburg, FL), Aug. 31, 1961.

3 Bob Thomas, "Coburn Reviews 60 Years," *The Evening Independent* (St. Petersburg, FL), Mar. 8, 1950.

4 Ibid.

5 "Charles Coburn," *Internet Broadway Database,* Mar. 20, 2012, *http://ibdb.com/person. php?id=14450.*

6 Theodore Strauss, "A Man and His Monocle," *New York Times* (New York, NY), Jan. 18, 1942.

7 Bob Thomas, "Coburn Reviews 60 Years," *The Evening Independent* (St. Petersburg, FL), Mar. 8, 1950.

8 Theodore Strauss, "A Man and His Monocle," *New York Times* (New York, NY), Jan. 18, 1942.

9 Bob Thomas, "Coburn Reviews 60 Years," *The Evening Independent* (St. Petersburg, FL), Mar. 8, 1950.

10 Ibid.

11 "Coburn Asserts Amateur Players Hope of Stage," *The Evening Independent* (St. Petersburg, FL), Jul. 8, 1941.

12 Hal Boyle, "Coburn Prove All Free Souls Are Not Youthful," *The Tuscaloosa News* (Tuscaloosa, AL), Apr. 13, 1953.

13 *The More the Merrier*, DVD, Dir.: George Stevens, Perf.: Jean Arthur, Joel McCrea, and Charles Coburn (1943; Hollywood: Columbia Pictures, 2004), Film.

14 "Coburn Wins Honor," *The Evening Independent* (St. Petersburg, FL), Mar. 3, 1944.

15 Hal Boyle, "Coburn Prove All Free Souls Are Not Youthful," *The Tuscaloosa News* (Tuscaloosa, AL), Apr. 13, 1953.

16 Bob Thomas, "Coburn Reviews 60 Years," *The Evening Independent* (St. Petersburg, FL), Mar. 8, 1950.

17 Theodore Strauss, "A Man and His Monocle," *New York Times* (New York, NY), Jan. 18, 1942.

18 Hal Boyle, "Coburn Prove All Free Souls Are Not Youthful," *The Tuscaloosa News* (Tuscaloosa, AL), Apr. 13, 1953.

19 Bob Thomas, "Charles Coburn Continues Drive to Aid Poker Players," *Reading Eagle* (Reading, PA), Oct. 16, 1951

20 Hal Boyle, "Coburn Prove All Free Souls Are Not Youthful," *The Tuscaloosa News* (Tuscaloosa, AL), Apr. 13, 1953.

21 Bob Thomas, "Charles Coburn Describes His Reactions to Monroe, Russell," *Reading Eagle* (Reading, PA), Dec. 16, 1952.

22 Ibid.

23 "Actor Charles Coburn Weds Pretty Widow," *Lodi News-Sentinel* (Lodi, CA), Oct. 17, 1959.

24 "Come to My Funeral Smiling, Actor Coburn Wrote in Will," *The Tuscaloosa News* (Tuscaloosa, AL), Sep. 3, 1961.

25 Hal Boyle, "Coburn Prove All Free Souls Are Not Youthful," *The Tuscaloosa News* (Tuscaloosa, AL), Apr. 13, 1953.

26 *The More the Merrier*, DVD, Dir.: George Stevens, Perf.: Jean Arthur, Joel McCrea, and Charles Coburn (1943; Hollywood: Columbia Pictures, 2004), Film.

GLADYS COOPER

1 Sheridan Morley, *Gladys Cooper* (New York: McGraw-Hill Book Co., 1979), p. 113.

2 Betsy Von Furstenberg, "Gladys Cooper 1889-1971," *New York Times* (New York, NY), Nov. 28, 1971.

3 Sheridan Morley, *Gladys Cooper* (New York: McGraw-Hill Book Co., 1979), p. 280.

4 Ibid, p. 16.

5 Ibid, p. 10.

6 Ibid, p. 12.

7 Ibid, p. 71.

8 "Gladys Cooper, British Actress, Dies," *New York Times* (New York, NY), Nov. 18, 1971.

9 "Actress Gets Damages," *New York Times* (New York, NY), Jan. 13, 1915.

10 Sheridan Morley, *Gladys Cooper* (New York: McGraw-Hill Book Co., 1979), p. 76.

11 Ibid, p. 77.

12 Ibid, p. 89.

13 Ibid, p. 80.

14 "Gladys Cooper," *Wikipedia*, Mar. 3, 2012, *http://en.wikipedia.org/wiki/Gladys_Cooper.*

15 Ibid, 144.

16 Ibid, p. xx.

17 "Actress Surprised on Arrival in City," *Montreal Gazette* (Montreal, Quebec), Nov. 21, 1938.

18 Sheridan Morley, *Gladys Cooper* (New York: McGraw-Hill Book Co., 1979), p. 162.

19 Bob Thomas, "Gladys Cooper Stays Busy at 74," *The Telegraph* (Nashua, NH), Aug. 30, 1966.

20 Betsy Von Furstenberg, "Gladys Cooper 1889-1971," *New York Times* (New York, NY), Nov. 28, 1971.

21 Sheridan Morley, *Gladys Cooper* (New York: McGraw-Hill Book Co., 1979), p. 213.

22 Ibid, p. 191.

23 *Now, Voyager,* DVD, Dir.: Irving Rapper, Perf.: Bette Davis, Paul Henreid, and Claude Rains (1942; Hollywood: Warner Bros., 2005), Film.

24 Ibid, p. 217.

25 Ibid, p. 243.

26 Ibid, p. 254.

27 *My Fair Lady,* DVD, Dir.: George Cukor, Perf.: Audrey Hepburn, Rex Harrison and Gladys Cooper (1964; Hollywood: Warner Bros., 2009), Film.

28 Sheridan Morley, *Gladys Cooper* (New York: McGraw-Hill Book Co., 1979), p. 268.

29 Ibid, p. 283.

30 Ibid, p. 286.

31 "Gladys Cooper, British Actress, Dies," *New York Times* (New York, NY), Nov. 18, 1971.

32 Ibid, p. 63.

33 "Gladys Cooper, British Actress, Dies," *New York Times* (New York, NY), Nov. 18, 1971.

HARRY DAVENPORT

1 "Harry Davenport, Veteran Actor, 83," *New York Times* (New York, NY), Aug. 10, 1949.

2 Ken Dennis, "Harry Davenport: Grand Old Man of the Golden Age," *Films of the Golden Age* (Muscatine, IA), Fall 2009.

3 Ibid.

4 Ibid.

5 "Dramatic and Musical," *New York Times* (New York, NY), Jan. 8, 1901.

6 Ken Dennis, "Harry Davenport: Grand Old Man of the Golden Age," *Films of the Golden Age* (Muscatine, IA), Fall 2009.

7 Ibid.

8 "Methodist Pastor OK's Theater Going," *New York Times* (New York, NY), Jan. 1, 1922.

9 Ken Dennis, "Harry Davenport: Grand Old Man of the Golden Age," *Films of the Golden Age* (Muscatine, IA), Fall 2009.

10 Ibid.

11 Ibid.

12 *Gone With the Wind,* Video, Dir.: Victor Fleming, Perf.: Clark Gable, Vivien Leigh, and Thomas Mitchell, (1939; Hollywood: Selznick International Pictures, 1998), Film.

13 Ibid.

14 "Harry Davenport, Veteran Actor, 83," *New York Times* (New York, NY), Aug. 10, 1949.

15 *Meet Me in St. Louis,* Video, Dir.: Vincent Minnelli, Perf.: Judy Garland, Margaret O'Brien, Mary Astor (1944, Hollywood: M-G-M, 1944), Film.

16 Rita Piro, *Judy Garland: The Golden Years* (New York, NY: Great Feats Press, 2001), p. 154.

17 Elizabeth Pallette, "A Trip to the Actors' Hobby Mart," *New York Times* (New York, NY), Jan. 23, 1949.

18 "Harry Davenport: Noted Character Actor Has Long Career," *Toledo Blade* (Toledo, OH), Aug. 10, 1949.

19 *King's Row,* DVD, Dir.: Sam Wood, Perf.: Ann Sheridan, Robert Cummings, and Ronald Reagan, (1942; Hollywood: Warner Brothers, 2006), Film.

JAMES GLEASON

1 "James Gleason — His Struggles and Emergence," *New York Times* (New York, NY), Jan. 18, 1925.

2 "James Gleason," *The Internet Movie Database,* Feb. 20, 2012,

3 "Hard-Boiled Mr. Gleason," *New York Times* (New York, NY), Aug. 3, 1941.

4 Ibid.

5 "Hard-Boiled Mr. Gleason," *New York Times* (New York, NY), Aug. 3, 1941.

6 "Author Needs to Know Slang," *Boston Daily Globe* (Boston, MA), Aug, 23, 1925.

7 "James Gleason, Actor, 72, Dead," *New York Times* (New York, NY), Apr. 14, 1959.

8 "James Gleason — His Struggles and Emergence," *New York Times* (New York, NY), Jan. 18, 1925.

9 "Author Needs to Know Slang," *Boston Daily Globe* (Boston, MA), Aug, 23, 1925.

10 Arthur Kober, "Mr. Gleason Talks it Over," *New York Times* (New York, NY), Oct. 2, 1927.

11 Ibid.

12 "Hard-Boiled Mr. Gleason," *New York Times* (New York, NY), Aug. 3, 1941.

13 Ibid.

14 Ibid.

15 "Hollywood Defended by James Gleason," *Spokane Daily Chronicle* (Spokane, WA), Jun. 4, 1947.

16 Matme Ober Peak, "Lucile and Jimmy Gleason Celebrate 25th Anniversary," *Daily Boston Globe* (Boston, MA), Sep. 23, 1931.

17 Ibid.

18 "James Gleason, Actor, 72, Dead," *New York Times* (New York, NY), Apr. 14, 1959.

19 *The Clock,* Video, Dir.: Vincente Minnelli, Perf.: Judy Garland, Robert Walker, and James Gleason (1945; Hollywood: M-G-M, 1992), Film.

20 Ibid.

21 Film Actor's Son Plunges to Death," *The Miami News* (Miami, FL), Dec. 26, 1945.

22 "James Gleason, Actor, 72, Dead," *New York Times* (New York, NY), Apr. 14, 1959.

23 "Hard-Boiled Mr. Gleason," *New York Times* (New York, NY), Aug. 3, 1941.

MARGARET HAMILTON

1 John P. Shanley, "Voice of Emily Tipp," *New York Times* (New York, NY), Mar. 27, 1960.

2 Ibid.

3 Ibid.

4 Howard Thompson, "The 'Oz' Witch Recalls a Happy Time," *New York Times* (New York, NY), Mar. 14, 1979.

5 Aljean Harmetz, *The Making of The Wizard of Oz* (New York: Trafalgar Square, 1989), p. 12.

6 Ibid, p. 124.

7 " 'Wicked Witch' Recalls Role," *Youngstown Vindicator* (Youngstown, Ohio), Dec. 18, 1978.

8 "Wicked Witch of West — Today," *The Leader Post* (Regina, Saskatchewan), Dec. 5, 1977.

9 *Nothing Sacred*, DVD, Dir.: William Wellman, Perf.: Fredric March, Carole Lombard, and Charles Winninger (1937; Hollywood: Selznick International Pictures, 2011), Film.

10 Howard Thompson, "The 'Oz' Witch Recalls a Happy Time," *New York Times* (New York, NY), Mar. 14, 1979.

11 Aljean Harmetz, *The Making of The Wizard of Oz* (New York: Trafalgar Square, 1989), p. 123.

12 L. Frank Baum, *The Wonderful Wizard of Oz* (New York, NY: Scholastic, Inc., 1958), p. 80

13 Aljean Harmetz, *The Making of The Wizard of Oz* (New York: Trafalgar Square, 1989), p. 162.

14 Ibid, p. 162.

15 Ibid, p. 162.

16 Ibid, p. 274.

17 Ibid, p. 277.

18 "Wicked Witch of West — Today," *The Leader Post* (Regina, Saskatchewan), Dec. 5, 1977.

19 "Margaret Hamilton, 'Oz' Witch Is Dead," *The Evening Independent* (St. Petersburg, FL), May 17, 1985.

20 "One-Woman Show Set," *New York Times* (New York, NY), Jun. 1, 1959.

21 "Wicked Witch of West — Today," *The Leader Post* (Regina, Saskatchewan), Dec. 5, 1977.

22 "Cora Pours Her Last Drop as Young Coffee Drinkers Take Over," *St. Petersburg Times* (St. Petersburg, FL), Dec. 29, 1979.

23 Margaret Hamilton, "Porpoises Under Peril," *New York Times* (New York NY), Dec. 13, 1980.

24 "Wicked Witch of West — Today," *The Leader Post* (Regina, Saskatchewan), Dec. 5, 1977.

25 Henrietta Leith, "Cagney Misses Star-studded Tribute," *The Lewiston Journal* (Lewiston, ME), Sep. 24, 1983.

26 "Margaret Hamilton, 'Oz' Witch Is Dead," *The Evening Independent* (St. Petersburg, FL), May 17, 1985.

27 Cynthia Lowry, "She Has Ridden Many a Broomstick Since 'Oz'," *Ocala Star-Banner* (Ocala, FL), Dec. 22, 1959.

EDWARD EVERETT HORTON

1 "Fluttery Master of Comedy Horton Dead at 84," *Montreal Gazette* (Montreal, Quebec), Oct. 1, 1970.

2 "Edward Everett Horton," *Internet Movie Database*, Nov. 15, 2011, *http://www.imdb.com/ name/nm0002143/.*

3 Hedda Hopper, "Stars Don't Fade Away," *The News-Courier* (Athens, AL), May 30, 1965.

4 Ibid.

5 Bob Thomas, "Edward Everett Horton: 50 Years of Sly Tricks," *Evening Independent* (Massillon, OH), June 13, 1960.

6 "It's Edward Everett Horton 'Cause Eddie Has His Reasons," *Rochester Journal* (Rochester, NY), May 5, 1936.

7 Eve Golden, *Bride of Golden Image* (Albany, GA: BearManor Media, 2009), p. 80.

8 Bob Thomas, "Edward Everett Horton's Mansion Has Great Charm," *The Owosso Argus-Press* (Owosso, MI), Oct. 9, 1962.

9 Hedda Hopper, "Stars Don't Fade Away," *The News and Courier* (Athens, AL), May 30, 1965.

10 Ibid.

11 "The Meek Do Inherit the Earth," *The Milwaukee Journal* (Milwaukee, WI), Sep. 6, 1931.

12 Bob Thomas, "Edward Everett Horton: 50 Years of Sly Tricks," *Evening Independent* (Massillon, OH), June 13, 1960.

13 "The Meek Do Inherit the Earth," *The Milwaukee Journal* (Milwaukee, WI), Sep. 6, 1931.

14 Henry Hewes, "Mr. Dewlip of 'Springtime'," *New York Times* (New York, NY), Mar. 11, 1951.

15 Donald Deschner, *The Complete Films of Cary Grant, (*New York: Citadel Press, 1991) p. 77.

16 Ginger Rogers, *Ginger: My Story* (New York: HarperCollins, 1991), p. 165.

17 Eve Golden, *Bride of Golden Images,* (Albany, GA: BearManor Media, 2009), p. 114.

18 *The Gay Divorcee*, Video, Dir.: Mark Sandrich, Perf.: Fred Astaire, Ginger Rogers, and Edward Everett Horton (1934; Hollywood: RKO, 2006), Film.

19 Bob Thomas. "Edward Everett Horton: 50 Years of Sly Tricks," *Evening Independent* (Massillon, OH), June 13, 1960.

20 "Fluttery Master of Comedy Horton Dead at 84," *Montreal Gazette* (Montreal, Quebec), Oct. 1, 1970.

21 "Edward Everett Horton Will Play Lead in Rib-Tickling 'Springtime for Henry'," *St. Petersburg Times* (St. Petersburg, FL), Feb. 19, 1950.

22 Hedda Hopper, "Stars Don't Fade Away," *The News and Courier* (Athens, AL), May 30, 1965.

23 Henry Hewes. "Mr. Dewlip of 'Springtime'," *New York Times* (New York, NY), Mar. 11,. 1951.

24 "Edward Everett Horton Will Play Lead in Rib-Tickling 'Springtime for Henry'," *St. Petersburg Times* (St. Petersburg, FL), Feb. 19, 1950.

25 Hedda Hopper, "Stars Don't Fade Away," *The News and Courier* (Athens, AL), May 30, 1965.

26 Henry Hewes, "Mr. Dewlip of 'Springtime'," *New York Times* (New York, NY), Mar. 11, 1951.

PATSY KELLY

1   Mollie Merrick, "Hollywood in Person," *The Sunday Morning Star* (Wilmington, DE), Aug, 25, 1935.

2   Ibid.

3   Charles Stumpf, "Patsy Kelly: Ugly Duckling with an Enlarged Funny Bone," *Classic Images* (Muscatine, IA), March 1999.

4   Vernon Scott, "Patsy Kelly Recalls How She Was Almost Married to Faye," *Times Daily* (Tuscumbia, AL), Oct. 11, 1967.

5   Charles Stumpf, "Patsy Kelly: Ugly Duckling with an Enlarged Funny Bone," *Classic Images* (Muscatine, IA), March 1999.

6   Ibid.

7   Bob Thomas, "Patsy Kelly, Wise-Cracker, Finally Back in Movies," *Reading Eagle* (Reading, PA), Nov. 26, 1959.

8   Ruth White, "Humor Will Go as Far as Beauty in Hollywood," *Eugene Register-Guard* (Eugene, OR), May 1, 1937.

9   Charles Stumpf, "Patsy Kelly: Ugly Duckling with an Enlarged Funny Bone," *Classic Images* (Muscatine, IA), March 1999.

10 Ibid.

11 "Patsy Kelly, 'North St. Irregulars'," *The Evening News* (Newburgh, NY), Feb. 11, 1979.

12 Harold Heffernan, "Stop Worrying, Eat Anything Is Patsy's Creed," *The Milwaukee Journal* (Milwaukee, WS), May 2, 1937.

13 "Patsy Kelly, 'North St. Irregulars'," *The Evening News* (Newburgh, NY), Feb. 11, 1979.

14 *The Girl from Missouri*, DVD, dir. Jack Conway, perf. Jean Harlow, Franchot Tone, and Patsy Kelly (1934; Hollywood, CA: M-G-M, 2011), Film.

15 Harold Heffernan, "Stop Worrying, Eat Anything Is Patsy's Creed," *The Milwaukee Journal* (Milwaukee, WS), May 2, 1937.

16 Ibid.

17 Ruth White, "Humor Will Go as Far as Beauty in Hollywood," *Eugene Register-Guard* (Eugene, OR), May 1, 1937.

18 Charles Stumpf, "Patsy Kelly: Ugly Duckling with an Enlarged Funny Bone," *Classic Images* (Muscatine, IA), March 1999.

19 Earl Wilson, "Of All Stars Named Kelly, Patsy Ranks Among Best," *Toledo Blade* (Toledo, OH), Jul. 22, 1972.

20 Bob Thomas, "Patsy Kelly, Wise-Cracker, Finally Back in Movies," *Reading Eagle* (Reading, PA), Nov. 26, 1959.

21 "Patsy Kelly, 'North St. Irregulars'," *The Evening News* (Newburgh, NY), Feb. 11, 1979.

22 Charles Stumpf, "Patsy Kelly: Ugly Duckling with an Enlarged Funny Bone," *Classic Images* (Muscatine, IA), March 1999.

23 Bob Thomas, "Patsy Kelly, Wise-Cracker, Finally Back in Movies," *Reading Eagle* (Reading, PA), Nov. 26, 1959.

24 Ibid.

25 Earl Wilson, "Of All Stars Named Kelly, Patsy Ranks Among Best," *Toledo Blade* (Toledo, OH), Jul. 22, 1972.

26 Ruth White, "Humor Will Go as Far as Beauty in Hollywood," *Eugene Register-Guard* (Eugene, OR), May 1, 1937.

ELSA LANCHESTER

1   Elsa Lanchester, *Elsa Lanchester Herself* (New York: St. Martin's Press, 1983), p. 133.

2   Kevin Kelly, "It May Be Life, Elsa, But Dearie Ain't It Slow," *Boston Globe* (Boston, MA), Nov. 7, 1960.

3   "Elsa Proves It Pays to Be Unattractive," *Boston Globe* (Boston, MA), Sep. 8, 1968.

4   Arthur Gelb, "Theatre: Elsa Lanchester," *Boston Globe* (Boston, MA), Nov. 5, 1960.

5   Elsa Lanchester, *Elsa Lanchester Herself* (New York: St. Martin's Press, 1983), p. 14.

6   Arthur Gelb, "Theatre: Elsa Lanchester," *Boston Globe* (Boston, MA), Nov. 5, 1960.

7   Elsa Lanchester, *Elsa Lanchester Herself* (New York: St. Martin's Press, 1983), p. 57.

8   William McPeak, "Elsa Lanchester," *Internet Movie Database*, Mar. 25, 2012, *http://www. imdb.com/name/nm0006471/*.

9   Elsa Lanchester, *Elsa Lanchester Herself* (New York: St. Martin's Press, 1983), p. 83.

10 Ibid, p. 115.

11 Ibid, p. 128.

12 Bob Thomas, "Key For Movie Marriages: More Fame For Husband," *Sarasota Herald-Tribune* (Saratoga, FL), Dec. 26, 1946.

13 Elsa Lanchester, *Elsa Lanchester Herself* (New York: St. Martin's Press, 1983), p. 133.

14 Olga Curtis, "Elsa Dislikes Crowds, Garlic, Togetherness," *Boston Globe* (Boston, MA), Apr. 23, 1961.

15 "Elsa Lanchester Can Make Things Sound Quite Naughty," *Lewiston Morning-Tribune* (Lewiston, ID), Mar. 12, 1961.

16 "Elsa Lanchester Can Make Things Sound Quite Naughty," *Lewiston Morning-Tribune* (Lewiston, ID), Mar. 12, 1961.

17 *Witness for the Prosecution*, DVD, Dir.: Billy Wilder, Perf.: Charles Laughton, Tyrone Power, Marlene Dietrich (1957; Hollywood: M-G-M, 2001), Film.

18 Ibid.

19 Arthur Gelb, "Theatre: Elsa Lanchester," *Boston Globe* (Boston, MA), Nov. 5, 1960.

20 Elsa Lanchester, *Elsa Lanchester Herself* (New York: St. Martin's Press, 1983), p. 331.

21 *That Darn Cat!*, DVD, Dir.: Robert Stevenson, Perf.: Hayley Mills, Dean Jones, Roddy McDowell (1964; Hollywood: Walt Disney, 2005), Film.

22 "Elsa Lanchester-Theory and Fact," *The Montreal Gazette* (Montreal, Quebec), Nov. 8, 1965.

23 William McPeak, "Elsa Lanchester," *Internet Movie Database*, Mar. 25, 2012, *http://www. imdb.com/name/nm0006471/*.

24 Kevin Kelly, "It May Be Life, Elsa, But Dearie Ain't It Slow," *Boston Globe* (Boston, MA), Nov. 7, 1960.

25 "Elsa Proves it Pays to Be Unattractive," *Boston Globe* (Boston, MA), Sep. 8, 1968.

MARJORIE MAIN

1   "Marjorie Main Dies of Cancer," *Waycross Journal-Herald* (Waycross, GA), Apr. 11, 1975.

2   Howard Thompson, "'Ma Kettle Sings Out,'" *New York Times* (New York, NY), May 23, 1954.

3   Nancy Anderson, "Marjorie Main: There's Still a Lot of Steam in Her Kettle," *The Miami News* (Miami, FL), Aug. 18, 1973.

4   "Marjorie Main Vetoes Any Off-Color Scenes," *The Miami News* (Miami, FL), Apr. 18, 1954.

5   Bob Thomas, "Marjorie Main Names Self as The Worst-Dressed Woman," *The Owosso Argus Press* (Owosso, MI), Jan. 4, 1950.

6   Aline Mosby, "Marjorie Main Not Bothered By 'Worst Dressed' Title," *The Newburgh News* (Newburgh, NY), Jan. 17, 1957.

7   Nancy Anderson, "Marjorie Main: There's Still a Lot of Steam in Her Kettle," *The Miami News* (Miami, FL), Aug. 18, 1973.

8   Ibid.

9   Louella O. Parsons, "Hard-Boiled Marjorie Main Can Be Sympathetic, Too," *St. Petersburg Times* (St. Petersburg, FL), Jul. 6, 1941.

10 Ed Stephen, "Marjorie Main," *Internet Movie Database*, Feb. 15, 2012, *http://www.imdb.com/ name/nm0537685/*.

11 Louella O. Parsons, "Hard-Boiled Marjorie Main Can Be Sympathetic, Too," *St. Petersburg Times* (St. Petersburg, FL), Jul. 6, 1941.

12 "Marjorie Main Dies of Cancer," *Waycross Journal-Herald* (Waycross, GA), Apr. 11, 1975.

13 "Swamp Melodrama At Garden Is Done Well," *The Portsmouth Times* (Portsmouth, OH), Jul. 18, 1938.

14 Nancy Anderson, "Marjorie Main: There's Still a Lot of Steam in Her Kettle," *The Miami News* (Miami, FL), Aug. 18, 1973.

15 Howard Thompson, "'Ma Kettle Sings Out,'" *New York Times* (New York, NY), May 23, 1954.

16 Frederick C. Othman, "Marjorie Main Got Her Start in Chautauqua," *St. Petersburg Times* (St. Petersburg, FL), Oct. 14, 1941.

17 Ibid.

18 Ed Stephen, "Marjorie Main," *Internet Movie Database*, Feb. 15, 2012, *http://www.imdb.com/ name/nm0537685/*.

19 Louella O. Parsons, "Hard-Boiled Marjorie Main Can Be Sympathetic, Too," *St. Petersburg Times* (St. Petersburg, FL), Jul. 6, 1941.

20 "Swamp Melodrama at Garden Is Done Well," *The Portsmouth Times* (Portsmouth, OH), Jul. 18, 1938.

21 *Meet Me in St. Louis*, DVD, Dir.: Vincent Minnelli, Perf.: Judy Garland, Margaret O'Brien, Tom Drake (1944; Hollywood: M-G-M, 2011) Film.

22 Ibid.

23 *The Harvey Girls*, DVD, Dir.: George Sidney, Perf.: Judy Garland, John Hodiak, Angela Lansbury (1945; Hollywood: M-G-M,), Film.

24 *Ma and Pa Kettle at the Fair*, DVD, Dir: Charles Barton, Perf: Marjorie Main, Percy Kilbride, and James Best (1952; Hollywood: Universal Pictures, 2004), Film.

25 Howard Thompson, "'Ma Kettle Sings Out,'" *New York Times* (New York, NY), May 23, 1954.

26   Ibid.

27   Nancy Anderson, "Marjorie Main: There's Still a Lot of Steam in Her Kettle," *The Miami News* (Miami, FL), Aug. 18, 1973.

28   Howard Thompson, "'Ma Kettle Sings Out,'" *New York Times* (New York, NY), May 23, 1954.

29   Ibid.

30   Ed Stephen, "Marjorie Main," *Internet Movie Database*, Feb. 15, 2012, *http://www.imdb.com/name/nm0537685/*.

31   Aline Mosby, "Marjorie Main Not Bothered By 'Worst Dressed' Title," *The Newburgh News* (Newburgh, NY), Jan. 17, 1957.

32   Ibid.

33   Vernon Scott, "Marjorie Main Soon To Be 79 Years Old," *The Times-News* (Burlington, NC), Mar. 4, 1969.

34   Nancy Anderson, "Marjorie Main: There's Still a Lot of Steam in Her Kettle," *The Miami News* (Miami, FL), Aug. 18, 1973.

35   Howard Thompson, "'Ma Kettle Sings Out,'" *New York Times* (New York, NY), May 23, 1954.

36   Ibid.

37   "Likes Own Cooking Better," *Meriden Record* (Meriden, CT), Jul. 2, 1954.

38   Bob Thomas, "Marjorie Main May Quit Acting, And She May Not," *Times Daily* (Florence, AL), Feb. 19, 1954.

39   "Marjorie Main Biography (1890-1975)," *Filmreference.com*, Aug. 3, 2009, *http//www.filmreference.com/film/16/Marjorie-Main.html*.

40   Aline Mosby, "Marjorie Main Not Bothered By 'Worst Dressed' Title," *The Newburgh News* (Newburgh, NY), Jan. 17, 1957.

HATTIE MCDANIEL

1   Carlton Jackson, *Hattie: The Life of Hattie McDaniel* (London: Madison Books, 1990), p. 163.

2   Monica L. Haynes, "TV Preview: Hats Off to Hattie McDaniel," *Post-Gazette*, Aug. 5, 2001, *http://old.post-gazette.com/ae/20010805hattie0805fnp3.asp*.

3   Norman Vincent Peale, "Confident Living," *The Portsmouth Times* (Portsmouth, OH), Jul. 4, 1953.

4   Carlton Jackson, *Hattie: The Life of Hattie McDaniel* (London: Madison Books, 1990), p. 8.

5   "Biography of Hattie McDaniel," *Encyclopedia of World Biography*, May 2, 2012, *http://www.notablebiographies.com/Ma-Mo/McDaniel-Hattie.html*.

6   Carlton Jackson, *Hattie: The Life of Hattie McDaniel* (London: Madison Books, 1990), p. 10.

7   Ibid, p. 12.

8   Ibid, p. 18.

9   Hedda Hopper, "Hattie McDaniel Makes Good In Films Despite Obstacles," *The Miami News* (Miami, FL), Dec. 14, 1947.

10   Ibid.

11   Carlton Jackson, *Hattie: The Life of Hattie McDaniel* (London: Madison Books, 1990), p. 18.

12   Ibid, p. 25.

13 Monica L. Haynes, "TV Preview: Hats Off to Hattie McDaniel," *Post-Gazzette,* Aug. 5, 2001, *http://old.post-gazzette.com/ae/20010805hattie0805fnp3.asp.*

14 Carlton Jackson, *Hattie: The Life of Hattie McDaniel* (London: Madison Books, 1990), p. 30.

15 Ibid, p. 26.

16 Margaret Mitchell, *Gone With the Wind* (New York: Warner Books, 1936), p. 25.

17 Carlton Jackson, *Hattie: The Life of Hattie McDaniel* (London: Madison Books, 1990), p. 52

18 Ibid, p. 54.

19 Ibid, p. 70.

20 Monica L. Haynes, "TV Preview: Hats Off to Hattie McDaniel," *Post-Gazzette,* Aug. 5, 2001, *http://old.post-gazzette.com/ae/20010805hattie0805fnp3.asp.*

21 Carlton Jackson, *Hattie: The Life of Hattie McDaniel* (London: Madison Books, 1990), p. 31.

22 Ibid, p. 85.

23 Norman Vincent Peale, "Confident Living," *The Portsmouth Times* (Portsmouth, OH), Jul. 4, 1953.

24 *Since You Went Away,* DVD, Dir.: David O. Selznick, Perf.: Claudette Colbert, Jennifer Jones, Shirley Temple, (1944; Hollywood: Selznick Studios, 2004), Film.

25 Carlton Jackson, *Hattie: The Life of Hattie McDaniel* (London: Madison Books, 1990), p. 86.

26 Hedda Hopper, "Hattie McDaniel Makes Good in Films Despite Obstacles," *The Miami News* (Miami, FL), Dec. 14, 1947.

27 Carlton Jackson, *Hattie: The Life of Hattie McDaniel* (London: Madison Books, 1990), p. 121.

28 Ibid, p. 123

29 Ibid, p. 128.

30 Ibid, p. 144.

31 Norman Vincent Peale, "Confident Living," *The Portsmouth Times* (Portsmouth, OH), Jul. 4, 1953.

32 Carlton Jackson, *Hattie: The Life of Hattie McDaniel* (London: Madison Books, 1990), p. 160

33 Ibid, p 57.

UNA MERKEL

1 "Una Merkel Is Dead at 82; Was 'Nitwit' Blonde in Movies," *The Vindicator* (Youngstown, Ohio), Jan. 4, 1986.

2 Nancy Anderson, "Una Was Numero Dos," *Reading Eagle* (Reading, PA), Sep. 15, 1978.

3 "Comic Gift Her Best Bet," *The Pittsburgh Press* (Pittsburgh, PA), Sep. 7, 1946.

4 Ward Morehouse, "Una Merkel in First Musical After 100 Motion Pictures," *The Milwaukee Journal* (Milwaukee, WI), Feb. 23, 1960.

5 Ibid.

6 Ibid.

7 Ibid.

8 Frances Morrin, "Una Envies Her Grandmother," *Boston Globe* (Boston, MA), Jun. 7, 1936.

9 "Una Merkel Doubled for Lillian Gish in Films," *Boston Globe* (Boston, MA), Nov. 18, 1928.

10 Frances Morrin, "Una Envies Her Grandmother," *Boston Globe* (Boston, MA), Jun. 7, 1936.

11 Paul Harrison, "Film Comedienne Fired, Changed Type, Now She's Una Merkel, Tragedienne," *The Milwaukee Journal* (Milwaukee, WI), Jun. 19, 1939.

12 Ibid.

13 *Red-Headed Woman,* DVD, Dir.: Jack Conway, Perf.: Jean Harlow, Chester Morris, Una Merkel (1932; Hollywood: M-G-M, 2006) Film.

14 Grace Wilcox, "I've Got It All, Says Miss Merkel," *The Milwaukee Journal* (Milwaukee, WI), Jul. 25, 1937.

15 Ibid.

16 Nancy Anderson, "Una Was Numero Dos," *Reading Eagle* (Reading, PA), Sep. 15, 1978.

17 Frances Morrin, "Una Envies Her Grandmother," *Boston Globe* (Boston, MA), Jun. 7, 1936.

18 John Ferris, "Between Phone Calls, Una Merkel Tells All — Wants One Serious Role," *The Milwaukee Journal* (Milwaukee, WI), Mr. 10, 1942.

19 Grace Wilcox, "I've Got It All, Says Miss Merkel," *The Milwaukee Journal* (Milwaukee, WI), Jul. 25, 1937.

20 Paul Harrison, "Film Comedienne Fired, Changed Type, Now She's Una Merkel, Tragedienne," *The Milwaukee Journal* (Milwaukee, WI), Jun. 19, 1939.

21 "Una Merkel Felled By Gas, Mother Dies," *New York Times* (New York, NY), Mar. 6, 1945.

22 "Una Merkel Is Dead at 82; Was 'Nitwit' Blonde in Movies," *The Vindicator* (Youngstown, Ohio), Jan. 4, 1986.

23 "Una Merkel Critically Ill," *The Sydney Morning Herald* (Sydney, Australia), Mar. 5, 1952.

24 Bob Thomas, "Una Merkel Says She Never Felt Better in Life," *The Meridan Daily Journal* (Merridan, CT), Jul. 23, 1952.

25 Ibid.

26 Ibid.

27 Ward Morehouse, "Una Merkel in First Musical After 100 Motion Pictures," *The Milwaukee Journal* (Milwaukee, WI), Feb. 23, 1960.

28 Harold Heffernan, "Una Merkel Jubilant Over Chance at Oscar," *The Calgary Herald* (Calgary, Canada), Mar. 14, 1962.

29 Ibid.

30 Ibid.

31 Nancy Anderson, "Una Was Numero Dos," *Reading Eagle* (Reading, PA), Sep. 15, 1978.

32 Ibid.

33 Ibid.

THOMAS MITCHELL

1 Paul P. Kennedy, "An Actor Views the Fuller Life," *New York Times* (New York, NY), Aug. 13, 1944.

2 Ibid.

3 "Thomas Mitchell, Actor, Dead; Star of Stage and Screen, 70," *New York Times* (New York, NY), Dec. 18, 1962.

4 Paul P. Kennedy, "An Actor Views the Fuller Life," *New York Times* (New York, NY), Aug. 13, 1944.

5 Louis Calta, "Thomas Mitchell to Essay Musical," *New York Times* (New York, NY), Aug. 19, 1952.

6 "Music, Farce, and a Dash or Two of Melodrama," *The Pittsburgh Press* (Pittsburgh, PA), Nov. 3, 1929.

7 "She Was Five and He Was a Hero," *Daily Boston Globe* (Boston, MA), Jan. 3, 1932.

8 " 'Little Accident' Wins the Megrue Prize," *The New York Times* (New York, NY), June 18, 1929.

9 Heywood Broun, "It Seems to Me," *The Pittsburgh Press* (Pittsburgh, PA), Sep. 9, 1931.

10 Ibid.

11 William McPeak, "Thomas Mitchell," *Internet Movie Database,* Dec. 5, 2011, *http://www. imdb.com/name/nm0593775/.*

12 "She Was Five and He Was a Hero," *Daily Boston Globe* (Boston, MA), Jan. 3, 1932.

13 Paul P. Kennedy, "An Actor Views the Fuller Life," *New York Times* (New York, NY), Aug. 13, 1944.

14 William McPeak, "Thomas Mitchell," *Internet Movie Database,* Dec. 5, 2011, *http://www. imdb.com/name/nm0593775/.*

15 Paul P. Kennedy, "An Actor Views the Fuller Life," *New York Times* (New York, NY), Aug. 13, 1944.

16 Ibid.

17 Ibid.

18 Herb Bridges and Terryl C. Boodman, *Gone With the Wind: The Definitive, Illustrated History, The Book, the Movie and the Legend* (Lady Lake, FL:Fireside Books, 1989), p. 193.

19 *Gone With the Wind,* Video, Dir.: Victor Fleming, Perf.: Clark Gable, Vivien Leigh, and Thomas Mitchell (1939; Hollywood: Selznick International Pictures, 1998), Film.

20 *Stagecoach,* DVD, Dir.: John Ford, Perf.: John Wayne, Claire Trevor, and Thomas Mitchell (1939; Hollywood: Walter Wanger Productions, 2010), Film.

21 "Thomas Mitchell, Actor, Marries Former Wife," *Los Angeles Times* (Los Angeles, CA), Jul. 1, 1941.

22 Paul P. Kennedy, "An Actor Views the Fuller Life," *New York Times* (New York, NY), Aug. 13, 1944.

23 *It's a Wonderful Life,* Dir.: Frank Capra, Perf.: James Stewart, Donna Reed, and Lionel Barrymore (1946; Hollywood: Republic Pictures, 2006), Film.

24 " 'Death of a Salesman' Soars Season at Nixon," *Pittsburgh Post-Gazette* (Pittsburgh, PA), Mar. 7, 1950.

25 William McPeak, "Thomas Mitchell," *Internet Movie Database,* Dec. 5, 2011, *http://www. imdb.com/name/nm0593775/.*

26 "Mitchell Leaves Estate to Wife," *St. Joseph News-Press* (St. Joseph, MO), Dec. 23, 1962.

27 Ben Jonson, "Ben Jonson Quotes," *Brainyquote.com,* Dec. 14, 2011, *http://www.brainyquote. com/quotes/authors/b/ben_jonson.html#ixzz1gYcmRfDd*

AGNES MOOREHEAD

1   Mayme Ober Peak, "Widely Varied Roles Please Boston-Born Agnes Moorehead," *Daily Boston Globe* (Boston, MA), Apr. 11, 1945.

2   Warren Sherk, *Agnes Moorehead: A Very Private Person* (Philadelphia, PA: Dorrance and Company, 1976), p. 123.

3   Ibid, p. 17.

4   Ibid, p. 11.

5   Ibid, p. 24.

6   "No Talent to Nudity: Agnes Moorehead," *Boston Globe* (Boston, MA), Nov. 23, 1969.

7   Ibid, p. 31.

8   "Anxious Agnes," *Daily Boston Globe* (Boston, MA), Oct. 25, 1936.

9   John P. Shanley, "Queens to Witches," *New York Times* (New York, NY), Sep. 18, 1960.

10 Warren Sherk, *Agnes Moorehead: A Very Private Person* (Philadelphia, PA: Dorrance and Company, 1976), p. .

11 Ibid, p. 11.

12 *Since You Went Away,* DVD, Dir.: , Perf.: Claudette Colbert, Jennifer Jones, and Shirley Temple (1944; Hollywood: Selznick International Pictures,), Film.

13 Warren Sherk, *Agnes Moorehead: A Very Private Person* (Philadelphia, PA: Dorrance and Company, 1976), p. 77.

14 "Agnes Moorehead Is Happy Over 'Glamour' Treatment," *The Pittsburgh Press* (Pittsburgh, PA), Oct. 4, 1947.

15 Mayme Ober Peak, "Widely Varied roles Please Boston-Born Agnes Moorehead," *Daily Boston Globe* (Boston, MA), Apr. 11, 1945.

16 Warren Sherk, *Agnes Moorehead: A Very Private Person* (Philadelphia, PA: Dorrance and Company, 1976), p. 93.

17 Ibid, p. 67.

18 "Actor Accuses Wife of Berating Him Over Dress," *The News and Courier* (Charleston, SC), Oct. 5, 1950.

19 "Agnes Moorehead Seeks Separation," *Daily Boston Globe* (Boston, MA), Aug. 26, 1945.

20 Warren Sherk, *Agnes Moorehead: A Very Private Person* (Philadelphia, PA: Dorrance and Company, 1976), p. 66.

21 Ibid, p. 60.

22 Marjory Adams, "Cambridge- Born Agnes Moorehead Says Movies Are Turning to Religion," *Daily Boston Globe* (Boston, MA), Jul. 13, 1954.

23 I.S. Mowis, "Agnes Moorehead," *Internet Movie Database,* Mar. 15, 2012, *http://www.imdb.com/name/nm0001547/.*

24 Warren Sherk, *Agnes Moorehead: A Very Private Person* (Philadelphia, PA: Dorrance and Company, 1976), p. 50.

25 Ibid, p. 70.

26 I.S. Mowis, "Agnes Moorehead," *Internet Movie Database,* Mar. 15, 2012, *http://www.imdb.com/name/nm0001547/.*

27 Warren Sherk, *Agnes Moorehead: A Very Private Person* (Philadelphia, PA: Dorrance and Company, 1976), p. 92.

28 "And Then There Were Three," in *Bewitched* (1966; Hollywood: Ashmont Productions,), Television.

29 Percy Shain, "Agnes Moorehead: Dedicated Actress," *Boston Globe* (Boston, MA), Sep. 3, 1967.

30 Warren Sherk, *Agnes Moorehead: A Very Private Person* (Philadelphia, PA: Dorrance and Company, 1976), p. 77.

31 Percy Shain, "Agnes Moorehead: Dedicated Actress," *Boston Globe* (Boston, MA), Sep. 3, 1967.

32 Karen G. Jackovich and Mark Sennet, "The Children of John Wayne, Susan Hayward, Dick Powell Fear That Fallout Killed Their Parents," *People* (Los Angeles, CA), Nov. 10, 1980.

33 Warren Sherk, *Agnes Moorehead: A Very Private Person* (Philadelphia, PA: Dorrance and Company, 1976), p. 17.

34 Ibid, p. 115.

35 "Be It Ever So Mortgaged," in *Bewitched* (1964; Hollywood: Ashmont Productions), Television.

FRANK MORGAN

1 Aljean Harmetz, *The Making of The Wizard of Oz* (New York: Trafalgar Square, 1989), p. 119.

2 Mickey Rooney, "If I Were Frank Morgan," *The Deseret News* (Salt Lake City, Utah), May 4, 1943.

3 "Frank Morgan," *Internet Movie Database*, May 23, 2012, *http://www.imdb.com/name/ nm0604656/.*

4 "Taking the Bitters with the Sweet," *The New York Times* (New York, NY), Mar. 10, 1935.

5 "Bounding Heroes Are Not for Him," *Daily Boston Globe* (Boston, MA), Feb. 8, 1931.

6 "Taking the Bitters with the Sweet," *The New York Times* (New York, NY), Mar. 10, 1935.

7 Ibid.

8 Ibid.

9 "Bounding Heroes Are Not for Him," *Daily Boston Globe* (Boston, MA), Feb. 8, 1931.

10 "Frank Morgan Enjoys Life in a Musical Production," *Daily Boston Globe* (Boston, MA), Jan. 17, 1932.

11 "Bounding Heroes Are Not for Him," *Daily Boston Globe* (Boston, MA), Feb. 8, 1931.

12 Ibid.

13 L. Frank Baum, *The Wonderful Wizard of Oz* (New York, NY: Scholastic, Inc., 1958), p. 109.

14 Aljean Harmetz, *The Making of The Wizard of Oz* (New York: Trafalgar Square, 1989), p. 120.

15 Ibid, p. 180.

16 Ibid, p. 181.

17 Ibid, p. 180.

18 Ibid, p. 180.

19 Mickey Rooney, "If I Were Frank Morgan," *The Deseret News* (Salt Lake City, Utah), May 4, 1943.

20 "Morgan Clinches Yacht Race While Slumbering," *Daily Boston Globe* (Boston, MA), Jul. 22, 1947.

21 Si Steinhauser, "Frank Morgan Loses His Vacation Because He's Funny on the Radio," *The Pittsburgh Press* (Pittsburgh, PA), Feb. 16, 1938.

22 Frederick C. Othman, "Frank Morgan: Tiredest Old Man You Ever Saw," *Pittsburgh Post-Gazette* (Pittsburgh, PA), Feb. 5, 1942.

23 "Oldster Morgan Taking Two at a Time," *Ottawa Citizen* (Ottawa, Ontario), Nov. 20, 1948.

24 Mickey Rooney, "If I Were Frank Morgan," *The Deseret News* (Salt Lake City, Utah), May 4, 1943.

25 Ibid.

26 Aljean Harmetz, *The Making of The Wizard of Oz* (New York: Trafalgar Square, 1989), p. 180.

27 "Frank Morgan," *Internet Movie Database*, May 23, 2012, *http://www.imdb.com/name/nm0604656/*.

JULES MUNSHIN

1 Marjory Adams, "Jules Munshin Says No Man So Wordly He Knows What to Tip," *Daily Boston Globe* (Boston, MA), Jan. 18, 1953.

2 Jules Munshin, *Dear Anybody* (New York: Crown Publishers, 1957), p. 7.

3 Ibid, p. 7.

4 "Comedian Jules Munshin Likes His Role Opposite Helen Hayes in 'Mrs. McThing'," *Daily Boston Globe* (Boston, MA), Dec. 28, 1952.

5 "Jules Munshin, Comedy Actor in Film and on Stage Dies at 54," *New York Times* (New York, NY), Feb. 20, 1970.

6 Ibid.

7 Marjory Adams, "Jules Munshin Says No Man So Wordly He Knows What to Tip," *Daily Boston Globe* (Boston, MA), Jan. 18, 1953.

8 *Easter Parade*, Video, Dir.: Charles Walters, Perf. Fred Astaire, Judy Garland, and Ann Miller (1948; Hollywood: M-G-M, 2000), Film.

9 Marjory Adams, "Jules Munshin Says No Man So Wordly He Knows What to Tip," *Daily Boston Globe* (Boston, MA), Jan. 18, 1953.

10 Ibid.

11 Ibid.

12 "Comedian Jules Munshin Likes His Role Opposite Helen Hayes in 'Mrs. McThing'," *Daily Boston Globe* (Boston, MA), Dec. 28, 1952.

13 Ibid, p. 139.

14 Ibid, p. 15.

15 Ibid, p. 20.

16 Ibid, p. 115.

17 "At the Palace," *New York Times* (New York, NY), May 29, 1954.

18 *Silk Stockings*, DVD, Dir.: Rouben Mamoulian, Perf.: Fred Astaire, Cyd Charisse, and Peter Lorre (1957; Hollywood: M-G-M, 2003), Film.

19 Hugh Fordin, *M-G-M's Greatest Musicals* (New York, NY: Da Capo, 1996), p. 114.

20 Jules Munshin, *Dear Anybody* (New York: Crown Publishers, 1957), p. 171.

21 Ibid, p. 172.

22 Ibid, p. 90.

23 "Dear Anybody," *The Milwaukee Sentinel* (Milwaukee, WI), Jan. 26, 1958.

24 William Ewald, "Television in Review," *Meriden Journal* (Meriden, CT), Mar. 6, 1958.

25 "Jules Munshin, Comedy Actor in Film and on Stage Dies at 54," *New York Times* (New York, NY), Feb. 20, 1970.

26 Jules Munshin, *Dear Anybody* (New York: Crown Publishers, 1957), p. 90.

VIRGINIA O'BRIEN

1 *Thousands Cheer,* DVD, Dir. George Sidney, Perf.: Gene Kelly, Kathryn Grayson, and Mickey Rooney (1943; Hollywood: M-G-M, 2009), Film.

2 "Virginia O'Brien," *The Guardian* (London, England), Jan. 24, 2001.

3 Bill Takacs, "Virginia O'Brien," *Internet Movie Database,* Dec. 2, 2011, *http://www.imdb.com/name/nm0639877/*

4 "Virginia O'Brien," *The Guardian* (London, England), Jan. 24, 2001.

5 "Virginia O'Brien Quotes," *Whosdatedwho.com,* Dec. 20, 2011, *http://www.whosdatedwho.com/tpx_32679/virginia-o-brien/quotes.*

6 Vernon Scott, "Deadpan Singer Virginia O'Brien Makes Movie Comeback," *Montreal Gazette* (Montreal, Quebec), July 8, 1975.

7 Ibid.

8 Ibid.

9 "Virginia O'Brien Quotes," *Whosdatedwho.com,* Dec. 20, 2011, *http://www.whosdatedwho.com/tpx_32679/virginia-o-brien/quotes.*

10 Ibid.

11 "Virginia O'Brien," *The Guardian* (London, England), Jan. 24, 2001.

12 Ibid.

13 *Dubarry Was a Lady,* DVD, Dir.: Charles Walters, Perf.: Red Skelton, Lucille Ball, and Gene Kelly (1942; Hollywood: M-G-M, 2007), Film.

14 Earl K. Brent, "Say We're Sweethearts Again" from *Meet the People,* DVD, Dir.: Charles Reisner, Perf.: Dick Powell, Lucille Ball, and Virginia O'Brien (1944; Hollywood: M-G-M, 2009), Film.

15 Earl K. Brent and Roger Edens, "Bring on the Wonderful Men" from *Ziegfeld Follies,* DVD, Dir.: Vincente Minnelli, Perf.: Fred Astaire, Lucille Bremer, and William Powell (1945; Hollywood: M-G-M, 2006), Film.

16 *The Harvey Girls,* Video, Dir.: George Sidney, Perf.: Judy Garland, John Hodiak, and Virginia O'Brien (1946; Hollywood: M-G-M, 1992), Film.

17 Johnny Mercer and Harry Warren, "The Wild, Wild West" from *The Harvey Girls,* Video, Dir.: George Sidney, Perf.: Judy Garland, John Hodiak, and Virginia O'Brien (1946; Hollywood: M-G-M, 1992), Film.

18 Vernon Scott, "Deadpan Singer Virginia O'Brien Makes Movie Comeback," *Montreal Gazette* (Montreal, Quebec), July 8, 1975.

19 "Virginia O'Brien," *The Guardian* (London, England), Jan. 24, 2001.

20 "Singer Is Happy As She Wins Her Divorce," *Kentucky New-Era* (Hopkinsville, KY), June 25, 1955.

21 Vernon Scott, "Deadpan Singer Virginia O'Brien Makes Movie Comeback," *Montreal Gazette* (Montreal, Quebec), July 8, 1975.

22 Ibid.

23 Bill Takacs, "Virginia O'Brien," *Internet Movie Database,* Dec. 2, 2011, *http://www.imdb.com/name/nm0639877/*

24 Vernon Scott, "Deadpan Singer Virginia O'Brien Makes Movie Comeback," *Montreal Gazette* (Montreal, Quebec), July 8, 1975.

25 "In Loving Memory: Virginia O'Brien," *Lucyfan.com,* Nov. 25, 2011, *http://www.lucyfan.com/virginiaobrien.html*

26 Ibid.

EDNA MAY OLIVER

1 Thomas McWilliams, "Edna May Oliver," *Internet Movie Database,* Dec. 19, 2011, *http://www.imdb.com/name/nm0646829/.*

2 Hal Erickson, "About This Person," *New York Times* (New York, NY), Dec. 20, 2011.

3 Thomas McWilliams, "Edna May Oliver," *Internet Movie Database,* Dec. 19, 2011, *http://www.imdb.com/name/nm0646829/.*

4 Gary Cahill, "Edna May Oliver: Queen of the Old Maids," *Scene Stealers,* Jan. 5, 2011, *http://www.moviefanfare.com/scene-stealers/edna-may-oliver/.*

5 "Edna May Oliver Dies in Hollywood," *New York Times* (New York, NY), Nov. 10, 1942.

6 "Chuckle at Mention of Edna May Oliver," *Spokane Daily Chronicle* (Spokane, WA), Jan. 22, 1932.

7 "Edna May Oliver Dies in Hollywood," *New York Times* (New York, NY), Nov. 10, 1942.

8 "Chuckle at Mention of Edna May Oliver," *Spokane Daily Chronicle* (Spokane, WA), Jan. 22, 1932.

9 Gary Cahill, "Edna May Oliver: Queen of the Old Maids," *Scene Stealers,* Jan. 5, 2011, *http://www.moviefanfare.com/scene-stealers/edna-may-oliver/.*

10 "Edna May Oliver Back," *New York Times* (New York, NY), Jul. 28, 1927.

11 "Edna May Oliver Weds," *New York Times* (New York, NY), Jan. 25, 1928.

12 "Katharine Hepburn," *Internet Movie Database,* Jun. 19, 2012, *http://www.imdb.com/name/nm0000031/bio#quotes.*

13 "Hubby 'Fettered' So She Frees Him," *Milwaukee Sentinel* (Milwaukee, WI), Aug. 12, 1931.

14 Ibid.

15 "Edna May Oliver Hit With Audience," *Spokane Daily Chronicle* (Spokane, WA), May 13, 1932.

16 "The Screen," *New York Times* (New York, NY), Mar. 4, 1935.

17 Thomas McWilliams, "Edna May Oliver," *Internet Movie Database,* Dec. 19, 2011, *http://www.imdb.com/name/nm0646829/.*

18 *David Copperfield*, DVD, Dir.: George Cukor, Perf.: Freddie Bartholomew, Roland Young, Edna May Oliver (1935; Hollywood: M-G-M, 2006), Film.

19 "Edna May Oliver Dies in Hollywood," *New York Times* (New York, NY), Nov. 10, 1942.

20 *A Tale of Two Cities*, DVD, Dir.: John Conway, Perf.: Ronald Coleman, Elizabeth Allan, Edna May Oliver (1935; Hollywood: M-G-M, 2006), Film.

21 Ibid.

22 "Long Screen Career of Edna Mae Oliver Ends on 59th Birthday," *Ludington Daily News* (Ludington, MI), Nov. 10, 1942.

23 "By Remote Control," *Spokane Daily Chronicle* (Spokane, WA), Dec. 19, 1935.

24 Mollie Merrick, "Favorite Actors All Dead," *The Spokesman Review* (Spokane, WA), Feb. 7, 1934.

25 "Edna May Oliver, Character Star, Dies Quietly on 59th Birthday," *The Montreal Gazette* (Montreal, Quebec), Nov. 10, 1942.

26 Gary Cahill, "Edna May Oliver: Queen of the Old Maids," *Scene Stealers,* Jan. 5, 2011, *http://www.moviefanfare.com/scene-stealers/edna-may-oliver/.*

27 Ibid.

28 Ibid.

29 *Lydia,* Video, Dir.: Julien Duvivier, Perf.: Merle Oberon, Joseph Cotton, Edna May Oliver (1941; Hollywood: Samuel Goldwyn Studios, 1995), Film.

30 "Edna May Oliver Dies in Hollywood," *New York Times* (New York, NY), Nov. 10, 1942.

31 *David Copperfield*, DVD, Dir.: George Cukor, Perf.: Freddie Bartholomew, Roland Young, Edna May Oliver (1935; Hollywood: M-G-M, 2006), Film.

CLAUDE RAINS

1 "Film Star Claude Rains Dies at 77," *The News and Courier* (Charleston, SC), May, 31, 1967.

2 Sanford L. Cooper, "Magnificent Film of Edwin Drood," *The Pittsburgh Press* (Pittsburgh, PA), Mar. 30, 1935.

3 David J. Skall, *An Actor's Voice* (Lexington, KY: University Press of Kentucky, 2009), p. 170.

4 Ibid, p. 2.

5 Ibid, p. 2.

6 Ibid, p. 27.

7 Ibid, p. 30.

8 Ibid, p. 33.

9 Ibid, p. 35.

10 Ibid, p. 35.

11 "Film Star Claude Rains Dies at 77," *The News and Courier* (Charleston, SC), May, 31, 1967.

12 David J. Skall, *An Actor's Voice* (Lexington, KY: University Press of Kentucky, 2009), p. 82.

13 Ibid, p. 42.

14 William McPeak, "Claude Rains," *Internet Movie Database*, Jan. 11, 2012, *http://www.imdb. com/name/nm0001647/*.

15 Ibid, p. 45.

16 Ibid, p. 47.

17 Ibid, p. 62.

18 Saul Pett, "TV Actors Rehearse in the Oddest Places," *The Miami News* (Miami, FL), May 10, 1956.

19 Bob Thomas, "Meet Claude Rains: Master of Monsters Deplores Current Crop," *The Portsmouth Times* (Portsmouth, OH), Oct. 29, 1958.

20 Ibid.

21 *The Invisible Man*, DVD, Dir.: James Whale, Perf.: Claude Rains, Gloria Stuart, Henry Travers (1933; Hollywood: Universal Studios, 2009), Film.

22 William McPeak, "Claude Rains," *Internet Movie Database*, Jan. 11, 2012, *http://www.imdb. com/name/nm0001647/*.

23 David J. Skall, *An Actor's Voice* (Lexington, KY: University Press of Kentucky, 2009), p. 89.

24 Ibid, p. 103.

25 Ibid, p. 170.

26 *Casablanca*, DVD, Dir.: Michael Curtiz, Perf.: Humphrey Bogart, Ingrid Bergman, Paul Henreid (1942; Hollywood: Warner Brothers, 2010), Film.

27 David J. Skall, *An Actor's Voice* (Lexington, KY: University Press of Kentucky, 2009), p. 141.

28 Ibid, p. 153.

29 Claude Rains, "Rains Discusses His Hardest Role," *New York Times* (New York, NY), Mar. 18, 1951.

30 David J. Skall, *An Actor's Voice* (Lexington, KY: University Press of Kentucky, 2009), p. 153.

31 "Film Star Claude Rains Dies at 77," *The News and Courier* (Charleston, SC), May, 31, 1967.

32 David J. Skall, *An Actor's Voice* (Lexington, KY: University Press of Kentucky, 2009), p. 181.

33 Ibid, p. 87.

THELMA RITTER

1 Dick Kleiner, "Thelma Ritter, Once Famous on Broadway, Makes Stage Comeback," *Middlesboro Daily News* (Middlesboro, KY) Jun. 17, 1957.

2 Hal Boyle, "Thelma Ritter Thinks Hollywood Should Rank Actors as Pentagon Does Generals," *Ocala Star-Banner*(Ocala, FL), May 1, 1959.

3 Dick Kleiner, "Thelma Ritter, Once Famous on Broadway, Makes Stage Comeback," *Middlesboro Daily News* (Middlesboro, KY) Jun. 17, 1957.

4 Hedda Hopper, "One-Line Role into Stardom Character Actress Parlayed," *The Miami News* (Miami, FL), Feb. 4, 1951.

5 Howard Thompson, "Out of Character," *New York Times* (New York, NY), Oct. 8, 1950.

6 Hedda Hopper, "One-Line Role into Stardom Character Actress Parlayed," *The Miami News* (Miami, FL), Feb. 4, 1951.

7   Hal Boyle, "Thelma Ritter Thinks Hollywood Should Rank Actors as Pentagon Does Generals," *Ocala Star-Banner*(Ocala, FL), May 1, 1959.

8   Milton Z. Esterow, "Ingenue to Star," *New York Times* (New York, NY), Sep. 1, 1957.

9   Marjory Adams, "Thelma Ritter: Stalwart Screen Mother to Stars," *Boston Globe* (Boston, MA), Sep. 15, 1963.

10 Marjory Adams, "Thelma Ritter, Now Film Star, Enjoys Bus-to-Pullman Change," *Daily Boston Globe* (Boston, MA), Mar, 8, 1951.

11 Howard Thompson, "Out of Character," *New York Times* (New York, NY), Oct. 8, 1950.

12 Hal Boyle, "Thelma Ritter Thinks Hollywood Should Rank Actors as Pentagon Does Generals," *Ocala Star-Banner*(Ocala, FL), May 1, 1959.

13 Howard Thompson, "Out of Character," *New York Times* (New York, NY), Oct. 8, 1950.

14 Hedda Hopper, "One-Line Role into Stardom Character Actress Parlayed," *The Miami News* (Miami, FL), Feb. 4, 1951.

15 Howard Thompson, "Out of Character," *New York Times* (New York, NY), Oct. 8, 1950.

16 *All About Eve*, DVD, Dir.: Joseph Mankiewicz, Perf.: Bette Davis, Anne Baxter, and Celeste Holm (1950; Hollywood: Twentieth Century Fox, 2003), Film.

17 Hedda Hopper, "One-Line Role into Stardom Character Actress Parlayed," *The Miami News* (Miami, FL), Feb. 4, 1951.

18 Marjory Adams, "Thelma Ritter, Now Film Star, Enjoys Bus-to-Pullman Change," *Daily Boston Globe* (Boston, MA), Mar, 8, 1951.

19 Milton Z. Esterow, "Ingenue to Star," *New York Times* (New York, NY), Sep. 1, 1957.

20 Marjory Adams, "Thelma Ritter: Stalwart Screen Mother to Stars," *Boston Globe* (Boston, MA), Sep. 15, 1963.

21 Hal Boyle, "Thelma Ritter Thinks Hollywood Should Rank Actors as Pentagon Does Generals," *Ocala Star-Banner*(Ocala, FL), May 1, 1959.

22 *Rear Window*, DVD, Dir.: Alfred Hitchcock, Perf.: James Stewart, Grace Kelly, and Thelma Ritter (1954; Hollywood: Paramount Pictures, 2001), Film.

23 "Thelma Ritter Wrecking Idol Pattern," *Herald Journal* (Spartanburg, SC), Jul. 28, 1957.

24 Milton Z. Esterow, "Ingenue to Star," *New York Times* (New York, NY), Sep. 1, 1957.

25 Ibid.

26 Ibid.

27 Marjory Adams, "Thelma Ritter: Stalwart Screen Mother to Stars," *Boston Globe* (Boston, MA), Sep. 15, 1963.

28 Ibid.

29 Dick Kleiner, "Thelma Ritter, Once Famous on Broadway, Makes Stage Comeback," *Middlesboro Daily News* (Middlesboro, KY) Jun. 17, 1957.

30 Milton Z. Esterow, "Ingenue to Star," *New York Times* (New York, NY), Sep. 1, 1957.

31 Ibid.

32 Howard Thompson, "Out of Character," *New York Times* (New York, NY), Oct. 8, 1950.

33 Hedda Hopper, "One-Line Role into Stardom Character Actress Parlayed," *The Miami News* (Miami, FL), Feb. 4, 1951.

S.Z. SAKALL

1 "S.Z. Sakall," Class Act, Feb. 19, 2012, *http://www.classicmoviemusicals.com/actorss.htm.*

2 Hal Erikson, "About This Person: S.Z. Sakall," New York Times, Feb. 20, 2012, *http://movies. nytimes.com/person/62678/S-Z-Sakall.*

3 S.Z. Sakall, The Story of Cuddles: My Life Under the Emperor Francis Joseph, Adolf Hitler, and the Warner Brothers (London: Cassell and Co. Ltd, 1954), p. 12.

4 Ibid, p. 13.

5 Ibid, p. 22.

6 Ibid, p. 81.

7 Philip K. Scheur, "S.Z. Sakall Gets Name Unravelled," Los Angeles Times (Los Angeles, CA), Sept. 30, 1945.

8 "A Jowling Success," New York Times (New York, NY), Sept. 13, 1942.

9 Philip K. Scheur, "S.Z. Sakall Gets Name Unravelled," Los Angeles Times (Los Angeles, CA), Sept. 30, 1945.

10 S.Z. Sakall, The Story of Cuddles: My Life Under the Emperor Francis Joseph, Adolf Hitler, and the Warner Brothers (London: Cassell and Co. Ltd, 1954), p. 109.

11 Ibid, p. 126.

12 Ibid, p. 126.

13 Ibid, p. 129.

14 Fred Hift, "The Accent Boys," New York Times (New York, NY), Oct. 9, 1949.

15 S.Z. Sakall, The Story of Cuddles: My Life Under the Emperor Francis Joseph, Adolf Hitler, and the Warner Brothers (London: Cassell and Co. Ltd, 1954), p. 150.

16 Ibid, p. 177.

17 Ibid, p. 177.

18 Karen Thomas, "Biography: S.Z. Sakall," Cinema's Exiles, December 2, 2008, *http://www.pbs. org/wnet/cinemasexiles/biographies/the-actors/biography-s-z-sakall/219/.*

19 S.Z. Sakall, The Story of Cuddles: My Life Under the Emperor Francis Joseph, Adolf Hitler, and the Warner Brothers (London: Cassell and Co. Ltd, 1954), p. 213.

20 Ibid, p. 198.

21 Ibid, p. 198.

22 Ibid, p. 199.

23 Ibid, p. 199.

24 Casablanca, DVD, Dir.: Michael Curtiz, Perf.: Humphrey Bogart, Ingrid Bergman, Paul Henreid (1942; Hollywood: Warner Brothers, 2010), Film.

25 S.Z. Sakall, The Story of Cuddles: My Life Under the Emperor Francis Joseph, Adolf Hitler, and the Warner Brothers (London: Cassell and Co. Ltd, 1954), p. 192-93.

26 Christmas in Connecticut, DVD, Dir.: Peter Godfrey, Perf.: Barbara Stanwyck, Dennis Morgan, S.Z. Sakall (1945; Hollywood: Warner Brothers, 2005), Film.

27 Ibid.

28 Fred Hift, "The Accent Boys," New York Times (New York, NY), Oct. 9, 1949.

29 Ibid.

30 Ibid.

31 S.Z. Sakall, The Story of Cuddles: My Life Under the Emperor Francis Joseph, Adolf Hitler, and the Warner Brothers (London: Cassell and Co. Ltd, 1954), p. 206.

32 Fred Hift, "The Accent Boys," New York Times (New York, NY), Oct. 9, 1949.

33 Edwin Schallert, "Drama," Los Angeles Times (Los Angeles, CA), May 19, 1951.

34 "S.Z. (Cuddles) Sakall Dies on Coast; Widely Known Film Character Actor," New York Times (New York, NY), Feb. 14, 1955.

35 Ibid, p. 228.

36 Ibid, p. 231.

LEWIS STONE

1 Sheila Graham, "Stone Plays Judge Hardy For 8 Years — Character Now," The Miami News (Miami, FL), Aug. 4, 1943.

2 Grady Johnson, "A Milestone for Lewis Stone," New York Times (New York, NY), Mar. 27, 1949.

3 Ibid.

4 Bob Thomas, "Lewis Stone Eyes TV After 20 Years of Entertaining," The Owosso Argus-Press (Owosso, MI), Apr. 4, 1951.

5 "Judge Hardy Signs Up," New York Times (New York, NY), Mar. 8, 1942.

6 Bob Thomas, "Lewis Stone Eyes TV After 20 Years of Entertaining," The Owosso Argus-Press (Owosso, MI), Apr. 4, 1951.

7 "Judge Hardy Signs Up," New York Times (New York, NY), Mar. 8, 1942.

8 Ibid.

9 Ibid.

10 "Lewis Stone," Internet Movie Database, Jan. 2, 2012, http://www.imdb.com/name/nm0832011/.

11 Grady Johnson, "A Milestone for Lewis Stone," New York Times (New York, NY), Mar. 27, 1949.

12 Grand Hotel, DVD, Dir.: Edmund Goulding and Roy Mack, Perf.: Greta Garbo, John Barrymore, Joan Crawford (1932; Hollywood: M-G-M, 2005), Film.

13 Grady Johnson, "A Milestone for Lewis Stone," New York Times (New York, NY), Mar. 27, 1949.

14 Ibid.

15 John H. Rothwell, "Lewis Stone: Perennial 'Prisoner of Zenda'," New York Times (New York, NY), Jun. 1, 1952.

16 Life Begins for Andy Hardy, VHS, Dir.: George B. Seitz, Perf.: Mickey Rooney, Lewis Stone, Judy Garland (1941; Hollywood: M-G-M, 1992), Film.

17 Bob Thomas, "Lewis Stone Eyes TV After 20 Years of Entertaining," The Owosso Argus-Press (Owosso, MI), Apr. 4, 1951.

18 Sheila Graham, "Stone Plays Judge Hardy for 8 Years — Character Now," The Miami News (Miami, FL), Aug. 4, 1943.

19 Grady Johnson, "A Milestone for Lewis Stone," *New York Times* (New York, NY), Mar. 27, 1949.

20 "Judge Hardy Signs Up," *New York Times* (New York, NY), Mar. 8, 1942.

21 Ibid.

22 Ibid.

23 Bob Thomas, "Lewis Stone Eyes TV After 20 Years of Entertaining," *The Owosso Argus-Press* (Owosso, MI), Apr. 4, 1951.

24 Ibid.

25 Ibid.

26 John H. Rothwell, "Lewis Stone: Perennial 'Prisoner of Zenda'," New York Times (New York, NY), Jun. 1, 1952.

27 "Actor Lewis Stone Dies After Routing Vandals," *Pittsburgh Post-Gazette* (Pittsburgh, PA), Sep. 14, 1953.

28 Bob Thomas, "Impressed By Lewis Stone," *Park City Daily News* (Bowling Green, KY), Jan. 14, 1959.

29 John H. Rothwell, "Lewis Stone: Perennial 'Prisoner of Zenda'," *New York Times* (New York, NY), Jun. 1, 1952.

HENRY TRAVERS

1 Stephen Cox, *It's a Wonderful Life: A Memory Book.* (Nashville, TN: Cumberland House, 2003), p. 70.

2 *It's a Wonderful Life*, DVD, Dir.: Frank Capra, Perf.: James Stewart, Donna Reed, Lionel Barrymore (1946, Hollywood: Republic Pictures, 2006), Film.

3 Stephen Cox, *It's a Wonderful Life: A Memory Book.* (Nashville, TN: Cumberland House, 2003), p. 70.

4 Mieka Smiles, "Wonderful Life of Henry Travers Revealed," *The Journal*, Dec. 18, 2010, www.journallive.co.uk.

5 "Who's Who on Stage," *New York Times* (New York, NY), Oct. 14, 1923.

6 Ibid.

7 Mieka Smiles, "Wonderful Life of Henry Travers Revealed," *The Journal*, Dec. 18, 2010, www.journallive.co.uk.

8 "Who's Who on Stage," *New York Times* (New York, NY), Oct. 14, 1923.

9 "Henry Travers," *Internet Broadway Database*, Dec. 8, 2011, *http://ibdb.com/person.php?id=62596.*

10 Hal Erikson, "About This Person: Henry Travers," *New York Times,* Dec. 8, 2011, *http://movies.nytimes.com/person/71634/Henry-Travers?scp=1&sq=henry%20travers&st=cse.*

11 "Henry Travers," *Internet Broadway Database*, Dec. 8, 2011, *http://ibdb.com/person.php?id=62596.*

12 "Henry Travers's Start in Life," *New York Times* (New York, NY), Aug. 6, 1933.

13 "Who's Who on Stage," *New York Times* (New York, NY), Oct. 14, 1923.

14 "Henry Travers," *Internet Broadway Database*, Dec. 8, 2011, *http://ibdb.com/person.php?id=62596.*

15 Ibid.

16 Ibid.

17 "The Play," *New York Times* (New York, NY), Nov. 17, 1931.

18 Mollie Merrick, "Man's Day in Pictures," *The Spokesman Review* (Spokane, WA), Jun. 8, 1933.

19 "Henry Travers's Start in Life," *New York Times* (New York, NY), Aug. 6, 1933.

20 *Mrs. Miniver*, DVD, Dir. William Wyler, Perf. Greer Garson, Walter Pidgeon, Teresa Wright (1941, Hollywood: M-G-M, 2004), Film.

21 *Shadow of a Doubt*, Video, Dir.: Alfred Hitchcock, Perf.: Teresa Wright, Joseph Cotton, MacDonald Carey (1943, Hollywood: Universal Studios, 1999), Film.

22 Hal Erikson, "About This Person: Henry Travers," *New York Times*, Dec. 8, 2011, *http://movies.nytimes.com/person/71634/Henry-Travers?scp=1&sq=henry%20travers&st=cse.*

23 *The Bells of St. Mary's*, DVD, Dir.: Leo McCarey, Perf.: Bing Crosby, Ingrid Bergman, Henry Travers (1946, Hollywood: Republic Pictures, 2002), Film.

24 *It's a Wonderful Life*, DVD, Dir.: Frank Capra, Perf.: James Stewart, Donna Reed, Lionel Barrymore (1946, Hollywood: Republic Pictures, 2006), Film.

25 Jeanine Basinger, *The 'It's a Wonderful Life' Book* (New York, NY: Knopf, 1986), p. 7.

26 "Good Cast, Comedy in Playhouse Film," *St. Petersburg Times* (St. Petersburg, FL), Aug. 6, 1949.

27 Stephen Cox, *It's a Wonderful Life: A Memory Book.* (Nashville, TN: Cumberland House, 2003), p. 70.

28 Mieka Smiles, "Wonderful Life of Henry Travers Revealed," *The Journal*, Dec. 18, 2010, www.journallive.co.uk.

29 Ibid.

30 Stephen Cox, *It's a Wonderful Life: A Memory Book.* (Nashville, TN: Cumberland House, 2003), p. 71.

NANCY WALKER

1 Robert Windeler, "TV's Funny Woman." *People* (Los Angeles, CA), May 26, 1975.

2 Hugh Martin, *Hugh Martin: The Boy Next Door* (Encinitas, CA: Trolley Press, 2010), p. 148.

3 Good Night, Mrs. Morgenstern," *People* (Los Angeles, CA), Apr. 13, 1992.

4 "Nancy Walker," *Internet Movie Database*, Sep. 20, 2011, *http://www.imdb.com/name/nm0908055/.*

5 Robert Windeler, "TV's Funny Woman." *People* (Los Angeles, CA), May 26, 1975.

6 Nancy Walker, *Turner Classic Movies*, Sep. 15, 2011, *http://www.tcm.com/tcmdb/person/200956|116079/Nancy-Walker/.*

7 Hugh Martin, *Hugh Martin: The Boy Next Door* (Encinitas, CA: Trolley Press, 2010), p. 135.

8 Ibid, p. 148.

9 Ibid, p. 147.

10 Hugh Martin and Ralph Blane, "The Three B's," from *Best Foot Forward*, DVD, Dir.: Charles Walters, Perf.: Lucile Ball, Tommy Dix, and Virginia Weidler, (1943; Hollywood: M-G-M, 2006), Film.

11 *Best Foot Forward,* DVD, Dir.: Charles Walter, Perf.: Lucille Ball, Tommy Dix, and Virginia Weidler, (1943; Hollywood: M-G-M, 2006), Film.

12 Hugh Martin, *Hugh Martin: The Boy Next Door* (Encinitas, CA: Trolley Press, 2010), p.136.

13 Betty Comden and Adolph Green, "I Can Cook, Too!" from *On the Town,* Play, Dir.: George Abbott, Perf.: Adolph Green, Nancy Walker, and John Battles (1944-1946; New York: Shubert Organization), Theater.

14 *Girl Crazy,* Video, Dir.: Busby Berkeley, Perf.: Mickey Rooney, Judy Garland, and Guy Kibbee (1943; Hollywood: M-G-M, 1992), Film.

15 Brooks Atkinson, "Our Lady Buffoon," *New York Times* (New York, NY), Feb. 8, 1948.

16 Brooks Atkinson, "At the Theater," *New York Times* (New York, NY), Jan. 14, 1949.

17 Nancy Walker, *Turner Classic Movies,* Sep. 15, 2011, *http://www.tcm.com/tcmdb/ person/200956|116079/Nancy-Walker/.*

18 Robert Windeler, "TV's Funny Woman." *People* (Los Angeles, CA), May 26, 1975.

19 Ibid.

20 Doc Quigg, "Nancy Walker, Comedienne," *St. Petersburg Times* (St. Petersburg, FL), Jun. 4, 1961.

21 "Good Night, Mrs. Morgenstern," *People* (Los Angeles, CA), Apr. 13, 1992.

22 Robert Windeler, "TV's Funny Woman." *People* (Los Angeles, CA), May 26, 1975.

23 "The Chest Pains," in *Rhoda* (1974; Hollywood: MTM Enterprises), Television.

24 Ibid.

25 "The Death of Nancy Walker," *Findadeath.com,* Sep. 15, 2011, *http://www.findadeath.com/ Deceased/w/Nancy%20Walker/nancy_walker.htm.*

26 "Good Night, Mrs. Morgenstern," *People* (Los Angeles, CA), Apr. 13, 1992.

27 Ibid.

28 Robert Windeler, "TV's Funny Woman." *People* (Los Angeles, CA), May 26, 1975.

H.B. WARNER

1 Marjory Adams, "H.B. Warner, in Ibsen Play, Back on Stage After 18 Years," *Daily Boston Globe* (Boston, MA), Apr. 22, 1945.

2 " 'King of Kings' Impressive Film," *Boston Daily Globe* (Boston, MA), Jun. 14, 1927.

3 "Actor's Mission Is to Amuse," *Boston Daily Globe* (Boston, MA), Dec. 10, 1922.

4 Marjory Adams, "H.B. Warner, in Ibsen Play, Back on Stage After 18 Years," *Daily Boston Globe* (Boston, MA), Apr. 22, 1945.

5 "H.B. Warner's Wife Dies in Auto Smash," *New York Times* (New York, NY), Apr. 21, 1913.

6 "Actor's Fortune Quick to Change," *Boston Daily Globe* (Boston, MA), May 5, 1912.

7 Jon C. Hopwood, "H.B. Warner," *Internet Movie Database,* Jan. 1, 2012, *http://www.imdb.com/ name/nm0912478/.*

8 "Actor's Fortune Quick to Change," *Boston Daily Globe* (Boston, MA), May 5, 1912.

9 "H.B. Warner's Forty-Week Visit Has Lasted 29 Years," *The Montreal Gazette* (Montreal, Quebec), Jun. 9, 1934.

10 "Actor's Fortune Quick to Change," *Boston Daily Globe* (Boston, MA), May 5, 1912.

11 Ibid.

12 "English Actor's American Home," *Boston Daily Globe* (Boston, MA), Aug. 29, 1913.

13 "Actor's Fortune Quick to Change," *Boston Daily Globe* (Boston, MA), May 5, 1912.

14 "An Optimistic Actor," *New York Times* (New York, NY), Jan. 30, 1910.

15 "H.B. Warner's Wife Dies in Auto Smash," *New York Times* (New York, NY), Apr. 21, 1913.

16 "Actor's Mission Is to Amuse," *Boston Daily Globe* (Boston, MA), Dec. 10, 1922.

17 Marjory Adams, "H.B. Warner, in Ibsen Play, Back on Stage After 18 Years," *Daily Boston Globe*(Boston, MA), Apr. 22, 1945.

18 " 'King of Kings' Impressive Film," *Boston Daily Globe* (Boston, MA), Jun. 14, 1927.

19 "Actor's Mission Is to Amuse," *Boston Daily Globe* (Boston, MA), Dec. 10, 1922.

20 *Lost Horizon*, DVD, Dir: Frank Capra, Perf: Ronald Colman, Thomas Mitchell, and H.B. Warner (1937; Hollywood: Columbia Pictures, 1999), Film.

21 *You Can't Take It with You*, Video, Dir: Frank Capra, Perf: James Stewart, Jean Arthur, and Lionel Barrymore (1938; Hollywood: Columbia Pictures, 1997), Film.

22 Marjory Adams, "H.B. Warner, in Ibsen Play, Back on Stage After 18 Years," *Daily Boston Globe*(Boston, MA), Apr. 22, 1945.

23 Ibid.

24 Stephen Cox, *It's a Wonderful Life: A Memory Book.* (Nashville, TN: Cumberland House, 2003), p.33.

25 "Actor's Mission is to Amuse," *Boston Daily Globe* (Boston, MA), Dec. 10, 1922.

26 Stephen Cox, *It's a Wonderful Life: A Memory Book.* (Nashville, TN: Cumberland House, 2003), p.32.

MARY WICKES

1 "Mary Wickes: A Treasure in Greasepaint," *Lucyfan Enterprises,* 2005, *http://www.lucyfan.com/marywickes.html.*

2 Ibid.

3 Mel Gussow, "Mary Wickes, 85, Character Actress for 50 Years," *New York Times* (New York, NY), Oct. 26, 1995.

4 Jean Lewis, "Veteran Actress Mary Wickes Thought Actors 'Nother Race," *The Evening News* (Jeffersonville, IN), Oct. 1, 1975.

5 Ibid.

6 Jerry Buck, "Wickes' 'Father Dowling' role familiar," *Kentucky New Era* (Hopkinsville, KY), Aug. 15, 1990.

7 Jean Lewis, "Veteran Actress Mary Wickes Thought Actors 'Nother Race," *The Evening News* (Jeffersonville, IN), Oct. 1, 1975.

8 Ellen Koteff, "Mary Wickes: A White Witch Driving Men Wild," *Palm Beach Daily News* (Palm Beach, FL), Feb. 8, 1979.

9 Ibid.

10 *The Man Who Came to Dinner*, Video, Dir.: William Keighley, Perf.: Bette Davis, Ann Sheridan, and Monty Woolley (1942; Hollywood: Warner Brothers, 1995), Film.

11　Jerry Buck, "Wickes' 'Father Dowling' Role Familiar," *Kentucky New Era* (Hopkinsville, KY), Aug. 15, 1990.

12　"Homeliness Pays," *St. Petersburg Times* (St. Petersburg, FL), Aug. 8, 1943.

13　Evan Levine, "Mary Wickes Finds Time to Talk," *The Durant Daily Democrat* (Durant, OK), Aug. 26, 1990.

14　*White Christmas*, DVD, Dir.: Michael Curtiz, Perf.: Bing Crosby and Rosemary Clooney (1954; Hollywood: Paramount, 2009), Film.

15　"Mary Wickes: A Treasure in Greasepaint," *Lucyfan.com*, 2005, *http://www.lucyfan.com/mary-wickes.html*.

16　Vernon Scott, " 'Doc' Nurse Likes Antiques," *The News-Dispatch* (Michigan City, IN), Dec. 3, 1975.

17　"Mary Wickes," *Internet Movie Database*, Dec. 1, 2011, *http://www.imdb.com/name/nm0926897/*.

18　Ibid.

19　Ellen Koteff, "Mary Wickes: A White Witch Driving Men Wild," *Palm Beach Daily News* (Palm Beach, FL), Feb. 8, 1979.

20　Ibid.

21　Vernon Scott, " 'Doc' Nurse Likes Antiques," *The News-Dispatch* (Michigan City, IN), Dec. 3, 1975.

22　Ibid.

23　Jerry Buck, "Wickes' 'Father Dowling' Role Familiar," *Kentucky New Era* (Hopkinsville, KY), Aug. 15, 1990.

24　Ellen Koteff, "Mary Wickes: A White Witch Driving Men Wild," *Palm Beach Daily News* (Palm Beach, FL), Feb. 8, 1979.

25　"Mary Wickes: A Treasure in Greasepaint," *Lucyfan .com*, 2005, *http://www.lucyfan.com/mary-wickes.html*.

26　"Mary Wickes," *Internet Movie Database*, Dec. 1, 2011, *http://www.imdb.com/name/nm0926897/*.

27　Ibid.

28　Ibid.

CHILL WILLS

1　"Chill Wills Has No Urge for Stardom," *The Miami News* (Miami, FL), Jan. 11, 1951.

2　"Chill Wills Visits with His Family," *The Deseret News* (Salt Lake City, UT), Sep. 7, 1956.

3　Vernon Scott, "Chill Wills Chilling Texan Guy," *The Pittsburgh Press* (Pittsburgh, PA), Sep. 21, 1971.

4　"Chill Wills Creates His Own Comedy Style in *High Lonesome*," *Times Daily* (Florence, AL), Sep. 26, 1950.

5　Vernon Scott, "Chill Wills Chilling Texan Guy," *The Pittsburgh Press* (Pittsburgh, PA), Sep. 21, 1971.

6　"On Chill Wills, Tenor from Texas," *New York Times* (New York, NY), Sep. 15, 1940.

7   Johna Blinn, "Chill Wills Cooks 'Man's Food'," *The Victoria Advocate* (Victoria, TX), Jun. 7, 1973.

8   "Chill Wills Grateful for Early Schooling," *The Pittsburgh Press* (Pittsburgh, PA), Jul. 15, 1956.

9   "On Chill Wills, Tenor from Texas," *New York Times* (New York, NY), Sep. 15, 1940.

10   Marjory Adams, "Chill in Hub: No 'Pedestal Actor' But He'd Like Oscar," *Boston Globe* (Boston, MA), Sep. 30, 1963.

11   Nancy Anderson, "Chill Wills Just Needs a Little Summer Money," *Kingsport Post* (Kingsport, TN), Mar. 3, 1977.

12   Johna Blinn, "Chill Wills Cooks 'Man's Food'," *The Victoria Advocate* (Victoria, TX), Jun. 7, 1973.

13   Ibid.

14   Ibid.

15   "On Chill Wills, Tenor from Texas," *New York Times* (New York, NY), Sep. 15, 1940.

16   *The Harvey Girls,* Video, Dir.: George Sidney, Perf.: Judy Garland, John Hodiak, and Virginia O'Brien (1946; Hollywood: M-G-M, 1992), Film.

17   "Chill Wills Creates His Own Comedy Style in *High Lonesome,*" *Times Daily* (Florence, AL), Sep. 26, 1950.

18   Hedda Hopper, "Inside Hollywood," *The Pittsburgh Press* (Pittsburgh, PA), Apr. 18, 1946.

19   "Chill Wills Has No Urge for Stardom," *The Miami News* (Miami, FL), Jan. 11, 1951.

20   Gene Handsaker, "Hollywood Sights and Sounds," *Prescott Evening Courier* (Prescott, AZ), Aug. 24, 1950.

21   Harold Heffernan, "Will May Play Will Rogers," *Daily Boston Globe* (Boston, MA), Oct. 17, 1951.

22   Ibid.

23   "Chill Wills Visits with His Family," *The Deseret News* (Salt Lake City, Utah), Sep. 7, 1956.

24   *Giant,* Video, Dir.: George Stevens, Perf.: Elizabeth Taylor, Rock Hudson, and James Dean (1956; Hollywood: Warner Brothers, 1996), Film.

25   Joe Hyams, "Wayne Gets Hot as Wills Chases Oscar," *Pittsburgh Post Gazette* (Pittsburgh, PA), Apr. 2, 1961.

26   "Chill Wills Has Not Made Up His Mind About the Race," *The Bonham Daily Favorite* (Bonham, TX), Sep. 7, 1967.

27   Nancy Anderson, "Chill Wills Just Needs a Little Summer Money," *Kingsport Post* (Kingsport, TN), Mar. 3, 1977.

28   Vernon Scott, "Chill Wills Chilling Texan Guy," *The Pittsburgh Press* (Pittsburgh, PA), Sep. 21, 1971.

29   Johna Blinn, "Chill Wills Cooks 'Man's Food'," *The Victoria Advocate* (Victoria, TX), Jun. 7, 1973.

30   "Sidewalk Star Is Unveiled for Western Actor Chill Wills," *The Press-Courier* (Milwaukee, WS), Dec. 16, 1970.

31   Nancy Anderson, "Chill Wills Just Needs a Little Summer Money," *Kingsport Post* (Kingsport, TN), Mar. 3, 1977.

32 "Sidewalk Star Is Unveiled For Western Actor Chill Wills," *The Press-Courier* (Milwaukee, WS), Dec. 16, 1970.

33 Ibid.

CHARLES WINNINGER

1 *Babes in Arms*, DVD, Dir.: Busby Berkeley, Perf.: Mickey Rooney, Judy Garland, and June Preisser (1939; Hollywood: M-G-M, 2012), Film.

2 Bob Thomas, "Charles Winninger Isn't Ready For Rocking Chair," *Times Daily* (Florence, AL), Dec. 8, 1952.

3 Buck Herzog, "Up and Down Amusement Row," *The Milwaukee Sentinel* (Milwaukee, WI), Aug. 9, 1948.

4 Paul Harrison, "The Theater Finds Its Glamor in Personalities," *The Tuscaloosa News* (Tuscaloosa, AL), Jun. 3, 1935.

5 Charles Winninger, "Two 'Captain Henry's' Tell Favorite Stories of Their Early Days," *The Pittsburgh Press* (Pittsburgh, PA), Aug. 25, 1935.

6 Bob Thomas, "Charles Winninger Isn't Ready for Rocking Chair," *Times Daily* (Florence, AL), Dec. 8, 1952.

7 Paul Harrison, "The Theater Finds Its Glamor in Personalities," *The Tuscaloosa News* (Tuscaloosa, AL), Jun. 3, 1935.

8 Bob Thomas, "Charles Winninger Isn't Ready for Rocking Chair," *Times Daily* (Florence, AL), Dec. 8, 1952.

9 Paul Harrison, "The Theater Finds Its Glamor in Personalities," *The Tuscaloosa News* (Tuscaloosa, AL), Jun. 3, 1935.

10 "Charles Winninger Is Proud of His Golf Prowess," *Daily Boston Globe* (Boston, MA), May 5, 1929.

11 Bob Thomas, "Charles Winninger Isn't Ready for Rocking Chair," *Times Daily* (Florence, AL), Dec. 8, 1952.

12 "Blanche Ring Weds," *Daily Boston Globe* (Boston, MA), Nov. 12, 1912.

13 Richard and Paulette Ziegfeld, *The Ziegfeld Touch* (New York: Harry N. Abrams, Inc. Publishers, 1993), p. 251.

14 "Minute Biographers: Charles Winninger," *The Milwaukee Sentinel* (Milwaukee, WI), Sep. 15, 1932.

15 "Charles Winninger Is Proud of His Golf Prowess," *Daily Boston Globe* (Boston, MA), May 5, 1929.

16 Ibid.

17 "News of the Stage; Mr. Winninger Breaks a Leg but Not a Tradition," *New York Times* (New York, NY), Dec. 7, 1934.

18 Gary Brumburgh, "Charles Winninger," *Internet Movie Database*, Mar. 10, 2012, *http://www.imdb.com/name/nm0935415/*.

19 Ibid.

20 " 'Can't Bunk Public Anymore,' Asserts Charles Winninger," *The Palm Beach Post* (Palm Beach, FL), Feb. 24, 1932.

21 "Show Boat," VHS, Dir.: James Whale, Perf.: Irene Dunne, Allan Jones, Helen Morgan (1936; Hollywood: Universal Pictures, 1990) Film.

22 Ibid.

23 " 'Can't Bunk Public Anymore,' Asserts Charles Winninger," *The Palm Beach Post* (Palm Beach, FL), Feb. 24, 1932.

24 *Babes in Arms,* DVD, Dir.: Busby Berkeley, Perf.: Mickey Rooney, Judy Garland, and June Preisser (1939; Hollywood: M-G-M, 2012), Film.

25 Edward Gallagher and Al Shean, "Mr. Gallagher and Mr. Shean" (1922), from *Ziegfeld Girl,* DVD, Dir.: Robert Z. Leonard, Perf.: Judy Garland, Lana Turner, Hedy Lamarr (1941; Hollywood: M-G-M, 2004), Film.

26 Buck Herzog, "Up and Down Amusement Row," *The Milwaukee Sentinel* (Milwaukee, WI), Aug. 9, 1948.

27 "Veteran Actor Succumbs," *The Dispatch* (Lexington, NC), Jan. 28, 1969.

28 Billy Rose, "Charles Winninger Revives the Days of Vaudeville," *The Evening Independent* (St. Petersburg, FL), Jun. 30, 1948.

SHELLEY WINTERS

1 Howard Thompson, "Testament by the Untamed Winters," *New York Times* (New York, NY), Aug. 30, 1964.

2 Gary Brumburgh, "Shelley Winters Mini Biography," *Internet Movie Database,* Feb. 26, 2012, *http://www.imdb.com/name/nm0001859/.*

3 Shelley Winters, *Shelley: Also Known as Shirley* (New York: William Morrow and Co., 1980), p. 16.

4 Ibid, 27.

5 Ibid, p. 86.

6 Howard Thompson, "Testament by the Untamed Winters," *New York Times* (New York, NY), Aug. 30, 1964.

7 Shelley Winters, *Shelley: Also Known as Shirley* (New York: William Morrow and Co., 1980), p. 191.

8 Ibid, p. 197.

9 Ibid, p. 220.

10 Herbert Mitgang, "Portrait of a Mild Winters," *New York Times* (New York, NY), Apr. 29, 1956.

11 Shelley Winters, *Shelley: Also Known as Shirley* (New York: William Morrow and Co., 1980), p. 234.

12 *A Place in the Sun,* DVD, Dir.: George Stevens, Perf.: Montgomery Clift, Elizabeth Taylor, and Shelley Winters (1951; Hollywood: Paramount Pictures, 2001), Film.

13 "Shelley Winters Heaves Mirror," *Greensburg Daily Tribune* (Greensburg, PA), Mar. 24, 1954.

14 *The Night of the Hunter,* DVD, Dir.: Charles Laughton, Perf.: Robert Mitchum, Shelley Winters, and Lillian Gish (1955; Hollywood: Paul Gregory Productions, 2000), Film.

15 Herbert Mitgang, "Portrait of a Mild Winters," *New York Times* (New York, NY), Apr. 29, 1956.

16 Ibid.

17 Ibid.

18 Howard Thompson, "Testament by the Untamed Winters," *New York Times* (New York, NY), Aug. 30, 1964.

19 Gary Brumburgh, "Shelley Winters Mini Biography," *Internet Movie Database*, Feb. 26, 2012, *http://www.imdb.com/name/nm0001859/.*

20 Ibid.

21 Ibid.

22 Vincent Canby, "M is for the Mothers That She Gave Us," *New York Times* (New York, NY), Jul. 7, 1968.

23 Gary Brumburgh, "Shelley Winters Mini Biography," *Internet Movie Database*, Feb. 26, 2012, *http://www.imdb.com/name/nm0001859/.*

24 Howard Thompson, "Testament by the Untamed Winters," *New York Times* (New York, NY), Aug. 30, 1964.

25 Vincent Canby, "M is for the Mothers That She Gave Us," *New York Times* (New York, NY), Jul. 7, 1968.

26 Shelley Winters, *Shelley: Also Known as Shirley* (New York: William Morrow and Co., 1980), p. 283.

27 Lewis Funke, "Shelley Winters, Author," *New York Times* (New York, NY), Oct. 11, 1970.

28 Ibid.

29 Carol Lawson, "Behind the Best Sellers: Shelley Winters," *New York Times* (New York, NY), Aug. 3, 1980.

30 Shelley Winters, *Shelley: Also Known as Shirley* (New York: William Morrow and Co., 1980), p. 506.

31 Herbert Mitgang, "Portrait of a Mild Winters," *New York Times* (New York, NY), Apr. 29, 1956.

MONTY WOOLLEY

1 *The Man Who Came to Dinner*, Video, Dir.: William Keighley, Perf.: Bette Davis, Ann Sheridan, and Monty Woolley (1942; Hollywood: Warner Brothers, 1995), Film.

2 "Monty Woolley Dies in Albany," *St. Petersburg Times (St. Petersburg, FL)*, May 7, 1963.

3 Robert A. Schanke and Kimberley Bell Marra, *Passing Performances: Queer Readings of Leading Players in American Theater* (Ann Arbor, MI: University of Michigan Press, 1998), p. 262-276.

4 Judith Ann Schiff, "Before He Came to Dinner," *Yale Alumni Magazine* (New Haven, CT), Apr. 1999.

5 Ibid.

6 William McBrien, *Cole Porter*, (New York: Vintage Publishing, 2000), p. 37.

7 Ibid, p. 44.

8 Ibid, p. 38.

9 Ibid, p. 108.

10 Ibid, p. 111.

11 Judith Ann Schiff, "Before He Came to Dinner," *Yale Alumni Magazine* (New Haven, CT), Apr. 1999.

12 Ibid.

13 Ibid.

14 "Monty Woolley Dies in Albany," *St. Petersburg Times (St. Petersburg, FL),* May 7, 1963.

15 Robert A. Schanke and Kimberley Bell Marra, *Passing Performances: Queer Readings of Leading Players in American Theater* (Ann Arbor, MI: University of Michigan Press, 1998), p. 262-276.

16 "Monty Woolley Dies in Albany," *St. Petersburg Times (St. Petersburg, FL),* May 7, 1963.

17 Robert A. Schanke and Kimberley Bell Marra, *Passing Performances: Queer Readings of Leading Players in American Theater* (Ann Arbor, MI: University of Michigan Press, 1998), p. 262-276.

18 *The Man Who Came to Dinner*, Video, Dir.: William Keighley, Perf.: Bette Davis, Ann Sheridan, and Monty Woolley (1942; Hollywood: Warner Brothers, 1995.), Film.

19 Ibid.

20 *Since You Went Away,* DVD, Dir.: John Cromwell, Perf.: Claudette Colbert, Jennifer Jones, and Shirley Temple (1944; Hollywood: Selznick International Pictures, 2004), Film.

21 Robert A. Schanke and Kimberley Bell Marra, *Passing Performances: Queer Readings of Leading Players in American Theater* (Ann Arbor, MI: University of Michigan Press, 1998), p. 262-276.

22 "Monty Woolley Snorts at Liberace, Bore Bars," *Ottawa Citizen (Ottawa, Ontario),* June 27, 1955.

23 "Monty Woolley Dies in Albany," *St. Petersburg Times (St. Petersburg, FL),* May 7, 1963.

24 Hedda Hopper, "Hedda Says: Monty Woolley Lets Loose Blast at Hollywood's Acting Schools," *Pittsburgh Press (Pittsburgh, PA),* Apr. 29, 1944.

25 Ibid.

ROLAND YOUNG

1 "Roland Young: Actor Best Known for 'Topper' Movies. *Toledo Blade* (Toledo, OH), Jun. 7, 1953.

2 "Roland Young," *The Internet Movie Database,* Nov. 25, 2011. *http://www.imdb.com/name/nm0950019/bio.*

3 "Roland Young (1887-1953)," *Tripod.com,* 2007. *http://jchoma.tripod.com/young.htm. Nov. 20, 2011.*

4 "The Story of Roland Young," *New York Times* (New York, NY), Dec. 23, 1917.

5 Ibid.

6 Ibid.

7 "Roland Young," *Internet Broadway Database,* Nov. 20, 2011, *http://ibdb.com/person.php?id=65943*

8 Alexander Woollcott, "The Play," *The New York Times* (New York, NY), Aug. 6, 1920.

9 "Roland Young (1997-1953)," *Tripod.com,* 2007, *http://jchoma.tripod.com/young.htm.*

10 "Roland Young," *Internet Movie Database,* Nov. 25, 2011. *http://www.imdb.com/name/ nm0950019/bio.*

11 "Roland Young: Actor Best Known for 'Topper' Movies," *Toledo Blade* (Toledo, OH), Jun. 7, 1953.

12 Donald Deschner, *The Complete Films of Cary Grant (*New York: Citadel Press, 1983), p. 33.

13 Roland Young, *Not for Children* (New York: Garden City Publishing, 1945).

14 "Roland Young Drawings; Actors and Others," *New York Times* (New York, NY), May 17, 1925.

15 Mollie Merrick, "Loves Penguins for Themselves," *The Calgary Herald* (Calgary, Canada), Aug. 4, 1931.

16 "Roland Young (1997-1953)," *Tripod.com,* 2007, *http://jchoma.tripod.com/young.htm.*

17 "THE VERY 'UMBLE MR. 'EEP; Disguised as Roland Young, Uriah Shudders Once for Benighted Hollywood," *New York Times* (New York, NY), Jan. 20, 1935.

18 Thorne Smith, *Topper (*New York: Modern Library, 1999), p. 1.

19 Mollie Merrick, "Hates Food But Has to Eat," *The Spokesman Review* (Spokane, WA), Sep. 10, 1934.

20 Donald Deschner, *The Complete Films of Cary Grant* (New York: Citadel Press, 1983), p. 108.

21 *Topper,* Video, Dir.: Norman Z. McLeod. Perf.: Roland Young, Constance Bennett, Cary Grant, and Billie Burke (1937; Hollywood: Hal Roach Studios, 1987), Film.

22 Donald Deshner, *The Complete Films of Cary Grant* (New York: Citadel Press, 1983) p. 108.

23 *The Young in Heart*, Video, Dir.: Richard Wallace. Perf.: Janet Gaynor, Douglas Fairbanks Jr., Roland Young, and Billie Burke (1938; Hollywood: Selznick International Studios, 1999), Film.

24 *The Philadelphia Story*, DVD, Dir.: George Cukor, Perf.: Katharine Hepburn, Cary Grant, and James Stewart (1940; Hollywood: M-G-M, 2005), Film.

25 "The Adventures of Topper ," *ThorneSmith.net,* Nov. 20, 2011, *http://www.thornesmith.net/ Adventures-of-Topper.html.*

26 "Roland Young." *Internet Movie Database,* Sep. 20, 2011, *http://www.imdb.com/name/ nm0950019/bio. Nov. 20, 2011.*

27 "Roland Young." *Internet Broadway Database,* Sep. 20, 2011, *http://ibdb.com/person. php?id=65943. Nov. 21, 2011.*

28 "Roland Young," *Internet Movie Database,* Sep. 20, 2011, *http://www.imdb.com/name/ nm0950019/bio. Nov. 20, 2011.*

29 Mollie Merrick, "Roland Young Still Sane," *The Spokesman Review* (Spokane, WA), Nov. 23, 1932.

ABOUT THE AUTHORS

CYNTHIA AND SARA BRIDESON have been studying classic film from the time they were seven years old. Their special areas of expertise are in musicals, particularly those of producer Arthur Freed and Florenz Ziegfeld Jr. As twin sisters, they are inseparable and have several future writing projects in the works which they are penning together. Currently, they are working on a book about Jews and the creation of the American musical as well as a historical fiction novel set in 1927. Currently, they reside in Sacramento, California with their family and two cats.

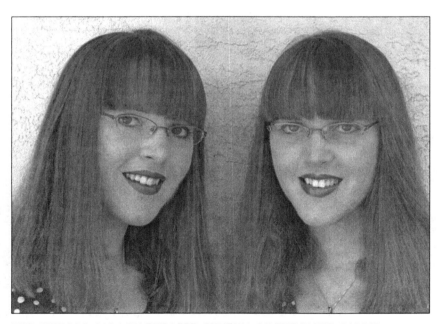

THE AUTHORS, SARA ON THE LEFT, CYNTHIA ON THE RIGHT, IN 2012.

INDEX OF NAMES

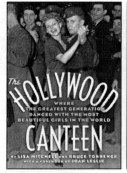

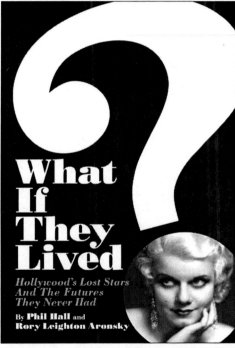

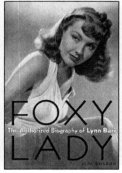

CPSIA information can be obtained at www.ICGtesting.com
Printed in the USA
BVOW010653151212

308012BV00007B/165/P